The
MINISTRY
of the
WORD

Published by
The Bible Reading Fellowship
First Floor, Elsfield Hall,
15–17 Elsfield Way, Oxford OX2 8FG
ISBN 1 84101 117 7

First published 2000
1 3 5 7 9 10 8 6 4 2
All rights reserved

Acknowledgments
Unless otherwise stated, scripture quotations are taken from
The New Revised Standard Version of the Bible, Anglicized Edition,
copyright © 1989, 1995 by the Division of Christian Education
of the National Council of the Churches of Christ in the USA,
and are used by permission. All rights reserved.

Scripture quotations taken from the Holy Bible, New International
Version, copyright © 1973, 1978, 1984 by International Bible
Society, are used by permission of Hodder & Stoughton Limited.
All rights reserved. 'NIV' is a registered trademark of International
Bible Society. UK trademark number 1448790.

Scripture quotations from the New Jerusalem Bible published and
copyright © 1985 by Darton, Longman & Todd Ltd and les
Editions du Cerf, and by Doubleday, a division of Bantam
Doubleday Dell Publishing Group, Inc. Used by permission of
Darton, Longman and Todd Ltd, and Doubleday, a division of
Random House, Inc.

Revised English Bible with the Apocrypha copyright © 1989 by
Oxford University Press and Cambridge University Press.

The Message © 1993 by Eugene H. Peterson, NavPress,
Colorado Springs.

Extracts from the Authorized Version of the Bible (The King James
Bible), the rights in which are vested in the Crown, are reproduced
by permission of the Crown's patentee, Cambridge University Press.

Extracts from the College Hymn of St John's College, Durham,
reprinted by kind permission of Christopher Jones.

A catalogue record for this book is available from the British Library

Printed and bound in Finland

The
MINISTRY
of the
WORD

A Handbook for Preachers
on the Common Worship Lectionary

EDITED BY NAOMI STARKEY

PREFACE

In 1980, BRF published a commentary on the new ASB lectionary—*The Ministry of the Word*. By popular demand, we have compiled a similar volume for the *Common Worship* lectionary. Drawing together nine contributors, we have produced a volume of short commentaries on the readings for the Principal Service every Sunday, covering all three years of the lectionary. It also includes the readings for other special services and festivals in the Church Calendar. These commentaries are designed to offer a way into the given passage, providing material to stimulate thought and get the creative processes flowing.

As a guide to the structure of the *Common Worship* lectionary, we recommend *The Christian Year: Calendar, Lectionary and Collects* (Church House Publishing) as well as the books recommended by Anna de Lange at the end of her helpful introduction to *The Ministry of the Word* (page 12).

Contibutors are as follows.

The Revd Dr Robert Fyall

Lecturer in Old Testament at Cranmer Hall, St John's College, Durham, and minister of Claypath URC Church. He has written on Job, Daniel, preaching and pilgrimage and is currently writing a commentary on 1 and 2 Kings.

The Revd Dr Alan Garrow

Tutor in New Testament Studies for the St Albans and Oxford Ministry Course, he also serves as a parish priest in one of Oxfordshire's rural benefices. He is author of *Revelation* (New Testament Readings, Routledge, 1997).

The Revd Dr Michael Gilbertson

Vicar of All Saints, Stranton in Harlepool, and editor of the theological journal *Anvil*. Before entering full-time ministry he was a civil servant in the Department of Trade and Industry.

Mrs Margaret Killingray

Tutor for the London Institute for Contemporary Christianity, where she contributes to programmes on interpreting the Bible in the modern world. She has degrees in sociology and theology.

The Revd Dr Ian Paul

An Associate Minister in Poole, Dorset, Theological Adviser in Salisbury Diocese and Managing Editor of Grove Books Ltd. He has written both popular and academic material about the Bible, and has a special interest in the book of Revelation.

The Revd John Proctor

Works for the United Reformed Church as New Testament lecturer at Westminster College, Cambridge. He studied for church ministry at Glasgow University and served at a Church of Scotland parish in Glasgow from 1981 to 1986.

Dr Deborah Rooke

Lecturer in Old Testament Studies at King's College, London. She has wide experience of church life and ministry and is trained as a minister in the Baptist denomination. Her particular interest is making the Bible come alive for those who read it.

The Revd Preb Gill Sumner

Local Ministry Officer for the Diocese of Hereford, with a particular interest in the Old Testament and biblical interpretation. She was formerly Associate Principal of the Oxford Ministry Course and has also been a tutor in Biblical Studies at a theological college and on courses for both lay people and ordinands.

Dom Henry Wansbrough

Benedictine monk of Ampleforth, at present Master of St Benet's Hall, Oxford, where he teaches in the Theology faculty. After studying for degrees at Oxford, Fribourg, Jerusalem and Rome, he taught for 25 years at Ampleforth. He has lectured widely in Europe, Africa and America and is the only English member of the Pontifical Biblical Commission.

CONTENTS

THE COMMON WORSHIP LECTIONARY: AN INTRODUCTION

Anna de Lange, Member of the Church of England's General Synod and Liturgical Commission

Over the past thirty years or so, the worship of the Church of England has undergone a sea change: no longer is every word we use written down and said every week. Yet some things remain the same. Ask the person on the Clapham omnibus for a Christmas reading from the Bible, and the choice will vary: some would cite one of the Gospel nativity stories (or a conflation of the two); others might remember the beginning of John's Gospel. Few, however, would think of the parables or the events of Holy Week in this context. The Christmas passages are well known because they have been used at Christmas for centuries; they are part of our culture, our heritage, as well as part of our Christian faith. The Christian calendar has shaped the readings laid down for each Sunday, each festival, each day of the year. Season by season the Christian story unfolds, as the events which shape our faith are retold.

The basis for any lectionary is as simple as that: a cycle of readings linked to the Christian calendar and covering a range of Bible texts. There are two main, and complementary, approaches. The first is to arrange the readings by season or theme related to the calendar; the second is to read consecutive, or nearly consecutive, passages from one book of the Bible so that the flow and story of scripture can be covered. Most lectionaries use a combination of the two styles.

WHY USE A LECTIONARY?

Readings from the Bible give us not only the passage for preaching, but also remind us day by day and week by week of the story of salvation. Granted that scripture has to be chosen by someone, why should we use a lectionary rather than just selecting passages to be used?

- **Calendar:** the Church's year tells the story of salvation; its seasonal rhythm, both complementing and contrasting with the natural and secular cycles, will rightly inform the choice of readings. A lectionary ensures that all aspects of the gospel story from all parts of the Bible have their place.

- **Coverage**: the lectionary gives a balanced coverage of the Bible over time. It takes us into parts of the Bible that we might otherwise neither read nor use as a basis for preaching. We, and the congregation, have to wrestle with the difficult passages and subjects as well as the favourites we might prefer to choose. The three-year cycle of the Common Worship lectionary allows more of the Bible to be read than the two-year ASB lectionary.
- **Common prayer**: use of the authorized lectionary provision can help to unite churches who, even though their services may differ, are reading the same passages and preaching on similar topics week by week. Other churches in this country and elsewhere have introduced a very similar lectionary.

FEATURES OF THE COMMON WORSHIP LECTIONARY

The pattern of readings

The lectionary follows a three-year cycle, with provision for three readings and a psalm each Sunday. The years are designated A, B and C. In each one, the Gospel readings concentrate on one of the synoptic Gospels (Matthew, Mark and Luke), read seasonally where possible and using a semi-continuous approach at other times. John's Gospel is shared between all three years. Other books of the Bible are also read semi-continuously. The lectionary is seasonal, but not often thematic.

The New Testament readings do not relate to the Gospel, and each book is read semi-continuously. The Old Testament readings relate to the Gospel in the Christian seasons, but there is a choice of track out of the seasons, which is explored below. The psalm usually relates to the Old Testament reading.

Provision has also been made for Feasts, Holy Days and Festivals. Other weekdays, including the commemorations in the Calendar, have a separate lectionary.

The pattern of services

There is provision for three services each Sunday. These are designated 'Principal Service', 'Second Service' and 'Third Service' rather than being differentiated by liturgy as in the ASB. This gives continuity at any particular service where the pattern of worship varies week by week, and flexibility as to which lectionary is used for which service.

In most churches, the 'Principal Service' lectionary will be used at the main act of worship, with the 'Second Service' lectionary at a secondary act of worship such as Evening Prayer. The 'Third Service' lectionary has been designed with a Sunday Office (or short said service) in mind, but is suitable for use on other occasions.

The 'Principal Service' lectionary is based, with a few amendments, on the Revised Common Lectionary (often referred to by the initials RCL), which was itself adapted from a Roman Catholic lectionary. However, RCL contains provision for only one service, while it is common in the Church of England to have two or more. Therefore, two further cycles have been newly compiled for the second and third services, and are designed to complement RCL.

The disappearance of themes

There are no weekly themes set for each Sunday, a major departure from the lectionary in the ASB. It has become apparent that the themes are tired after twenty years, and that they have led to sermons being preached with the theme in mind rather than with openness to the message of the Bible passage and the church context. Of course every service will have a theme, but those planning worship and preaching will determine what the theme should be; it might emerge from any of the readings, but should not be sought from all three. The commentaries in this book are designed to help the preacher to engage with one of the readings, not to discern a thread running through all three.

A consequence of the decision to abandon the thematic approach is that the Collect (often called the Prayer of the Day) now relates to the calendar rather than to the lectionary, and may or may not illuminate the readings. In addition, there is no provision for weekly sentences: if a sentence is required to start the service or at some other point, any suitable passage can be selected.

Ordinary time

The lectionary year is divided into two types of 'season' (quite apart from the seasons of the Christian year)—open, or ordinary, time; and closed time. During the closed seasons, the authorized provision must be used: they run from Advent until the Presentation of Christ in the Temple and from Ash Wednesday to Trinity Sunday. The rest of the year is ordinary time, when alternative lectionaries, including those constructed by churches for their own use, may be used. Thus, when a note or rubric in any service contains words such as 'the readings are governed by authorized lectionary provision', this includes permission to deviate from the given readings in ordinary time. Many people do not realize that this flexibility exists.

Making choices

There are several points in the new provision where choices have to be made if repetition and confusion are to be avoided.

- Occasionally (such as on Christmas Day and Easter Day), there are alternative readings; care is needed to ensure that readings are not repeated unintentionally, whether on the one day or from year to year.
- In churches where the principal service is Holy Communion, but only two readings are used, a choice has to be made whether to opt for a series of Old Testament or New Testament readings before the Gospel. Semi-continuous reading of a book requires different planning from the ASB's thematic approach.
- A similar type of choice has to be made in the summer and autumn season of ordinary time, when there are two options for Old Testament readings. One set provides for the semi-continuous reading of scripture to continue, while the other set relates the Old Testament reading to the Gospel set for the day. The choice of track needs to be made before the season begins, as it would be most unhelpful to both preachers and the congregations for the tracks to be mixed arbitrarily. As the psalm is generally linked to the Old Testament reading, those planning the music need also to be aware which track is in use.

PLANNING THE PREACHING WITH THE COMMON WORSHIP LECTIONARY

If the scriptures are to speak for themselves, then paradoxically there is a need for more planning. This will certainly need to be done when the lectionary is first adopted and when there is a change in the worship pattern of a church, but will also be necessary at various points during the year. It becomes even more important if several people share the preaching, so that each knows the choices that are being made.

- Which lectionary goes with which service? In some cases it may be obvious, but in multi-church benefices or in large churches with a number of Sunday services, the decision may be less clear-cut. It is permissible to use one lectionary at more than one service if, for example, two morning services are run 'back-to-back' for different congregations.

- Which track is to be followed when there is a choice? In ordinary time, it is necessary to decide whether to follow the semi-continuous or the related track for the Old Testament readings.
- Are the sermons to form a series? For example, it is possible to concentrate on the Gospel one year, and at another time to preach on the New Testament or Old Testament passages.
- Will an introductory sermon be needed when a new book of the Bible is begun, or a concluding one at the end of the series?
- Remember to ask what readings or lectionary track are used if you are invited to preach in another church.

A FINAL HEALTH WARNING

This introduction has been necessarily brief and somewhat sweeping in its generalizations, and contains very little on the calendar, which forms the backdrop against which the Bible and the lectionary should be used. Further information and commentary can be found elsewhere, and some suggestions follow.

Trevor Lloyd, Peter Moger, Jane Sinclair and Michael Vasey, *Introducing the New Lectionary: Getting the Bible into worship*, Grove Books, Worship Series 141, 1997

The Christian Year: Calendar, Lectionary and Collects, Church House Publishing, 1997

Lectionary Training Pack, Praxis, 1997

Michael Perham, *Celebrate the Christian Story*, SPCK, 1999

THE FIRST SUNDAY OF ADVENT

YEAR A

Isaiah 2:1—5

The prophet promises foreign pilgrims to Jerusalem guidance for a new way of life (v. 3b). The law is not just a new set of rules, more of a map for the journey. It offers a wealth of instruction about living as God's people, in harmony with him, with each other and with the creation. They will also hear 'the word of the Lord', the direct guidance of God through the oracles of the prophets.

The prophet also promises the nations peace—based not on their own attempts to avoid war, but on submitting to the judgment of God. The court of Yahweh replaces the battlefield. Their differences will be settled by his just arbitration as his rule brings order into a fragmented world. Living at peace, they will turn their energy and resources to making the earth fruitful.

But these halcyon 'latter days' are yet far off. Meanwhile the editor adds an appeal to his own contemporaries (v. 5). It is not enough for us in Advent to hold out hope for a splendid new world order at the end of time. 'Come, let *us* walk in the light of the Lord'—now.

Note: The first four verses of this oracle are identical to Micah 4:1-3. It is possible that it was used in the temple liturgy and that verse 5 represents a corporate response from the congregation.

Romans 13:11—14

Paul has just summarized the Torah: 'Love is the fulfilling of the law' (13:10).

'Let us then...' (v. 12) echoes the Old Testament reading, but Paul's appeal carries a greater sense of urgency, for he is conscious of living in the end time. The Day of the Lord seems an immediate prospect. The familiar language of darkness (evil, Godless) versus light (good, God-filled) is interwoven with images of throwing off civilian clothing and seizing armour ready for battle.

Conduct that might escape censure under cover of darkness seems shameful in the light of day (cf. 1 Thessalonians 5:5-8). Paul's list of behaviour to be condemned is not confined to over-indulgence in wine and sex. A tendency to pick unnecessary arguments, a secret hint of jealousy—

these are less obviously dramatic faults but just as destructive of human relationships and Christian communities.

Paul offers his readers no opportunity for complacency or holier-than-thou attitudes: 'the flesh', the old nature, is still unreformed, ready to reassert its pull over us (cf. Colossians 3:5–10). Christians have a pattern for living in God's Son, who took our nature upon him, so that we could take his nature upon us. There is, as it were, an exchange of clothing. We are offered the privilege of 'wearing Christ'—and not just as a cover-up.

Matthew 24:36–44

The coming of God to his people under the old covenant or the new has three recurring motifs:

- **It will be unexpected.** Those who led self-contained lives in total disregard of God, or in which God was an irrelevance, found their complacency shattered when the flood came.
- **It will be divisive.** Noah and his family were saved, his contemporaries died. Men working alongside each other on the land, the women who had taken their grain together to be ground—each is separated from the neighbour who shares the same daily occupations.
- **It will be terrifying.** The cataclysmic flood struck with appalling finality. The householder's security is shattered by the intrusion of the thief.

Christians have no inside knowledge of the timing of the final consummation of the age. Even Jesus could not know. And yet they need not be caught unawares. They are to prepare for the great event, not by speculating about the date, but by living in a constant state of responsiveness to God. For them, the 'coming' of the Son of Man is an event to look forward to with eager expectation.

GS

YEAR B

Isaiah 64:1–9

'Don't just stand there, do something!' There is a holy frustration in Isaiah's prayer. This reading expresses the longing that we can also feel when everything is falling apart and God appears to be absent, silent or inactive.

Isaiah longed that God would tear open the heavens and put an end to his silence (v. 1). After a very profound silence, when the age of prophets seemed to have died out altogether, God did tear the heavens open. Mark

1:10 says, 'And just as [Jesus] was coming up out of the water, he saw the heavens torn apart and the Spirit descending like a dove on him.' In the same Gospel, the curtain that represents the veil between heaven and earth is also torn: 'And the curtain of the temple was torn in two, from top to bottom' (Mark 15:38).

Sometimes it is at the points of deepest despair, when nothing seems to be happening or when only bad things are taking place, that the grace of God intervenes in power. Isaiah was right to cry out to God, but he needed faith to believe that his prayer would be answered, even after hundreds of years had elapsed.

1 Corinthians 1:3–9

Waiting is a permanent feature of life. It is also a very particular feature of Christian life as we wait for the realization and fulfilment of that which we hope for. However, there are two kinds of waiting. One is characterized by boredom and inaction, the other by a positive working towards the goal that is sought.

Paul begins his largely critical first letter to the Corinthians with something positive. He rejoices that as they wait for the revealing of our Lord Jesus Christ they have speech, knowledge and every spiritual gift (vv. 5, 7). However, it is telling that Paul attributes all these positives to the grace of God (v. 4). Unfortunately, as the rest of Paul's letter reveals, the Corinthians have done even worse than the servant who buried his talent (Matthew 25:14ff.); they have used their gifts to negative effect.

We too have been offered the gifts of God's grace as we wait for the culmination of his purpose. We need to recognize those gifts where they exist and use them for the building of his Kingdom, and not for further dividing and weakening the body of Christ.

Mark 13:24–37

To know the future is a possibility that fascinates human beings. Jesus' disciples have asked him eagerly about the signs of the end of the age (13:4) and Jesus responds in a highly enigmatic fashion.

In our desire to know the future, it is tempting to read passages such as Mark 13 as a straightforward map of our present and future history. However, there is every indication that this was not Jesus' purpose. The chapter arises from a question regarding the timing of the destruction of the temple (13:1–2, 4). For Jesus, the temple is destroyed at his crucifixion and the ordering of the whole universe is radically altered at his resurrection. Thus, in one sense, the events described in Mark 13 have already happened. Even the final ingathering of the elect (v. 27) is already taking place. That is to say that people from all nations are being baptized into the life of the new and eternal Kingdom and are joining to share in the food of that Kingdom at the Eucharist.

This is not to say that the end of the age has already come. It is simply to observe that we are not waiting for the future hour of Christ's return as people might wait for a bus. Instead we keep watch for that future hour by living as people who have already begun to dwell within it.

AG

YEAR C

Jeremiah 33:14–16

Promises are only worth the ability of the promiser to deliver or, indeed, the truthfulness of that person. Here is a promise, however, which cannot be broken. Here the earlier promise of Jeremiah 23 is underlined with some significant details added.

This is first a 'gracious' promise. The failures and sins of Israel and Judah have not destroyed God's love for them because it was not their merits that caused his love in the first place. God's love is unconditional, a message which is at the heart of Advent. As the carol *Christians awake* says: 'Rise to adore the mystery of Love' (John Byrom, 1691–1763).

Second, this king embodies God's purposes in creation—'Branch' and 'spring up' (v. 15) are words which speak of the new life of God surging through the soil in the dark soil of exile. We may remember that wonderful scene from *The Lion, the Witch and the Wardrobe*: '"This is no thaw," said the dwarf, suddenly stopping. "This is Spring… This is Aslan's doing."'

Since Aslan has landed, spring is already at work. At Advent, in the darkness of the year, when the season is at its bleakest, the corner has been turned and we can already glimpse 'the high midsummer pomps' (Matthew Arnold) where the King already reigns.

1 Thessalonians 3:9–13

The letters to the Thessalonians repeatedly ring the note that the Lord is coming. The Church is a community waiting for the Son of God from heaven. This is an important reminder that for the early Church, Advent was not a frenetic preparation for Christmas but a waiting for the return of Christ. We are always in Advent, which is the period between the comings.

This does not lead to 'other-worldliness' but to an effective and expectant engagement with life. The more firmly we believe that Christ will one day wind up the affairs of this world and usher in a better one, the more urgently we will engage in all lawful and worthy activities until he comes.

Here Paul mentions three things which will mark the community as it waits for Advent. The first will be overflowing and generous love, the kind of love the King himself showed us (v. 12). The second will be a strong and disciplined life so that we will not be ashamed when he comes (v. 13). The third is a vibrant expectancy as we wait for him.

None of this is the old 'gospel of works' smuggled in by the back door. Rather, this is the work of God, a rescue operation from outside. When Christians respond in love, holiness and expectant hope, the Kingdom is already at work in their lives and thus the coming of the King is anticipated.

Luke 21:25–36

All through our Advent readings has run a continuous thread of the effect the coming of the King will have on creation. This is not simply to be a domestic gathering of the King and his people but an event which will profoundly affect heaven and earth. Here in the vivid language of apocalyptic and cosmic imagery, Luke speaks of what that coming will mean.

First, Luke links this event with other great events in the Bible's unfolding drama. The heavens themselves will be affected as they were at the first coming (vv. 25–26). The nations, as in Psalm 2, will rage like the troubled sea as God installs his King on the holy hill of Zion. Wesley, in his powerful Advent hymn, catches this emphasis: 'Lo he comes with clouds descending'.

Second, this will be a public and visible event (v. 27). The first coming was incognito; the young Prince of Glory landing in disguise behind enemy lines. This time it will be unveiled. Wesley, again: 'Every eye shall now behold him, robed in dreadful majesty'.

Third, like the Thessalonians passage, this is an impetus to strong and forward-looking faith (v. 36). The basis for this is the abiding and unshakeable word of God which will outlast the created universe. This is the word that links Jeremiah in the darkness of exile, Paul in his missionary journeys and Luke the evangelist. This is the message of Advent which will not only strengthen the individual but will confront institutional evil and the dark powers with the triumph of the Lamb.

RF

THE SECOND SUNDAY OF ADVENT

YEAR A

Isaiah 11:1–10

Isaiah has prophesied the downfall of Israel's oppressor, Assyria—like a majestic tree cut down in its prime (ch. 10). Now Israel, her empire reduced to a shattered stump by her mighty overlord, begins to show signs of new life—a healthy shoot. An ideal ruler will emerge, a descendant of David. He will discern truth beneath falsehood, he will right the genuine grievances of those unable to defend themselves. He will 'wear' righteousness and faithfulness, attributes of God himself, for he is God's viceroy.

So far, the prophecy could be describing a return to the golden age of Solomon. Verses 6–9 carry us into a vision of paradise where creation is at peace with itself and human beings have nothing to fear. 'Knowledge of the Lord' now belongs not only to the king (v. 2), but to the whole earth. This is a new age and a new world order.

'In that day' (v. 10) alerts us to the beginning of a new oracle. The *root* of Jesse (contrast v. 1) might well refer to the whole people of Israel who in the new age will stand like a flag, a rallying point, upon a hilltop.

Will Israel respond to this glorious calling? The New Testament sees the prophecy fulfilled in Jesus (Luke 2:30–32) and in the proclamation of the gospel (Acts 13:47).

Romans 15:4–13

Christian believers have hope (v. 4). Looking to the past, the record of God's dealings with his people and his promises to them encourage the Roman Christians to live with a steady sense of purpose in the present, and joyful anticipation for the future.

Interwoven with hope is the theme of harmony. For Jew and Gentile to live united in community is at least as revolutionary as the cow and the bear feeding together! A new age has dawned. Christ has fulfilled God's ancient promises for Jew and Gentile alike. It is in Christ that Jew and Gentile can open their lives to each other.

The Gentiles have hope (v. 12), for they are now part of the believing community. While Gentiles were strangers to the covenant of promise, they were 'without hope and without God in the world' (Ephesians 2:12, NIV). Now in Christ they have found God's mercy (v. 9) and that transforms their situation. They too are under his just and gentle rule (v. 12).

Above all, **God himself is the source of hope** (v. 13). Christian hope depends not on inside information about heaven or the timescale of God's plan. It is focused on the nature of God himself—his unwavering faithfulness and encouragement, his unchanging purpose of mercy. This is why Christian hope is a certainty, not just a supposedly safe bet.

Matthew 3:1–12

The new age, the rule of God, is about to break like a storm upon Israel, demanding immediate action.

Above all, what is needed is radical repentance. Repentance includes being sorry for wrongs committed and good deeds omitted. True repentance finds practical expression ('fruit', v. 8) More than that, however, repentance has echoes of prophets calling Israel to 'return to the Lord'. It requires a change of mindset, a deliberate turning towards God, setting out to live a God-centred life.

For the crowds confessing their sins, John offers baptism as a sign of repentance and desire for cleansing. The Pharisees and Sadducees, coming out of curiosity to investigate this latest religious movement (note 'to the baptism', not 'to be baptized'), are castigated for their complacency. The claim to be God's people requires more than descent from Abraham.

John's appearance is like Elijah (cf. 2 Kings 1:8); his outspoken preaching of coming wrath is in good prophetic tradition. Yet he sees himself not as occupying the centre stage, but as a humble forerunner. The Coming One will bring God's judgment with purifying fire and 'Holy Spirit'. Like wind sifting the tossed grain at wheat harvest, the Spirit will sift the committed believer from the lightweight dilettante.

Note: 'Wind' and 'spirit' are the same word in Greek.

GS

YEAR B

Isaiah 40:1–11

People who feel like failures can show this in their posture. Their steps are slow and their heads hang down. A good captain of a losing sports team will call out, 'Head up' when these signs of defeat appear. God speaks through Isaiah with that kind of voice of encouragement to disconsolate Israel (vv. 1, 9). After years in exile (v. 2), her assessment of herself has been brought very low, she cannot believe that there is anything lovable left in her, anything that would cause God to rescue her.

Like a prisoner whose sentence is suddenly ended, Israel is gently led back into the light of hope. The obstacles to her restoration that seemed insuperable are being supernaturally overcome. A path to a reunion with God has been made across the hostile desert. In a crescendo of exultation, Isaiah's prophecy pictures Israel being welcomed home by a torrent of praise to the God who leads them safely in like a shepherd (v. 11). It is this picture that opens Mark's Gospel (Mark 1:1).

2 Peter 3:8–15a

Waiting is the subject of this reading. Peter faces a congregation who are disillusioned by the non-appearance of the Lord in glory. They are like children who 'want it *now*'. Peter tries to introduce to them the idea that they can realize and hasten that for which they wait, by being 'at peace, without spot or blemish' (v. 14).

In our own time, this kind of impatience is rare. Some people have an opposite problem to that experienced by Peter's audience: they would rather that the Lord didn't appear just yet because things are quite all right as they are, thank you. Despite the possibility of different attitudes to Christ's return, Peter's message still applies. We need to be ready for the unknown moment by living as communities where righteousness is already at home.

Mark 1:1–8

The picture is one of the desert road leading from exile into homecoming. Mark picks up this image from Isaiah 40:3 and applies it to the events that he is about to record.

This preparation for reunion with God and the reinstatement of his rule is begun by John's ministry of baptism, but it doesn't stop there. The whole of Mark's Gospel is a description of how the mountains of sin are laid low and the waste places of death are made good, culminating in the resurrection of Jesus Christ. As we read Mark, we too are invited to prepare the way of the Lord. We begin this in our baptism and experience its full effects as we continue to follow Christ in his resurrection.

Isaiah spoke to people who were far from any hope, who needed a miracle. We are also those people, and the miracle we need, and the miracle we have received, is Jesus.

AG

YEAR C

Malachi 3:1–4

Much of our thinking about Advent tends to be sloppy and sentimental. Talk about helpless babies and innocent children tends to create an atmosphere where 'baby Jesus' ('no crying he makes'!) is banished to the nursery along with Santa Claus. How different is Malachi's picture of the coming.

First, it will be unexpected: 'suddenly' he will come and everything will change (v. 1). Yet he will be the one of whom the ancient patriarchs and prophets spoke—'the messenger of the covenant'.

> *This is he whom seers of old time,*
> *Chanted of with one accord.*
> *Whom the voices of the prophets*
> *Promised in their faithful word.*
> **Prudentius (348–c.413), trs. J.M. Neale (1818–66)**

It will also be terrifying: 'Who can endure?' (v. 2). It will not be tinsel, holly, docile beasts and a smiling infant dressed from Mothercare. The fire of judgment, the washing away of filth and the refiner's fire will purge and purify (vv. 2–3).

It will also be transforming. Like Jeremiah, two centuries before him, Malachi sees that this coming will transform society. The offerings will be as they once were (perhaps in the days of Josiah, worthiest of David's sons to sit on his throne) (v. 4). But this will be no repetition of a nostalgic past, because this time it will be no mere representative who sits on the throne but the King himself.

Philippians 1:3–11

Advent is a time of expectancy when the future casts its light on the present. Paul here speaks twice (vv. 6, 10) of 'the day of Christ', which is the Day of the Lord of which the old prophets spoke. To prepare for that is to live now in the light of then, confident that the 'good work' of the first coming will continue and grow until the second.

A number of characteristics will mark those who are living this way and thus anticipate the Kingdom. The first is the wonderful sense of fellowship engendered by our 'sharing in the gospel' (v. 5). Paul loves sincerely those to whom he had brought the gospel and strikes the characteristic note of 'joy' which is such a prominent feature of this letter. This joy is not one dependent on circumstances; Paul is 'in chains', yet the Advent gospel affirms that Christ is Lord and the last word will be his.

There will also be growth in knowledge and insight to enable the Christians to be at their most effective in the cause of Christ. Living in the time between the comings needs sharp perception and a deepening understanding of the gospel (vv. 9–10).

Also, as in Malachi, there will be growth in transformed living and holiness as Christ is formed in his people and his righteousness becomes the firstfruits of the harvest that will result at his coming. The King will already be reigning in hearts and lives and thus glory will be given to God (v. 11).

Luke 3:1–6

On Jordan's bank, the Baptist's cry
Announces that the Lord is nigh.
Charles Coffin (1676–1749)

Luke here plunges into the world of power politics with the roll-call of the great and the good. The mighty Roman Empire, under the increasingly paranoid Tiberius, is represented in Judea by Pontius Pilate—the man destined for ever to be remembered in the Apostles' Creed. Jewish power and prestige are represented politically by the Herod family and religiously by Annas and Caiaphas. Then, in one swift stroke, the evangelist marginalizes the entire world establishment: the word of God comes to John as it came to the ancient prophets. Indeed the fulfilment of these prophecies is now happening (vv. 1–2).

As in our last two passages, we have here a message of transformation. This is going to be an inner transformation. Baptism, the outward ritual of the cleansing of sin, is to be real because of the inward turning of the heart to God which is repentance. The inner deserts of sin, selfishness and rebellion have to be made ready for the coming of the King.

There is to be an outward transformation. The deserts and rough terrain will become a highway for God. This is a reminder that when the King comes again, not only will his people be saved but creation will be restored. Only a few had recognized the Advent of the King—Mary, Joseph, shepherds, Simeon and Anna—but on that day the King will be universally seen and acknowledged.

RF

THE THIRD SUNDAY OF ADVENT

YEAR A

Isaiah 35:1–10

The prophet unfolds God's plan for a new age, painting for the dispirited exiles a glowing picture of restoration.

Three particular aspects focus the prophet's attention:

- **Fertility for the land** (vv. 1–2). In the Old Testament, the land of Israel shares the fortunes of the people. When king and people are in harmony with God, the land prospers and is fruitful. When God's judgment falls upon them, the land becomes desolate. So as a sign of God's blessing, regions hitherto infertile and lacking water for crops will now be covered with rich pasture and trees.
- **Healing for the exiles** (vv. 3–6). For many, after generations in exile, the call to a journey back 'home' was a frightening prospect. But the promise is of an intervention of God, punishing the oppressor, rescuing his people. In the new age there will be no sickness or disability—all will be made whole.
- **A highway for God's people** (vv. 8–9). Those whom God has freed will walk in safety, with relief and joy. It is also a *holy* way, for those who are dedicated to following God in trust and obedience.

The boundaries between literal expectations and visionary ideals are blurred, for God's transforming power has no limits.

James 5:7–10

'Behold...' (vv. 7, 9, 11). James draws three comparisons to emphasize his message.

The rhythm of the countryside is an apt analogy to encourage those who are waiting for the coming of the Lord. The farmer has planted all his carefully husbanded seed but can do nothing to hurry the process if the vital rain is delayed. As the time for harvest approaches, he and his family may go hungry but still he must be patient. So those who face hardship and poverty must endure until the coming of Christ rights all wrongs.

Yet the coming Lord is about to break in upon them, like the Judge standing at the door—perhaps at the city gates where the judicial assembly met—ready to begin the day's proceedings. As they wait, they must not give way to doubt or allow frustration to erupt into criticizing others, but must remember that they too will face the discerning eye of the Judge.

Encouragement comes from looking back to others who have been similarly tested. The prophets and other heroes of the faith certainly faced persecution. Some may have been tempted to give up. But in fact they endured. As Christians wait with patience, they are in good company.

Matthew 11:2–11

In prison, John was mystified. He had been so sure that Jesus was God's chosen one; yet surely the Messiah, coming to bring God's judgment (3:12), would by now have taken control and vanquished the opposition? John hears of miracles of healing and teaching about loving your enemies, tales of a man who does not fast as a pious Jew should and who consorts with sinners as a pious Jew should not. Doubts creep in: can *this* be the Messiah?

Jesus' response is to ask John to think over the evidence. The miracles of healing and the proclamation of good news fulfil Old Testament prophecy of God's servant ushering in a new age (Isaiah 35:5–6; cf. 61:1). Many people 'took offence' (literally 'were tripped up') at a Messiah who failed to live up to their expectations, defied the conventions. Those who have the spiritual discernment to see God's hand at work are indeed 'blessed'!

Jesus turns the incident into an opportunity to challenge the crowd. What had drawn them like a magnet into the desert? Whether they realized it or not, they were responding to the compelling urgency of God's word through his chosen messenger.

Yet John was the last of the old order. To share in the fulfilment is better than to be the bearer of the promise.

GS

YEAR B

Isaiah 61:1–4, 8–11

It is sometimes observed that while Greek culture perceived history as proceeding in cycles, Hebrew culture understood history as travelling in a straight line towards a goal. This is a slight over-simplification. Time in the Bible certainly progresses towards an ultimate goal, but it does so in repeating patterns. We can see something of this as, from a Christian point of view, we read Isaiah 61. Jesus appropriates these words to himself as he sets out his own manifesto for the restoration of Israel (Luke 4:17–21).

Isaiah, and subsequently Jesus, addressed himself to those who were at the very lowest point of existence and promised that their situation would be reversed. Jesus announces in Luke 4:21 that he is the agent of God's table-turning action. However, it is noteworthy that this revolution is not the kind where the oppressed immediately becomes the oppressor. Rather, this is the Kingdom where the new ruler is the Suffering Servant himself.

This song is sometimes grouped with the Servant Songs of Isaiah and it provides a fitting climax to them. The means by which the restoration of God's people is possible is via the suffering that is a mark of the Servant's life and death (Isaiah 42:1–4; 53:10–12).

1 Thessalonians 5:16–24

'Rejoice always' (v. 16) may not seem like the most tactful instruction to give the Thessalonians. They had been experiencing persecution and had every reason to lick their wounds and feel sorry for themselves. However, Paul's letter is full of encouragements to go on living out the Christian life with ever-increasing commitment and passion (3:12; 4:1, 10). Paul longs for these Christians to step into a complete experience of God's grace and presence; and he asks that God would sanctify them *entirely* (v. 23). As the Thessalonians live in this new reality with increasing wholeheartedness, it will become entirely natural for them to rejoice always in their new and intimate experience of God, to converse with him without ceasing (v. 17), and to give thanks in all circumstances (v. 18)—despite the trials that they are experiencing in their earthly life.

From our standpoint, it is possible to view such unadulterated joy in the face of trouble as facile or unrealistic. However, it is precisely our vivid appreciation of the *reality* of God's Kingdom, in the present and beyond death, that will enable us to see our difficulties in new perspective. This is an instance where what we cannot see has a greater effect on our thoughts and feelings that what we can see.

John 1:6–8, 19–28

This passage is part of an interplay of descriptions of John and Jesus, but the lectionary only allows us one strand of the comparison here. The Gospels suggest that there was a complex relationship between John and Jesus. They are closely bound at the beginning of their ministry and yet John is left unclear as to Jesus' identity later in the story (Matthew 11:2–3). By the time we reach Acts 19, there is the suggestion that perhaps a strand of John's teaching had continued in Christian circles. The details with which we are provided are certainly sketchy, so it is difficult to reach any firm conclusions.

The central concern of this passage, however, is to show that John is a signpost to Jesus. He is the man, a very noble man, who prepares the ground for the one who will come after. As such, he is worthy of considerable respect, but he is not where the focus of our attention should lie. In our own context, we must be constantly aware of the temptation to make people who point to Christ, rather than Christ himself, the focus of our attention.

AG

YEAR C

Zephaniah 3:14–20

From my window I have a splendid view of Durham Cathedral, which looks as if it were rising immediately behind some houses at the other side of the allotments that face our streets. What cannot be seen from here is that between these houses and the cathedral lies the deep gorge of the River Wear. So it was that the old prophets peering across the centuries did not perceive the gap that would intervene between what we call the first and second comings. In a profound sense they were right: both comings are part of that great invasion of God into human affairs which will lead to the crowning of the King.

Zephaniah here breaks into song and, in what is in effect a little psalm, he rejoices that the Lord is enthroned in Zion. Here the emphasis is on God's presence with his people—Immanuel is there. As Revelation 21:3 says, 'See, the home of God is among mortals. He will dwell with them as their God'. The Saviour who rescued them from the enemy is also the Lover who cherishes and delights in his Bride (vv. 14–15).

This will result in blessing which will undo the rebellion and oppression of the first part of the chapter. Verse 18 is somewhat obscure but probably means that worship will be renewed and filled with God's presence. Further, God will honour his people, and the disadvantaged, the dispossessed and the dispersed will be restored and their deepest longings and hopes realized. This will be the result of the coming of the King and partially fulfilled in his first coming.

Philippians 4:4–7

At first sight, this passage is most embarrassing. First we are told to 'rejoice', which sounds rather like 'grin and bear it'. Then we are told that the way to peace is to tell God what we need. Even if this does not mean that God does not know what our requests are, at the very least he needs to be continually reminded. This is another pointer to the radical changes the coming of Christ makes in our lives.

Notice first the phrase 'in the Lord' (v. 4). This is not a call to be optimistic and have a 'positive' outlook. It is a call to realize that Christ is Lord, and that (as chapter 2 says) every knee will bow to him. Whatever is happening now, we can still sing that triumph song.

Second, in the meantime, God cares and wants to share all that takes our joy away (v. 6). It is not that he needs to know what we need and want; it is that we need to know by spelling it out in his presence and seeing it with his eyes.

Third, that will result in peace (v. 7). Advent is about a peace which is far more than the absence of hostility. It is the life of God in our hearts, homes and communities, anticipating the life of the world to come. That will guard us in the meantime. It will guard our hearts: it will give us a warm love for the Lord. It will guard our minds: it will save us from mere emotionalism.

Luke 3:7–18

As an audience-friendly soundbite, 'brood of vipers', we may feel, leaves something to be desired. Yet it is another example of the thread running through our Advent readings, which is that the coming of Christ is disturbing and brings about radical changes. Luke 3:1–6 spoke of a transformation of the desert and the removing of obstacles to the King's coming; here this is translated into the spiritual and ethical spheres.

First, this King requires allegiance rather than simply descent from Abraham; baptism without repentance is meaningless (v. 8). That John's opening sallies, however uncomfortable, are effective is shown by the crowd's question: 'What then should we do?' (v. 10). John's answer takes us to the very heart of Advent. Two things need to be noted.

The first is the ethical transformation already foretold in Zephaniah. By sharing food, by fair taxes, by equable administration of justice, anticipations of the Kingdom would already be seen. In an occupied and humiliated province, this was indeed radical good news (vv. 11–14).

The second is the apocalyptic language of baptism with fire which shows that Advent is far more than changes in society. This is the coming of God himself. The fire that accompanies his coming recalls the flaming sword at the gates of Eden, the bush that burned, the fiery pillar and other manifestations of God's holiness. It also looks forward to Pentecost when one of the signs of the coming of the Spirit is tongues of fire (vv. 16–17).

RF

The Fourth Sunday of Advent

Year A

Isaiah 7:10–16

Faced with a coalition besieging Jerusalem, the challenge to Ahaz, king of Judah, is clear: 'If you do not stand firm in faith, you shall not stand at all' (v. 9; cf. v. 2).

'Put your trust in Yahweh,' says Isaiah. But Ahaz was already putting his faith in an alliance with the might of Assyria, to secure his own position.

Isaiah's counsel of neutrality is based partly on political foresight. Assyria would conquer Syria and northern Israel regardless of Ahaz's actions and involvement, so their plot to depose him will fail. The proposed alliance will leave Judah as a vassal state.

Much more important for Isaiah, however, is the damage Ahaz is doing to the relationship between Yahweh and his people. Ultimately, salvation for the nation depends upon trusting God to be faithful to his promises. (cf. 2 Kings 16:10–18).

Intent on his own plans, Ahaz will not even consent to asking Yahweh for a sign to guide his decision. Exasperated, Isaiah announces that he will get one whether he likes it or not! A child will be born, bearing a sign-name as a word from Yahweh. In all this danger and complexity, 'God is with us'. There is nothing to fear: before the child is weaned, the threat will have dissolved.

Ahaz spurned Isaiah's assurance and effectively turned his back upon Yahweh. The sign-name of promise is turned into a threat of judgment (v. 17). But Immanuel becomes a reality in the birth of Jesus.

Romans 1:1–7

Paul sets the scene for his great exposition of 'the gospel of God'.

The subject of the good news is Jesus. By his human birth, he is 'great David's greater son', thus fulfilling promises made by generations of prophets. By his resurrection, he is defined as Son-of-God-in-power.

The purpose of the good news is to open up the possibility of faith in God for all the nations (v. 5), Gentiles as well as Jews. And because Jesus Christ is *Lord*, faith will mean not only belief but also obedience to his will.

The effect of the good news is that men and women respond to the call of God:

• All are called to belong to Jesus Christ (v. 6).

- Christians, beloved of God, are called to be saints (v. 7), progressively being made holy.
- Paul (v. 1) and others (v. 5) are called to be apostles, messengers.

The power of the good news is grace, God's love in action. The apostles live by grace (v. 5); 'grace to you' is Paul's greeting (v. 7).

Every person of the Trinity is involved in this good news—the Father from whom it originates (vv. 1, 7), the Son who is its focus (v. 3), the Holy Spirit who reveals it (v. 4).

Matthew 1:18–25

Matthew's 'nativity' does not describe the birth of Jesus but rather explains his origin, seen from Joseph's perspective.

Joseph's ancestry is important. In Matthew's genealogy, the line runs back though David to Abraham, father of the nation. Jesus is a true Israelite. The angel addresses Joseph as 'son of David'. The expected Messiah would be a descendant of David. Joseph taking Jesus into his house confirms his legal lineage.

Joseph's character is important. As a morally upright, law-abiding man, Joseph could, and in the eyes of his contemporaries probably should, have divorced Mary publicly. Her story no doubt presented him with a dilemma, but he is a man of generous spirit (v. 19).

Joseph's openness to God is vital. A man in tune with God, he is able to accept the unimaginable as the word of God. Obedient to God, he acts on his convictions, living no doubt with the innuendoes and scorn of his acquaintances Taking Mary as his wife, he gives her care and protection but denies himself the sexual intimacy of marriage until the child is safely born.

Joseph has a key role in the divine plan, leaving an example of faith, courage and obedience.

GS

YEAR B

2 Samuel 7:1–11, 16

Most of our actions express a tangle of conflicting motives. It is likely that David's desire to build a temple for the Lord was no exception. Towards the end of his reign he was struck by the thought that it was not seemly that the Lord should dwell in a tent while he lived in a palace (v. 2).

While this may seem like an entirely generous and pious notion, it is one that is fraught with confused motives and misperceptions. Among these he may have been driven by a desire to win God's favour by a generous act.

All this was, however, entirely wrongheaded. God revealed, through Nathan, that he didn't need a place to live provided for him and David certainly did not need to invent tasks for himself in order to win God's approval. In response, God turned the whole project on its head and revealed that it was David who would be the recipient of a house (v. 11), not one made of wood or stone, but a dynasty to reign before God for ever (v. 16).

Romans 16:25–27

In closing his letter to the Romans, Paul returns to two important themes— first, that something new has been revealed by God, and second, that this revelation calls for a response of faith (v. 26).

The something new that has been revealed may seem anything but new to us at the beginning of the twenty-first century. However, we should remember that something profoundly mysterious and valuable has been made available to all people and to us. This gospel should not lose its preciousness because it has been laid open. Rather, that openness should inspire praise to the One who has made it so.

It is a natural human instinct not to trust that which we cannot completely control or understand. Paul urges his readers to open their eyes to the revelation of God's purpose and to walk in 'the obedience of faith' (v. 26) the road that, through Christ, he has set before us and that leads into the fullness of his presence.

Luke 1:26–38

After all the trials, failures and ultimate collapse of the Davidic dynasty, the thread of the story of God's involvement with his people is rejoined. In the Old Testament reading, God made a promise to give David a house (2 Samuel 7:11, 16). Now, in Luke's account, that same house re-emerges into the foreground (v. 27), in preparation for the completion of the promise.

At the centre of this account, however, is Mary rather than Joseph (v. 27). There is something significant in the fact that God chose to fulfil his promise to David, the hope of a Messiah for Israel, through a teenage girl. Once again we can see God setting his own agenda and fulfilling his purpose according to his own nature.

Mary was the right girl for the job. It is unlikely that others would have considered her to be suitable for anything more spectacular than the ordinary life that seemingly stretched before her. God, on the other hand, was able to see more. From the humble starting-point of Mary's willingness to be God's servant, he was able to bring the means of our salvation into being.

AG

YEAR C

Micah 5:2–5a

'Once in our world there was a stable which had something in it which was larger than the whole world.' These wonderful words from C.S. Lewis' *The Last Battle* express something of the wonder of this passage. In the world of brutal power politics where the Assyrian superpower is devouring everything in its path, a Shepherd-King will arise from an obscure village and establish another kingdom. Three things are noteworthy in this passage.

The first is the link with God's activity in the past. Bethlehem was 'royal David's city' and this King was to be David come again. God had saved his people through David in the past and this gave confidence that he would do so again (v. 2).

But the second is that something more fundamental than a new Davidic king is being spoken of. After all, they did have one in Micah's time— Hezekiah, who stood up to the Assyrian 'Goliath'. 'From of old' takes us back further than David, to the staggering realization that at Christmas we celebrate the fact that the Creator, like his creatures, was going to be born into the world (v. 2b).

> *Lo within a manger lies*
> *He who built the starry skies.*
> **Edward Caswall (1814–78)**

The third thing to note is that this King will reign over the whole earth and will do so for ever (vv. 4–5a). The result of his reign will be 'peace'. The great Hebrew word *shalom* gathers up all the associations of loving community and justice and security which have resonated throughout all our Advent readings.

Hebrews 10:5–10

One of the most beautiful sights in nature is to see a whole landscape, indeed skyscape, reflected in a deep lake. So it is that in the letter to the

Hebrews the whole landscape of the Old Testament is mirrored and re-defined. The old sacrificial system pointed beyond itself to the one sacrifice with which God was pleased. Christ has already been celebrated as Creator (1:2) and, throughout the letter, as Saviour. The old carol *The First Nowell* encapsulates this simply but powerfully

> *...our heavenly Lord,*
> *Who hath made heaven and earth of naught,*
> *And with his blood mankind hath bought.*

Here our author (vv. 5–7), quoting from Psalm 40:6–7, emphasizes the incarnation—'a body you prepared for me'. This was a real birth into an unfriendly world, and led to a real death. Moreover, this birth and this death were not stopgaps like the ancient cult. Rather, this was the reality to which they pointed.

Moreover, the sacrifice was voluntary (v. 9). The innumerable animals could do no other and could act as no more than an object lesson. Ultimately it needed someone who was fully human, and only Christ, who is one with God as well as one of us, could be the one 'full, perfect and sufficient sacrifice, oblation and satisfaction for the sins of the whole world' (*Book of Common Prayer*).

A most impressive painting shows Jesus in Mary's arms; beyond an open doorway stands a cross and, beyond that still, an open tomb. So Advent focuses and adumbrates the great saving events of the gospel.

Luke 1:39–45 [46–55]

'How beautiful upon the mountains are the feet of the messenger... who brings good news,' sings the prophet Isaiah (52:7). Mary, like countless of her people, travels the uplands of Judah, and, in her case, literally carried the Word. She 'went with haste', reads the text, and this conveys a sense of urgency as she sets out on a journey of probably some eighty miles from Nazareth to this unnamed 'Judean town in the hill country' (v. 39).

What did Advent mean to Mary and thus to us who, in a figurative sense, carry the Word? First of all, it is a call to courage and risk-taking. For her, there would be the hazards of bandits, wild animals and primitive caravanserais (like the one she is not allowed into in chapter 2!) For us, there will be unknown challenges, and following Christ will 'cost not less than everything'.

Second, on one level, Mary's shared joy with Elizabeth is entirely natural —two expectant mothers sharing the joy of childbearing. But there is something deeper. 'Elizabeth was filled with the Holy Spirit' (v. 41), which reminds the reader that the Creator is at work. In verse 43, her question, 'Why has this happened to me, that the mother of my Lord comes to me?' is reminiscent of 2 Samuel 6:9: 'How can the ark of the Lord come into my care?' Mary is indeed the ark of the covenant, carrying the glory of God.

Third, their shared joy is embodied in the word 'blessed' (vv. 42, 45), used several times in the passage. This means much more than 'happy', which is a feeling. It means rather the reality that God is favourably disposed whether we feel it or not. Advent is far more about what God has done and is doing; our response is important, but secondary.

RF

CHRISTMAS EVE

EUCHARIST

2 Samuel 7:1–5, 8–11, 16

In the long story of the Old Testament, no name shines more prominently (apart from Moses) than David, and our Christmas Eve readings focus on his part in the drama that led to the coming of his greater son. Yet the emphasis is on God's initiative and how he works throughout all the changing scenes and in all the different personalities to bring about his purposes. This passage is a crucial moment in the unfolding story and is given further significance by being the words of God spoken through the prophet Nathan.

David longs to build a temple to symbolize the settled presence of God among his people. Nathan's answer simultaneously disappoints in the short term and, in the long term, promises far more than a house for the Lord, but the Lord is going to build a house for David. 'House' has all the associations of palace, temple and dynasty.

Moreover, this promise will never be repealed. Sin will be punished, both in David and in his descendants. Verse 16, however, says 'Your house and your kingdom shall be made sure for ever'. What a mockery these words must have seemed at the Babylonian exile; but on Christmas Eve, as we stand on the threshold of the birth of David's greater son, we know that these words are true and in that we can rejoice. And our New Testaments open with the birth of the King, Jesus, Son of David.

Acts 13:16–26

Christmas Eve, and twelve of the clock,
Now they are all on their knees.

These nostalgic words from Thomas Hardy are redolent with associations such as holly, log fires, Christmas cards, festive food and the like, which most of us connect with this season. One of the problems of such things, beautiful in themselves, is that they can create a kind of unreal Christmas divorced from the rest of the biblical gospel. Nothing could be further from the truth. Paul's words here, like those of Nathan, link Christmas with the whole story of salvation and show us how, at Christmas, God intervened decisively in Christ. Three important facts emerge.

The first is that God's rescue plan for the world was entirely his initiative. Words like 'chose', 'made great', 'gave', 'have found' (vv. 17–22), show that the living God was and is at work in history.

The second is that God's purposes are not thwarted by human weakness. 'He put up with them in the wilderness' (v. 18) is a tribute to his love and his patience. The failure of Saul, likewise, did not prevent God fulfilling his promise.

And third, reminding us of Nathan's prophecy, the spotlight falls on David from whose descendants 'God has brought to Israel a Saviour, Jesus' (v. 23). Christmas is not simply a time when the oxen low, when carols fill the frosty air and gifts are given and received. Christmas is the promised time when God's love is revealed in the son of David who is also the Son of God.

Luke 1:67–79

Luke 1 is full of the songs of those whose salvation has drawn near and who, in words drawn from the deep wells of the Old Testament, celebrate the coming of the Messiah. Zechariah's song—often called the Benedictus—in glowing and rich words welcomes the rising sun from heaven. This majestic song gathers the great themes of divine providence and mercy which have been at the heart of our other Christmas Eve readings.

First, Zechariah recalls the great historic acts of salvation. 'Redeemed his people' (v. 68) especially recalls the exodus event which was the birthday of the nation. The promise to Abraham (v. 73) is about to be fulfilled. And again, the house of David is to rejoice in the birth of the greatest son, the King of kings (v. 69).

Second, Zechariah echoes the language of the Psalter, that great treasury of Israel's praise. Like Mary, he blends the liturgical and the personal. These words, while spoken on particular occasions and applicable to others, are particularly focused on the day which is about to dawn.

And that is the third thing. Zechariah, with awe, realizes that his own child, John, is to be the one who prepares the way of the Lord (v. 76). That way will involve repentance and forgiveness. It will be the beginning of a new creation where life will overwhelm death and light will swallow darkness. With bated breath, Zechariah stands on the very threshold of the new age when the ancient prophecies are to be fulfilled and God will visit his people (v. 75).

RF

CHRISTMAS DAY

YEARS A, B, C (SET I)

Isaiah 9:2–7

The scene is a royal coronation. The prophet sees in the young king a child of promise, who will walk in the steps of his great ancestor, David, and fulfil the hopes and aspirations of the nation. The time of war and oppression and suffering is over. On his accession to the throne, the king is acclaimed as God's son and heir. He is given 'throne names', royal titles for the royal task:

- **Wonderful Counsellor:** he will be a wise political leader.
- **Mighty God (better translated 'Divine Warrior'):** he will be strong in battle.
- **Everlasting Father (better translated 'Father for ever'):** he will care for the welfare of his people.
- **Prince of Peace:** his reign will bring stability, with prosperity. Never again will the nation's security be shattered.

In fact, not even the 'good kings' were able to live up to this ideal. But each Christmas we celebrate the birth of the child who *does* fulfil the prophet's promise. In the Christ-child are the wisdom, the strength, the compassion and the peace of God himself. Faith and hope are renewed as we work and wait for his rule to be established throughout the world.

Titus 2:11–14

Christmas can easily become a time of spiritual escapism, a refuge from the challenging realities of daily life. This letter offers a very different perspective.

We live in the end times, between grace and glory.

The grace of God *has* appeared (v. 11; cf. John 1:17). In the birth at Bethlehem, in the life and ministry of Jesus, this grace has taken human form—love in action, God's way of salvation.

The glory *will* appear (v. 13). It is there already in the child in the manger, but veiled by his weakness and vulnerability. The time will come when it will be made manifest to all—unmistakable, the universal revelation of God's purpose.

Keeping these two pivotal events in view—past and future—gives us a sense of direction in the present.

- **It is a spur to holiness** (v. 12). Grace has come into our lives to prepare us for glory.
- **It is a source of hope** (v. 13). We move forward in joyful expectation towards God's future.

But we cannot have Christmas without the cross (v. 14). In his death, as in his birth, is our grace and our glory.

Luke 2:1–20

He was born in Bethlehem because the bureaucrats were updating the taxation register. His cradle was a cattle trough because the pub was so overcrowded. The most important birth in the history of humankind is recorded in a single factual sentence (v. 7). Despite the baby's royal lineage, it seems that Luke is underlining the very *ordinariness* of it all.

This throws the story of the shepherds into sharper relief, for here the divine realm touches the human. For a brief moment, the shepherds are given a window into the joy and praise of heaven. Then the light and the voices fade and they are alone again on a bare hillside, with the sheep. No wonder they needed a sign to convince them that their experience was real!

Mary pondered, the shepherds rejoiced. Both responses are needed as we celebrate God's priceless gift. The incarnation remains a gift of mystery beyond all human definition: we can only meditate in awe and wonder. It is also a gift of joy, lifting us above and beyond human fears and anxieties. For God himself is with us, sharing our humanity.

All human life is transfigured by this moment. There is a fleeting glimpse of glory at Jesus' birth. Eternal glory is open to all who recognize in this very ordinary baby 'the Saviour who is Christ the Lord'.

GS

Years A, B, C (Set II)

Isaiah 62:6–12

'Do this in remembrance of me.' These familiar words from the communion service are perhaps most obviously understood, to today's readers at least, as meaning that part of the purpose of the Eucharist is to help us to remember Christ's sacrifice for us.

The reading from Isaiah, however, invites an additional understanding of the idea of remembrance. 'You who remind the Lord, take no rest' the prophet urges (vv. 6–7). The function of these 'reminders' was to keep calling out to God to fulfil his promise to Israel and to restore Jerusalem and his Kingdom on earth. Thus, the remembrance that takes place in the communion need not be solely concerned with *our* memory, it may also be in the sense of 'in remembrance of me before *God*'.

Today we celebrate the beginning of a decisive new phase in God's dealing with his creation. The coming of Jesus opens up the possibility of God's rule truly being restored, just as Isaiah had foreseen (vv. 11–12). The process begun on the night of Christ's birth has yet to be completed. We still pray, 'Your kingdom come, Your will be done on earth as it is in heaven.' In the Holy Communion that we celebrate today, we call out to God once again to answer that prayer more and more.

Titus 3:4–7

Sometimes, people's failure to respond to changed circumstances can be funny. Sitcom writers frequently create the type of situation where, for example, colleagues are lamenting their employer's dress sense while being unaware of the boss's unseen presence. Similarly, a 'fish out of water' scenario might place city slickers in a forbidding wilderness, or desert dwellers in a busy metropolis.

Paul urged Titus to remind his churches of their changed situation. They were no longer to act as they had formerly done (3:3), but to respond to their new situation as 'heirs according to the hope of eternal life' (3:7)—by living like it!

On Christmas Day, we celebrate the turning point in human history. How have we responded to that changed situation? Are we comically, or not so comically, out of touch?

Luke 2:[1–7] 8–20

When we have a piece of good news to tell, we generally make a beeline for those who we think will share our joy most wholeheartedly. It is significant, therefore, that God chose to share the news of Christ's birth with a group of shepherds. At the time of Jesus' birth, shepherds were despised, poorly paid and generally suspected of dishonesty. It was people just such as this who had the most to gain from the birth of Christ. The good news is said to be 'for all people' (v. 10), but it certainly wasn't good news for Herod and those who benefited from the *status quo*.

God's choice of the shepherds invites an interesting question in our present situation: if God was about to perform an act of power to bring about his justice in our own time, would he expect us to be pleased to hear about it? Those of us who are quite happy with things as they are might not be his first port of call.

A G

YEARS A, B, C (SET III)

Isaiah 52:7–10

A virtually forgotten poem by a virtually forgotten poet—*A Christmas Hymn* by A. Domet—catches neatly the indifference of high and low, Roman senator and 'weary boor', to the birth in a stable, in 'a paltry province', 'in the solemn midnight, centuries ago'. This 'strange indifference' still marks 'low and high', 'drowsed over common joy and cares'.

How different from this glorious passage which is a song of celebration about the Lord visiting and redeeming his people. This song goes to the heart of what Christmas is about: God's rescue mission will not only free Israel from exile, not only save the nations, but the whole of the cosmos will share in his redemption.

Jerusalem has suffered siege and destruction. Many a time, messengers must have come with evil tidings. Here a distant runner appears on the hills waving a victory palm and leaping in triumph. As he approaches the city, he bursts into song about how God's coming will bring joy, freedom and peace (v. 7).

The solo voice merges into a choir as the watchman on the city walls join the song (v. 8). The arm of God who had rescued from Egypt, Babylon and every other tyrant is bared, not to aggrandize himself but to rebuild, restore, renew and free those who are enslaved by sin, imprisoned in darkness and subject to tyranny. That song is more than an earthly one: it is to be taken up by the heavenly hosts who sing 'to you is born a Saviour who is Christ the Lord'.

Hebrews 1:1–4

In majestic language the author begins his exposition of the uniqueness of Jesus Christ which is the theme at the heart of every true celebration of Christmas. He tells us that nothing further about God can ever be known than the full revealing of himself in Jesus Christ. That said, such is the wonder and mystery that we will never fully understand it.

The author tells us that while God's coming in Jesus is unique, nevertheless he is the fulfilment of earlier revelation. The pages of the Old Testament rustle and sigh with expectation. God's written word fully and faithfully points to Christ, his living Word (vv. 1–2). Who is this final Word of God, born for us at Christmas?

He is God himself: 'Veiled in flesh the Godhead see'. He is the creator and sustainer of the whole universe and is thus both the reason for creation and its goal.

He is also the redeemer. The great twin Old Testament themes of creation and exodus meet at Bethlehem and continue to Calvary and beyond, to the new heaven and new earth (v. 3b).

The mention of the angels (v. 4) is another link with the Christmas story. Gabriel announced the wonder of the incarnation to Mary; the heavenly hosts celebrated it in the sky above the Bethlehem hillsides. But they were only messengers, the King himself has come and nothing can ever be the same again. This is what Christmas is about; in the words of John Betjeman, 'God was man in Palestine'.

John 1:1–14

When a biographer sets out to write the life of some great person, the first problem is finding the best place to begin. With the birth, with the parents, with the circumstances of the time or with a multitude of other possible starting points? John, with amazing words which echo the opening words of Genesis, takes us back to eternity itself (v. 1). Jesus Christ did not begin at Bethlehem. There never was a time when the Son was not with the Father (v. 2). Before the solar system wheeled through space, Jesus was there; when the continents were molten lava, Jesus was there; when the dinosaurs roamed the earth, Jesus was there.

As he comes into the world he brings the gifts that only the Creator can bring—light and life. But he did more: 'he became flesh and pitched his tent among us' (v. 14) as, long ago, God's glory was revealed in the tent in the desert and there he lived and travelled with his people. God has visited us in his Son, one with him who became one of us and is one of us still.

That coming which divides history also divides people into those who believe and those who do not (vv. 10–12). People have no natural ability to become children of God; it is a gift. Christmas (and all three readings have emphasized this) is the great rescue mission of God to win back his world. As we were helpless, lost and wandering, the living Word came among us, bringing us the gift of himself. So Christmas calls us to the life of faith and trust which has at its heart the great miracle that God has come to us in Jesus.

RF

THE FIRST SUNDAY OF CHRISTMAS

YEAR A

Isaiah 63:7–9

These verses lose their point if taken out of context. The chapter begins, 'Who is this?' as the Lord appears, alone, soaked in blood. This is the avenging God, who has rescued his people by trampling hostile nations like grapes in the wine press.

The warrior God contrasts sharply with the tender God who, in compassion, lifts and carries his people as a Father picks up his children (v. 9; cf. Hosea 11:3–4). In this song of thanksgiving the writer stresses Yahweh's overflowing kindness to Israel—steadfast love, goodness, mercy, pity. He feels the pain of his people personally; he intervenes personally to save them.

The tragic irony is that God trusts them (v. 8). They are his chosen people, adopted as his children. And yet—they rebel and grieve his Holy Spirit (v. 10). The anger of the warrior God is now vented on those he has called his own. The writer cries out 'Thou art our Father... (but) we have become like those over whom thou hast never ruled, like those who are not called by thy name' (vv. 16, 19).

In the coming of Christ, the steadfast love of God again intervenes to save, by sending his own Son. Will his people accept him? 'He came to his own home, and his own people received him not...' (John 1:11).

Hebrews 2:10–18

'*Cur Deus homo*?' asked Anselm. 'Why did God become man?'

His answer is that the injury caused by human sin is so great that no one less than God himself could make reparation. But since the debt is incurred by the human race, only a human being ought to pay it.

God's eternal purpose is to bring us as his children to live in the glory of his presence. Only by entering human experience could God open up a way that human beings could follow. Jesus, God's own Son, is the trailblazer for this rescue operation—at the cost of his own life.

Jesus has identified totally with us in our humanness.

- Dying as the perfect human being, he broke the fearful stranglehold of death (for the powers of evil had no legitimate claim on him).
- Offering the perfect sacrifice (himself) as our high priest, he secured forgiveness for all our sin.
- Being tested and suffering as our brother, he is able to help us when we are tested.

So he makes us 'holy', fit for the presence of God, his Father and ours (v. 11). 'He became what we are, so that we might become what he is' (Irenaeus).

Matthew 2:13–23

It is no accident that the reading for Holy Innocents Day so closely follows Christmas, although historically the events were separated by many months.

All through his life, Jesus appears as a threat to the vested interests of those who have power and influence. Wherever the truth and goodness of God are seen, a backlash of evil is provoked and others are caught in the crossfire. Victory will be won at unimaginable cost.

The suffering begins early—the little child a refugee, his parents driven from their home in fear. Other children are the innocent victims of Herod's paranoia; *their* parents grieve in anguish.

At one level, Herod is the chief protagonist, inflicting suffering to save his own position. Yet at another level, he plays a very minor role in the drama of salvation, for God is in control. Herod's actions serve only to demonstrate that God's plan is unfolding as he himself foretold (vv. 15 and 18). In God's economy, Joseph the carpenter from Nazareth has a far more privileged role than the king in Jerusalem.

Jesus, God's Son, has come to fulfil the role originally assigned to Israel, rescued from slavery (out of Egypt) to be God's servant (cf. Hosea 11:1).

GS

YEAR B

Isaiah 61:10—62:3

Now is the time for carols! The pressure to celebrate Christmas prematurely is too great to bear for many churches. Some, however, reserve the singing of carols until after the event that these songs celebrate. This may be a little hard for most people to understand, but it has a certain logic: we wait for Christmas, and then celebrate its consequences. Our more usual experience, however, is to run ourselves into the ground in the preparation for Christmas and then heave a huge sigh of relief that it's all over for another year.

The songs of exultation in Isaiah 61:10–11 are a wonderful expression of praise. There is praise from the inside out, as the 'whole being' exults. There is a gift from the outside in, signified by the robe and the clothing of the bride and bridegroom. We too receive this kind of new clothing when God, in his mercy, reckons us as righteous, through the saving work of his Son.

Isaiah 62:1 contains a note of pressing on towards the goal. So Isaiah rejoices in the vindication of the faithful, but he also looks forward to its complete fulfilment (62:2). The situation may be illustrated by a poor analogy. It is good to rejoice in the moment of buying a delightful tub of ice-cream, but in order to complete that joy it is necessary to get it home and eat it in company. The same may be said of our rejoicing in Christmas.

Galatians 4:4–7

Here is news that we might have dreamed of, but never believed would actually happen. A messenger comes to the door to tell us that we are the heir of a huge fortune.

The fortune that Paul speaks of is not, of course, the forgotten country seat in the Scottish Highlands, but it is membership of a true family. We, who were orphans, have been adopted into an intimate relationship as children of the living God (v. 5).

If this were not generosity enough, our given status as children, which we did not deserve by birth or by effort, makes us heirs to every blessing that our heavenly Father can bestow upon us. Sometimes we are given gifts that are too large for us to accept in an instant. This one certainly takes some digesting.

Luke 2:15–21

One of Mary's distinctive qualities, in Luke's account, was her ability to think over the extraordinary events that were going on within and around her (2:19, 51). This type of reflection is vital if the larger picture is to be pieced together. Sometimes we read, hear or experience something that does not fit in with our previous view of the world or of God. An ability to hold these things in mind means that later connections and clarifications are made possible.

The naming and circumcision of Jesus (v. 21), two seemingly innocuous events, express his connection with two important figures among God's ancient people. His circumcision links him to Abraham, the one through whose seed God promised to bless all nations. His name links him with Joshua, the 'saviour' who led the children of Israel from the desert, across the Jordan and into the promised land. The saviour Jesus fulfils God's covenant made with Abraham and leads his people, like Joshua, through the waters of death to dwell in the Kingdom of God.

AG

YEAR C

1 Samuel 2:18–20, 26

'The angels had left them and gone into heaven' (Luke 2:15) expresses what many of us feel when the presents are opened, the dinner is eaten and the sense of anticlimax comes, not least in the empty pews of the Sunday after Christmas. Our readings today remind us that God's work goes on and that Christmas is a beginning.

Here in 1 Samuel 2, amid the gross failure of Eli's sons and Eli's own pathetic weakness, God is preparing young Samuel in a way which astonishingly prefigures Jesus' own boyhood. Three things are worth noting.

The first is the practical love and care of his mother Hannah. Every year a new priestly garment was provided for her growing son. This is as much an evidence of genuine piety as more formal liturgical activity (v. 19).

The second is that Eli, compromised as he is, still prays, and these prayers are accepted by God and generously answered in Hannah's receiving of five other children for the one she had given to the Lord. Thus God's blessing overrules and overtops human sin and frailty. Where sin abounds, grace abounds so much more (v. 20).

Third, the comment in verse 26 on Samuel's growth and increasing maturity is taken up by Luke, who applies the same words to the boy Jesus (Luke 2:52). God is working his purposes out in old Israel which will one day culminate in one greater than Samuel who will perfectly exemplify what the prophet showed partially.

Colossians 3:12–17

There is always the temptation in our Christian lives to search for the spectacular and to ignore the steady growth of the life of faith—'How silently, how silently the wondrous gift is given'. However, the Christian life must grow and develop in the 'ordinary' times when the angels have gone back into heaven. Here Paul shows how, as Christ grew up in Nazareth, so the Christian community grows up as the word of Christ dwells richly in us.

The growing will be active—'clothe yourselves' (vv. 12–14). Being clothed with love is identical to 'put on the Lord Jesus Christ' (Romans 13:14). Love is not just one of the virtues such as compassion, kindness, and so on, but rather the atmosphere in which these other virtues will flourish.

This growing will be receptive—'let the peace of Christ rule in your hearts' (v. 15). This is not primarily a subjective feeling, rather it is the peace that Christ brings between God and us by his death (see Colossians 1:20). By appreciating that we are not perfect, but forgiven, we can then receive and share Christ's own reign of peace.

This growing will be worshipful—'teach and admonish and... sing' (v. 16). A church's growth will be fostered by great songs of praise which are truly and richly biblical and which sound a deep note of thankfulness.

This growing will be comprehensive—'whatever you do' (v. 17). The motivation to maturity is thankfulness for all God has done in Christ, and it involves a total lifestyle—'whatever you do, in word or deed'.

Luke 2:41–52

J.H. Newman's line that says, 'A second Adam to the fight and to the rescue came' can be much more widely applied. Here now is the 'second Samuel' perfectly fulfilling all that the first Samuel had attempted. Luke completes his birth narrative with this charming vignette which is the only account we have of Jesus' boyhood outside apocryphal accounts. There is a vivid blend of the awesome and the homely, as is characteristic of Luke.

Jesus, whom Colossians describes as the one 'in whom are hidden all the treasures of wisdom and knowledge' (2:3), engages the teachers in profound discussion of wisdom. Here is the mystery of the Word made flesh as he voluntarily subjects himself both to teachers and parents. Luke shuns the bizarre apocryphal legends of the young Jesus' magical powers.

We should notice, too, the subtle interplay of 'your father' (v. 48) and 'my Father' (v. 49). Luke, with marvellous restraint, suggests Jesus' growing consciousness of all that lay before him. Much later, in 21:6, Jesus is to speak of 'the days... when not one stone will be left upon another'. Just as young Samuel had heard the voice of the Lord in the shrine of that time at Shiloh, so the boy Jesus listens and obeys the voice of his Father as well as his earthly parents (v. 51).

Like Mary, we can only treasure these things in our heart. The veil now falls and it is some eighteen years before we meet Jesus again at the beginning of his public ministry. This is our Lord, one with God, who became one of us and is one of us still.

RF

THE SECOND SUNDAY OF CHRISTMAS

YEARS A, B, C

Jeremiah 31:7–14

The coming of Christ has long been seen as the end of exile for his people, and in this exuberant poem, Jeremiah celebrates the blessing God will give to the restored community. The oracle falls into three parts.

Verses 7–12 call the believing community to praise because of God's mighty acts in salvation. Salvation in this particular context involves reuniting God's people from all the nations of the world, a vision which is eventually to find fulfilment in 'a great multitude that no one could count, from every nation, from all tribes and peoples and languages, standing before the throne and before the Lamb' (Revelation 7:9). It further involves healing and cherishing of the weak, despised and vulnerable. God will be both Shepherd and Father and will make a way for them (v. 8).

Verses 10–12 address the surrounding nations who are given God's view of history. The exile was caused by God 'who scattered Israel' and will be reversed by him who will 'ransom' them. A new exodus is about to happen. Indeed, in a promise redolent of Eden and anticipatory of heaven, the land will blossom and flourish.

Verses 13–14 develop the theme of God's blessing as he undoes the exile. The language of mourning turning to joy and dancing and gladness goes far beyond the return from Babylon and looks forward to the last day when Christ will establish his Kingdom and God will make everything new.

Ephesians 1:3–14

The glowing promises of the Jeremiah passage are intensified in this glorious doxological passage which brings together the love of God before all ages, its revelation in the coming of Christ and its full reality in 'the fullness of time' (v. 10).

Notice first that the Trinity is the source of all our blessings. Father, Son and Holy Spirit have committed themselves to bringing the people not just back from exile but home to glory (see vv. 3, 5, 13).

See too how this vast eternal plan focuses on the cross and the forgiveness that flows from that (v. 7). More will happen than the redemption of God's people, though wonderful as that is. The universe will be made new and 'all things… in heaven and… on earth' will be under Christ.

This wonderful salvation will unite Jews—'we, who were the first to set our hope on Christ' (v. 12)—and the other nations—'you also were included in Christ' (v. 13, NIV). Paul is to develop this in chapter 2 and show how the divisions caused by sin and Satan will be—indeed already are—removed in Christ.

Further, the completion of this breathtaking plan is guaranteed by the presence of the Spirit. It is as if the Spirit says, 'Father, you've placed me in this child of yours to bring her, to bring him, to glory. We've a long way to go but we're going to make it.'

These mind-boggling realities will enable the Christian to live in the present for the praise of God's glory. The rest of the letter is to develop the wonder of our salvation and calls us to 'lead a life worthy of the calling to which you have been called' (4:1).

John 1:[1–9] 10–18

Running through all our Christmas readings has been the persistent theme that our salvation is a rescue operation from outside by God who comes right down among us. Nowhere is this more breathtakingly evident than in our passage here. Had John written, 'The Word loved flesh', 'The Word pitied flesh' or even 'The Word forgave flesh', that would have been good news indeed. But 'the Word *became* flesh': without ceasing to be God, he became fully human (v. 14).

Sadly, when the dramatist appeared on the stage, those who should have known better harried him off (v. 11). Yet this was not to lead to an abandoning of the play but to new and exciting developments, foreseen indeed, but only fully realized now.

Grace—the undeserved, unconditional love of God—became flesh. Truth—the final and perfect revelation of God—became flesh. Thus, in Jesus, heaven's love and heaven's justice find their perfect expression (v. 14).

Here is what the drama of redemption is about. Moses, one of the great early characters in the plot-line, was given the Torah with its revelation of God's holiness and his love. However, only the man who was God is the whole truth expressed. Moses longed to see God and was allowed to see part of this glory (Exodus 24:9–11). However, now in Jesus that full revelation of God has dawned for all who have eyes to see. Everything that is true about God is true about Jesus; everything that is true about Jesus is true about God.

THE EPIPHANY

YEARS A, B, C

Isaiah 60:1–6

Here is a picture of hope beyond darkness. Isaiah's hearers are called to act in response to the light that will come (v. 1), even though it is preceded by darkness (v. 2). They are asked to take a long view towards the time when the age of the Messiah dawns on the land and a reversal of circumstances is introduced. Then darkness will become light; then, instead of the Israelites' being taken off to foreign lands in exile, people from those lands will come to Zion (vv. 4–6).

Isaiah's vision is perhaps most readily interpreted as a reversal in material fortunes. Thus the Gentiles who once ruled over Israel will be subject to her rule and will bring her tribute (vv. 5, 6). While this picture is consistent with Jesus' teaching that the poor shall inherit the Kingdom of God and the hungry shall be filled (Luke 6:20–21), it does not represent the whole picture. Verse 6 states, 'They shall... proclaim the praise of the Lord', thus intimating that the Gentiles who come shall be co-beneficiaries of God's grace.

Ephesians 3:1–12

Paul was one of the few very early Christian leaders who recognized that the scope of God's mission to the world expanded beyond the bounds of ethnic Israel. It is hard for us to realize quite how revolutionary a thought this was. It was a shift of perception as great as the change from belief in a flat earth to belief in a round earth. For centuries of Israel's history, she had understood herself to be the object of a special and exclusive relationship with God. However, Paul perceives the wider picture and the fathomless extent of God's grace. He rails against those who try to limit that grace by funnelling Gentile converts into becoming second-class Jews.

47

For those of us who are not ethnic Jews, this passage expresses the enormous and undeserved privilege that we enjoy at God's hands: 'Gentiles have become fellow heirs, members of the same body, and sharers in the promise in Christ Jesus' (v. 6).

In most Western churches, the division between Jew and Gentile within our congregations is not one that we generally have to wrestle with. A more vivid parallel might perhaps be drawn between 'old' and 'new/young' church members. Neither these categories, nor any others, can divide the universality of God's grace.

Matthew 2:1–12

Two strands run particularly strongly through Matthew's birth narrative: Christ as the fulfilment of Old Testament prophecy and Christ as the superior of all other powers. The most obvious element of prophetic fulfilment in these verses is, of course, in the reference to the birthplace of the Messiah (vv. 1, 6; cf. Isaiah 7:14). On a broader scale, the account of Herod's animosity towards the child forms the part of Matthew's presentation of Christ's birth that parallels the birth of Moses (cf. Matthew 2:16 and Exodus 1:22).

The theme of superiority is expressed in the homage paid to Jesus by the Magi (v. 11). These characters represent the subordination of foreign lands, predicted in Isaiah 60, and also suggest a parallel with the honour paid to Solomon by the queen of Sheba (1 Kings 10:1–13). Astrology was important to eastern mystery cults, such as Mithraism, which grew up in the Roman empire alongside Christianity. The stars were also read as a source of omens in Roman culture. The homage of the Magi expresses the idea that not only foreign lands, but also pagan religion, should be seen as subordinate to Christ.

AG

THE BAPTISM OF CHRIST

(THE FIRST SUNDAY OF EPIPHANY)

YEAR A

Isaiah 42:1–9

The Servant Songs have been described as the 'Situations Vacant' column of the Old Testament. The prophet knows that God is calling someone/some people to undertake this role, but he does not know who it will be or what will be the timescale.

The 'job specification' is clear enough.

- Establishing a just society, without the use of violence or oppression and with a care for the weak and vulnerable (vv. 1–4).
- Bringing light where there is darkness, whether revealing to the Gentiles God's covenant truth or literally opening blind eyes (vv. 6–7).
- Liberating those who are imprisoned, whether literally or because they are outside the circle of God's covenant mercy (v. 7).

The identity and character of the 'employer' are clear enough. He is Yahweh and he alone is supreme (v. 8), and he is righteous (v. 6a).

His servant has been chosen in love and equipped for the task by his Spirit, guided and protected in preparation for this role.

Whoever the servant is to be, this is a totally new initiative God is taking. Will it be recognized when the time comes?

Note: There is a play on words in verses 3 and 4, which is brought out clearly in the RSV footnotes: the servant is contrasted with the exiles in that he himself will not 'burn dimly', nor will he be 'bruised', but he will use his strength to bring justice for those who are weak.

Acts 10:34–43

If the prophet declared God's 'new things', Peter is experiencing them.

He recounts to the Gentile Cornelius how 'good news' has been brought to Israel by Jesus. Healing and exorcisms in the power of the Spirit confirmed Jesus' message and the presence of God with him. There were many witnesses to his resurrection from death. At the beginning of his ministry, he was perceived simply as 'Jesus of Nazareth' (v. 38). Now all the evidence shows that he is the one chosen by God to judge the whole world (v. 42).

Peter is beginning to see a whole new horizon opening up, a gospel of reconciliation offered to any 'God-fearer', whatever his or her race (vv. 34–35). He is also beginning to see new meaning in the old prophecies which have shaped his upbringing as a Jew: they are actually disclosing that *every* believer will find forgiveness and acceptance with God, through the name of Jesus (v. 43). Peter is convincing himself as much as Cornelius!

Hardly are the words out of his mouth than God dramatically confirms the truth of his new insights. Not only does Peter order the household to be baptized, he stays—and presumably eats—with his Gentile hosts.

Matthew 3:13-17

John's baptism was itself something new. Gentile converts to Judaism had baptized themselves on becoming proselytes and the Qumran community also washed themselves repeatedly as part of their rituals. But John's baptism was for Jews and was apparently administered once only.

Jesus evidently came with others (cf. Luke 3:21), deliberately seeking baptism as an act of commitment to the crowd of penitents. Presumably he was also identifying himself with this new movement and with John's preaching of the imminent Kingdom. John's reluctance stems from the recognition that Jesus is the 'mightier one' sent by God. Yet Jesus takes the path of submission.

Jesus' words are enigmatic. 'Righteousness' as used by Matthew is the accomplishing of God's will in all its fullness. Jesus' baptism provides continuity between John's preparation and his own mission to bring the Kingdom to fulfilment.

The sequel is of vital importance to Jesus' understanding of his ministry. The vision confirms that he is acting in the power of God's Spirit as his representative. The voice confirms his special relationship to God, as his Son. Since the demise of prophecy, Israel's rabbis have only been able to refer to 'the echo of the voice': now God speaks again directly.

Commissioned and empowered by God, Jesus begins his saving work.

GS

YEAR B

Genesis 1:1-5

Woody Allen is famous for his refusal to watch the remainder of a film if he has missed the opening sequence. As a film-maker himself, he recognizes how vital the first lines of a narrative can be. It is here that the audience begins to grasp the central threads and movements of the ensuing story. Without this initial information, the whole point of the film can be lost.

The opening lines of Genesis give us some vital information that is relevant to our understanding of the rest of the book, and of the Bible as a whole. These verses reveal that God, and not humankind (as in parallel creation myths), is the central character about whom the narrative will speak (v. 1). This God is the one who sets everything in motion and who drives the action to its ultimate conclusion.

The creation story depicts a situation where, after the creation of heaven and earth (v. 1), there is simply a watery waste (v. 2). The possibility of life lies within it, but without God's action, through the Holy Spirit (v. 2), life and action cannot arise. This pattern is repeated again and again in the story of God's people, and is a feature of Jesus' baptism, which we celebrate today.

Acts 19:1–7

The believers whom Paul comes across in Ephesus have undergone a baptism of preparation, but new life has not actually come to them because they have not received the Holy Spirit. On receiving baptism in the name of the Lord Jesus, they publicly manifest gifts of tongues and prophecy (v. 6).

There is no indication that this particular manifestation is necessary to confirm that true baptism has taken place. However, this passage does show that a reception of the Holy Spirit is a necessary element of Christian baptism and, therefore, of Christian life. In all the debates that Christians engage in regarding the nature and timing of baptism, it is necessary to appreciate that true baptism is not to be recognized in a form of words, or in the time of life at which it is received, but by the manifestation of God's Spirit in the life of the recipient—that is, the manifestation of the likeness of Christ in the baptized individual.

Mark 1:4–11

What was Jesus doing when he received John's baptism (v. 9)? Early theologians wrestled with this question because John's baptism was one of repentance. However, without Jesus' baptism we would be without a host of images that help us to understand Christ's mission. First, there is his identification with us in our own baptism. Second, there is a parallel to the crossing of the Red Sea at the beginning of the journey of salvation for the children of Israel. Third, there is the image of a new creation rising from the water, a new beginning brought forth by the Spirit of God just as the first creation had been.

Beyond the Old Testament background to the combination of water and the activity of God, Mark gives us a precious account of God's approval of his Son. While it is a considerable understatement to say that the relationship of the Father and the Son is unique and uniquely intimate, it is nevertheless legitimate to observe that God's statement over Jesus is one that has an echo in our own baptism. We are baptized into Christ; we become members of his body (cf. Colossians 2:12); we too are God's beloved.

AG

51

Year C

Isaiah 43:1–7

The great biblical themes of creation and redemption are used here to inspire and re-energize people in exile. What has happened to God's ancient promises and purposes if they are to end in dreary and hopeless imprisonment by the waters of Babylon? Here the Lord, through the prophet, addressing his people directly, reminds them that the great saving events of creation and exodus have committed him too deeply to them to abandon them now. This passage is rich in its evocation of the presence of God with his people, pointing to the time when in a fuller and deeper way he would be physically present with them. Three consequences flow from this.

First, God will save his people by grace alone and he will do so because it is his nature to save and because he loves his people (v. 1).

Second, God will bring together his scattered people from the ends of the earth and thus fulfil the purpose for which he created them (v. 6).

Third, this passage points far beyond exile and return. Only in the coming of Christ and his coming at the end of the age for his people can the full realities of verses 5–7 be realized.

The powerful images of water and fire which we are to meet in our Gospel reading are both a reminder of creation and exodus and an anticipation of the great event of the coming of Christ.

Acts 8:14–17

The promised Messiah has come; he has fulfilled the scriptures by dying, rising again, ascending into heaven and sending his Spirit. All these events have been foretold in vivid language in the later chapters of Isaiah. In this part of Acts, a great new wave of mission has begun, bringing the knowledge of these events to an ever-widening circle. The evangelist Philip has gone to Samaria and wonderful blessing has followed his preaching. This is the background of the little incident in these verses where Peter and John are sent by the other apostles to see what is happening. People there had been baptized but had not yet received the Spirit (v. 16). What does this mean?

We must first realize that this is a narrative of a unique situation and not mandatory for later generations. The normative experience is to receive the Holy Spirit on believing (see, e.g., Acts 10:44). What can we make of it?

First we must remember the importance of apostolic authority. Thus the danger of starting a new 'Samaritan church' was avoided by associating this work with the authority of Christ's apostles.

Second, and we shall see this again in Luke 3, the passage emphasizes the importance of prayer. Nothing was to be done without its being saturated in prayer (vv. 15, 17).

Third, the passage shows the importance of holding together the unity of the Church and the diverse ways in which its mission will be carried out in different settings.

Luke 3:15–17, 21–22

Great events often have apparently insignificant settings and appear not to be very significant. An insignificant river, a wandering prophet and a hitherto unknown carpenter of Nazareth, along with a nameless crowd, seem hardly the stuff of which great drama is made. Yet here the Trinity is involved, the great drama of redemption reaches a new high point and the whole plot-line of scripture passes through this key event of the baptism of Jesus. It would be useful to mention five things.

First, this one who comes to be baptized fulfils God's ancient promises. He will be the one whose fire symbolizes the arrival of the last days and the harvest which will be the end of the world (v. 16).

Second, his coming is the coming of God himself. The words from the Father in heaven (v. 22), which echo Psalm 2, identify Jesus as the one in whom all the fullness of God dwells.

Third, this is the one in whom the Spirit dwells uniquely and fully. He is the anointed Servant of Isaiah 61:1 who says, 'The Spirit of the Sovereign Lord is on me.'

Fourth, the baptism is an event which springs out of Jesus' praying: 'When Jesus... was praying, the heaven was opened' (v. 21). Prayer was both the motivation and heart of Jesus' ministry.

Fifth, this is one of the great Trinitarian passages. As Jesus' mission begins, Father, Son and Holy Spirit are together in this event and all that it symbolizes and all it would lead to (vv. 21–22).

RF

THE SECOND SUNDAY OF EPIPHANY

YEAR A

Isaiah 49:1–7

This particular Servant Song focuses on the prophet himself.

The *initiative* comes from God. The prophet/servant has not chosen his career. He has been singled out by God from birth, gifted with perceptive eloquence that will go straight to its target, kept hidden by God until the time was ripe. God promises him success in his mission to Israel (v. 13).

The *experience* of the servant is very different. He meets indifference and rejection and feels he is wasting his time. Yet he remains convinced that he will be vindicated by Yahweh. His confidence is rewarded, for God calls him to an even greater role: he is to reveal God not just to the people of Israel, but to the nations, so that Yahweh's saving power may reach 'to the ends of the earth'.

The prophet may only have been referring to Jews scattered among the nations but Luke sees the coming of Christ as the fulfilment for both Jew and Gentile. Jesus too remained faithful to his mission despite rejection, he too suffered and was despised, and through him God's salvation reached out to all nations.

Note: Verse 3 names the servant as 'Israel', but this is difficult to square with the servant's mission *to* Israel in verses 5 and 6, and some commentators therefore omit the name. On the other hand, verse 7 appears to apply much more naturally to Israel as the servant.

1 Corinthians 1:1–9

Like the Servant of old, Paul is called by God (to be an apostle) and the whole Church is called—to be 'saints', dedicated to God's service.

If the prophet was, so to speak, short-sighted, unable to see the outcome of the message he had received, Paul's 'glasses' are tinted—he sees everything Christ-coloured! Every verse mentions Christ (verse 2 twice).

It is 'in Christ' that they are being made holy, shaped to his image. It is in Christ that they receive God's grace and in him they receive their gifts. In him they are part of a fellowship community—in Corinth and across the churches (v. 2).It is Christ they acknowledge as Lord, for they recognize in him the Son of God and worship him (v. 2). And it is to Christ that they bear witness (v. 6) as they respond to their calling.

Jesus is God's complete revelation: 'God is Christlike, and in him is no unChristlikeness at all' (John Taylor). Yet we are still waiting, as they waited, for the unmistakable 'showing forth' of that revelation to the whole world. Only then shall we fully understand our calling into the fellowship of his Son (v. 9; cf. 1 Corinthians 13:9–12).

John 1:29–42

The fourth evangelist has set out his case in the Prologue. Now he begins to present the evidence.

'I myself did not know him,' says John the Baptist emphatically (vv. 31, 33). As he fulfilled his own calling from God, John did not know the identity of the Messiah for whom he prepared.

Only by direct revelation from God did John understand, and this insight was confirmed by a sign. So John becomes the first witness to be called. He testifies that Jesus is both Lamb of God and Son of God, that he will take away the sin of the world and baptize with the Holy Spirit. Each of these mind-blowing concepts will require demonstration.

Two of John's disciples act on his repeated testimony and approach Jesus. Their apparently mundane question meets an equally mundane answer. But in John's Gospel, words have different levels of meaning:

• 'Stay' also means 'dwell with' or 'abide in' (e.g. ch. 15).
• 'See' also implies spiritual understanding (e.g. 14:19).

Those who put their trust in Jesus and follow him ('come') will be given spiritual insight—to recognize that Jesus abides in God, and in Jesus God abides in human hearts.

The two came and saw and stayed (v. 39). Curiosity was satisfied at the immediate level. But Andrew, with growing insight and commitment, is able in turn to bear witness (v. 41).

GS

YEAR B

1 Samuel 3:1–10, [11–20]

Where water is scarce, each drop is of tremendous value. 1 Samuel opens on a barren landscape. The religion of the people is being abused by the sons of Eli. Eli himself, who should be a spiritual leader of the people, is weak and resigned. The whole atmosphere is one of emptiness and impurity.

In this sullied context shines a particular point of purity. Samuel is a child growing up in the midst of priestly malpractice (2:12–17) and yet, through Hannah's pure offering (1:26–28) and Samuel's simple response (3:10), God begins to usher in a new era in the history of Israel, the era that reaches its height in the reign of David the king. The beginning of that process of redemption is not, however, a pleasant one. Samuel is immediately given a terrifying message of judgment to pass on to his master, Eli (3:11–14).

Samuel, like every other great instrument of God's purposes, had to be prepared to respond directly to God's call, however unpalatable to himself or to those around him.

Revelation 5:1–10

The scroll that John sees (v. 1) is the container of 'what must soon take place' (cf. 1:1, 19; 4:1). It tells the story of the persecution that God's people will endure, the punishment of their persecutors and the salvation of the persecuted. This is a scroll that can only be opened by the Lord of history, since only this Lord can determine history's final outcome.

Christ's Lordship is won by his faithful death and resurrection. In taking on death and defeating it, he has gained dominion and, with it, the right to history's final say. Thus whatever happens in the course of this world's life, its ultimate destination will always be the victory of Christ, the Lamb who was slain (v. 6).

Successful sports teams tend to have more followers than unsuccessful ones because people like to be associated with winners. Revelation calls its audience to recognize and to follow the one who, despite initial appearances to the contrary (v. 6), ultimately conquers (vv. 9–10). That victory is won through the painful path of undying faithfulness to God. Those who follow him are called to this same path.

John 1:43–51

Nathanael is a character with whom it is easy for many people to identify. He was sceptical of Philip's optimism and understandably so. Philip was claiming to have found what had been longed for for centuries past, but why should this man be the right one? Worse still, the one whom Philip believed to be the fulfilment of the words of Moses and the prophets apparently came from the unlikely town of Nazareth (v. 46a). Philip's enthusiasm, however, persuaded Nathanael to 'come and see' (v. 46b).

Nathanael, in his encounter with Jesus, is taken from scepticism to belief. The words, 'I saw you under the fig tree before Philip called you' (v. 48) have a transformative effect on him. We can only speculate as to the nature of their significance for him. Perhaps Nathanael had been praying for the restoration of Israel as he sat under the tree?

Nathanael is instantly bowled over, but Jesus indicates that there is a much longer and more extraordinary road ahead. At its culmination, any small expectations that Nathanael might have had will have been infinitely surpassed (v. 51). In our own experience, when scepticism turns to faith, we may still be one step short of the true scale of what we have begun to believe in.

AG

YEAR C

Isaiah 62:1–5

Epiphany takes place in a low period of the year. Christmas is a memory and the season is not far enough advanced to anticipate Easter and summer. In this time, the glowing words of Isaiah remind us that in spite of appearances, the Lord will work ceaselessly for his people. God will be God and the world will know it.

Two rich images foreshadow this coming vindication of God's promises. Verses 1–3 focus on glory—the blazing splendour and utter reality of God which is at the heart of salvation (see especially Isaiah 6). That glory of God will shine from a restored and rejuvenated Israel. This will be a sign to the whole world that the Lord is reigning.

Verses 4 and 5 speak of the new Jerusalem as the Lord's Bride, and the marriage which follows crystallizes the new relationship of God and his people.

All this can seem 'pie in the sky' until we remember that this passage follows the Servant/Messiah passages in which God's purposes are to be brought to fruition in a coming Saviour. In him the glory of God is to be seen: he is the Bridegroom who loved the Church and gave himself for her, and whose marriage is celebrated at the end of the book of Revelation. That was good news in Isaiah's day and it is good news in ours.

1 Corinthians 12:1–11

Birthdays, weddings and anniversaries of various kinds are marked by gifts, and how often these become the centre of complaint and argument. Here in the church at Corinth, the gifts of the Spirit had become the occasion for bitter controversy, personal rivalry and arrogance instead of the cause of grateful thanks to God. Here Paul, introducing his teaching on the gifts of the Spirit, turns the church's attention to the great centralities of the faith and to Christ himself, the embodiment of every gift God has for us. He makes three assertions.

The first (vv. 1–3) is that the sign of the Spirit's presence is the acknowledgment and conviction that Jesus is Lord. A Spirit-filled church is one centred on and submissive to Jesus Christ.

The second (vv. 4–6) is that unity itself is a gift of the Spirit. Whatever kind of gift or service or activity individuals may be given or called to, they all come from the same Spirit. God has only one worker, the Holy Spirit.

The third (vv. 7–11) is that within this unity there is rich diversity. No comment is made at this point about the exact nature or practice of these gifts; some of that is to follow. The point is more fundamental here. These gifts are not for self-aggrandizement but 'for the common good' (v. 7). They are not our work but the work of the Spirit himself (v. 11a). They are not jobs for which we volunteer but gifts we are given (v. 11b). No better comment can sum up this passage than Paul's own in his second letter to the Corinthians (9:15): 'Thanks be to God for his indescribable gift'.

John 2:1–11

This passage is well known particularly because of its use in wedding services, and that is not wrong, but verse 11 suggests that the point of the story lies elsewhere. Verse 11 ties this incident closely to the developing plot-line of scripture and the centrality and uniqueness of Christ in that story.

The changing of water into wine was the first of the 'signs' performed by Jesus. In the first twelve chapters of John's Gospel, we are to encounter several others, such as feeding the crowds, stilling the storm and raising the dead. These all point unerringly to the fact that the Creator is present in this creation.

Second, this sign reveals Jesus' glory. Glory is the splendour of God which rested on the tent and the temple in old days, which shone through creation and is glimpsed in history. Now it is concentrated in one person—Jesus of Nazareth.

Third, 'his disciples put their faith in him' (v. 11, NIV). Notice that they were already his disciples; we have read in John 1:35ff. of the call of various people such as Andrew and Peter. However, this faith must be a growing one, for no relationship can remain static. Just as this wedding at Cana (we have no idea whose wedding it was) was only the beginning of a life together, so the initial following of Jesus is a beginning of not just a lifelong but an eternal relationship with him who is the way, the truth and the life.

RF

THE THIRD SUNDAY OF EPIPHANY

YEAR A

Isaiah 9:1–4

The light of God shines in the darkness of suffering.

The land of Zebulun and Naphtali was part of the area annexed by the Assyrians from Israel in 733BC and treated harshly. The three regions—the way of the sea, the land beyond Jordan, and Galilee of the nations—correspond to the three Assyrian provinces created.

The prophecy clearly relates to the accession of a new king. The disobedience of King Ahaz had caused God to hide his face from his people—now, with a new king, there is new hope and high excitement. The oppression of the occupying power (symbolized by the yoke, the staff and the rod) will be broken, as when Gideon defeated the Midianites!

The prophecy was an inspiration to future generations, and was reinterpreted whenever Israel faced a prolonged time of exile or depression. When there was no prophetic word, the covenant people felt cut off from the source of light and life and God's face seemed hidden. Yet at the moment of deepest darkness, light will appear in a glory hitherto unknown.

And the light will again come from Galilee (of all places), despised as the backwoods of Judah. The deeper the shadows, the more dramatic is the ring of light—like the corona of the sun when eclipsed by the moon.

1 Corinthians 1:10–18

The Corinthian church seems to have viewed the proclamation of the gospel as a Eurovision Song Contest, with votes for preachers.

Paul is horrified by their attitudes. His appeal for unity is made in the strongest language, in the very name of Christ, for he and he alone is the foundation of the gospel. There is no 'gospel of Paul' for he was not crucified on their behalf, nor can they be baptized into his name. He has no desire for a fan club.

The effectiveness of the gospel depends not on the persuasive performance of the preacher but on the power of the cross. Rhetorical flourishes and the eloquent conventions of Greek oratory are totally inappropriate to the stark picture of the cross, and no human wisdom can fathom its awesome mystery.

A gospel based on a Saviour crucified as a common criminal can only appear ridiculous by the world's standards. But the answer is not to dress it up in fine language which will only mask the message. Those who receive this gospel find that the transforming power of God himself has broken into their lives.

Matthew 4:12–23

Jesus begins his ministry with an apparent retreat.

What did it mean for him, the news that John had been arrested? At a personal level, he had identified with John's movement and been encouraged by John to understand his own role. The experience of the wilderness temptations had taught him that his mission would involve a lonely spiritual battle. Now it appeared that it would involve physical danger and confrontation with authority.

So he returns to Galilee, far from the centre of power. He begins his ministry not in his home village but in the centre of the local fishing industry, where trade draws the crowds. He picks up where John left off, preaching the same message (v. 17). He looks for support, calling local fishermen to join him in this vital task of calling men and women to turn to God, bringing in the Kingdom revolution.

This is, however, more than a reprise of John's ministry. Matthew recognizes that now Isaiah's prophecy is fulfilled—'light will shine' becomes 'light has dawned'. In Jesus, the rule of God is already breaking in.

The first disciples respond to an authority they perhaps only half understand but which they feel impelled to obey. Family obligations, business interests, urgent practical tasks are set aside without question.

GS

YEAR B

Genesis 14:17–20

Abraham's meeting with Melchizedek (v. 18) is m⸱ terious in that we have almost no further information about him. Psalm 110:4 has God swearing to David, 'You are a priest forever, according to the order of Melchizedek', indicating that the king of Salem (probably Jerusalem) was somehow a forerunner of David. Hebrews 5—7 uses the figure of Melchizedek to explain the existence of a separate and greater priesthood, alongside the Levitical priesthood, to which Christ belongs.

Melchizedek represents the permanent presence of that which we only occasionally see, and even more partially understand. Any religious hierarchy may be tempted to believe that it has the divine revelation entirely in its grasp. Melchizedek reminds us that what we are given to know isn't all that there is to know.

The meal that Abraham and Melchizedek shared may have been a sign of treaty between them (v. 18). In this respect it has resonances for us of the mysterious covenant meal of bread and wine that we, the offspring (through faith) of Abraham, are given to share with the king-priest Jesus.

Revelation 19:6–10

After the destruction of the city of Babylon (16:19), which had been responsible for the persecution of God's faithful people, there is a shift of key to one of celebration that the feast of vindication is imminent.

The image of a great feast at the culmination of history is an important and recurring biblical image. In Psalm 23, David looks forward to having a table spread before him in the face of his enemies. The parable of the great banquet (Luke 14:15–23) opens with the remark, 'Blessed is the man who will eat at the feast in the kingdom of God' (NIV).

The marriage supper of the Lamb (v. 9) refers to the meal at which Christ and his Church are made one in the new heaven and new earth. This feast is one that is anticipated in Holy Communion. Thus, whenever we eat and drink the bread and wine, we declare our identification with the slain and risen Christ who has defeated evil and who has inaugurated the great wedding feast.

John 2:1–11

As is characteristic of John's Gospel, this miracle has many layers of depth. It is not the case that Jesus simply has compassion and so decides to save the acute embarrassment of the bridegroom. Jesus indicates that this is an act that carries a particular significance, by his statement that it relates to an 'hour' that has not yet come. This invites us to consider what 'hour' Jesus may have been referring to. Perhaps the most likely answer is Jesus' ultimate provision for the Messianic banquet.

John says that the miracle reveals Jesus' glory so that his disciples put their faith in him (v. 11). If Jesus' glory is that he is the Messiah, rather than simply that he is a welcome guest at a party, then the act of abundant wine provision (more than one hundred gallons on this occasion) may be seen as an important clue to this identity. In a similar vein, the miraculous feeding (John 6) also points to Jesus' Messianic person in his provision of a super-abundant feast for the five thousand.

Throughout John's Gospel, there are references to eating and drinking with Jesus. It is as if John is seeking to invite us to identify with the characters within his Gospel, not only in imagining their experiences but also in participating in them. Thus, as we take the wine of Communion we become another of the guests at the wedding, and also perceive his glory.

AG

YEAR C

Nehemiah 8:1–3, 5–6

All our passages today (including 1 Corinthians) have as a major focus hearing the word of God. Here, in a significant moment for the returned exiles, Ezra the scribe and priest reads and expounds the Torah. The symbolic significance is profound. Deuteronomy speaks of Moses assembling the people to hear and obey the Torah of Yahweh (Deuteronomy 4:1–2) and adds the command to 'make them known to your children and your children's children' (Deuteronomy 4:9). Many times this command was neglected, and that neglect led to the exile. It is, however, significant that the great reformation of King Josiah was marked by the rediscovery, the reading of and obedience to the Torah.

So here Ezra is setting the standard for the returned exiles, which is faithfulness to the Torah. Some important principles for hearing the word of God emerge from this story. First is the communal nature of listening to scripture (v. 1). Of course there is an absolute need for private reading, but listening to scripture together is at the heart of a community's growth in faith.

Second, there is the willing response of the people (v. 3), who stood for some five or six hours listening eagerly.

Third, this exposition takes place in the context of worship (v. 6). This was no mere intellectual exercise but involved openness to God and praise to his name.

Fourth, to jump a little ahead (vv. 7–8), the Torah was expounded, not to give people something more important, but to send them back to it with renewed understanding. These remain indispensable conditions for the preaching and hearing of the word of God.

1 Corinthians 12:12–31a

This is a rich passage and the subject of much controversy. Today's comment cannot deal with this debate and simply suggests a few guidelines following on from last Sunday's comment.

Verses 12–14 introduce the metaphor of the body and of diversity in unity. However, in this section the basic presupposition is unity. That unity in Christ comes from the common experience of conversion, expressed in two vivid metaphors as being drenched or baptized in the Spirit and drinking deeply from that same Spirit. Verse 14 focuses on the many parts of the body as an introduction to the next section.

Verses 15–26 apply the body metaphor to both unity and diversity. The metaphor is detailed and quite complex but the underlying emphasis is that the true nature of the body is divinely created and thus every part, while distinctive, is interdependent. The dangers of pride and self-sufficiency are vividly highlighted by personifying certain parts of the body. Paul is concerned to hold in balance the twin realities of diversity and the need for mutual concern.

Verses 27–31 apply the body metaphor directly to the working of spiritual gifts in the Church and thus illustrate in what way members of the body of Christ can operate together. Two striking and complementary emphases are important. The first is that this is an *ad hoc* list, without any claim to be exhaustive or in rank order. The second is that the foundational gifts of apostle and prophet are first both in time and in significance. Thus the gift of teaching, the unfolding of the prophetic and apostolic word, is a necessary environment for the other gifts to operate effectively.

Luke 4:14–21

Here the Word made flesh reads and expounds the written word and presents himself as its fulfilment. Here he specifically reveals himself as the Messiah and Servant of Yahweh and the full flowering of the prophetic ministry represented by Elijah and Elisha. Three points are worth noting.

The Spirit's power is first represented by the proclamation of the word. Verses 14 and 15 link Jesus returning in the power of the Spirit with his teaching in the synagogues. This draws heavily from the Word/Spirit theology of Isaiah 40ff. which lies behind much of this passage.

Second, we have a fascinating glimpse of Jesus' use of the Old Testament. He does not (as he does not on the Emmaus road in Luke 24) say, 'You don't need the Bible, you've got me'. Rather he expounds his own person and ministry in the words of the Old Testament. In these words from Isaiah 61, the 'good news to the poor' is expressed in a variety of liberating metaphors.

Third, as in Nehemiah and, in a different way, in 1 Corinthians, the importance of response to the word is emphasized by 'hearing' (v. 21). All this requires the response of faith. It was not self-evident in an occupied province that the prisoners were being freed and the oppressed being released. Blindness was heavy on the land and the 'year of the Lord's favour' seemed an idle dream. But the King had come and his liberating word was about to sweep through the land.

RF

THE FOURTH SUNDAY OF EPIPHANY

YEAR A

1 Kings 17:8–16

In the revelation of God's purposes, obedience counts for more than worldly common sense.

Elijah, keeping out of Ahab's way, has already been sent by God out into the desert. The stream on which he relied was bound to dry up, if God's own forecast of drought was fulfilled. Now he is sent in another apparently pointless direction. Zarephath is outside Israel: who in time of drought is going to feed a foreigner? The woman is a widow. She will be struggling to feed her own family. Yet Elijah obeys.

The widow is in effect down to her last crust. She has a child. Traditionally, in famine, what little there is is given to the young and those who can work the land, for they are the future—not idle visitors. She cannot expect favours from the God of Israel (he is 'the Lord *your* God', v. 12).

Does she sense divine authority behind the prophet's unlikely promise, or is this just clutching at a straw? She obeys—and obedience is rewarded by a miracle.

The word of the Lord came to Elijah (v. 1), the word of the Lord comes through Elijah to the woman (v. 16). The word of the Lord may run counter to all human wisdom, but his powerful word always effects what it promises.

1 Corinthians 1:18–31

Paul develops his contrast between the wisdom of the world and the wisdom of God.

Worldly wisdom has three representatives:
- The 'scribe', expert in Jewish law (Torah), understood God's favour to rest on those who kept his law.
- The 'wise man' was heir to the Old Testament Wisdom tradition in which the favour of God was seen in prosperity and social success.
- The 'debater', the Hellenistic philosopher, understood divine favour to rest on those of superior knowledge and high-minded morals.

But none of these traditions, each admirable in its own way, has brought humankind to 'know' God, to live in harmonious relationship with their Creator.

The wisdom of God also has three representatives:

- **The Corinthian Christians,** not very intellectual or influential.
- **Paul and his fellow apostles,** preaching 'good news' that appears scandalous to their religious fellow countrymen and utterly silly to educated intellectuals.
- **Christ himself,** a figure stripped of all human glory and pretensions, ending his life an evident failure.

Surely God has reversed all human perspectives and values? For it is in this Christ that God's wisdom and power are to be found.

John 2:1–11

A very ordinary village event becomes the setting for the first of Jesus' 'signs'.

Wedding celebrations could easily last a week, and the wine running out did nothing for the host's reputation.

Three strands are interwoven through the story:
- **Power:** Jesus' simple instructions effect a miracle. His word had the same transforming power as 'the word of the Lord'.
- **Faith:** His mother trusts him, despite an apparent rebuff. The servants obey him, despite the improbable nature of what they are asked to do. The disciples believe in him.
- **Revelation:** Signs in the synoptic Gospels are spectacular events demanded by the faithless. In John's 'book of signs', they are pointers to the incarnation, to Jesus' being Son of God. They allow those with the eye of faith a glimpse into a heavenly dimension. The glory that is revealed is the glory of the eternal God.

Yet both the disciples' faith and Jesus' revelation are incomplete. The 'hour' which has not yet come (v. 4) points forward to the cross.

Only when Jesus' glory is revealed through the cross and the empty tomb will the disciples recognize the truth.

GS

YEAR B

Deuteronomy 18:15–20

The children of Israel had requested a mediator between God and themselves when they were terrified by God's awesome presence at Mount Horeb (5:23–27). Moses had been that mediator, and here he assures the people that, in future, God will raise up prophets as mediators. This promise establishes an important principle regarding the way in which God chooses to communicate with his people. It makes clear that contemporary practices of divination (such as reading the entrails of birds or animals) were unnecessary as well as forbidden.

Through the ages, God has sent prophets to speak his word plainly. This method of communication is not always welcome because it is usually possible to make entrails, tea leaves, or the stars say what we would like to hear; the words of a prophet are not always so amenable.

The promise of future prophecy lends itself to messianic interpretation; from here comes the question to John the Baptist, 'Are you the prophet?' (John 1:21). Matthew is particularly keen to bring out the features of Jesus' ministry that emphasize his particular fulfilment of God's promise through Moses, with numerous parallels between the ministries of Moses and Jesus, particularly in his birth narrative and the Sermon on the Mount.

Revelation 12:1–5a
Revelation is arranged in concentric circles so that, in simple terms, everything from 6:1 to 11:19 mirrors and builds up to everything that happens from 12:1 to 22:5. Revelation 12:1 thus stands right at the centre of the book and represents its turning point.

A simple outline of the events described here is as follows. The woman clothed with the sun (v. 1) represents the community of God's faithful people from whom, and to whom, the Messiah is born. This figure does not specifically represent Mary, although the obedient community depicted here is certainly epitomized by her. The dragon (v. 3) is Satan, who attempts to snuff out the threat to his power that is represented by the vulnerable newborn child (v. 4), whose destiny is to fulfil the role of the judging and saving Messiah.

The lectionary leaves us in suspense as to what happens next. We are left with the dragon's jaws poised around the baby's body! The passage goes on (v. 5b) to describe how the Messiah is snatched up to heaven, an act that holds together Christ's death, resurrection and ascension. This then becomes the focal moment of the whole book. Because of these events, the pattern of history that leads ultimately to the establishment of the new heaven and new earth (21:1ff.) are set in train.

Mark 1:21–28
Mark has a somewhat frustrating habit of telling us that Jesus' teaching caused people to be amazed, while failing to record more than the tiniest

morsel of what that teaching contained. Its consequences are, however, informative in this regard. Jesus is said to teach something that is of a kind with the scribes, possibly an exposition of the Law, but which is 'new' and 'with authority' (v. 22). To this extent, the Sermon on the Mount (placed in the equivalent position in Matthew's Gospel: Mark 1:20ff. = Matthew 4:22ff.) may give us a helpful indication of the type of subject that Jesus addressed, and the way in which it was treated.

This teaching has the effect of revealing Jesus' true identity and purpose to the unclean spirit (vv. 23–24). This spirit feels threatened and exposed by Jesus and is ultimately expelled by him (vv. 25–26). In this brief incident, therefore, the pattern is set for the course of Jesus' ministry. His grand battle with evil and death is played out in miniature in the demon-possessed man.

AG

YEAR C

Ezekiel 43:27—44:4

Today's readings (again, though less specifically, the Corinthians passage) centre on the temple, God living with his people. At the end of the Epiphany season, this is an important reminder that the Word became flesh and by doing so has opened the possibility for God and humans to live together in perfect fellowship.

In the grim days of exile, Ezekiel has faced up to and preached that God has removed his glory from his ancient city (11:23). From that gloomy perspective he has a powerful vision of a new city and a new temple and in eight chapters he gives a full and vivid account of God restoring Zion. Our reading is a small part of that and tells of the consecration of the altar as a response to the return of Yahweh's glory.

That altar is to be used for the two offerings which symbolize the very heart of worship (43:27). The burnt offering symbolizes total devotion to the Lord, and the fellowship offering symbolizes peace and unity among the worshippers.

But there is a gate as well as an altar, and this is the east gate through which Yahweh's glory will return (44:1–2). The closed gate shows the permanence of his presence; the tragedy of 11:23 will not be repeated.

A problem arises in 44:3 about the identity of the prince who alone may eat sacrificial meals before Yahweh, yet who is to enter by another way. It may be an indication that no one, however important, can take the place of Yahweh. 'The Lord is there' (48:35) is not only the name of the city, but its nature.

1 Corinthians 13:1–13

This is one of the Bible's best-known passages; particularly in the sonorous words of the King James version, it has been read on numerous public occasions, quoted on many more and been the subject of innumerable books and sermons. Yet, all too often, the context has been ignored and it has not been sufficiently understood that it is primarily a stern rebuke to the pride and spiritual arrogance of Corinth. It is profoundly Christological; love is no abstraction but its embodiment is the Christ who comes to us in the Word of the cross.

Verses 1–3 speak of the necessity of love. Tongues, prophecy and knowledge, along with faith and sacrifice, are not devalued but put in their proper place. 'Tongues of angels' may suggest that there were those in Corinth who thought they were in heaven already and speaking its language.

Verses 4–7 speak of the character of love both positive and negative, active and passive. The unselfconscious, unself-seeking and unostentatious nature of love is crystallized in a few vivid words.

Verses 9–12 speak of the permanence of love. The gifts are valuable but belong to now, whereas love belongs both to now and then. The concern in Corinth has overwhelmingly been for the 'now', hence their overemphasis on the gifts, especially the more spectacular of them. This is where our reading links with the Old Testament and the Gospel. We have Christ now, but not yet in the full sense that we shall when Ezekiel's vision is fulfilled and Simeon's salvation is consummated. Now we do not see 'a poor reflection' (NIV) or 'through a glass, darkly' (KJV) but rather an indirect and not yet complete vision of God. In the final glory, love will reign supreme.

Luke 2:22–40

This is the Gospel reading for two Sundays; this note will concentrate on Simeon and Anna and next week's on verse 40. Simeon and Anna represent the faithful remnant who, all through the long centuries, had kept faith and hope alive as they waited for the moment of fulfilment.

Simeon's prayer—the 'Nunc dimittis' (vv. 29–32)—brings together many of these aspirations. There is a sense of great gratitude and trust. He knows that he can now go in peace and that God is in control.

The salvation of God is now crystallized in this baby he holds in his arms. This is not natural insight, but faith responding to revelation, made possible because Simeon's whole life was lived in the presence and power of the Holy Spirit.

This salvation, so profoundly Jewish, was also to be universal (v. 32). Jesus himself is to embody God's glory and thus be the reality to which the temple pointed. Simeon's words (vv. 34–35) reveal the importance of faith and vision; only as people look at Christ as Simeon did will they recognize him as God's salvation.

Anna has known long widowhood, yet has found a meaning for her life in the service of God's temple. How fitting that such devotion should be rewarded with a sight of the Christ himself. Like the shepherds, her response is praise and gratitude, which is an encouragement and challenge to others. How little they saw—no miracles, no inspired words, no death, no resurrection—yet how much they saw and how shining an example their faith and courage are.

RF

THE PRESENTATION OF CHRIST IN THE TEMPLE

(CANDLEMAS)

YEARS A, B, C

Malachi 3:1–5

'Humankind cannot bear very much reality,' said T.S. Eliot (*The Four Quartets*), and part of the prophet's (and the preacher's) task is to open people's eyes to reality. The people of Malachi's time, a low-key, disillusioned community who had indeed returned from exile but had not found the desert blossoming as a rose, imagined they wanted the Lord to come but were living in a fool's paradise when they supposed that his coming would be pleasant. The prophet warns them that three things will happen, all related to the covenant they had neglected.

First, his coming would be like blazing fire (v. 3), recalling the burning bush and Mount Sinai. This would mean a burning out of dross, pointing to the Baptist's words about Jesus as the one who will 'baptize you with the Holy Spirit and fire' (Luke 3:16). More especially, this purifying will affect the Levites as those most responsible for the community's holiness.

Second, his coming will lead to restored worship (vv. 3 and 4). 'Former years' may refer to the reforms of Josiah (see 2 Kings 22 and 23 and 2 Chronicles 34 and 35). Malachi has already castigated unworthy offerings (1:6ff.) because these ultimately treat God with contempt. Because the attitude is wrong, the action cannot be right.

Third, his coming will lead to changes in society. Both social injustice and occult practices, often condemned in the earlier prophets, will be severely judged. The root of the problem is the failure to fear the Lord (v. 5) and thus the lack of godly wisdom.

(See also the comment on this passage for the Second Sunday of Advent.)

Hebrews 2:14–18

The early readers of Hebrews would have been familiar with the stories of Hercules, one of whose labours was wrestling with Death in order to rescue Alcestis. Even more, they would have recalled the rich Old Testament pictures of Yahweh the warrior as champion of Israel. One of the most vivid is Isaiah 25:7 where he swallows up death for ever. This is probably an allusion to the grim Canaanite god of death, Mot the Swallower, whose jaws reached from heaven to earth. The Swallower himself is to be swallowed, a theme we shall explore in 1 Corinthians 15 over the next few weeks.

So here our author sees Christ as the champion who defeats death, and not only so but death's master, the devil. But with clear pastoral insight he sees Christ also, for the first time in this letter, as high priest. Both are representative roles, the one emphasizing protection and the other compassion. Two elements, essential to the continuing argument of the letter, deserve attention.

The first is the total solidarity of Jesus with his people—'he too shared in their humanity' (v. 14, NIV)—which underlies the reality of both his incarnation and his death. This means that his death opens the way into the presence of God for others (a theme particularly developed in chapters 4—9).

The second is the continuing liberation which the death of Jesus ensures. Verse 18 speaks of his continuing help to ordinary, struggling people. The letter is addressed to Christian communities, probably in Rome, which were in danger of falling away. Strengthened by their champion and upheld by their priest, they will be able to continue running the race.

Luke 2:22–40

Anna and Simeon, as we saw in last week's comment, represent the faithful remnant who longed for that coming which Malachi prophesied and the author of Hebrews celebrated. Today our attention will be on verse 40 with its astonishing blend of the everyday and the miraculous.

'The child grew'—and how we would love to know some of the details of that home and family. But undoubtedly much of it would be the humdrum and everyday routines of ordinary living. Just as, back in 1:80, the childhood of the Baptist is described in the same way, so here the angels have gone and the astonishing secret of this humble home remains unknown.

However, we have two hints of what is happening. First, 'he was filled with wisdom', which anticipates 4:14: 'Jesus, filled with the power of the Spirit, returned to Galilee'. This wisdom is to be evidenced in the next passage where Jesus appears with the teachers in the temple. Behind this are all the rich Old Testament associations of the wisdom of God which is so closely linked with creation.

But second, 'the grace of God was upon him'. Mary in 1:30 had found 'favour' or 'grace', and in 2:14 the message of the favour of God is part of the message of the angels. This is different, though, because here the grace of God is permanently dwelling in this child.

How little is told us, how much is suggested; and the only appropriate response is that of Mary who 'treasured and pondered' all these things.

RF

PROPER 1

YEAR A

Isaiah 58:1–9a [9b–12]

Verse 3 may well be a quotation from a lamentation made on one of the regular fast days observed after Jerusalem was destroyed in 587BC. Public fasting has previously been a spontaneous reaction to national disaster. Now it is part of the liturgical calendar (see Zechariah 7—8), when the whole community pleads for God's blessing and full restoration of the city. Why does God not accept their fasting and prayer?

Two complementary answers are given:

First, their behaviour belies their religious rituals (vv. 3b–4). Even while fasting, they are preoccupied with their own interests rather than giving themselves to prayer. They are exploiting their workers unjustly; they are given to conflict and violence. Such superficial fasting implies no real devotion to God or his law.

Second, fasting has apparently become an alternative for social action, an excuse for *not* providing freedom and food, shelter and clothing—basic human rights for the needy (vv. 6–7). Fasting is not just about personal breast-beating: it can become a self-indulgence.

There is an irony in the injured protests of those who fast, as they seek God's 'righteous judgments' (v. 2)—for the judgment when it comes is their condemnation. Only when they satisfy the needs of the destitute (v. 10) will the Lord satisfy *their* desires and renew their strength (v. 11).

1 Corinthians 2:1–16

The contrast between the wisdom of God and the wisdom of the world has implications for Paul's approach to preaching. He takes a conscious decision to focus attention exclusively on Christ and particularly upon his death on the cross. He avoids the grand style (v. 1) and also the rhetoric of persuasion (v. 4) practised by contemporary orators. If his hearers are convinced of the gospel truth, this is a clear indication that the power of God's Spirit is at work.

The Corinthian converts are privileged to receive understanding too deep to be found by human logic. It can only be communicated by the Holy Spirit and received by those in whom the Spirit dwells. Paul, however, clearly expects them to apply their minds to the truth as it has been revealed to them.

So Paul does 'speak wisdom' but only with the mature Christians, whose minds are shaped by the Holy Spirit. He does not proclaim it *to* them, but *among* them: this wisdom is not the prerogative of certain experts, but is potentially shared by all as they grow into spiritual maturity (cf. 3:1–3a).

'This age' (v. 8), however splendid and superior (scientific?) it may appear, represents the creature's vain attempt to claim independence from the Creator. Inevitably, it is in conflict with divine and eternal wisdom.

Matthew 5:13–20

What outlook and behaviour are required of a citizen of the Kingdom of heaven?

Salt (v. 13) is a cleansing agent and a preservative. In a corrupt society, disciples are to be distinctive by their high moral standards. Salt also gives flavour: in an apathetic and negative society, they are to bring out the good news—the truth, mercy, peace of God.

However, just as the impure salt of the Dead Sea could lose its salinity when the sodium chloride dissolved, so there is a danger that the distinctiveness and commitment of the disciple may be watered down.

Light (v. 14) exposes what many would prefer to remain hidden. But it also illuminates darkness, allowing people to find their way, to do their work, to see each other clearly, to appreciate the beauty of creation. The mindset and lifestyle of the disciple should bring the Christ-light to bear on every aspect of human life.

However, just as lamplight can be masked by a cover, so the disciple's impact can be overshadowed by other preoccupations.

Scrupulous obedience to the law's tenets, as practised by scribes and Pharisees, is insufficient (v. 20). The law is fulfilled by 'a greater righteousness' in which the whole quality of life reflects the character of God.

GS

YEAR B

Isaiah 40:21–31

How can we compare a limerick with an epic poem? How can we compare a statue with a living God? Isaiah is struggling here with the limits of language. The transcendence of God in comparison to idols is his theme in 40:12–20. From 40:21 Isaiah turns to a comparison of God with earthly rulers, the influence of which would have been all too apparent to Isaiah's listeners. In verses 21–26, Isaiah records the impossibility that God may be compared with anything or anyone else, by virtue of his transcendent greatness. However, this is not a greatness that removes the Almighty from close relationship with his people. Verses 27–31 make clear the other side of God's character, that he is more closely concerned with his people than human rulers could ever be, even if they attempted to be so. His interest cannot be deflected by other concerns (v. 27), weariness (v. 28) or lack of strength (v. 29).

Isaiah closes this passage (v. 31) with advice to his hearers in response to the nature of this God. We are to wait for him, his timing and his power. Then his purposes will be our purposes and they will be achieved, no matter what.

1 Corinthians 9:16–23

This passage is part of an extended argument concerning the eating of food sacrificed to idols, which runs from 8:1 to 11:1. In chapter 9, Paul uses himself as an example of someone who has the right to material support but who chooses not to take it up. By this means, Paul hopes to persuade his readers that, although they have the right to eat food sacrificed to idols, they should not, for the sake of others, take up that right.

Our passage forms a small digression in the course of chapter 9. Paul, having just explained that he does not want a material reward for his work (v. 15), breaks into a celebration of his experience of preaching the gospel. Here Paul lives Marshall McLuhan's observation that 'the medium is the message'. Thus Paul preaches, free of charge, the gospel that is God's free gift of grace. Paul incarnates himself to the situation of those under the law

(v. 20) and those not under the law (v. 21), the weak (v. 22) and those in every situation (v. 22), just as Christ incarnates himself to our earthly life. He will suffer any indignity to make available what God has made available through the passion of Christ.

Paul has tremendous integrity in his preaching. He is not looking over his shoulder at the church treasurer, and he does not alter his message to improve sales. He is what he preaches, and as such presents a challenge to every Christian leader and community.

Mark 1:29–39

What started with one individual (1:23) now becomes concerned with many. The signs of the Kingdom are beginning to grow. First there is Simon's mother-in-law (vv. 30–31), then there is a multitude at the door (vv. 32–34). Mark emphasizes, with one of his famous repetitions, that this happened in the evening, after sunset (v. 32). Sunset marked the beginning of a new day. The particular day in question is one that is rich with significance for Christians. The day after the Sabbath of the first creation marks the beginning of God's new creation. The language that we use to describe Jesus as the second Adam and the firstborn from the dead combines with our celebration of Sunday as the day of resurrection, the first day of the new Kingdom.

Despite his instant fame and popularity, Jesus is able to keep his true goal in view. We are perhaps more inclined to pray when things are going badly than when they are going well. However, at this moment of success Jesus retreats to consider his next move (v. 35). He wants that move to be motivated and guided by the Father, rather than in response to the immediate pressure to meet the expectations of others.

AG

YEAR C

Isaiah 6:1–8

Each of today's passages focuses on the call of God and the message embodied in that call. Here first is one of the great 'call narratives' of the Bible. Three things cry out for attention.

The first is the time—'the year that King Uzziah died' (v. 1). For the better part of forty years, Uzziah's reign had spelt peace and prosperity for his people. Now he was gone and an uncertain future faced his country, with the hordes of Assyria ready to pounce. The prophet, painfully aware of this, contemplates the empty throne and then has a vision of a throne that can never be emptied.

The second is the vision itself—the awesome throne, the majestic and mysterious seraphim, the trisagion (the threefold 'holy'), the fire, the smoke and the weight and awesomeness of Yahweh of hosts as he partly reveals and partly conceals himself. This God is wholly other and utterly real. His 'glory', from the Hebrew verb 'to be solid, heavy' conveys his utter blinding presence, compared to which the gods of the nations are a puff of wind and less than nothing (vv. 2–3).

The third is the confession and the cleansing. This is a divine initiative because the seraph is sent to the prophet with a live coal from the perpetual fire on the altar (v. 6; see Leviticus 6:12–13) which symbolizes both God's holiness and his provision for sin. Now God speaks. It is as if the prophet has not been fit to hear until this point but now he is able to respond and to offer himself (v. 8).

Alternative reading: Isaiah 6:9–13

One of the problems of separating verses 9–13 from verses 1–8 is that we can ourselves set the agenda for 'Here am I. Send me'. We can decide to whom and for what we are going to be sent. However, verses 9–13 make it plain, uncomfortably so, what the prophet is to say.

First there is the strange commission (vv. 9–10). The prophet is sent to tell the people that the message will in fact be one of stern judgment. Here is the burden of the prophet: the message which alone can heal will bring judgment if rejected. Yet, since it is true, it must be preached with the accompanying danger that the next rejection will harden hearts beyond recovery. This passage made a deep impression on the early Church, as is seen by its quotation at two critical points in the New Testament. It is mentioned in Matthew 13:14–15 where Jesus applies the prophecy to the parables of the Kingdom, whose point people fail to grasp because they are not serious in their desire to know him. It is mentioned again in Acts 28:25–27, where Paul sees its fulfilment in the rejection of the gospel by his compatriots and thus turns to the Gentile mission.

Then there is the message of judgment now and hope in the future (vv. 11–13). This points not just to the Assyrian devastation of Judah (see chs. 36—37) but to the Babylonian exile, for there is no mention here of Jerusalem being saved. The curses of Deuteronomy 28 and 29 are being fulfilled and the Lord is punishing his people. Beyond the holocaust there is a hope, and here emerges the idea of the remnant which is to be crystallized in the messianic figure of chapters 7—9 and the renewed land of chapters 11—12.

1 Corinthians 15:1–11

'Last of all... he appeared also to me' (v. 8). With these words Paul expresses his sense of call and his confidence in the gospel he received from the risen Lord. Here we have an example of the kind of things Christians were saying some twenty years or so after the great saving events. Paul sees these events and their proclamation as 'of first importance' (v. 3).

First, we are dealing with historical and datable events: Christ 'died' and 'he was buried' (v. 4), which emphasizes the physicality of the event. The fact that he rose 'on the third day' emphasizes that this too is a physical event which cannot be collapsed into myth and symbol. It is on the factuality of these great saving events that the gospel depends and in subsequent weeks our readings are going to explore part of Paul's passionate conviction of the reality of the resurrection.

Second, we have interpretation. Why did Christ die? The explanation here is 'for our sins' (v. 3). Paul affirms rather than develops here the idea of Christ dying as our substitute, which is almost certainly a reflection of Isaiah 53:5.

Third, Paul states that if we want to understand the meaning of these events we must study the Old Testament because these things happened 'in accordance with the scriptures' (v. 3). This probably means the overall thrust of the scriptures as pointing to Christ, but plainly such passages as Isaiah 53, alluded to here, and Psalm 22 would be important and significant. Since much of this passage uses creation imagery, the fundamental thrust of Genesis 1 (the transcendent God 'out there') combined with the immanent God of Genesis 2 (who comes 'down here') would be significant in establishing the pattern which runs through the whole of scripture.

Luke 5:1–11

Here we have a call narrative of the first disciples, similar to those in Matthew 4:18–22 and Mark 1:16–20. However, Luke's account is fuller and, in particular, uniquely has the incident of the encounter of Jesus and Peter. It is this incident which we shall examine. Jesus (as he does also in John 21) gives the odd command to the experts to fish again where they had hitherto failed. Simon demurs but does obey.

Here the narrative echoes Isaiah 6 very clearly. Simon is not simply overwhelmed by a sense of his smallness and inferiority but by his own sinfulness (v. 8). Peter, like Isaiah, must take his place as a sinner before he can preach the gospel of salvation. Like Paul, he needs to repent and be changed into a follower of Jesus.

This is followed by the declaration about 'catching people' (v. 10). It is significant that Jesus tells him not to be afraid, which is in effect a declaration of forgiveness and which gives Peter the strength to carry out the implied command to catch people. This 'catching' is not predatory but gracious, and points to the wide horizons which Luke is to describe in Acts.

Although, unlike some of the other accounts, Luke does not mention Jesus' command to follow him, this is in fact what they do. Luke adds the detail that they left everything. This does not mean that all their former skills and talents were abandoned, rather that they were applied to higher purposes.

RF

PROPER 2

YEAR A

Deuteronomy 30:15–20

God desires to bless his chosen people. His *law* has been given for their instruction and guidance, with a view to their welfare and prosperity. His *promise*—many descendants, and a land to possess—is now renewed. The fulfilment depends, however, on their response. If their allegiance wavers or is given to other gods, the promise is forfeit.

The 'sermons' of Deuteronomy often sound like an ancient vassal treaty—setting out conditions in the form of blessings and cursings. More significant is the stark choice between life and death (vv. 15, 19) with the emphatic appeal to choose life. (Good and evil are not used here in a moral sense: the contrast is life/prosperity, death/misfortune.)

Loving God (v. 20; cf. v. 6) is closely linked to obedience. (In a treaty there is often a clause that the vassal should 'love' the suzerain.) 'Cleaving' encompasses commitment, loyalty, constancy. It involves 'heart and soul and strength', much more than a formal arrangement (Deuteronomy 6:5).

The choice of allegiance is urgent, amid the dangers of entering Canaan. The message is edited and reapplied in the upheavals of the seventh century BC. Yet the people have just been reassured that the commandment of God is not too hard or too distant (v. 14). God is reaching out to them in love.

1 Corinthians 3:1–9

'Oh, *do* grow up!'—the familiar cry of an exasperated parent to a wayward teenager. Paul is more polite but the message is the same.

Whose responsibility is it to grow disciples?

As men of the world, physically and mentally the Corinthians are adult, but as Christians they are immature, mere babies. God's wisdom is spiritual food for the spiritually mature. Forming fan clubs for their favourite apostle, dividing into factions and trying to score points off each other—all this merely demonstrates their immaturity. Arguing about the most effective preacher is evading their own responsibility.

Various Christian leaders with a variety of gifts may play a part in 'growing disciples'. From one perspective they are 'merely' servants, equipped to carry out a defined task. From another perspective, they have the immense privilege of being fellow workers with God. Whatever their role, they are all on a level (equal pay for equal work!)

Above all, both church members and church leaders need to remember that they depend on *God* for spiritual growth (vv. 6–7).

Moses could set out the issues of life and death: God alone *gives* life. Paul and Apollos could offer disciples teaching and support: God alone gives growth.

Matthew 5:21–37

'You have heard… but *I* say…' Jesus gives examples of how the principles relating to the law would work in practice. Growing as a disciple requires a new dimension of obedience to God's will, a dimension that is not less than keeping the law, but infinitely more.

Murder is prohibited by the law—but violent anger and contemptuous abuse are inadmissible. So—be reconciled before the evening sacrifice. Adultery is prohibited by the law—but uncontrolled lust is inadmissible. So—ruthlessly cut out the occasion of temptation. Divorce is permitted by the law—but divorce creates the scenario for adultery. So—(implied) you should not use this legal concession. False oaths are prohibited by the law— but swearing is presumptuous even if it avoids the name of God, for heaven and earth all belong to him. So—make your word your bond in truth and integrity.

In each case, Jesus is probing causes and consequences.

- Is this a counsel of perfection, an ideal to aim at, or is it a practical programme for all disciples? It seems that this is the ethic of the Kingdom of heaven, beginning to be realized now, but only perfected in the age to come.
- Is this 'justification by works'? The whole framework of the sermon is the gift and grace of God. Where disciples fail to live up to the ideal, they are driven back to the gospel and their need of God's grace.

Jesus alone, not the teachers of the law, can interpret the law for the new age of the Kingdom.

GS

YEAR B

2 Kings 5:1–14

When Naaman went to Israel to be healed, he went with certain expectations: to deal first with the king (v. 5), perhaps as the prophet's employer; to pay a reward (v. 5), or to enter into a business transaction; to deal with his healer personally (v. 11) and to take part in some mysterious and suitably elaborate ritual (v. 11). All this is entirely understandable, not only because of Naaman's culture, but because this is our natural human instinct. We want to be able to pin our faith on something we can see, or on some mysteriously authoritative person. However, Elisha avoids getting between Naaman and God. He doesn't make himself, or any magical words or ointments, the focus of attention—the waters of the Jordan are suitable for the washing precisely because they are no different from any other river. Elisha also refuses payment. Thus he prevents Naaman from going away with the impression that the power of God can be located in people or things that can be owned or traded.

Naaman thus discovers the power of God, and not the power of an individual or of a special oil or action. As we seek, in our churches, to be God's priests to the world, we need to ensure that it is God and nothing else that is the focus of attention and the recipient of all glory.

1 Corinthians 9:24–27

Paul continues in his efforts to persuade the Corinthians to avoid food sacrificed to idols. Here he is not suggesting that we are in competition with one another to reach a heavenly podium (v. 24). Rather, he is urging his hearers to keep their eye on the finishing line, or 'on the ball', to use another sporting metaphor.

The force of his argument here is simply that they are focusing on something that does not help them or anyone else towards salvation. It seems that some of the Corinthian Christians may have been taking positive pride in eating food sacrificed to idols as a way of flaunting their new-found 'knowledge' that idols are nothing at all (8:4). This type of behaviour has no positive benefit; its only function is to demonstrate a false spiritual superiority.

The athletic image Paul uses is sometimes interpreted as expressing his ideal of the Christian life. Paul is thus cast as some kind of a striving workaholic who loves to break sweat. In fact, Paul's point is simply that, by any reckoning, the Christian life is amazingly hard. It is folly, therefore, to make it even harder by introducing side issues that only serve to increase the difficulty of the journey. In today's Church, we equally need to identify the 'finishing line' and then keep our eye fixed firmly on it.

Mark 1:40–45

This leper has no letter of recommendation, no status and no handsome reward to offer his healer (cf. 2 Kings 5:1–14). He simply throws himself on God's mercy and puts his trust in Jesus (v. 40).

The man's skin disease made him unclean and therefore cast out of the community of Israel. It is a testimony to Jesus' reputation for compassion that this man even considered the possibility of Jesus' being willing to heal him. In touching the man (v. 41), Jesus made himself unclean and thus identified with his condition.

In our own prayers for healing, this passage contains an important lesson. We cannot bargain with God; we can only depend on his mercy. That mercy, seen on a grand scale in Jesus' incarnation and crucifixion, is seen in its personal and particular nature in the way that Jesus treated this particular individual.

AG

YEAR C

Jeremiah 17:5–10

This is an uncompromising passage and one of the Bible's challenges about the two ways. The language and imagery particularly recall Psalm 1. We have no way of knowing who influenced whom, although it is likely that the collection we know as the Psalter, whenever it was finally collected, existed in some form at an early stage in Israel's history.

What Jeremiah presents is not two alternative lifestyles; the imagery used, especially that of water, shows that this is a matter of life and death. The personal urgency of the passage suggests that the prophet himself has experienced his times of dryness and deadness, his 'dark nights of the soul'. He has survived these and is anxious that others should choose life.

The way that leads to death (vv. 5b–6) is one of dryness and fruitlessness. It is one of pride and complacency, relying on human achievement and turning away from God. It leads not only to barrenness but to a solitary and dehumanizing existence.

By contrast, the way that leads to life (vv. 7–8) is the way of trust and fruitfulness. It is part of the creating love of God which causes the desert to blossom as a rose, and is independent of hostile forces represented by heat and drought.

Verses 9 and 10 underline the dependence of all this on Yahweh. He cannot be deceived, however much the human heart, fertile in stratagems, tries to deceive him. There is a day of reckoning which is both certain and utterly fair. Here we have both warning and assurance.

1 Corinthians 15:12–20

Paul is asserting the centrality of the resurrection of Christ, without which neither Christian living nor Christian preaching are possible. He is determined to prove that resurrection does not simply mean survival but involves future bodily life beyond the grave. If no such resurrection can be hoped for, then plainly Christ's body still lies in Joseph's tomb and the preaching that Paul has so passionately advocated in verses 1–11 is hollow. Later he is to develop the argument that since Christ has been raised, there must be a resurrection of the dead, but now he wants to show the theological consequences of his opponents' position.

First of all, they have nothing to preach (v. 14). They have no gospel to proclaim. Both the preaching which led the Corinthians to faith, and the faith itself, are futile.

Worse, their preaching becomes a tissue of lies. If Christ was not raised, then God has failed to do what he promised to do, and that is ultimately a denial of the gospel altogether (vv. 15–16).

There are further disastrous consequences. The first is that the living are still in their sins and all the present experiences of the Spirit as a foretaste of the life to come are bogus. The second is that those 'who have died in Christ' (v. 18) are lost as if they had never believed the gospel at all. Thus (v. 19) the Christian faith becomes a miserable and pointless 'this world' gospel.

All this is dismissed in the triumphant affirmation of verse 20—Christ has risen and thus all who are 'in Christ' will be raised with him.

Luke 6:17–26

This week's and next week's Gospel readings include a large part of what is usually called the 'Sermon on the Plain'. Verses 17–19 remind us of Jesus' wider ministry, including exorcism and healing. The following verses are densely packed and all we can do is to mention some leading ideas.

Luke's version of the Beatitudes focuses on basic attitudes: he wants to ensure right responses to poverty, hunger, sorrow, society and ostracism. 'Blessed' is better than 'happy' because it emphasizes that this is the final truth to be revealed on the last day rather than simply a feeling of well-being. The basic criterion is whether people are genuine disciples of Christ.

In sharp contrast to the blessings are the 'woes' (vv. 24–26). If the blessings reflect the words of the Magnificat—'he has filled the hungry with good things'—the woes reflect the latter part of that verse (1:53)—'and sent the rich away empty'. The rich are not condemned because they are rich but because they have chosen present indulgence instead of future blessing. Similarly, those who are full now are those who are not hungry for God. Those who laugh are those whose laughter is heartless and at the expense of others. Those who have unusually high reputations are in the line of the false prophets, who always said what they knew would be popular.

These words go to the very heart of Christ's teaching. No life of faith and love is possible if basic attitudes are this—worldly and self-centred. In spite of appearances, there are only two types of people—those who love God and others and those whose horizons are limited by wealth and status.

RF

PROPER 3

YEAR A

Leviticus 19:1–2, 9–18

It is immediately obvious that these verses recall many of the ten commandments. Yet they are set in a very diverse collection of laws.

The basic principle that governs all Old Testament Torah is set out in verse 2: 'You shall be holy, for I the Lord your God am holy.' The holiness of God is never defined: holiness is simply what God is. In every aspect of life, the law is there to enable the people of God to reflect the character and the actions of God himself. So the passage is punctuated with reminders of this motive—'I am the Lord (your God)' (vv. 3, 4, 10, 12, 14, 16, 18).

Many of the commands reflect God's care for 'the poor'—the weak and defenceless, those who are vulnerable physically or economically (e.g. vv. 13–14). God as Judge of his people requires just dealings to be a hallmark of human society (v. 15). God who does not condemn expects his people to reason with each other, not store resentment (cf. Isaiah 1:18). God who is truth abhors lying and slander. Even the sabbath is to reflect God's rest after creation (v. 3) and the prohibition against mixing species is to preserve the order of the natural world as God created it (v. 19).

Verse 18 offers a summary: the love we give to our neighbour is just an echo of God's sacrificial love for his people.

1 Corinthians 3:10–11, 16–23

In verse 9, Paul has described the Corinthians as 'God's building'. This leads him to compare his own ministry to the work of a master builder.

Whatever the superstructure (vv. 12–13), a building is worthless without a strong foundation. If Christian disciples are to be God's building, the only foundation that can be laid is in Jesus Christ himself.

Christians are not just any building, but a temple, where God's Spirit dwells. So they are protected against attack by God himself.

Faith cannot be secure if it rests on human intellect or human personality (vv. 18–22). The post-enlightenment West has frequently tested gospel acceptability (God incarnate, a crucified Saviour) against the constructs of the human mind—and found a credibility gap. Paul, wrestling with a pre-scientific but equally sceptical philosophical culture, would not have been surprised. Nor would he have been unduly impressed by the 'choose your own foundation' of post-modernism. The *only* foundation for the gospel, in his view, is Christ—incarnate in Jesus, crucified and risen. If that makes Christian believers look fools in the eyes of the world, so be it. For in Christ they possess all things and are themselves possessed by God (vv. 22–23).

Matthew 5:38–48

How literally did Jesus intended this teaching to be understood? Cutting off hands and plucking out eyes to avoid temptation is plainly hyperbole; but what about inviting your assailant to have another go? And is it never legitimate to refuse a beggar?

Luther offered one solution: the Christian lives in two realms. In the Church, disciples are literally to obey these injunctions; in the world, natural law prevails. Albert Schweitzer suggested that these demands only made sense as an 'interim ethic', where people lived in expectation that the end of the world was imminent.

The *lex talionis*, an eye for an eye, etc., was primarily a way of *limiting* personal vengeance. Jesus says simply, 'Do not resist evil at all'. His three examples show that disciples should not only forgo their rights, but actively offer *more* than is demanded. This surprise generosity reflects their experience of unexpected grace.

The Old Testament does not specifically teach hatred of enemies, although it was often inferred (and justified on the basis that they are also God's enemies! Cf. Psalm 139:21–22). 'Hate', however, often means 'less love' or 'not love'.

'One good deed deserves another' is common sense for the world. Loving and caring for your 'enemies' on the other hand is, for the Christian, simply a reflection of the Father's generosity.

GS

YEAR B

Isaiah 43:18–25

The verses immediately preceding this reading recall the exodus across the Red Sea. These verses look forward to the promise of a new and greater exodus. This future event is not simply concerned with the movement of a people from one location to another; it is rather a renewal of all creation (vv. 19–20), including God's chosen people (v. 20). In the initial instance, this applies to the return from the Babylonian exile. Beyond this, as numerous New Testament writers pick up, this image of a new exodus applies to the work of Christ.

The reaction of God's people to this new thing, however, is to miss it completely. They forget that they are in a covenant relationship with a *living* God and so they do not respond to him in living worship (vv. 22–24). All they do is add to their sins (v. 24).

Our God is not one who submits to formulae or who can be learnt about and then taped up. He is constantly at work in history. Isaiah 43:19 calls for perception of what God is doing. Such perception is impossible when our responses to God are founded on what we *assume* he is about, rather than what he is actually doing in the world today.

2 Corinthians 1:18–22

Paul is here defending his decision to call off a planned return visit to Corinth. His supposed vacillation, a serious accusation (cf. Matthew 5:37; James 5:12), was being used to call his integrity into question.

Paul appeals to the Corinthians to trust his integrity on the basis of their experience of him: he is true to his promise as God is true (vv. 18–19); he is in full agreement with all God's work among them (v. 20); he is a man

84

whom they had recognized as appointed and equipped by God to work among them (vv. 21–22). He explains that his decision to change his plans was motivated by love for them, so as not to cause them further pain (v. 23). The idea that anyone could accuse Paul of being a ditherer strikes us as extraordinary, so we can appreciate Paul's frustration.

Church leaders must be people of clear integrity. However, that integrity cannot be tested by gossip and rumour. This medium usually reveals more about the speaker than the person being spoken of. It is to the Corinthians' shame that they have forced Paul to plead his case as he does here. Paul's attitude to whoever has wronged him is, however, entirely forgiving (2:7, 10).

Mark 2:1–12

Jesus' identity and the scope of his mission continue to be mapped out in these opening chapters of Mark. Of course it is impossible for us to know exactly what Jesus was speaking about just before the paralysed man was lowered through the roof. However, it is reasonable to suppose that, as recorded in Mark 1:15 (cf. 1:38–39), his theme was 'The time is fulfilled, and the Kingdom of God has come near; repent and believe the good news.'

If this was the case, then the appearance of the man through the roof (v. 4) provided an opportunity to demonstrate the real availability of the good news that Jesus was preaching. If he had simply healed the man, then he could have been seen merely as a miracle worker. If he had simply pronounced forgiveness, then the benefits of the Kingdom would have been invisible and therefore doubtful. In forgiving *and* healing, Jesus made plain that something extraordinary and new was taking place, something more than the healing of bodies—the opportunity to heal the source of death itself, the sin that alienates us from God.

AG

YEAR C

Genesis 45:3–11, 15

Even in these days of biblical illiteracy, the story of Joseph is still reasonably familiar. This little vignette shows in full measure the marvellous qualities of the story, reminds us that story is at the very heart of the Bible and draws us into the plot with marvellous and vivid creativity. Four things can be noticed.

The first is the sheer skill of the narrative. The clearer repetition: 'I am Joseph' (v. 3) with its terrifying implications, and 'I am your brother, Joseph' (v. 4), with its blend of reassurance and warning. The psychology of the characters, the cross-currents of feeling, are powerfully conveyed. All this is a reminder of the need to enter imaginatively into the Bible's world.

Second, there is the doctrine of divine providence. This is more than a well-told story, it is part of the big story, the 'metanarrative' which is God's story. Four times (vv. 5, 7, 8, 9) the initiative in all these events is said to be God's. Thus is emphasized the importance of faith and vision.

But third, there is emphasized the human activity which is the response to God's providence. Joseph makes practical arrangements for his family to live in Goshen (vv. 9–11).

Fourth, and this is seen especially in verse 15, this is a deeply moving human story. With the practicalities attended to, an emotional reunion scene and reconciliation takes place.

With all these riches in the story, it is not surprising that many have seen in this a picture of Christ welcoming his estranged people and bringing them to share his glory.

1 Corinthians 15:35–38, 42–50

As Paul continues his exposition of the resurrection, he now argues that the created universe itself has bodily life beyond death written large across it. It is not disembodied existence in a shadowland that he is asserting; it is new bodily existence, because the whole person and not just a disembodied 'soul' is to be saved.

He takes the analogy of the seed as illustrating the principle that out of death springs new and vibrant life. God has already created the universe so that bodies can adapt to various kinds of existence. The plant does not look like the seed but is nevertheless in direct organic continuity with it. Thus God's purposes are not thwarted by death. Verse 38 emphasizes that this is not simply a 'natural' process but a direct activity of God. Thus, as Paul is to say in Philippians 3:20–21, God will 'transform our lowly bodies so that they will be like Christ's glorious body' (NIV).

In verses 42–50, Paul applies the analogies of the seed, animal life and the heavenly bodies to 'the resurrection of the dead'. He is now concerned to show that the illustrations drawn from nature can also be demonstrated from scripture. He establishes a series of contrasts between the mortal and immortal bodies—the primary one of decaying and imperishable, then of humiliation and glory, finally of weakness and power.

He buttresses this by the Adam/Christ contrast. In Adam we share in death; in Christ we will share in resurrection. The old creation story in Genesis 2:7 of the breath of life breathed into Adam's nostrils is the background of the imagery here.

The next stage of the argument is introduced in verse 50, which makes the important point that even those who are alive when the Saviour returns will need their mortal bodies to be transformed.

Luke 6:27–38

It would be easy to be only too happy to be ostracized (6:26) and for that to lead to a kind of misanthropy. Our Lord now speaks of the balancing grace of loving our enemies.

The first section (vv. 27–31) shows how Christian behaviour must exemplify a higher standard than that of the world, not least in not expecting any recompense for what is done. This applies in the realm of insults and injuries, of possessions and generosity. Here we must avoid the twin pitfalls of pedantic legalism and watering down the text. The spirit and attitude is all important and this is reinforced by the Golden Rule (v. 31), put in a positive form which raises it from mere prudence to an evidence of grace.

The second section (vv. 32–38) emphasizes that these attitudes and actions are only possible because we are our Father's children (vv. 35–36). We have a series of contrasts between the behaviour patterns of the Father's children and those of 'sinners'. Every sphere of relationships—God, society and possessions—is affected.

The fundamental nature of these attitudes is encapsulated first by 'Be merciful' (v. 36), which is a response to God's grace and love towards us. Second, we are told not to 'judge' here, made clearer by being in parallel with 'condemn'. Here it means not to be judgmental or censorious or to pass quick judgments without knowing all the facts. God alone will judge. Positively, the children of the Father will be marked by huge and overflowing generosity which is a response to God's own generosity.

RF

THE SECOND SUNDAY BEFORE LENT

YEAR A

Genesis 1:1—2:3

'And God said... and it was so.' Unlike the gods in Babylonian myths of creation, Israel's Creator God is transcendent. The world does not emerge from a conflict between good and evil in precarious dualism. Evil enters only *after* creation. The material world has every potential for good, and God's good order cannot ultimately be defeated.

All living creatures are blessed by God and join in procreation (v. 22) but only humankind, the apex of creation, is made 'in our image, after our likeness' (v. 26). The dominion that humankind is given (v. 23) consists therefore not in exploitation but in continuing God's work of creativity, fruitfulness and order.

God, who has brought chaos to cosmos in orderly sequence, takes the risk of putting this responsibility in the hands of human beings, seeking their free co-operation. (The fixed poetic pattern of verses 1–25 is broken as human beings are made.)

But there are limits set: humankind belongs on the earth, a creature who cannot usurp the role of the Creator.

Human beings turning in upon themselves, instead of being open to God, will destroy this harmony. But the God who creates intends salvation and he will recreate (cf. Isaiah 51).

Romans 8:18–25

'Creation waits...' (v. 19) 'and we wait...' (v. 23).

The story of the fall is the story of human rebellion and a broken relationship between God and humanity. The harmony between God and whole created order is also affected (Genesis 3:17–19). So the whole creation is frustrated, falling short of the full glory that God intended.

The destiny of the natural order is intimately bound up with the destiny of humankind. But there is hope for both (vv. 20, 24). Already individually we have the first instalment of the glory that will be ours, for the Spirit's power is at work within us.

This glory will be seen in all its perfection when we are transformed by the Spirit into the image of Christ. Then, revealed as children of God and heirs with Christ, we shall be set free from the grip of decay and death. Our mortal bodies (which link us to the natural order) will find new life in resurrection.

Then and not before, the whole of creation will share this 'liberty of glory'. Meanwhile, creation is in labour, we are in labour—but the pain is the harbinger of joyful new birth.

Matthew 6:25–34

A grand design of cosmic salvation inspired Paul. The Gospel reading focuses on the everyday needs of food and clothing for survival in this imperfect world. Yet the abundance and order of nature provide Jesus with examples of a divine perspective on human society.

Sowing, reaping, gathering (v. 26) were the immediate concerns of men in an agricultural community, whereas preparing food, finding water, making clothes were the preoccupations of the women (v. 31). Both need to look around them and learn not to be anxious. (In the Wisdom writings, the Greek word is associated with sleepless nights and premature ageing!)

That God provided food for the birds was a common Jewish thought. Wild flowers abounded in the fields—their life was short, for grass and weeds were common fuel for ovens. Jesus uses a rabbinic style of argument, from the lesser to the greater: 'Are not you of more value than... Is not the life more than... Will he not much more...'

The fact that in the twenty-first century wild flowers and birds can be decimated by pollution and the whole ecology distorted by human greed does not detract from God's generous provision for all his creatures (cf. Genesis 1:29–30).

Lent will be a time for reviewing priorities (v. 33).

GS

YEAR B

Proverbs 8:1, 22–31

Most cultures admire one quality above all others. In the West, in our own time, 'celebrity' is probably considered of greater worth than wisdom, but this was not the case in ancient Israel. Wisdom was so highly prized in Hebrew culture that it came to be seen as a personified entity who blessed those whom she considered worthy.

Through the course of Proverbs 8, Wisdom explains why people should listen to her. First, because of the truth and justice of what she says (vv. 4–11). Second, because of the practical value of her words in the working of a society (vv. 12–21). Third, because she was involved with God in the creation of the world, and so creation is ordered according to the laws of wisdom (vv. 22–31).

It is this final reason that has been used by Christian theology to explain how it is possible for the God who is One to have a co-creator in Christ. This passage underlies the theology expressed in Colossians 1:15–20 and John's Prologue.

Colossians 1:15–20

In Colossians 1:13–14, Paul describes what has happened to his readers. They have been rescued and transferred from one reality into another, from the power of darkness to the Kingdom of the Son. In verses 15–20, Paul uses a poem to illustrate, explain and celebrate how this is possible. This passage is overwhelmingly rich because it contains an entire theology of salvation.

The opening statements regarding the pre-existence of Christ and his role in creation do not serve as a basis for praise in isolation from what follows. These aspects of Christ's nature are fundamental to his ability to achieve the effect that has been described in verse 13. Only the Creator can forge a new creation. Only the One who is over all powers and dominions can transfer subjects from one kingdom to another. Only the One who is God can do the work that only God can do (vv. 15–17).

In the first creation, as it is described in Genesis, God first of all creates habitats (light and dark; sky, sea and land) and then fills them with inhabitants (sun and moon; birds, fish and animals). A parallel pattern appears here. In the new creation, Christ is the firstborn inhabitant, a new Adam. Through his blood on the cross (v. 20) he makes possible the transfer of new inhabitants into this creation. This is our experience, with the Colossians, when we receive Holy Communion. Then we too accept the work of Christ and experience its transforming power. And, having been so transferred, we benefit from the type of prayers that Paul offers in 1:3–6, 9–14.

John 1:1–14

John's prologue, like Colossians 1:15–20, expresses an understanding of Jesus' relationship with God that is grounded in the work that Christ achieves. The parallel with Genesis' account of creation is particularly strong.

It is the scope of God's plan in Christ that is expressed so remarkably here. First, it is boundless in its breadth: it reaches back to the very origin of all things (v. 1); it is part of the warp and weft of the nature of creation itself (v. 3). Second, it is specific and intimate in its focus (vv. 10, 13). Jesus, who reveals to us everything that is true about the nature of God, meets us in flesh and invites us to enter a new experience of intimacy with God as his own children.

As we grow up from babyhood to adulthood, we struggle to understand the nature of our environment so as to learn how to respond to it appropriately. John reveals here a fundamental truth about the universe, of which we should be aware—that Jesus, in all that he is, reveals the nature of the One who is sovereign over all things from beginning to end.

AG

YEAR C

Genesis 2:4b–9, 15–25

Having had the panorama of creation in chapter 1, the scene switches to close-up and particularly concentrates on humans and their environment, culminating in the marriage story. The name of God characteristic of this section—'Yahweh Elohim'—underlines that the God who made heaven and earth is also Yahweh, the covenant Lord committed to his people by promises which he will not break.

So the context here is not a universe but a garden. All the emphasis is on the creating power of God to make a garden from a desert and a human from dust. In that garden grow trees—the tree of life which reappears in the heavenly city (Revelation 2:7; 22:2, 14, 19) and the tree of the knowledge of good and evil 'whose mortal taste brought death into the world and all our woe with loss of Eden' (John Milton, *Paradise Lost*).

This is the setting for the task given to Adam and the creation of Eve. Eden is not magic; gardens need gardeners. An ominous note is struck by the threatened death sentence.

So far everything has been pronounced 'good' but now, in 2:18, comes the first negative note: Adam is incomplete without a companion. This new companion is a 'helper', with no sense of inferiority as the word is also used of Yahweh (e.g. Psalms 33:20; 146:5). Moreover, while Adam contributes his rib he is wholly passive and in no sense a co-creator. Adam's joyous shout (v. 23) is a recognition of a covenant and remains a clear statement of a new and total union. Both together are one flesh and represent mutuality— God's image.

Revelation 4

This is part of the great enthronement scene which continues into chapter 5. It is dominated by the throne of God towering above the troubled course of human history, and the scroll of destiny to be handed to the Lamb who, when the time comes, will bring history to a close. The great biblical themes of creation and redemption are underlined and these form the subject of the worship of heaven. Today's chapter focuses on creation and thus links with our other readings.

John, in a visionary experience, is given a glimpse of the heavenly throne-room (v. 2). Four things can be noted. First, John sees a throne symboliz-ing the absolute sovereignty of God, recalling the vision of Isaiah (Isaiah 6) and the 'enthronement psalms' (such as Psalm 93). God himself is not described but is portrayed as dazzling light reflected from precious stones, emphasizing his awesome purity. The rainbow is a reminder of God's covenant with Noah (Genesis 9:16–17).

Second, he sees around the throne of God twenty-four elders seated on thrones (v. 4). Some identify these as the twelve tribes and twelve apostles symbolizing God's people across the ages, others as angels. In any case, they render to God that perfect worship of which worship on earth is an imperfect echo.

Third, there are four living creatures (vv. 6–8) which may represent the worship of creation (cf. Psalm 148:1–10). They engage in ceaseless adoration and particularly praise God in his holiness which stretches from eternity to eternity.

Then there is the song (v. 11) which exalts God for his work in creation. 'You are worthy' may be a polemic against the emperor-cult, as these words and 'our Lord and God' were introduced as greetings to the emperor by Domitian. To churches threatened by persecution, the whole scenario is encouragement: Jesus, not Caesar, is Lord.

Luke 8:22–25

This story is one of the Gospel narratives often referred to as 'nature miracles', which demonstrate the biblical view of creation as not just an act in the past but a continuing involvement of God in his world. Its importance here and in Matthew 13 and Mark 4 is that it comes at the climax of a series of mighty acts—exorcisms, healings, unprecedented authority in preaching. All of these, of course, have many Old Testament parallels—for example, Saul's evil spirit exorcized by David's harp; healings and even raising the dead by Elijah and Elisha; the inspired utterances of the prophets. Thus there was inevitable controversy (most of it reflected within the disciples themselves) about who Jesus of Nazareth was, and, while most of his mighty acts were not unique, surely there was only one who could say to the proud waves, 'Thus far shall you come, and no farther'.

Thus Jesus is Lord of the universe, and Luke emphasizes the contrast between the fury of the storm and Christ's peaceful sleep. Moreover, his calm authority sharply exposes the disciples' panic (vv. 24–25).

Yet the abiding impression is not so much their lack of faith as the awe and trembling with which they look at Jesus with new eyes. 'Who then is this?' (v. 25) is massively important in the Christology of the Gospels, and this passage very directly anticipates Jesus' question at Caesarea Philippi— 'Who do you say that I am?' (Luke 9:20).

The Creator is present in his creation, and in subsequent generations the Church has often thought of herself as a boat tossed by turbulent and threatening waters. In such circumstances we rejoice in Jesus, who does what God does.

RF

THE SUNDAY NEXT BEFORE LENT

YEAR A

Exodus 24:12–18

Very ancient texts connect the appearing of Yahweh with Mount Sinai (Judges 5:5), and the cloud shrouding the peaks offered a vivid symbol of the awe-inspiring mystery of his presence. The Hebrew word for glory (*kabod*), originally meant a weight, and is used to express the overwhelming —and terrifying—presence of God. His glory is also symbolized by fire or blinding light (lightning in the storm clouds?) (cf. 19:16–19).

Only those whom God calls dare enter the glory of God's presence. Moses waits for six days in preparation, but then God speaks directly to him (cf. 33:11). Joshua, who will be his successor, is privileged to accompany him into the cloud, but not apparently to the encounter with God.

In the text as we now have it, this meeting of Moses with the Lord follows immediately on the sealing of the covenant between God and Israel. Moses has communicated the law, by spoken word and in writing (vv. 3–4). Now God himself is said to write the law and commandments on stone, a sign of their permanence and the divine authority behind them. They are given as Torah—instruction for life.

2 Peter 1:16–21

The author's phraseology suggests that he did not depend on the Gospels' accounts of the transfiguration, but on an independent tradition, perhaps his own knowledge of Peter's preaching.

The apostles' preaching about the *eschaton*, the new age to be inaugurated by Christ when he comes in glory and power, had evidently been written off by their opponents as cleverly concocted fabrications. This preaching, however, was based on eyewitness testimony, for they had been there on the mountain for that unique moment. Like a glimpse of the scene through a lighted window before the curtains are drawn, they had been given sight of what lay beyond. The 'glory and honour' Jesus received (v. 17), the words heard from heaven, were the signs of God's Messiah, enthroned as king on the holy mountain (Psalm 8:6–7) by God himself.

This gives great confidence in the Old Testament prophecies (v. 19). In a time of fear and persecution, his readers needed to hold on to such promises as a beacon of hope on a dark night. When the new age dawns, the daylight of God's coming will flood their lives (cf. Revelation 22:16).

Matthew 17:1–9

The description of the transfiguration of Jesus has several echoes of the exodus narrative. After the climax of Peter's confession (16:16), a period of six days elapses before Jesus goes up the mountain, taking close companions but leaving the rest behind.

When Jesus is transfigured, the description 'his face shone like the sun' inevitably recalls Moses' face after meeting with God. Moses and Elijah may represent the Law and the Prophets or, more probably, they appear because they were both expected to return before the coming of the Messiah (Deuteronomy 18:15–18, Malachi 4:5). Peter's inept suggestion is perhaps an attempt to make the experience permanent, as Moses set up the tent of meeting to indicate God's continuing presence with the Israelites in the desert.

The bright cloud of God's presence envelops them and the voice of God is heard—not giving commandments but bearing witness, as at the baptism of Jesus, to his Sonship and the divine authority of his teaching.

Plainly Jesus is being revealed as the new Moses. Even more significantly, the three disciples, bewildered and fearful after Jesus' prediction of his passion, are given a unique experience of his glory.

GS

YEAR B

2 Kings 2:1–12

Elijah was the first prophet whose ministry was conducted outside the seat of political power. This bruising experience left him feeling that he was entirely alone in his faithfulness to God (1 Kings 19:10). It was at his lowest point that God spoke to Elijah in the 'still small voice' (1 Kings 19:12) and commissioned him to anoint Elisha as his successor (1 Kings 19:16, 19).

Elijah, who had felt entirely alone, is unable to shake off his inseparable attendant Elisha (vv. 2–6). The journey of the two prophets is full of resonances from the exodus. Several of the places they visit featured in the initial conquest of the promised land. The parting of the Jordan river (v. 8) is again an echo of those events (cf. Joshua 3:17). Further, the succession of Elisha to Elijah's role (2:13–14) is parallel to Joshua's succession from Moses (both of which took place on the east side of the Jordan).

Elisha's succession from Elijah, like Joshua's from Moses before him, and like that of the disciples from Jesus (Acts 1—2 has a number of parallels with the Elijah and Elisha story), is a testimony to God's ability to continue a single work across the lifetime of more than one individual leader, or even across the whole expanse of history.

2 Corinthians 4:3–6

Paul is thought by some Christians to be an unattractive character who is rather too sure of his own rightness. Paul apparently displays this quality in this passage when he explains that those who can't understand his message are on their way to destruction (v. 3). Before judging Paul too harshly, we should recognize that he is battling not for his own reputation but for the very centre of the gospel itself.

Reading between the lines, it seems that Paul's opponents were adapting the gospel to make it more attractive or appealing in some way (4:1–2). Paul may have been defending the gospel against syncretism with pagan cults and mystery religions, or standing his ground with regard to the role of the Law in salvation. Whatever the circumstances, his only priority was to focus on Christ. 'Jesus Christ is Lord' (v. 5) was not a statement that he was at liberty to adapt to suit the circumstances. To do so would have been an unfaithfulness both to God and to his hearers.

Mark 9:2–9

The transfiguration offers a glimpse beyond. Moses and Elijah both looked forward to a new state of relationship between God and his people. Here they witness a prefigurement of Jesus' future glory and the dimension in which he will be revealed beyond the resurrection (v. 9).

Within the structure of Mark's Gospel, the transfiguration forms a parallel with Jesus' baptism. Thus, the first half of the story, from Jesus' baptism, leads up to Peter's confession of Christ in Mark 8:29. This is 'lesson one' of Jesus' teaching to the disciples. With the transfiguration, and God's reaffirmation of the beloved status of his Son (v. 7), lesson two begins. Thus, having established Jesus' status as the Messiah, the purpose of his Messiahship now unfolds. The ultimate destination of this purpose is foreseen in the glory on the mountain. The route to that goal, however, must take Jesus to the cross, towards which the story now moves.

In our Christian lives, we are also granted glimpses of future glory, perhaps especially when we gather together in worship. These glimpses sustain us through those periods when following Christ is anything but glorious.

AG

YEAR C

Exodus 34:29–35

The glory of the Lord is the theme that connects today's passages. The message of all three is that by God's grace mortals are permitted to share this uncreated glory. Moses here is the mediator of the old covenant whose essence is inscribed on the two stone tablets that he brings down from the mountain.

We notice first that this glory is connected with speaking to God. That conversation was a transforming one for Moses, and just as God's words caused light at the beginning of creation, so now they cause Moses' face to shine.

Second, we should notice Moses' humility. This echoes Numbers 12:3, which describes him as 'very humble, more so than anyone else on the face of the earth'. Here he is unaware that his face is shining. He is no demi-god or superhuman hero but a humble man, very conscious of his responsibility for standing between God and the people.

The veil is to protect the people from direct access to Yahweh's glory. This is another indication of the care Moses had for the people and his desire to protect them as much as he could. His previous descent from the mountain had been in anger over the incident of the golden calf (ch. 32) and he knew only too well that sinful people could not stand in the glory of God. The whole passage is a rich one, with the emphasis on the word of God which transforms and the subordinate but vital role of Moses.

2 Corinthians 3:12—4:2

In this passage, Paul is contrasting the old and new covenants, based on his meditation on Exodus 34:29–35. First he applies his argument of verses 7–11 that the glory of the old covenant was temporary. Paul himself knew well what the 'veil' was. He had sat in the synagogue Sabbath after Sabbath and heard the reading of the Torah, but was blind to the fact that it pointed to Christ. Only in him can the true meaning and glory of the old covenant be understood.

By contrast, he speaks now in verses 16–18 of the removing of the veil when someone turns to Christ. Much controversy has centred around the phrase 'Now the Lord is the Spirit' (v. 17), which cannot be engaged with here. What can be said is that the Spirit as he points to Christ is the proof that the new age has dawned and thus changed hearts and converted lives are possible. The following phrase 'the Spirit of the Lord', prevents an equating of the Spirit and Jesus. The freedom spoken of is a Spirit-empowered capacity to live in a right relationship with God. The goal of this is to be transformed from the 'glory' we first see when we turn to the Lord to the ultimate glory to be revealed when Christ returns.

This is the ministry that Paul now speaks of (4:1–2). Two consequences flow from this. One is negative—the avoidance of underhand behaviour and misrepresentations of the truth. The other is positive—a faithful and clear exposition of the gospel which will be seen to be truthful and penetrating. Paul is concerned that the Corinthians should see that his apostolic authority is from Christ.

Luke 9:28–36 [37–43]

Here is an incident which focuses the emphases of our other two passages, with its picture of the glorified Christ which points back to the exodus and forward to his coming. Three matters call for comment.

The first is the reality of the other world. For a brief period, the veil was drawn aside to allow a glimpse of the world normally invisible to us. Jesus was in contact with both worlds simultaneously and, while still on earth, he took on a splendour appropriate to the glory of that other world.

The second is the appearance of Moses and Elijah. Moses, the mediator of the old covenant, whose face shone at Sinai, is the great figure associated with the exodus; he now points to that greater exodus when Christ would lead his people out of the slavery of death (v. 30). Elijah was the one who would turn people's hearts back to the covenant (Malachi 4:4–6). Both had departed from the world in strange ways: Moses buried by God (Deuteronomy 34:6), and Elijah taken up to heaven in a whirlwind. Thus they draw attention to Jesus' central place in salvation history and point to the utter certainty of his second coming (see also 1 Peter 1:12–18).

The third is the uniqueness of Christ. Moses and Elijah, though outstanding, were not on the same level; this is implied by verse 32b, 'They saw his glory and the two men who stood with him', and it is confirmed by the voice from heaven. After the voice, Jesus is left alone. The next stage of salvation history can be accomplished by him alone. One day the whole universe will see his glory, but meanwhile the cross comes before the crown.

RF

ASH WEDNESDAY

YEARS A, B, C

Joel 2:1–2, 12–17

Drought has already spread death and despair. Now locusts remove the final vestiges of green and, with them, any last lingering hope.

A solemn assembly has been called in the drought, to fast and offer sacrifice and pray for God's mercy (ch. 1). With this latest disaster, what is the point? The sentence of death is upon them.

The prophet's message is that it is never too late to turn to God. Yet fasting, weeping, tearing garments as a sign of mourning, all will be of no avail unless their *hearts* are turned. (In Hebrew, the heart is the seat not only of emotions but of the mind and will, directing attitudes and actions.) Forgiveness depends ultimately not on their fasting and sacrifice, but on the gracious character of Yahweh (v. 13)—his grace and mercy, his patience and constant love, his desire to bless, not to punish.

When human beings turn away from God and do evil, the consequence, in the economy of God, is more evil rebounding upon them. 'Repent' is more often used of God than of humankind—not because God changes his mind but because the *relationship* between them is changed. When they turn towards him, his justice comes to them as love, not wrath.

For the alternative Old Testament reading, Isaiah 58:1–12, see comment on Proper 1, Year A.

2 Corinthians 5:20b—6:10

Joel's message is of hope—but uncertainty: 'Who knows? It may be...' In Paul's appeal, there is no doubt of the divine response, for God has already taken action (v. 19). The astonishing good news is that in the death of Jesus a paradoxical exchange has taken place (v. 21).

And yet—is it possible to receive this amazing grace 'in vain' (6:1)? Much of the Corinthian Christians' behaviour—especially their dissensions and status-seeking, resentment and critical spirit—belies the fact that in Christ they are a new creation.

Paul offers himself and his colleagues as examples of Christian integrity (vv. 3–8a). Whatever their circumstances and the hardships they face, their attitudes and actions are consonant with their calling.

Outward appearances can be deceptive (vv. 8b–10). Paul has none of the public acclaim the Corinthians seek for themselves and look for in others. Yet he is rich in grace, and through his ministry others find grace.

God has done his part (v. 2). Now it is time for the Corinthians, accepting God's gift of grace, to live in generosity of spirit, reflecting God's generosity to them. Only then will reconciliation with God and with each other be realized in their church community.

Matthew 6:1–6, 16–21

Matthew gives three examples from Jesus' teaching about personal piety.

Almsgiving was not optional, just for those who had money to spare and were feeling generous, but a religious duty for all Jews (Deuteronomy 15:7–11). With no welfare state, the poor depended on this well-organized charity for their support. Hypocrites (Greek, meaning 'actors') give ostent-atiously, performing for their audience, looking for applause.

Attendance at public prayer was also a regular duty. Those who wanted to be admired for devotion deliberately looked to say private prayer in a public place. By contrast, the disciple is to pray in the most secluded place he could find (literally a 'storeroom').

Fasting was a normal part of Jewish religious life (strict Pharisees fasted twice a week). A face smeared with dirt and ash left no one in doubt of your piety and self-discipline. Disciples too will fast, but look outwardly normal.

The 'performers' receive their wages in full: there is no more to come. By contrast, if almsgiving, prayer and fasting are known only to God, he will give recompense (literally 'give in return'). His blessing far exceeds any earned wages.

Lent offers the opportunity to review our own motives and integrity in Christ. Do we wear the actor's mask, either to play for applause or to disguise what lies behind?

John 8:1–11

Integrity is also the theme of the drama played out in the temple court.

The scribes and Pharisees come ostensibly to seek Jesus' opinion on a legal case. In practice, it was obvious to everyone that their concern was neither with the woman's morals nor the law of Moses (Deuteronomy 22:23–24) but with trapping Jesus into making an incriminating response. They are deliberately using the woman as a pawn.

The integrity of Jesus is on the line. If he disavows the Law of Moses, his credibility will be significantly undermined. On the other hand, he is known to forgive and restore the outcast. If he condemns the woman, is he operating double standards?

In a clear reference to Deuteronomy 13:9, Jesus overturns their assumption of superiority. The witness of the crime must be the first to throw the stones, and must not himself be guilty of this particular sin. The result is dramatic and tells its own story: the ring of accusers melts away and the woman is left with her rescuer.

The original question still hangs in the air. 'Neither do I condemn you...'—it would appear that compassion has won. 'Go and sin no more'— her adultery is not condoned and the moral law is upheld. Jesus alone can resolve the tension, for he alone can forgive sins; and the response to forgiveness is a new life.

Note: None of the most reliable manuscripts include this passage, which nevertheless has parallels with stories in the synoptic Gospels.

GS

THE FIRST SUNDAY OF LENT

YEAR A

Genesis 2:15–17; 3:1–7

The story unfolds from different angles. On God's side:

- **His purpose** in putting humankind in the garden is that human beings may care for it, share in God's own creativity and maintain God's order.
- **His provision** is that all are given what is needed to sustain life, not just enough for survival but a generous abundance of good things.
- **His prohibition** draws a boundary between the human and the divine, creature and creator. 'Knowledge of good and evil' is not primarily about morality, but about knowledge of all things. This is the prerogative of God alone: human beings should not encroach.

The man and woman are given choice: to fulfil God's purpose or not. Their co-operation is not taken for granted; but they are offered a real relationship with God, a free response to love.

The serpent is itself a creature, and therefore under God's control. It is also crafty. Insidious questioning, apparently innocent, sows doubt about God's word and God's intentions, giving a foothold for temptation.

The desire to be masters of their own existence becomes irresistible. The man and the woman clutch at divinity—but it eludes them.

Romans 5:12–19

To say no to God is to say no to life itself. Death (being cut off from God) was intended as a warning, not a punishment (Genesis 3:3). Death spread to everyone because everyone sinned, *not* because Adam sinned. Sin is not a congenital disease, not even a contagious disease and certainly not a 'sexually transmitted' disease as certain sections of the Church have taught. But once the disease has been introduced, those who put themselves at risk will catch it.

Paul makes two contrasts:

- The trespass—leading to judgment, then to condemnation and sentence of death—and the free gift, which is grace, leading to acquittal and a reign of life.
- Adam, as the first representative man, prefigures Jesus, the new representative man.

The effect of Adam's action (note: 'transgression', v. 14, means crossing a clearly defined boundary) is the death of many. The effect of Jesus' action is life for many (cf. Isaiah 53).

Both Adam and Jesus are fully human. There is solidarity between members of the human race. Between the first Adam and sinful humanity, between Jesus Christ and the community of the redeemed, there is an identity which Western emphasis on the individual makes it hard to appreciate.

Matthew 4:1–11

For forty days in the wilderness, Jesus lived with evil—led there by the Holy Spirit. This was a part of God's plan to prepare him for his mission.

The first temptation starts at the level of physical need. To use his divine power to satisfy extreme hunger seems reasonable enough. What use will he be in God's service if he is physically weak and unfit?

The second temptation sees the tempter seizing Jesus' own weapon, turning the words of scripture back upon him: 'It is written…' so surely it must not only be legitimate but also carry divine approval if he demonstrates his confidence in God's protection?

The third temptation is also carefully angled. Surely, it is in the interests of those he came to save that he should control the world as soon as possible?

Each temptation seeks to justify the means by the end. Each is related to Jesus' mission. Each will potentially undermine his relationship of trust to his Father. They are personal temptations, but about his role in the world.

Jesus' rejection of these temptations commits him to a life of hardship and self-denial, to patient trust in his heavenly Father's care and to achieving God's mission by God's means.

GS

YEAR B

Genesis 9:8–17

An essential moment in the process of creation was the separation of the waters (Genesis 1:6–7). By a further act of separation, God created land as distinct from the sea (Genesis 1:9). Thus the process of creation was, in the initial instance, about creating space that could be filled with living things.

In the flood, that which had been separated and kept apart was allowed to revert to its previous state. The process here was one of un-creation. Then, as the waters subsided and the land began to reappear, an act of re-creation took place (8:11–14). Noah and his family became a parallel to Adam and his family; a new creation was made available to them and they were invited to fill it (9:1, 7).

The pattern by which God makes his covenant with Noah and his descendants (vv. 8–17) is characteristic of the way in which God deals with his people throughout history. First, there is a faithful promise to act in a particular way (vv. 8–11). This is then accompanied by a sign that makes the promise graspable, concrete and real (vv. 12–17).

This combination of a promise accompanied by a physical sign is mirrored in our physical baptism and in the physical taste and touch of the bread and wine. In each case, the sign allows us to see and to take hold of God's faithful promise of forgiveness and salvation.

1 Peter 3:18–22

The purpose of this passage is to explain how Christ's experience of suffering provides a pattern for our own response to hardship, particularly that caused as a result of our faith (cf. 1 Peter 3:14, 16–17).

Peter catalogues the benefits won by Christ's suffering (vv. 18–20). Verse 18 is powerfully succinct; verse 19 is more difficult to follow. It is sometimes interpreted as referring to Christ's descent into hell. It is more likely, however, that the imprisoned spirits are visited by Christ in the course of his ascent to the right hand of God. The reference to Noah suggests that the characters in question are related to the angelic beings who sinned before the flood (Genesis 6:1–4). Peter's thrust here, whatever the details, is that

Christ's suffering led to a victory which could be proclaimed in every sphere of the universe.

In baptism, Peter argues, we pass through judgment (because of the work of Christ) to new life, just as Noah did. It is therefore an expected pattern of Christian life that we should suffer for righteousness just as Jesus did (cf. 1 Peter 2:21–23). The provocation of a hostile reaction is, in itself, no proof of righteous behaviour. True righteousness, however, rarely fails to provoke a negative response.

Mark 1:9–15

Why did Jesus' temptation occur at this point? Why did the Spirit deliberately drive Jesus into this situation? If we may suppose that Jesus was being tempted to diverge from the path set before him, then we may venture to answer both of these questions.

Jesus faced a journey with a particularly gruesome destination. Not only that, he also faced obstacles in reaching that destination, which would be erected by his enemies, friends (Mark 8:33; 14:43), and even himself (Mark 14:36). At the start of such a journey, it is vital to identify the destination with absolute clarity if there is to be any chance of staying on course. It is also necessary to be adequately prepared for the conditions that will be faced. In the wilderness, Jesus could focus on the ultimate and not just the immediate. At the same time, however, these spaces bring the big temptations to light. Usually, simple everyday concerns can distract us from our journey quite satisfactorily, but in periods of steady contemplation much heavier guns must be used to blow us off course.

Thus, as a final preparation for his public ministry, Jesus is given the opportunity to take stock of what lies before him, both the destination and the obstacles in between. We too need this constant refocusing, guided by the Spirit.

AG

Year C

Deuteronomy 26:1–11

Here we have one of the most important expressions of ancient Israel's self-understanding as the covenant people of Yahweh. This is a kind of creed where God's ancient people rejoice in their relationship with him and remember his mighty acts both in creation and history. Three factors call for comment.

The first is the emphasis that the land is Yahweh's gift (the Hebrew verb *natan* occurs in verses 1, 2, 3, 9, 10 and 11—although not always translated as 'give' in the English versions). The emphasis here is not on the battle to take the land nor the labour to work it but on God's grace and the fulfilment of his promise. Thus the giving of the first fruits expresses thanks to the Creator who graciously made the earth and has made this part of it available to his own people.

The second emphasis is on history (vv. 5–9), here traced back to the call of Abraham and sketching, in a few eloquent words, the exodus and the desert journey. No mention is made of Moses and Aaron; this is the gracious act of God. God who made heaven and earth remains powerfully active in the events of history.

The third emphasis is on worship and rejoicing (vv. 10–11). The land 'flowing with milk and honey' symbolized plenty and security and is a testimony to the faithfulness of God which is the ground for worship. Emphasis is also placed on the provision to be made for the Levites and aliens. Worship and gratitude will always lead to sharing and to including others in the benefits which flow from this gracious God.

Romans 10:8b–13

Here, as in the Deuteronomy passage, we have another confession of faith. Here what the ancient confessions anticipated is now embodied in Christ, the living Word to whom the written word points. Here Paul stresses the continuity of the old and new covenants and he underlines both the subjective and objective aspects of faith. This is both a gospel to proclaim— 'confess with your lips'—and a conviction of heart and mind—'believe in your heart' (v. 9).

Paul is echoing the language of Deutermonomy 30:14ff. where Moses presents the two ways of life and death and urges the Israelites to choose life. That life has now been uniquely embodied in the resurrection of the Lord Jesus Christ from the dead. Believing is no mere mental assent but the life-changing recognition that, with Christ, the last days have arrived. This has a number of important consequences.

First, the salvation of the believer is guaranteed. Isaiah 28:16 is quoted (v. 11) and now fulfilled because the foundation stone has been laid in Zion and God's temple is rising on that foundation.

Second, salvation is now available to the whole world because Jesus has been raised from the dead and given the name which is above every name (vv. 12–13). No longer are Jew and Gentile torn apart but, in fulfilment of the ancient scriptures, find unity in the life, death and resurrection of Christ.

Third, people must respond. Hence the emphasis is on 'calling on the name of the Lord' (v. 13). That call will certainly be met with a gracious response.

Luke 4:1–13

John Milton, in his poem *Paradise Regained*, well understands the importance of the story of Christ's temptation in the desert in the whole sweep of biblical narrative. This is 'Eden raised in the waste wilderness', and part of that great invasion of God into human affairs which is to culminate in the new heaven and the new earth. It also reminds us of the Lenten disciplines of resisting the world, the flesh and the devil. Jesus is to triumph where Adam failed and thus to be head of a new humanity.

The first temptation (v. 3) emphasizes Christ's divinity. It would not have been a temptation for us, for we have no power to turn stones into bread. Yet, as a human, Jesus is not going to step out of the path of obedience to the Father and live in a way inappropriate for a son of Adam. Adam fell, in spite of God's clear command; Christ was obedient to the word and refused to act independently of it.

The second temptation (vv. 5–7) turns on who has ultimate authority. Satan is demanding that Christ should acknowledge him as the ultimate power which cannot be overcome. Again Christ quotes that word which shows that worship belongs exclusively to God.

The third temptation (vv. 9–11) focuses on Christ's trust in scripture. As Shakespeare notes, 'the devil can cite scripture for his purpose' (*The Merchant of Venice*). There is great subtlety here: often believers have to trust God's word and step out in faith (so Abraham's story in next Sunday's reading). But no word had been given by God requiring Christ to jump off the temple. By refusing all three temptations, Jesus had indeed demonstrated that he was the Son of God.

RF

THE SECOND SUNDAY OF LENT

YEAR A

Genesis 12:1–4a

Abram's story revolves round the twin poles of call and promise, obedience and faith.

The *call* is to go from security and prosperity into uncertainty and risk. The *promise* seems improbable in the extreme. We already know that Sarai, Abram's wife, is barren (11:30). 'The land' is as yet unidentified. Being a blessing to the nations sounds like a desert mirage.

Yet Abram obeys. The economy of language (v. 4a) disguises the cost of obedience, the upheaval involving family, servants and stock, the breaking of ancestral bonds, the hardship and danger. To take such a step is an eloquent declaration of faith in God who has called and promised. That faith will be tested to the full.

The key word in the promise, however, is 'blessing'. Abram personally will be blessed; he will be a blessing to others; those who bless him will themselves be blessed; eventually the blessing will become universal.

Every stage of the journey (even the more questionable of Abram's actions!) is rewarded by a sign of God's blessing, by prosperity and—eventually—the longed-for child (24:35–36). Abram will not in his lifetime see the fulfilment of any specific part of the promise, but his obedience and faith are rewarded above all by the presence of Yahweh. Abram's God goes with him.

Romans 4:1–5, 13–17

Abraham, Father of the nation, was in Jewish eyes the supreme example of privilege and of merit. God had chosen him and established with him a covenant. Abraham had responded by total obedience. Privilege, being God's chosen people, and obedience, keeping the covenant Torah, are thus guarantees of 'righteousness', the status of being in relationship with God.

Paul's point is that this is a misreading of the story of Abraham, as scripture itself proves.

• If Abraham's obedience had earned his status before God, this would have been described as 'wages for work', not 'counted' or 'reckoned' as righteousness.

• Abraham's relationship with God predates the covenant with Israel and the sign of circumcision. Therefore it does not depend on being within the covenant. Still less does it depend on a covenant law, which comes later (v. 13).

It follows that Abraham's close relationship with God depends entirely on his faith in God's promise.

Abraham's faith is therefore a foreshadowing of the Christian's faith. Confidence and hope are not grounded in human achievement or potential.

The Christian's trust is wholly in God's promises and power. Faith means being absolutely open to receiving his gifts and giving glory only to him.

John 3:1–17

Nicodemus is the first of a series of individuals to have a direct encounter with Jesus. The conversation operates on two levels (v. 12):

- The earthly, in which Nicodemus takes Jesus' words literally, in terms of 'normal' human experience.
- The heavenly, in which spiritual perception brings the revelation of life in a new dimension—the Kingdom of God.

Jesus, Son of Man, Son of God, brings heavenly reality into the earthly sphere (vv. 13–16). Subtleties of language, difficult to reproduce in English, enable the evangelist to move between these two planes:

- Born 'anew' (v. 3) is taken by Nicodemus to mean repeating human childbirth. It can also mean born 'from above', the divine spiritual realm.
- The fact that *pneuma* means both 'wind' and 'spirit' (vv. 4–8) allows Jesus to illustrate the reality of the unseen Spirit by the daily human experience of the wind blowing.
- Signs (v. 2) are earthly events pointing to heavenly reality. Signs can be *seen* literally by anyone. Only those with spiritual insight can 'see' the divine truth and believe.

Ironically, Nicodemus, the teacher learned in the law and worship of Israel, cannot yet see/understand (v. 10).

The focus moves (v. 13) from the puzzled figure of Nicodemus to God's over-arching plan, the self-giving love that in his Son brings life to the world. But the passage is incomplete without the stark choice of verses 18–21. Judgment has come into the world...

GS

YEAR B

Genesis 17:1–7, 15–16

A promise is a remarkable thing. It changes the present by changing the future. If we are confident of the validity of a promise, then our behaviour can be quite radically affected. For example, someone who trusts a promise that they will receive a large cheque in the next morning's post may go out and make a purchase in the knowledge of the promise. Of course, absolute confidence in the promise is a prerequisite for real risk-taking.

God's promise to Abraham and Sarah was particularly demanding of their credulity (vv. 2, 4–7). Not only was the promise unthinkably enormous in its scope, it was seemingly physically impossible to fulfil (v. 1a). Worse still, in Abraham's eyes at least, it seemed unnecessary to promise a son to Sarah because he already had one by Hagar (v. 18). However, God was not interested in expedient plans or compromises, he wanted Sarah to be part of his plan (v. 16). This resolve, combined with his sovereign power, led to the creation of a great nation. More than that, by the ingrafting of Gentiles into Israel, we too, from all the nations of the world, can trace our ancestry to Abraham and Sarah and the impossible, but realized, promise that was given to them.

The promises of God for our future, therefore, should be sure enough to affect the way we live our present.

Romans 4:13–25

The power of a promise to change the future, and thus the present, is fundamental to Paul's argument here. For him, the righteousness of faith (v. 13) is the present result of belief in the future destination. Thus, my behaviour (my righteousness) is the direct result of my belief in God's promise for my future. This motivation for my behaviour is a product of a relationship, not a written code.

Thus, Paul argues, Abraham behaved as he did because he believed God's promise to him, not because he had a set of impersonal rules in front of him. Consequently, Abraham and his descendants received the fulfilment of the promise ('it came to him/them', v. 13), because his behaviour was motivated by his belief in the faithfulness of the promise, not because God had given him a set of rules to follow.

Ever since the Reformation, there has been confusion about what is meant by 'justification by faith'. There has been a tendency in some circles to equate faith with a kind of intellectual attribute which, once given by God, provides a ticket to being seen as righteous by God. I do not think that this is Paul's point. Paul seems to be arguing instead that the righteousness of faith is the righteousness that we *act* because we *believe* the promise of salvation given through Jesus. It is therefore a consequence of God's gift and a product of our relationship with him. It is not something that we screw up our faces to achieve; it simply flows out of believing that we shall, and do, belong to God's Kingdom through the work of Christ.

Mark 8:31–38

Our lives are always under pressure to conform to a short-termism. It is hard for us to focus on priorities beyond what is immediate to our own personal needs. Peter's response to Jesus is entirely human and instinctive (v. 32). His plans don't include the pain and disorientation of the great suffering that Jesus predicts.

Jesus demands of his followers an entirely new mindset. Jesus says that a long-termism which looks to the future fulfilment of the Kingdom of God will lead us to deny ourselves and take up our cross. What does this mean? He is not referring to the denials of chocolate or alcohol that we might be observing for Lent. Rather, he is calling us to see ourselves as dead to our old life and the will that directed it, and alive to a new life that shares in his resurrection.

AG

YEAR C

Genesis 15:1–12, 17–18

By any standards this is a remarkable chapter. God is the speaker for much of it. The New Testament in three significant places bases its teaching on this episode. In Galatians 3 and in Romans, Paul makes it the centrepiece of his exposition of the gospel of grace. James, in chapter 2 of his letter, uses it to demonstrate that Abraham's whole life proved his faith to be genuine. Three striking features of God's covenant with Abraham emerge.

The first is that God's promise was linked to Abraham's circumstances. Abraham had just won a great victory, but the kings, although defeated, were still alive and probably thirsting for revenge. Thus God says, 'Don't be afraid—I am your shield'. Had he been right to reject the king of Sodom's gifts? 'I am your reward,' says the Lord (v. 1, NIV).

The second is that God links the promise to his power to deliver it. So far no child and no land had been forthcoming. Ten years had passed since the promise was made and fifteen more were to elapse until the fulfilment. Yet God is the Creator, he had made the stars and he could and would make descendants for Abraham (v. 5).

Third, the promise becomes increasingly definite and specific and is made in the context of a covenant ceremony. The dramatic and sombre setting is an anticipation of that great covenant ceremony of Sinai and a reminder of the importance of this episode in the Bible's plot-line. Only briefly, in the days of David and Solomon, were the boundaries of verses 17–18 realized. This is a reminder that, as the author of Hebrews says, by faith Abraham 'stayed for a time in the land he had been promised, as in a foreign land' (Hebrews 11:9). This is a foretaste of the heavenly country, the city 'whose architect and builder is God' (Hebrews 11:10), and this links with our epistle.

Philippians 3:17—4:1

Paul knows well that only one motive will keep Christians faithful to Christ and that is living in the light of his coming. Far from this making people 'other worldly' and ineffective, nothing else will have such practical consequences. This is a question of heartland. Abraham's heartland was the city to come and thus his life was a practical expression of his faith. Here, the fact that the Philippian Christians are 'a colony of heaven' will mean both that they are not destined for destruction (v. 20) and that they can stand firm in the Lord (v. 21).

The first important thing about the Christian homeland is that it is the final phase of salvation brought about by the dying and rising of the Lord Jesus Christ (see 2:5–17). It is no theory; it is the culmination of that great plan of salvation, one of whose earlier stages is recorded in Genesis 15.

This heartland is not some disembodied state where spirits dressed in ethereal negligées float on clouds and strum harps. This is bodily and physical resurrection, where our mortal bodies are to be transformed 'so that they will be like his glorious body' (v. 21, NIV).

This will be part of the creation of a new heaven and a new earth as Christ brings the whole universe into complete harmony with his glorious and loving purposes. This will transform Christian living now, in that our efforts, struggles and failures all have a point and purpose. Paul wants us to anticipate being with Christ then, so that we can live for him now.

Luke 13:31–35

Here we have the other side of the graciousness of God's covenant which has been at the heart of both our Old Testament reading and Epistle. God will not coerce ('but you were not willing', v. 34) but in spite of all opposition and rejection God's gracious purposes will be fulfilled. This is part of that journey, not just to Jerusalem but to glory, which is such a prominent feature of the second part of Luke: 'When the days drew near for him to be taken up, Jesus set his face to go to Jerusalem' (Luke 9:51).

This means that all the machinations of Herod Antipas, 'the fox', are irrelevant. Christ will reach his goal and Herod will be the merest puppet. He will die in the appointed time and at the appointed place.

Yet human freedom is real and human responsibility great. Through the centuries, Jerusalem had rejected God's teaching and spurned his love. Thus the Messiah was to be killed in his own capital city. God's house had become 'your house' (v. 35); God will not overrule people's free choice.

When is verse 35 to be fulfilled? Palm Sunday is a partial but limited fulfilment. Rather his death would be the way Israel would come to repentance, and when he returns in glory then the whole purpose of his death will be recognized and he will be hailed and acknowledged as Lord.

RF

THE THIRD SUNDAY OF LENT

YEAR A

Exodus 17:1–7

Thirst—the terror of the desert. Deprivation and growing fear find expression first in mutterings and looking for someone to blame, then in open anger and the threat of riots and violence (vv. 3–4).

Despite the provision of food to stem their hunger (ch. 16), the people still do not have confidence in God's ability to provide. Focusing their uncertainties on Moses, God's representative, they blame him for present hardships. But they are effectively putting Yahweh to the test: is he there among them in power, or not? What sort of a God is he?

Or is the truth, ironically, that God is putting *them* to the test? What sort of people are they, and will they learn to trust him sufficiently to carry out their role as his chosen people?

When Moses in desperation pleads with him, God in mercy makes provision. Moses plays his part by his obedience. Harmony prevails until the next crisis of faith (ch 32).

For Paul (1 Corinthians 10), the Old Testament story gives a double warning for Christians:
• We must not put God to the test, for dire consequences may follow.
• We must not be complacent, for we too may fall to similar temptation.

Yet God is faithful to us: we will not be tested beyond our endurance.

Romans 5:1–11

Paul has established humanity's need for God's grace, and the essential role of faith in Christ alone for a right relationship with God. 'Therefore...' (v. 1) a new life has begun. Like a composer, Paul brings in new themes of peace, hope and love.

- Peace stems from being reconciled to God through Christ (v. 1).
- Hope 'exults' (REB) in the prospect of sharing through Christ in the glory of God (v. 2).
- Love is a present experience through the indwelling Spirit, 'poured' freely into our hearts (v. 5).

Hope is tested by suffering. For the believer, however, suffering leads not to complaints but to endurance, which in turn stamps us as a 'quality product', tempered like metal. So hope is strengthened.

But Paul is carried away by the amazing generosity of God's love. Like the rebellious Israelites, we have found God's mercy although we were opposing him. This is not cheap mercy. God's undeserved love finds expression in the death of his Son on behalf of sinners.

Our lost relationship with God restored, we are full of joy.

It all begins and ends 'through our Lord Jesus Christ' (vv. 1, 11).

John 4:5–42

Nicodemus the Jew was influential, a respectable citizen, orthodox, theologically trained. The Samaritan woman is despised, a moral outcast, heterodox and uneducated.

Again, the conversation is on two levels. Jesus himself is humanly vulnerable: the woman has access to water which he needs for physical life. He can offer to her the spiritual drink of eternal life.

The woman misunderstands, and remains earthbound. She sees a weary Jewish traveller; she thinks of the ancestors who used the well-spring. What a relief it would be not to come in the heat of the day to draw water! Jesus speaks of a fresh running spring (in contrast to the stagnant water of the storage cistern); 'living water' is the perfect metaphor for eternal life, constantly renewed.

Jesus cuts through the woman's preoccupations to the crucial point of her vulnerability. Startled by his knowledge of her life, she assumes he has the clairvoyance of the traditional prophet. She raises, as a diversion, or a challenge, the issues that divide Jew and Samaritan. Again Jesus cuts through to the essential: God is invisible, unknowable, yet revealing himself as life-giving, renewing—only those 'born of the Spirit' will recognize and worship him.

The climax of the conversation comes as Jesus openly declares his identity, with dramatic consequences.

- The woman in excitement abandons the water jar to share her tentative faith with others.
- The Samaritans listen both to her testimony and to Jesus' words, and many believe.
- The disciples are challenged about their priorities for mission.

GS

YEAR B

Exodus 20:1–17

What makes football different from hockey? What turns a collection of individuals into a community? What made Israel into the people of God? The answer in each case is 'rules'. The Ten Commandments were given by God to Israel as the central element of his covenant with them (19:1—24:11). It was these laws that shaped them into a distinctive community. The Ten Commandments begin by expressing their first distinctive: exclusive allegiance to and love of God (vv. 3–11). The remaining six commandments (vv. 12–17) flow from that love and describe the laws that bind members of the community together, as well as giving them individual rights to life (v. 13), marriage (v. 14) and property (v. 15).

A church, or a society, that keeps the Ten Commandments is a community that distinctively reflects the rule or 'Kingdom' of God. That was the case in the days of Moses, and it is the case now. However, they can only ever truly be kept if we have a relationship with God, made possible by the Spirit, that motivates us to keep these commands through an understanding of the depth of God's love for us and for our neighbour.

1 Corinthians 1:18–25

The Jews demanded a sign and the Greeks desired wisdom (v. 22). What do we demand? In what categories must we be able to explain the cross before it becomes understandable or palatable to us? There are still those who wish that God would make everything plain with a sign. Equally there are those who seek a rational explanation for the cross or scientific proof of the resurrection.

These desires are entirely natural but they are none the less intrinsically flawed. A God who conformed to our categories would be a God who met us on our terms, not his. Our terms for meeting new people are usually designed to give us maximum protection, and thus minimum connection. God, however, has no interest in impressing us! He shows himself in Christ crucified (v. 23) because there there is no defence. Where there is no defence, there is no barrier. Where there is no barrier, there is the possibility of reality and, thereby, of intimacy. A crucified God, Paul says, is offensive to Jews and ridiculous to Greeks (v. 23). But if God refused to stoop so low, there would never be any possibility of a point of contact between us and him.

John 2:13–22

A man walks into a dining-room, sweeps all the food off the laden table and sits on the table himself. What is he saying? There are several poss-ibilities. He could be complaining about the food; he could be saying that he is in need of psychiatric help. Alternatively, he could be saying, 'I am the meal.'

While Jesus' contemporaries might have thought that Jesus was insane when he cleared the temple, he was actually acting out a simple visual parable. The animals were on sale to be used as sacrifices (v. 15). By clearing them out and standing in their place, Jesus was saying, 'I am the true sacrifice that replaces this imperfect and abused (v. 16) sacrificial system.'

His statement about the temple follows the same pattern. Thus he explains that the temple's function, as the focus of God's relationship with his people, will be replaced and surpassed by, and in, himself.

AG

YEAR C

Isaiah 55:1–9

This great passage celebrates the gracious and universal invitation of God and is full of rich echoes of other scriptures. Commentators have noted the echoes both of the cries of street vendors and the cry of Wisdom as she invites people to her banquet (Proverbs 9:5–6). This is a good model for preaching—drawing from the deep wells of scripture and presenting the invitation in language familiar to hearers.

The water and bread show the necessity of what God offers. This is not mere luxury. This is the message which alone can create and sustain life. Yet these are no mere subsistence rations: wine and milk suggest abundance and generosity. The apparent paradox of 'buy without money' suggests that what is offered is not available for money, so valuable is it; yet 'buy' suggests a willingness and an eager response (vv. 1–2).

The spiritual nature of God's invitation is brought out by the command to hear and to come. The hearing is the equivalent of eating because the word of God must become part of the hearer. The coming is the visible response to the heart's desire to be fed and satisfied (v. 3).

This is now linked with God's purposes throughout history. The covenant made with David and his dynasty is to be embodied in a Davidic Messiah who is the guarantor of God's faithfulness (vv. 4–5).

All this requires a response which is articulated in verses 6–9. It is not mere information which people are to seek from the Lord, but his transforming grace. This involves a recognition that God's ways and thoughts are not ours and thus we must trust his promises and obey his commands.

1 Corinthians 10:1–13

Our Lenten readings have focused on the Bible's plot-line and many of the significant events in that. Here Paul is unpacking the spiritual significance of the exodus and desert wanderings and making more important remarks on the abiding relevance and importance of the Old Testament.

First Paul speaks of the profound meaning of these events. They signified the union of the people with God: his glory hovered over them; their passage through the sea signified baptism, foreshadowing their union with Christ; they were supplied with bread from heaven; and above all they were given water from the rock (vv. 1–3). The Rock is a name for God in the Old Testament (e.g. Deuteronomy 32:4; Psalm 18:2 and Isaiah 30:29). This identifies Jesus with Yahweh and as the Lord who would bring about the age to come.

These incidents are therefore not mere history but examples and warnings (v. 6). More especially, idolatry and immorality are not to be countenanced; they bring the judgment of God. Yet in spite of the unfaithfulness of his people, God does not abandon his covenant—'God is faithful' (v. 13) and makes generous provisions for our human frailty.

We live at 'the fullness of time' (see Ephesians 1:10) when Christ has inaugurated the last days, but the word of God remains relevant, indeed more relevant than ever, because the events of salvation history point so fully and faithfully to Christ. Only faithfulness to him and obedience to his word will keep us amid the temptations that surround us.

Luke 13:1–9

One of the problems of believing in God's providential control of events is how we interpret accidents and atrocities. Here Jesus warns that those who are victims of disasters and violence are not necessarily greater sinners than others. Rather the point is that we are all sinners and thus all caught up in 'the changes and chances of this mortal life' (*Book of Common Prayer*). The wonder is not that some people are overwhelmed by incidents such as those in verses 1–5 but that so many are spared. Death is inevitable and we must not draw wrong conclusions from such incidents as an atrocity ordered by Pilate or the collapse of a tower.

Luke follows this by the parable of the barren fig tree, whose purpose is to ensure that we draw the true conclusions from such incidents. First, Jesus is saying that we cannot indefinitely live in a way that is not pleasing to God (that is, bearing no fruit) and expect to evade his judgment.

Second, some three years had passed since the Baptist had announced, 'Even now the axe is lying at the root of the trees' (3:9). With the coming of Christ, judgment already has begun, although God graciously allows time to repent.

Third, the final judgment is inevitable and fixed. What is not fixed is the response of the human heart. Christ's contemporaries who first heard this parable, and all who subsequently read it, are being called to repentance and faith.

RF

THE FOURTH SUNDAY OF LENT

YEAR A

1 Samuel 16:1–13

To choose a national leader, most people would be looking for a commanding presence, proof of outstanding achievement and leadership, maturity and self-reliance. Particularly after the Saul fiasco, evidence of stability and wise judgment would be considered crucial for the next king of Israel.

David has none of these qualifications. He is a mere boy, despite his attractive appearance. As the youngest son, his previous responsibility has been limited to minding the sheep. He has no status or lineage or wealth to commend him. Only later does he develop as a courageous soldier, a shrewd diplomat, a natural leader.

What God actually saw when he 'looked on the heart', we are not told; but the historian's judgment later is that David's heart was 'wholly true to the Lord his God' (1 Kings 11:4). Despite moral lapses, David was characterized by integrity before God, a willingness to acknowledge his faults and steadfast trust in the Lord.

We respect achievement, status, power. God discerns truth, faith and potential. God chooses his own unlikely servants—and equips them with his own Spirit.

Ephesians 5:8–14

God knows what we are; but what we are also becomes visible in what we do and say.

Light both fosters growth and exposes dirt. Darkness is a symbol of lives untouched by the truth and goodness of God. Unbelief and evil behaviour feed each other, leading to alienation and ultimately to complete exclusion from God's presence—the darkness of death.

God, on the other hand, is light. Christ came as the Light of the world. Those who believe become in their turn children of light. The children of light are not, like electric light bulbs, automatically turned on or off by throwing a switch. Understanding what pleases God, living out 'what is good and right and true' demands lifelong learning, being gradually changed so that more and more of the Christ-light shines through us.

Exposing the 'works of darkness' does not imply deliberately looking for faults in others, or investigating unsavoury practices with a glow of righteous superiority. The brighter the Christ-light in us, the more the surrounding shadows will be illuminated. Then others will see clearly to make their own judgment.

John 9:1–41

John's sixth 'sign' presents us with a classic case of dramatic irony.

The man who is blind has been physically handicapped from birth. Trapped in his sightless world, he does not even approach Jesus hoping for healing. But in Jesus' touch of compassion and words of command, he recognizes an authority beyond the ordinary—and obeys. His physical sight restored, he continues a spiritual journey. He acknowledges his own ignorance at each stage but he 'sees' more and more as the sceptical opposition grows.

He starts with a simple statement of what the 'man called Jesus' had done. Under questioning, he moves to greater understanding: 'He is a prophet' (v. 17). With courage and integrity, he refuses to deny the truth of his experience and in the face of threats takes another step of understanding (vv. 31–33). Found by Jesus again, the final step of recognition leads to faith.

Meanwhile, the Pharisees, claiming to see and understand the will of God and confident in their own righteousness, lack the spiritual insight to recognize the truth of God when it stands before them. The brightness of the light of Christ only increases their blindness.

The very things that should have illuminated their understanding prove to be barriers. They are blinded by their own religious observance.

GS

Year B

Numbers 21:4–9

Israel had already been in the desert for forty years when they faced another setback. Unable to pass through Edomite territory, they had to go around it, and were thus forced back towards the Red Sea. The people's discontent at this stage is understandable, but their complaints were endangering the entire mission. This doubling back was stretching their faith in God, but that faith was more necessary, rather than less, precisely because of their circumstances. If they had given up at this stage, when they were so close to their goal, then everything that they had been through beforehand would have been worthless.

God took radical action and sent snakes into the camp (v. 6) so that the people could be saved from them (v. 9). This may seem perverse but it had the effect of forcing Israel to look to God rather than their own resources.

When difficulties multiply in the course of enterprises that we have entered into under God, then our reaction needs to be to look to him all the more keenly, rather than to give up in despair.

Ephesians 2:1–10

What is the visible difference between death and life? According to Paul, it is an ethical difference. Thus, the dead are characterized by trespasses, sins and living according to the passions of the flesh (vv. 1, 3). In life, by contrast, we are created for good works, which God prepared beforehand to be our way of life (v. 10).

This gives the impression that salvation is by works, but Paul plainly states that it is not (v. 9). Instead Paul claims that it is by grace alone that we have been saved (vv. 5, 7, 8). Thus our salvation is not the *result* of works, but works *do* result from our salvation. How does this happen?

The crucial difference between death and life is the role of Christ. Thus, we are made alive together with Christ (v. 5), raised up and seated with him in the heavenly places (v. 6). The imagery is of transference: we have been set in an entirely new context because of God's gracious gift to us in Christ.

We are part of him (v. 6b). The ethical consequences of such a change are obvious. If we receive the gift of membership of Christ, then we leave behind our own bad government (v. 3), and become instead governed by Christ, with very different consequences for our actions (v. 10).

John 3:14–21
John portrays a world that is already lost. It lives according to its own 'lights' which give no light at all. The situation is parallel to that in the camp of Israel (Numbers 21:4–9). There people were losing faith in God and were resorting to faith in themselves, with potentially disastrous consequences. In that chaotic situation in the desert, God acted and provided a focus (the bronze snake on a staff), as a sign of his saving involvement with them.

John reuses that image of God entering a situation of chaos to provide a means of escape. He presents Jesus as the snake that is lifted up as a sign to the people of God's faithful love for them, his desire to pull them through to the promised land (vv. 14–15). John combines this image with that of light coming into darkness. Jesus is like a raised torch that brings order to chaos, hope to despair. As with the bronze serpent, there are two ways of responding to God's action in Jesus. We can turn away for shame (v. 20) or we can turn and be forgiven (v. 21). Unless we are perfect we will always be embarrassed by the light, but if we allow it to reveal who we really are, then God's healing work of forgiveness can take place.

AG

YEAR C

Joshua 5:9–12
This is a richly nuanced passage which looks back on the exodus from Egypt and forward to the next phase of the story. It links the extraordinary and the everyday, the supernatural and the 'normal', and by doing so shows that they are part of the same reality. Gilgal, where the first Passover in the land was celebrated, was to become the base for military operations (Joshua 10:15, 43). The prophets, however, tend to refer to it in a negative way: Hosea attacks it for being a centre of evil (Hosea 4:15); Amos sees it as the city which will lead the nation into exile as it has once been associated with entering land (Amos 5:5). This emphasizes the need for continuing faithfulness to the Lord of the covenant.

The Passover stands at the heart of old Israel's covenant faith and speaks richly of lives rescued by the blood of a substitute. It recalls the years of slavery in Egypt and became the occasion for the recounting of salvation history to subsequent generations. Yet subsequently the celebration was not always followed. Only in the reigns of the great reforming kings, Hezekiah and Josiah (see 2 Kings 23 and 2 Chronicles 30—35) was there anything like a full and worthy celebration.

Finally the manna ceased because food was now readily available (v. 12). Both sources of food were divine, whatever the method of acquiring it. Thus, in this season of Lent, this old story speaks with power of the faithfulness of God shown in rescue from enemies and providing bread from heaven. It speaks also of the need for disciplined obedience and renewed faithfulness.

2 Corinthians 5:16–21

This is one of the great passages about the inner meaning of the new covenant and emphasizes how it is rooted in history and yet transcends history. Paul is certainly not saying that knowing the 'historical Jesus' is of no value but rather that the new age has dawned in him and nothing can ever be the same again. This transformation is no mere external change; it is a new creation.

At the heart of this passage is the theme of reconciliation (vv. 18–20) which is at once what happens to Christians and the content of their message. This reconciliation is first and foremost with God whom our sin has outraged, and it can only happen in Christ.

Christ became the sin offering where heaven's love and justice meet when he became the substitute for humans and 'paid the price of sin'. Thus a new people is created who are right with God.

This creates a radically altered view of people in which external appearances and distinctions no longer matter. The initiative—as always—is from God who, as Creator, breathes new life into his creatures. Not only that, he calls them to spread this message so that others may be reconciled. This comes with the authority of God because those called to preach this message are described as 'ambassadors', a technical term used of a legate of Caesar. None of this creates a sense of compulsion or coercion: 'We entreat you on behalf of Christ' (v. 20). As we have seen often in our Lent readings, the sovereign initiative of God does not preclude a responsible acceptance of the message.

Luke 15:1–3, 11b–32

The radical nature of the new covenant is nowhere more clearly seen than in Christ's fellowship with 'tax collectors and sinners', which, according to the

120

Pharisees and teachers of the law, was condoning their immorality. In the three stories in this chapter—the lost sheep, the lost coin and the lost son—the main subject of our reading reveals that Christ's true motive was to bring them back to God, to reconcile them to him as in our epistle.

Three elements in the so-called 'prodigal son' parable invite attention. The first is that, like the Pharisees, the older brother interpreted the father's generosity as a reward for sin and selfishness and a snub for years of faithful service (vv. 29–30). The Pharisees failed to rejoice both in God's grace and in the rehabilitation of the lost.

The second is that neither the older brother nor the Pharisees had any joy, any sense of acceptance with God or any assurance of salvation. They believed that to be accepted with God they had to satisfy him with years of good works and strict legal rectitude.

The third is that we must not expect one parable to say everything. It has been alleged that here we have no cross and no sacrifice. This ignores the place of this parable in Luke, which is as part of the section on the way to the cross, begun in 9:51 (see comment on Luke 13:31–35, Second Sunday of Lent). Moreover, it ignores the fact that the father can discern in his younger son a genuine repentance even before he has said anything.

RF

MOTHERING SUNDAY

YEARS A, B, C

The popular hype that now accompanies 'Mothers' Day' has made it at worst an occasion of artificial sentimentality and commercial profit, at best an occasion for saying 'thank you' to mothers for all they do and 'thank you' to God for all mothers.

The stories of mothers in scripture are in a sense incidental, told for the sake of their sons, who have a major part in the drama of salvation. Yet in each case the mother's role is crucial to the fulfilment of God's plan.

Exodus 2:1–10

From a human perspective, God's great rescue plan for his people has a fragile beginning. At the heart of the story are three women:

The **Hebrew mother** risks her own life to defy the edict of Pharaoh. She needs courage and resourcefulness to protect the child: her skill and care in preparing the basket are all that stand between him and death. Totally committed to his safety, she unselfishly gives up her own claims on him to ensure his future.

The **sister** is in the same mould. The baby is not abandoned to his fate, for she keeps a careful watch and adapts to the situation as it develops, cleverly seizing the opportunity to negotiate for the mother to become wet nurse for the child.

The **Egyptian princess** is presented in a very positive light. She too is taking risks, for she knows this is a Hebrew child. Yet she is compassionate —and practical. She also shows longer-term commitment.

Other characters are in the shadows behind the story—Pharaoh, cruel and callous, is duped by shrewd and God-fearing Hebrew midwives. God is not mentioned but his watchful presence is felt as his plan unfolds through the human drama.

1 Samuel 1:20–28

To be childless was an acutely painful situation, and not only because of Hannah's natural longing to have a child. Failure to produce children carried a social and religious stigma: what, her neighbours would ask, had she done wrong that God did not favour her with children?

Anger, frustration and grief are poured out in prayer to God. Her vow (v. 11) is a reaching out in desperation, yet her trust that God is *able* to help never wavers.

Hannah's integrity is tested to the limits. When God grants her petition and the precious child is born, how can she bear to give him up as she has promised? The depth of her love is seen in the costly sacrifice she makes on Samuel's behalf (v. 24), in her continued care as she journeys to the temple each year with her present, watching his progress.

In keeping faith with God, Hannah plays an important part in his purpose for Israel. In return, Hannah and her kindly, faithful and supportive husband are blessed by God with three sons and two daughters. And they have the joy of knowing that Samuel, 'lent to the Lord', has the special privilege of growing up 'in the presence of the Lord' (2:21).

NOTE ON THE NEW TESTAMENT READINGS

The emphasis on mothers—and the Western ideal nuclear family—leaves many feeling on the margins and even excluded. In the New Testament readings from 2 Corinthians and Colossians, Paul is talking to whole Christian communities: what does it mean to be part of God's household? The qualities required to live together in families are the same Christ-like qualities required of all Christians in the local church.

2 Corinthians 1:3–7

Paul stresses three essential qualities to cope with painful situations:

- **Praise** (v. 3). This is not a gritted-teeth cheerfulness or inappropriate heartiness, but a profound, heartfelt recognition of God's mercy and encouragement. Living in this frame of mind towards God enables Paul to look at people differently: whatever they have done, he always starts with praise of the good points rather than nagging criticism.
- **Patience** (v. 6). This would be high on anyone's shopping list of virtues needed for family life! Paul, however, is not talking just of 'putting up with things' or even of stoic acceptance of life's problems. This is patience with a purpose. Patience means self-restraint, forbearance, deliberately allowing space and time to resolve a situation, not lashing out in anger or pain, which only causes more hurt and frustration. Patience increases endurance, a greater ability to cope positively over long periods.
- **Hope** (v. 7). Paul does not get bogged down in resentment or gloom. His hope is not just a vague optimism that everything will get better, but a total conviction that God is in control and has power to transform people, situations, the entire world. Hope will only be fully realized in God's future, but it changes attitudes to the present.

Paul focuses not on his own failures or other people's shortcomings, but on God.

Colossians 3:12–17

At baptism, believers do not just commit themselves to adjusting their moral standards. They undertake a radical transformation—their old way of life is put to death, nailed to the cross of Christ, and they enter the new life of the risen Lord. Their outward, visible behaviour must correspond to the new inner reality.

So what are the new garments of grace? Outgoing care for others (compassion, kindness), and a humility about ourselves which puts others first (lowliness, meekness, v. 12). Forbearance and forgiveness come into play when there is an argument or someone is offended. Love holds all of these in place. These are not fashion accessories, constantly changing, but everyday clothes to match our new inner personality.

All of this might sound like clothes for angels rather than for ordinary human beings. As always for Paul, everything depends on Christ:

- The **example** of Christ (v. 13) inspires us to forgive, realizing how much we are forgiven.
- The **peace** of Christ (v. 15) 'umpires' in our conflicts of motives and principles.
- The **word** of Christ (v. 16) guides our thinking and makes us sing for joy.
- The **name** of Christ (v. 17) hallows everything we say and do.

Luke 2:33–35

In the temple, Simeon greets Mary and Joseph with a blessing and the most amazing words of prophecy: this helpless infant will bring in God's promised salvation, opening the eyes of the world to the truth of God, leading Israel to fulfil her glorious destiny.

Mary and Joseph marvel—as well they might! There is a darker side to this prophecy, however. Luke's nativity stories have been told through Mary's eyes and it is to Mary that Simeon speaks.

- Because of this child there will be revolution and division in Israel.
- The child is a sign from God, yet he will be opposed and rejected.

This is the beginning of the road to the cross for Mary, the burden that accompanies the privilege of being the mother of God's Son.

The role of most parents is a mixture of pride and anguish, joy and sorrow, and anxiety about the future. For Mary as a mother, this occasion, like the announcement of Jesus' conception, was a cause of amazement, delight and apprehension. Being 'highly favoured' came at great cost. She could only try to understand the present and trust God for the future.

John 19:25–27

Our children are not our personal possession. In a very real sense, they belong to God and must be released to find for themselves his call and his plan. Like Moses and Samuel, Jesus has to be handed over to the greater purposes of God.

In Mary, the privilege and the price of motherhood are etched in sharp relief. She has watched Jesus move from popular acclaim to public derision. A child full of promise, he has been consorting with dubious companions and courting danger. Now he dies a criminal's death. With the faith that has never let her down, does she even begin to see God's hand in this? Or is there nothing but darkness?

For Jesus in the hour of death it is enough that she is there, together with John, 'the beloved disciple'. In the depths of pain and rejection, his love and compassion overflow in care for them both. They are brought close together by their common devotion to Jesus and a new relationship is forged through their experience of the cross.

Mutual love marks those who are followers of Christ. The community of the Church, God's family, is the place where mothers in any kind of difficulty should find compassionate listening and loving care—in memory of Mary and in the name of her son.

GS

THE FIFTH SUNDAY OF LENT

YEAR A

Ezekiel 37:1–14

Cuttings—a row of brown sticks poking out of the cold winter earth—and suddenly, at the first hint of spring, there are green shoots of new life. Ezekiel's vision has the same sense of the miraculous, although it is doubtful that he expected literal resurrection.

The identity of wind/breath/spirit in one Hebrew word allows the subtle interplay between the wind blowing up the valley, the breathing that is the sign of life coming into the reconstructed shells of human bodies, and the Spirit of God who gives life.

The exiled Israelites face the death of a nation (v. 11). The deadness is not denied, for they are broken and hopeless after the fall of Jerusalem. The promise of God is that they will be restored, not as shadowy ghosts, but to health and vigour. A host of skeletons will become again a mighty nation (vv. 9–10). They will repossess their God-given homeland.

The initiative belongs to God. It is his word that recreates living beings from death as it created the world *ex nihilo*. It is his Spirit that gives the breath of life (cf. Genesis 2:7). It is his deliverance that will take them back to their own land. In this act of power, God's glory is displayed, his honour vindicated and trust restored. 'You shall *know* that I (am) Yahweh' (vv. 6, 13, 14).

Romans 8:6–11

This passage is a nightmare for translators. Paul uses two words in Greek which could both be rendered 'body' in English, yet they are very different.

Sarx and *soma* are both sinful and mortal. *Sarx* ('flesh') stands for our fallen nature and is fundamentally hostile to God. The *soma* of the believer, however, is already being renewed by the Spirit and will one day be completely restored in the resurrection.

When Paul speaks disparagingly of living 'according to the flesh' (Greek *sarx*) he is not suggesting that our physical bodies, or the material universe, are in themselves evil. Rather he seems to be talking of people whose horizons are limited to this world and whose focus is on self: self-preservation, self-gratification.

This self-indulgent existence might *look* as if it is extracting every ounce of self-fulfilment from life; but a mindset that excludes God is in fact death. Paradoxically, those whose minds are Spirit-directed are truly alive even when their mortal bodies (*somata*) are physically decaying.

If we are turned in on ourselves, the reality of Easter and resurrection life will pass us by. If we have used Lent to develop minds focused on God, the life of the risen Christ will already be at work in our lives.

John 11:1–45

Throughout the story of Lazarus, the focus is on believing in Jesus.

- Jesus offers the unique gift of eternal life to anyone who believes (v. 25).
- Martha and later Mary greet him with 'Lord, if you had been here…' (vv. 21, 32). Their trust is real, but their horizons of belief limited.
- Jesus' gentle challenge to Martha (v. 26) encourages her to move from abstract belief to a personal faith.
- Her response (v. 27) is a classic statement of belief.
- At the tomb, Jesus reminds her that believing trust will be met by God's revelation of himself (v. 40).
- Jesus performs the miracle 'that they may believe' (v. 42) and many indeed are persuaded (v. 45).

John also brings out the humanness of Jesus. Although his initial delay on the surface looks callous, in the depth of his own grief he shares the pain of the family he loves. He is also angered/outraged (vv. 33, 38)—perhaps by the power of death that causes such devastation and perhaps by the *un*belief in the mourning around him.

Lazarus is raised, restored to ordinary human life, but still mortal. The miracle is only a foreshadowing of Easter. Meanwhile, the man Jesus is revealed as the Christ, sent by God (vv. 27, 42). In him, the Father is revealed as the God of compassion and of power, the source of life.

GS

YEAR B

Jeremiah 31:31–34

The new, or possibly renewed, covenant that Jeremiah looks forward to is fulfilled in the initial instance by the return of the exiles from Babylon to Judah in the years following 539BC. However, Jeremiah's prophecy looks for a renewal that goes beyond those remarkable events. For one thing, this covenant includes 'Israel' as well as Judah, even though the northern kingdom did not exist in Jeremiah's day. For another, the covenant with the Sinai generation is not simply going to be restored, it is going to be supremely surpassed (v. 32).

The New Testament teaches that Jeremiah's prophecy (v. 33) is fulfilled in Jesus (Hebrews 8:7–13; 9:15). The indwelling of the Holy Spirit means that the Law is something internal rather than external, the product of a relationship and an outworking of love, rather than a never-ending struggle motivated by fear. As a consequence, one of the marks of our possession of, and response to, the law of the heart is that we are less interested in comparisons. The law of the book is all about measuring ourselves against an external standard, and is therefore bound to be concerned with external appearances. The law of the heart, however, inspires us actually to love—an attitude and activity that defies comparison with others.

Hebrews 5:5–10

The appointment of the high priest under the old covenant (5:1–4) is compared with Jesus' appointment to this role in the new. Thus, the high priest is selected and appointed by God (v. 1), he is concerned with the people's relationship with God (v. 1) and he identifies with the people in their weakness (v. 2). In all these dimensions, Jesus shows a continuity with the stream of past tradition while at the same time surpassing and augmenting it: he is God's appointment (v. 5), but as God's Son, not as an official; he is concerned with the people's relationship with God; and, beyond what the priests could achieve, he becomes a source for eternal salvation (v. 9). Jesus also identifies with us 'in the days of his flesh' (vv. 7, 8), and sympathizes with our weakness (4:15).

The writer to the Hebrews uses the figure of Melchizedek as a further means of showing how Jesus' priesthood is comparable to, yet separate from and surpassing, the priesthood of the old covenant. Melchizedek, the mysterious king of Salem, mentioned in Genesis 14 and Psalm 110, is quite independent of the Levitical system and apparently superior to Abraham (Hebrews 7). By citing Melchizedek, the writer shows that beyond the boundaries of the people's familiar means of dealing with God, there is scope for something more ancient and more powerful than what they had hitherto experienced.

John 12:20–33

It is impossible to tell precisely what the Greeks wanted to talk to Jesus about (v. 21). All that seems likely is that the answer they got was very, very different from what they expected. Paul mentions in 1 Corinthians 1:18–25 that the cross was foolishness to the Greeks. It may be unfair to tar these people with the same brush, but it is likely that, like most people, they wanted information that would somehow enhance or glorify their current lives. Instead, Jesus spoke to them about glory coming through suffering and death (vv. 23–26).

Whether or not Jesus' words were unpalatable to his Greek enquirers, it is certain that they are hard for us to hear. Western culture is obsessed with the preservation and enhancement of this life. Interest in spirituality is almost wholly motivated by a desire to feel better about ourselves, to become more fulfilled and rounded people.

Jesus challenges us to look beyond the boundaries of our current experience and to consider what is truly valuable. Do we want to see our lives invested for a great harvest (v. 24)? Do we seek eternal life (v. 25)? Do we seek the presence of God and to be honoured by the Father (v. 26)? If we do, then following Jesus has to be more than a subject for interesting discussion; it has to be a way of life that leads to the death of our selves.

AG

YEAR C

Isaiah 43:16–21

This part of Isaiah has as its overall theme the gracious salvation of God and the way he will use his servant Israel to bring this about. Here, this is related to his nature shown both in creation and history. Two aspects of God in particular are woven together: one is his constant faithfulness and the other is his constant bringing about of change.

The exodus, so prominent in this section of Isaiah, is celebrated in verses 16–17. Yet the main verbs, a fact obscured by most of the translations, are present tense and thus the exodus is not merely an event of the distant past. Israel's faith must not be in past events but in the living God.

Thus God says, 'Forget the past' (v. 18)—not, of course, to forget the great saving events themselves but rather to avoid using them as a strait-jacket, as if God was committed always to work in the way he once did. God here is speaking of a new exodus, indeed a new creation. God who dried up the sea can irrigate the desert, he provides for every living thing. He is not a prisoner in the world he has created.

The reason for all this is given in verse 21. The people he formed (an echo of 43:1) have been created to praise him—not only so but to 'proclaim' his praise. His people are to tell to the nations of the world what God has done. Doxology is the basis for mission. Only those who have experienced the creating and saving love of God can adequately declare that God to others.

Philippians 3:4b–14

Paul here, like Isaiah, rejects the wrong use of the past—in this case, his own past. It is not that his upbringing as a Jew and knowledge of the Torah are bad, rather that compared with Christ they are rubbish to be discarded. Christ is the reality to whom his early upbringing pointed and so the governing passion of Paul's life is to know him.

For Paul, knowing Christ is no vague theory; rather it results in a transformed life—'a righteousness that comes through faith in Christ' (v. 9). Knowing Christ is only possible because of 'the power of his resurrection' (v. 10). The power of the risen Christ is in Paul and provides both his motive for living and his effectiveness in serving.

But this resurrection life enables Paul to identify with the sufferings of Christ which are both at the heart of his message and the pattern of his living. Paul has earlier in this letter written 'For to me, living is Christ and dying is gain' (1:21), and here he is indicating something of the cost involved.

Verse 11 does not mean that Paul thinks that a self-denying asceticism will earn the reward of resurrection on the last day. He has no doubt of that (see comments on readings for the Second Sunday of Lent). What he does not know is how long it will be and what circumstances will intervene before that goal is reached. For the present, he wants to anticipate the goal by living a Christ-filled life, so that in his own body and experiences the life of the crucified and risen Saviour will be evident.

John 12:1–8

As we come to the end of our Lenten readings, we linger on this passage, rich both in theological significance and human interest. As Jesus enters the week leading to the cross, we have a blend of warm affection and hostile enmity as well as misunderstanding. These three reactions will form the substance of our meditation.

Mary's loving extravagance (v. 3) mirrors and anticipates that greater love which is to be poured out (see 13:1). Just as Jesus is to wash the disciples' feet, so she anoints his and cares nothing for hostile reactions. The shadow of the cross lies over the whole incident and Mary wants to declare her love unmistakably.

But there is also the dark presence of the betrayer (v. 4), so prominent in John's Passion narrative. John alone adds the detail 'he was a thief' (v. 6). Judas' chilling market economies show his inability to understand extravagant love and thus a failure to grasp the heart of the gospel.

Yet the silent crowd who neither defend Mary nor grasp the greater significance of the event are characteristic of the indifference of the masses which is to be a feature of the crucifixion itself. Passionate, overflowing love is at the heart of the Passion story which we by God's grace now remember and proclaim.

> *Here is love vast as the ocean,*
> *Loving kindness like the flood.*
> *When the Prince of Life, our ransom*
> *Shed for us his precious blood.*
> **Robert Lowry (1826–99)**

RF

PALM SUNDAY

YEAR A

Matthew 21:1–11 (Liturgy of the Palms)

What exactly happened? Mark, the earliest Gospel, mentions not the 'very large crowd' but only 'those who went ahead and those who followed' (Mark 11:9). Perhaps Jesus was going up for the festival among the other pilgrims gathering from all parts of the known world (Josephus tells us that over a million pilgrims went up for Passover). They regularly sang this hymn, Psalm 118, and carried palm branches for several festivals. It was perhaps only afterwards that the disciples saw the significance of the moment: this was not just a common crowd, but here was the Messiah solemnly and royally entering his holy city and taking possession of it.

As the allusion to Zechariah makes clear, the entry is true to Jesus' whole style of Messiahship. A donkey is a dignified and delicate little animal, but not grand. Jesus enters his holy city not as a great secular liberator but in simplicity and service. This will be the keynote of the whole week. Also present is the note of irony which so dominates the Passion story: one after another, the onlookers and participants, crowds, chief priests, Pilate, mockers, all recognize Jesus for what he is, without realizing that they are doing so.

Isaiah 50:4–9a (Liturgy of the Passion)

This third Song of the Servant of the Lord is used also on Wednesday of Holy Week (see comment there). On Palm Sunday, just before the recitation of the Passion it is perhaps appropriate to reflect on the first verse, with its emphasis on a disciple's tongue and listening like a disciple (NJB). It was Jesus' obedience and listening to his Father's will, and his proclaiming the Father's Kingship, that led him inevitably to his Passion. His proclamation of the bankruptcy of Judaism as it was being lived, and of the need for the renewal of Judaism to accord with the true Kingship of God, brought him into conflict with the Jewish authorities.

The controversies with the Pharisees over the Law needed to be completed by his symbolic destruction of the rites of the temple. Jesus' act of 'cleansing' the temple was no act of bravado, but was the logical consequence of all his previous ministry, bringing his mission of declaring the bankruptcy of Judaism to its very centre. The Gospels make clear that this act was intolerable to the Sadducees who controlled the temple. Such an act of defiance could not be allowed to recur during the festival of the Passover, and Jesus must be eliminated. It was therefore his action as servant and disciple of his Father which led inevitably to his death. Those who condemned him did not have an open ear, 'to listen like a disciple' (v. 4, NJB), and refused to listen to the message he brought them.

Philippians 2:5–11

In this very ancient Christian poem, incorporated by Paul into his letter to the Philippians, the obedience of Christ, which brought salvation, is contrasted with the disobedience of Adam, which brought disaster. Both were in the image of God. But while Adam strove in proud disobedience to be like God and to escape death, Christ did not think the godhead a thing to be grasped and exploited, but in humble obedience accepted the form of a servant and was obedient even unto death.

The outcomes similarly correspond. While Adam was humiliated by being cast out of the garden, Christ was exalted and vindicated by his resurrection, even to receiving the sacred Name which is above every name, that of 'Lord'. With a mindblowing audacity, the poem applies to the exalted Christ the homage of every creature, quoting the homage paid in Isaiah to the Lord God alone, the Holy One of Israel. This, one of the most daring New Testament expressions of the divinity of Christ, creates no rivalry between two Gods, for the homage redounds 'to the glory of God the Father'.

Matthew 26:14—27:66 or 27:11–54

The irony of the Passion account according to Matthew is almost unbearable. Again and again the evangelist stresses that Jesus is the Messiah of Israel, fulfilling all the promises of scripture. Again and again the Jews not merely fail to recognize him and insist on his condemnation, but mock him, even biblically, and precisely for what he is. At the trial scene, the members of the Sanhedrin itself mock him as the messianic prophet. At Pilate's trial, while Pilate washes his hands, the crowds roar for Jesus' condemnation and call down his blood upon themselves. Even the soldiers mock him as 'King of the Jews'. At the cross, the official representatives of Judaism use the biblical formulae of the book of Wisdom to taunt him as King of Israel and Son of God.

For his part, Jesus' dignity shines out. He goes to his death fully aware that 'my time is near'. In the garden, he uses the words which form the central petition of the Sermon on the Mount and of the Lord's Prayer, 'Thy will be done'. Before his judges he maintains a dignified silence as the Servant of the Lord. The end of Judaism is presaged by the tearing of the temple veil, the beginning of the new era by the dead rising again and going into the holy city.

HW

YEAR B

Mark 11:1–11 or John 12:12–16
(Liturgy of the Palms)

One image or symbol can be interpreted by ten different people in as many different ways. The picture of Jesus entering Jerusalem on a colt or foal is capable of inspiring a range of reactions.

For those travelling with Jesus from Galilee, the sight of their 'local hero' riding into Jerusalem in the guise of the messianic king may have inspired a regionalistic fervour. They were used to being looked down on by the inhabitants of the great city, but now a Galilean was coming to take his place of kingship there. Others viewing Jesus' approach may have been inspired by the hope of political liberation from Roman rule, or made anxious by this apparent threat to what was, for some, a comfortable *status quo*. For the disciples, this must have seemed like the moment they had been waiting for, the possibility of power and glory for themselves by association with their ascendant master. Of course, we cannot tell what was going through Jesus' own mind, although his choice of transport suggests that he was conscious of fulfilling the prophecy of Zechariah 9:9 (cf. Matthew 21:5). Whatever Jesus was thinking, he did not allow the adulation of the crowd to divert him from completing the journey through death that he was about to undertake for their sake.

Isaiah 50:4–9a (Liturgy of the Passion)

The pattern of Jesus is the pattern of the servant in this third Servant Song. The resources that he has to share with others come from a discipline of listening to God daily (v. 5). The fact that God has given him the gift of being able to sustain the weary (v. 4) suggests that the instruction he has received gives him a cause for hope. Hope derives from a perception of the future that gives cause for optimism despite more immediate evidence to the contrary. It is this long-term vision that also enables the servant to endure pain and insult (v. 6); he sees beyond it to God's help and vindication (vv. 6–8).

Jesus set his face like flint and endured the torture that was laid on him because he had an unshakeable grasp of where his priorities lay and what his life was for. There are all kinds of pressures which, while not of the same order as those endured by Jesus, are constantly capable of blowing our churches, and Christian lives, off course. We must be constantly aware of God's future purpose for us if we are to avoid being pressured into comfortable, but ultimately useless, cul-de-sacs.

Philippians 2:5–11

Paul's plea for unity which precedes this passage uses the following logic. The benefits of being a Christian (2:1) can only be achieved in a united church (2:2), and such unity can only be achieved through humility (2:3–4). The extraordinary passage in verses 5–11 then presents Christ's humility as an example to follow.

This 'hymn' emphasizes the extreme heights and extreme depths of Christ's experience. Thus, even though he was higher than any other, 'in very nature God' (v. 6, NIV), he became lower than any other, a slave (v. 7) suffering a cruel and humiliating execution (v. 8). It is this half of the hymn that really serves Paul's point. There is a silent appeal to those who have status in the church to let go of it. People in general are obsessed with what other people think of them. Our status and reputation are perhaps our most prized possessions. To lose hold of them is consequently one of the hardest demands of Christian living. Paul may be referring to this struggle when he speaks of working out our salvation 'with fear and trembling' (2:12), and the need for God's power to make it happen (2:13).

Mark 14:1—15:47 or Mark 15:1–39 [40–47]

From the adulation accompanying the triumphal entry, these chapters move towards an ever-increasing isolation. The die is cast in 14:1 when the chief priests and teachers of the law determine to kill Jesus. Everything else that happens from here on leads inevitably towards that destination. Judas' betrayal (14:43) comes to fruition just after Peter, James and John fail to stay awake in Gethsemane (14:32–42). Strangers then testify against Jesus falsely (14:56) and one of his closest friends, Peter, disowns him (14:66–72). Before Pilate, Jesus suffers not only these intimate desertions but also desertion by the general population (15:6–15). Eventually he is even forsaken by God himself (15:34).

In all this pattern of increasing darkness and loneliness, there is a point of light and faithfulness in the actions of the women. First, there is the woman who anoints Jesus at Bethany (14:3–9), then the women who stay at the crucifixion (15:40–41) and even wait to discover the place of Jesus' burial (15:47). They are able to show a love that is unrestricted by the boundaries of their society, and to maintain a faithfulness which the men, in fear for their lives, are unable to match.

AG

YEAR C

Luke 19:28–40 (Liturgy of the Palms)

The journey to glory by way of Jerusalem, which began in 9:51, now reaches a decisive stage. The heir to the throne of David enters Zion riding on a donkey as the prophet Zechariah (9:9) had foretold. This episode, like much else in the Gospels, combines the most momentous events with the most everyday routine.

Two aspects of this story are significant. The first is the repeated 'The Lord needs it' (vv. 31, 34). This is a marvellous example of the gracious providence of God. Though Lord of all, he will use the disciples, use the colt and allow them to contribute to this immensely significant occasion. The fact that Zechariah had prophesied this centuries before did not rule out careful and routine preparation. There is not rigid determinism here, rather a blend of divine sovereignty and human response.

The second is the very different response to this triumphal entry. His disciples leave us in no doubt that they are hailing him as the promised Messiah, and gladly and spontaneously acclaim him as king. This claim is rejected by the Pharisees. Jesus no longer tells his disciples to remain silent (cf. 9:21). The time for decision has come: Jerusalem must crown or crucify her king.

Luke 22:14—23:56 (Liturgy of the Passion)

When reading Luke's Passion narrative, one is constantly reminded of the French philosopher Renan's description of this Gospel as 'the most beautiful book ever written'. There is far too much material here to cover in one short meditation: the institution of the Lord's Supper; the agony in Gethsemane, the arrest, Peter's denial, the trial, the execution and Jesus' burial. Thus we shall concentrate on Luke's Gethsemane account (22:39–46).

All the accounts (Matthew 26:36–46; Mark 14:32–42) emphasize Jesus' utter loneliness: the outcome depends on him alone. Now he kneels on that very Mount of Olives down which he had come in triumph only a few days before. This prayer shows no evading of the issues, no pretending that the cup would be sweet. Unlike Peter, he does not have rash enthusiasm and superficial devotion. Here is total dedication to the will of the Father. Just over the hill lay Bethany and a home where he would be welcome and safe, but the moment had come and he would not shirk it.

Two details are unique to Luke. An angel appears from heaven to strengthen Jesus (v. 43). The unseen world is concerned with this conflict; all eternity depends on it. Dark, cosmic cross-currents are swirling around.

The other is the intensity of his agony in the blood-like sweat. Some early manuscripts do not, indeed, have verses 43 and 44 which contain these details. Nevertheless they must be authentic; no one would have dared to invent such embellishments.

Some weeks later, he is to lead them out to that same neighbourhood and an angel is to tell the now-rejoicing disciples that the Conqueror will return. For the moment, we must watch and pray with him. The cup must be drunk and the agony endured.

See from his head, his hands, his feet,
Sorrow and love flow mingled down.

Did e'er such love and sorrow meet
Or thorns compose so rich a crown?
Isaac Watts (1674–1748)

Luke 23:1—49

Once again, as in the account of the dying criminal (see comment on readings for Christ the King), Luke preserves a unique incident in verses 27–31 where a group of sympathetic women meet Jesus. This will be the subject of our meditation. Incidentally, this is very much in line with Luke's respect for women seen in his delicate and sensitive stories of Elizabeth and Mary and in the tragedy of the widow of Nain,

Yet we must not sentimentalize this episode. Probably they felt natural human sympathy at seeing a young man dragged off to a hideous death. Jesus wanted no pity; rather he wanted them to face up to the reality of what was happening. It was human sin that was driving him there, sin which would have terrible consequences (v. 27).

The fact that he addresses the women as 'daughters of Jerusalem' underlines the fact that this city which had rejected him would in a few decades suffer a terrible fate. Echoing 21:23 on the cruelty to pregnant women when the city is sacked, he warns them to fear the day of Jerusalem's doom. Quoting from Hosea 10:8, a prediction of the destruction of Samaria, he shows the awful consequences of rejecting God's grace (vv. 28–30).

The green tree (v. 31) represents the normal life of a stable society and thus the dried-up trunk of a pagan and evil society will suffer even more severely. The owner of the vineyard (20:9–19) would not stand idly by while his son was thrown out and killed. Yet as the rest of the chapter is to show, repentance is possible and then forgiveness will follow.

RF

MONDAY OF HOLY WEEK

YEARS A, B, C

Isaiah 42:1—9

The first readings of Monday to Wednesday are the first three of the four Songs of the Servant of Yahweh in Isaiah. The fourth Song, specifically of the Suffering Servant, forms the first reading for Good Friday. Scholars dispute over the identity of the Servant in the original prophecy. Is it the prophet himself? Is it the nation of Israel? Is it an unknown contemporary figure? Christian tradition sees the Songs as foreshadowing the role of Jesus, God's beloved Son, who gives himself freely for the salvation of others.

Today's first Song opens with the words used by the divine voice at the baptism of Jesus which triggered his mission of proclaiming the Kingship of God. In Mark's Gospel, the earliest, these divine words were addressed to Jesus himself, and must be read as a revelation to the Son of his role of service, as the Servant of the Lord who is to establish God's Kingship on earth. He will not break the crushed reed, and will establish fair judgment on earth by opening the eyes of the blind and freeing captives from prison. The constant recurrence of the message of service in the words of Jesus show how deeply this call struck home.

Hebrews 9:11–15

The second reading also sets the tone for the week with its focus on the priesthood of Jesus, contrasting it with the ineffective sacrifices of the old Law that foreshadowed it. The picture given by the reading takes us back to the tent of meeting set up by Moses in the desert. That was the scene of the annual sacrifice of atonement, when the high priest symbolically washed away the sins of the people by the blood of sacrifice. The blood was sprinkled half over the people and half over the 'mercy-seat', the place of God's dwelling on the ark of the covenant.

To us, the ritual of sacrifice may seem unnecessary or even repellent. It is the primitive recognition that all life comes from God. In Judaism there is no purification except by blood because, as the symbol of life, blood belongs to God. Blood is surrounded by every kind of reverence because of the sacredness of God-given life. This is why Jesus, in his sacrifice, is pictured as bearing his own blood into the sanctuary. But the blood ritual is only a metaphor, and the letter to the Hebrews also makes clear that the essence of Christ's sacrifice lay in his obedience to the Father, 'made perfect by obedience'.

John 12:1–11

The anointing at Bethany six days before the Passover, an expansive act of love, prepares Jesus for his burial. As the practical Judas remarks, it is a completely senseless waste of money, nearly a year's wages on one pot of ointment, and yet Jesus himself approves this act of homage and devotion. Not every gesture in life has to be logical or useful, and when it comes to the expression of emotion there are limits to the tyranny of good sense. Jesus was thoroughly at home in this family of two sisters and brother. Was Mary lavishly expressing her gratitude for the raising of Lazarus? There is an irony in Mary in return anointing Jesus for the burial from which no human being will raise him.

There is further irony in the fact that the chief priests decide to put Jesus to death, and Lazarus too, because of his gift of life. Jesus came so that his followers might have life, and have it more abundantly, but it is precisely this gift of life that brings him to his death.

HW

TUESDAY OF HOLY WEEK

YEARS A, B, C

Isaiah 49:1–7

The preparation for the Passion continues with this song about the mysterious Servant of the Lord. The Servant himself feels that all his labours have gone for nothing. Already, therefore, there is the hint of the Passion, the toil, the sorrow, the pain and the loneliness that Jesus must have suffered. We now learn also that the mission of the Servant is not only to reunite Israel to the Lord, but to bring in the nations as well, to 'reach to the end of the earth' (v. 6). And in awe of the Holy One of Israel, at the sight of it kings will stand up, princes bow low.

The Songs of the Servant are shot through with the dual aspect of Christian suffering. Suffering is faced squarely, without any attempt to pretend that it does not exist or that it is not painful and distressing. At the same time, there is the confident hope that the sufferer is lapped in the care of God and will never be deserted. The words of Jesus on the cross, 'My God, my God, why have you forsaken me?' are the opening words of the Psalm which passes through the deepest suffering, but ends with the vindication of the sufferer and the glory of God (Psalm 22).

1 Corinthians 1:18–31

Paul starts his letter, immediately after the greeting, with this strong statement of the paradox of the cross, folly in human eyes but wisdom to God. In modern times we do not know the full horror of crucifixion, nor do we wish to advert to it; it is simply too depraved and humiliating. We do not like to think of our Lord and Saviour in that state. The Gospels themselves hurry over the moment of crucifixion with a word or two, hastening to explain it to the eyes of faith. In the first centuries of Christianity, when the reality of such agonized corpses was only too familiar, all realism of representation was avoided by setting jewels in the place of a figure on the cross.

Paul, too, sees only the glory of the cross, the fulfilment of all God's promises which was achieved through Christ's sacrifice. It is, therefore, the summit of God's creative wisdom, the accomplishment of God's plan for the world. It is through his wisdom that God creates the world. So, no matter how foolish and how humiliating the cross may be by human reckoning, it is Christ who is both the power and the wisdom of God.

John 12:20–36

John stresses that Jesus goes to his hour, the hour of his glorification, the single hour both of his Passion and of his resurrection, in full consciousness. He has been looking forward to this hour throughout his ministry, from the marriage at Cana onwards. This is the hour when he will be 'lifted up', an exaltation whose sense is full of overtones and Johannine double meaning.

Here, early in Holy Week, we have the same saying which is at the heart of the agony in the garden—only the Johannine account is far different from that of the synoptic Gospels. In the other Gospels, Jesus prays passionately that the cup may pass him by, only to accept in perfect love the will of his Father. In John, his soul is again troubled, and his obedient union with his Father is absolute. But he cannot pray that the cup should be taken from him, for 'it is for this reason that I have come to this hour' (v. 27).

There is also all the grim symbolism of darkness. Jesus has shown himself as the light of the world, giving sight to the blind. Now the hour of darkness has come, just as, when Judas went out from the supper, we are told, 'It was night' (John 13:30).

HW

WEDNESDAY OF HOLY WEEK

YEARS A, B, C

Isaiah 50:4–9a

The accent on suffering increases through each of the Songs of the Servant of the Lord. Here, in the third Song, we are reminded chiefly of the trial scenes in the Passion of Jesus. Fulfilment of scripture is an important element in the Passion narratives, not only that the Passion fulfils the movement and hope of God's promises to Israel as a whole, but also in detail, so that the evangelists point out repeatedly the fulfilment of tiny details of the scripture. This is in accordance with the contemporary interpretation of scripture as it is found in the Dead Sea Scrolls, where the prophecies are seen to be fulfilled in minute detail by contemporary events. So, in this reading from Isaiah, the Servant's submission to insults and spitting reminds us of the insults and spitting to which Jesus was subjected at the end of the trial scene before the Sanhedrin. The challenge to 'appear in court together' (v. 8, NJB) must also be seen as taken up in the travesty of justice which was that trial, when Jesus' 'justice' shone out in his starburst claim to be the Christ, the Son of the Blessed One and the Son of Man seated at the right hand of the Power—a claim which his judges ironically interpreted as blasphemy.

Hebrews 12:1–3

Perseverance in the face of trial and persecution is one of the dominant themes of the letter to the Hebrews. The chapter which precedes this reading has passed in review a series of Old Testament heroes as examples of perseverance in faith and hope under trial, though none of them reached perfection. In this letter to the Hebrews, the greatness of Christ's work is presented by contrast to the figures of the Old Testament. They are described with respect and wonder, but Christ himself with even more respect and wonder. Now, as the climax of these great figures of perseverance, Jesus is presented. By enduring the cross, he reached that perfection which they never achieved, and 'took his seat at the right hand of the throne of God' (v. 2).

It is striking that Jesus is presented as a figure of faith. Despite his divinity, as a human being, deserted, tortured and betrayed, he must have clung to the one strand of hope and faith in his Father, convinced that his Father would somehow vindicate him from his humiliation, loneliness and agony.

John 13:21–32

The Gospel reading reflects the traditional English name of this day, 'Spy Wednesday', the story of the betrayal of Jesus, or rather the story which illustrates the treachery of Judas' action in handing Jesus over. Again, Jesus' awareness of what is destined to happen to him is underlined by his final warning to Judas. By any standards, to go out and betray for money a friend with whom one has just shared a meal is abhorrent, but in Near Eastern society the sacred laws of hospitality make it even worse.

There has been endless speculation about Judas' motives. Was he a nationalist Zealot, who had joined Jesus in the hope of a revolutionary uprising, and later cast him aside on discovering that this was not Jesus' purpose? Was he simply amoral and avaricious, out to make money by the betrayal? Did he (a recent theory) merely mean to put Jesus in dialogue with the authorities so that they could sort out certain differences of opinion? Whatever the case, his treachery is balanced by the fidelity of the beloved disciple, the model of all disciples, who will stay faithful through the Passion and will be the first to recognize the meaning of the empty tomb.

HW

MAUNDY THURSDAY

YEARS A, B, C

Exodus 12:1–4 [5–10] 11–14

The Christian eucharist is founded on the festival of the Passover, the prescriptions for which are given here. Some scholars argue that careful reading of these instructions shows how this festival in turn was founded on a primitive pastoral ritual, the sacrifice of a prime hope of the flocks as an offering to avert the jealousy of the deity at the beginning of the new year (after the spring solstice on 21 March), as the nomadic shepherds began their annual move from winter to summer pastures. So the meal is eaten standing ready to leave, with the unleavened bread of the nomad, the bitter herbs of the desert, the meat roasted to save precious water. The full moon may also betoken some original connection with a moon-goddess. This festival at the beginning of the annual trek received additional sense and symbolism when it was overlaid to become the commemoration of the greatest trek of all, the journey of forty years in the desert after the escape from Egypt. The blood on the doorposts, originally a charm to avert evil spirits, became a sign to the angel of the Lord, and the Passover became a festival in honour of the Lord.

1 Corinthians 11:23–26

This passage is one of the two precious pieces of tradition that Paul reports word for word, as 'received from' the Lord and 'handed on' to his converts—using the two technical terms of rabbinic tradition. The other is 1 Corinthians 15:3–5 on the tradition of the death and resurrection of Jesus. They have minor differences of language from Paul's own way of expressing himself, so that we can know that he himself learnt them by heart. They are the nucleus of the historical tradition of Jesus. The very close verbal accord with the accounts of the institution of the eucharist in the Gospels confirms their reliability: they were already deep in the Christian tradition a dozen years after the events.

'This is my body' is shocking enough, but to say over the cup, 'This is the new covenant in my blood' was staggering to the hearers. For the Jews, blood is the symbol of life, sacred to God, and to consume it is impious. For Jesus, the cup of his blood sealed his own new covenant, just as the blood of the sacrificial victim sealed the covenant on Sinai, making his disciples his own new people and giving to them his own life's blood.

John 13:1–17, 31b–35

John's Gospel has no account of the institution of the eucharist at the last supper. Instead he recounts Jesus' parable in action which shows the significance of what he is about to do in his Passion, a different expression of the same act of service which he is about to perform. Careless of his own dignity or convenience, he serves his own disciples and, in serving, cleanses them. In the Christian liturgical re-enactment of this act of service, well-prepared and already well-washed feet are presented to the Christian minister. The gnarled, habitually unwashed and travel-stained feet of the original disciples can have spared Jesus little.

Afterwards. Jesus explains what he has done, and he goes on to relate the Passion to the glory of the Father and the glorification of the Son. How can this dreadful suffering reveal God's and Jesus' glory? It must be in the relationship of their love for each other, revealed fully in this act of total obedience, and mirrored in the love which Christians are to have for one another. This reveals God's 'saving justice', his faithfulness to his promises and his loving generosity to his creation.

HW

GOOD FRIDAY

YEARS A, B, C

Isaiah 52:13—53:12

The fourth Song of the Suffering Servant of the Lord is the climax of these mysterious poems from the book of Isaiah which have been read during the week. It describes the suffering and humiliation of a Servant of the Lord who willingly takes upon himself the sins and the guilt of others. Even if the original author understood it of his own sufferings or those of the nation of Israel, it has been understood since the earliest Christian tradition as predicting Jesus' voluntary and vicarious offering of himself for the sins of many. The experience described at the baptism of Jesus and the allusions to this poem in his words at the last supper leave no doubt that Jesus himself understood his open-ended gift of himself to the Father in these terms.

Like Psalm 22, used on the cross, the poem moves through the darkest agony to the vindication of the sufferer and the glory of God. Even amid mockery and pain, the sufferer is sustained by trust and confidence in the God who he knows will rescue him and win his glory by the justification of many. Only so can the dreadful fact of human guilt be faced and overcome.

Hebrews 10:16–25

Like so much of the letter to the Hebrews, this reading gains its sense by reference to the book of Leviticus, the ritual in which the high priest passed through the curtain of the Holy of Holies on the Day of Reconciliation to offer the annual sacrifice of atonement. The symbolism is rich and multiple, combining the purification of the Day of Atonement with the idea of entry into the promised land. The true high priest, superior to all the temporary high priests of the old dispensation, is Jesus. Not only does he enter into the true sanctuary, which the Israelites never reached, but also we, the members of his body, enter with him. We must be purified in heart and—here we must surely have reference to Christian baptism—'washed with pure water' (v. 22). Already, therefore, this Good Friday reading looks forward to the baptism which is the climax of the Easter ceremonies, by which the baptized are purified and enter into the body of Christ.

Hebrews 4:14—5:9

One keynote of this reading is that Jesus reached perfection by his obedience in suffering, and so his prayer was heard. This is a full-bodied assertion of the real humanity of Jesus, who could suffer and so attain to perfection.

John 18:1—19:42

Throughout the Gospel of John, Jesus has been looking forward to his 'hour', the moment both of his suffering and of his being 'lifted up', exalted both on the cross and in glory. The narrative reflects this aspect of glorification. When they come to arrest him, they fall back in involuntary homage at the divine word, 'I am He' (18:5). At the trials, it is Jesus, the prisoner, who leads the questioning, continuing his mission of teaching. On the cross itself, Jesus reigns in triumph, not only as King of the Jews (as Pilate emphatically asserts), but totally in charge. He dies only when he has formed the new Israel from the loving community of Mary and the beloved disciple and has declared that his task is complete. Only then does he 'breathe forth his Spirit', imparting life to the Church.

Prominent in John's narrative is also the theme of judgment. The Father has given all judgment to the Son, but the Son judges no one. Throughout the Gospel, people have judged themselves by their reaction to Jesus— the disciples, the Pharisees, the Samaritan, Nicodemus. The climax of this comes at the trial before Pilate: the Jewish leaders think they are witnessing the condemnation of Jesus. In fact, before Jesus, crowned and enthroned as judge, they tragically condemn themselves and Judaism with the words, 'We have no king but Caesar' (19:15).

HW

EASTER EVE

YEARS A, B, C

Job 14:1–14

No worst, there is none. Pitched past pitch of grief,
More pangs will, schooled at forepangs, wilder wring.
Comforter, where, where is your comforting?

Like Gerard Manley Hopkins, many have asked the question, 'Where is God when it hurts?' Job speaks of the futility and despair of this experience. If God planned it all and knows every moment of our lives, he asks, then why does he continue to hound us?

- Job's bitter reaction to the inevitability of death does not lead to a denial of God, and there is a hint that death is not the end (see Job 19:25). God honours those who cling in faith to small signs of hope.
- All the hopes of the Old Testament are wonderfully fulfilled in tomorrow's Easter dawn. The resurrection promises purpose, vindication, justice and triumphant love for those whose battle with despair may never be completely won in this life.

- When human writers, Job or Hopkins, use words with such power and beauty to communicate their inner battles, they give us a creative sign that our lives are worth far more than just days to enjoy 'like labourers' (v. 6).

Lamentations 3:1–9, 19–24

The full horror of exile and imprisonment, brought about by God's hand as a punishment for Israel's sin, is described vividly and compellingly—the worst kind of dungeon, being driven and beaten, darkness, sickness and physical ill treatment, walls and chains. Unlike Job in his despair, the writer can see the broad justice of the terrible fate that has befallen the nation. 'Jerusalem has sinned grievously' (1:8). In all the violence and wars of the ages, the directly guilty have sometimes paid a terrible price, but often it is the uninvolved, 'the innocent', who suffer most.

One of the great themes of the Old Testament is remembrance, recall of what God has done in the past. So the lamenter remembers his affliction and is bowed down, but he 'calls to mind' (v. 21) what he knows of the Lord; by an act of will he remembers, and therefore has hope.

Our other Easter readings remind us of the Passion of Jesus, bearing in his own body the sins and griefs of the world, going through the depths of outer darkness, but we know that he too is not consumed, and new in the morning will be the risen Christ (v. 22–23), so that we have a sure and certain hope.

1 Peter 4:1–8

The example of the suffering of Christ is one of the main themes of this letter. His submission in obedience to the will of God seems to have made a deep impression on Peter. This explains the rather enigmatic first sentence of this passage. Christ suffered physical injustice as a righteous person. Christians may well suffer, but we are called to submit, arming ourselves with Christ's attitude, with the same intention to live by the will of God, whatever the outcome. We are done with past sin, outlined here in rather lurid terms (v. 3), and we will not go back on that, however difficult life gets.

We will live changed lives, even though the consequences may be uncomfortable. We may indeed be called to live such changed lives that we are an affront to some of our friends. But we still live 'in the flesh' and in this passage 'flesh', which translates so many different Greek ideas, seems to mean simply our earthly lives. Two things help us along through suffering and through the effects of sin: the end that is near (v. 7), bringing vindication and judgment, and the love of our fellows, outweighing our faltering failures and their consequences (v. 8).

Matthew 27:57–66

Two small groups are presented in the aftermath of the crucifixion—some disciples, but not the eleven remaining apostles, and some prosecutors.

The two Marys and Joseph of Arimathea may well have been feeling all the despair and loss of hope described in our Old Testament readings. But they keep faith even in despair, both with customary acts of respect for the dead body of Jesus (vv. 59–60; Luke 24:1) and with the Sabbath, getting the body away before the Sabbath begins and waiting until dawn on Sunday to finish the task.

Matthew's intention in this passage may have been to emphasize that Jesus was really dead. He is also conscious of the fulfilment of prophecy, and Isaiah 53 is implicit in the Passion narratives; here, Isaiah 53:9—'They made his grave with the wicked and his tomb with the rich'—may have led Matthew to mention Joseph's wealth (v. 57).

Many rumours must have circulated in Jerusalem after the resurrection, and Matthew ensures that some of them are silenced. Later (in Acts 5:38–39), Gamaliel, the Pharisee, tells the Council that if this new movement is of God they will not be able to overthrow it. The futility of their attempts to prevent the Lord of creation from raising Jesus from the dead must in the end have been clear even to some of them.

John 19:38–42

The alternative reading covers the same incident, and the points above apply. John links Nicodemus (v. 39) in with Joseph in the act of respect and generosity that lays Jesus' body in a substantial tomb. John tells us that these men were both influential and afraid. They, unlike many of Jesus' more humble followers, had a lot to lose.

Pilate in this reading seems to be living out his hand-washing, just anxious to get the whole episode behind him. The Romans usually left the bodies of crucified victims to rot on the crosses and flung them in a common unmarked grave. Did he care what happened to Jesus' body, and did he still feel some regret?

MK

Easter Vigil

Year A

The readings at the Easter Vigil carry us dramatically through the history of salvation in preparation for the re-creation celebrated with the resurrection of Christ.

Genesis 1:1—2:4a

The burden of the first creation narrative is God's effortless control over all creation. In this awesome account, God disposes each element where he pleases. The sun, the moon and the stars, those gods of the pagan nations, are relegated to the position of mere cuckoo clocks to mark the times and seasons. Here is no attempt to explain the scientific or evolutionary origin of the universe. In a scientific classification, the account describes the ongoing relationship of things to God: first the framework (the firmament), then fixed objects (sky, sea and land), then the objects that move in each (birds, fish and animals). And humanity is the crown of God's creation. It is an optimistic account: at each stage 'God saw that it was good', for evil had not yet entered in.

Genesis 7:1–5, 11–18; 8:6–18; 9:8–13

It is not long before disaster sets in and human sin becomes so all-enveloping that God finds that there is no alternative to destroying the whole human race—or almost. It may seem surprising that none of the earlier stories about the origin of evil is included, Adam and Eve or Cain and Abel. The story of the flood has a drama and an obvious universality about it which gives it immense force. Two other reasons conspire to make it especially suitable: first, it concludes with the story of the covenant symbolized by that potent symbol, the rainbow. (In fact, what distinguishes the biblical stories of evil from other mythical stories about evil is that they all end with hope and a promise that evil will not finally triumph.) Second, new life from the waters links with the symbolism of baptism which is so important at the Easter Vigil.

Genesis 22:1–18

This agonizing story, so tenderly recounted, portrays the ultimate test of Abraham's trust in God. The father's love is evident in every line: Abraham

carefully carries the fire and the knife himself, lest Isaac burn or cut himself.
Contrast Isaac's bouncy prattle with his father's heavy and painful reply,
and notice the slowing of the pace as the story approaches its climax. And
yet this tender love does not impede Abraham's absolute obedience. 'The
binding of Isaac' was always a favourite story in Judaism, already in Jesus'
time, with the elaboration that Isaac himself positively co-operated by offering his own hands to be bound. The ancient story mirrors the offering of
God's own Son in sacrifice, especially with this detail of elaboration that the
Son himself joins in the offering.

Exodus 14:10–31; 15:20–21

Again a story of deliverance by water and by the power of God, again
preparing for the climax of baptism. Like all good stories, the story has
grown in the telling, for the earliest version is simply Miriam's song of
triumph, 'Horse and rider he has thrown into the sea' (15:21). But this too
was a miracle of God's guidance of history to the miserable group of dis-
heartened and grousing fugitives whom God was about to turn into his
own special people. The crossing of the sea was the immediate prelude to
that great experience on Sinai which marked Israel for ever, when God
concluded the covenant with this runaway rabble and so created them a
people.

Isaiah 55:1–11

After a big jump in the history of salvation comes this invitation to participate
in the new and everlasting covenant. The long history of the monarchy in
Israel is simply recalled by the phrase 'in fulfilment of the favours promised
to David' (v. 3, NJB), those promises which were the foundation of all the
messianic hope, even in the darkest days of Israel's exile in Babylon. In its
pressing invitation (reminiscent of the invitations of Wisdom to her banquet,
Proverbs 9:1–4), this reading looks backwards to the revelation on Sinai of
God as a God rich in forgiveness and mercy, but it also makes a new
departure by looking forward to the participation of the Gentile nations in
those promises.

Proverbs 8:1–8, 19–21; 9:4b–5

This is the only reading at the Easter Vigil from the Wisdom Literature.
Wisdom was seen as the special gift of God, and as the outworking of God
in the world. God, so awesomely holy that he cannot mix in the world,

sends his wisdom as the means by which he makes himself known. By wisdom, God enables people to partake of what is most intimate to him and to come close to him. The invitation of Wisdom to partake of her banquet is full of reminiscences of the Gospel of John, where Jesus invites all those who are thirsty to drink of the living water which flows from him, and invites all people to partake of the banquet of the Bread of Life. The reading is thus a preparation for the eucharist in which the baptized are joined to the risen Christ.

Ezekiel 36:24–28

The tragedy of the exile to Babylon signalled that Israel had irrevocably broken the covenant made on Sinai. The persistent infidelity and idolatry of Israel left no alternative to a radical rupture in the cycle of disobedience. Israel had relied on those institutions which seemed to guarantee God's favours, monarchy, temple and its ritual. But the break was not to be permanent, for God's love found another way, the personal dedication of each individual's heart. The punishment was therefore also a re-education. Again the means of return is indicated by God's washing his people with water, a presage of baptism.

Ezekiel 37:1–14

This reading takes up the hint of the Spirit of the Lord in the previous reading with the dramatic vision of the Spirit bringing back to life the bones of Israel which seemed to be so utterly dead. The vision may be read on two levels: primarily it is a prophecy of the return to life of the nation of Israel which seemed so dead in Babylon, an encouragement to the exiles not to give up hope. Secondarily it must be read also in a Christian sense as a prophecy of the resurrection celebrated on this night. The resurrection of Christ is the firstfruits and the promise of the resurrection of his people. It is also a presage of the Spirit at baptism, for Christian baptism brings new life in water and the Spirit.

Zephaniah 3:14–20

The final Old Testament reading is a hymn of joy in the unfailing love of God, heralding the return from exile and the renewal of the Kingship of God. The warrior-saviour God will liberate and renew his people with dancing and shouts of joy. This is the Kingship of God which Jesus came to proclaim. In his ministry he met with little response, the crucifixion being the final sign of failure and rejection. And yet in his resurrection the Kingdom is definitively established. This is the restoration promised so long ago.

Romans 6:3–11

With the reading from Romans, we begin to concentrate on the baptismal element in the liturgy. The Easter Vigil reaches its climax in baptism into Christ, either the baptism of a new Christian or the renewal of baptism on the part of existing Christians. Paul is teaching that by being 'plunged' (for that is what 'baptism' means) into Christ's death, the Christian shares Christ's death, and not only his death but his whole history. The rhythms of Christ's body become those of the Christian's, and the rhythms of the Christian's body become those of Christ's, so that there is a complete sharing of life. Paul shows this by inventing a whole series of words compounded with the Greek *syn-* (as in 'synchronized'): co-heirs with Christ, con-buried with him, con-raised with him, con-glorified with him. Sharing in his death and burial has occurred for the Christian already in baptism. Sharing in his resurrection and glorification is still, in Romans, in the future. In a slightly different formulation, the later letters to the Colossians and Ephesians put it that the Christian already shares in Christ's resurrection, but it has still to be manifested.

Matthew 28:1–10; Mark 16:1–8; Luke 24:1–12

Each of these three evangelists has his own special message about the empty tomb. Mark (read in Year B) is probably the earliest account, which Matthew (Year A) and Luke (Year C) both enlarge.

The extraordinary thing about Mark's account is that it constitutes the very end of the Gospel. His record of 'the good news of Jesus' ends with the women running away and saying nothing to anyone. There is no attempt to check that the tomb is in fact empty; that is taken for granted. All the accent is on the interpretation of this fact provided by the young man clad in white (and so obviously a heavenly messenger). Despite his encouragement not to be afraid, all the emphasis is on their fear and terror and amazement. It was the common belief of Jews that at the last day, when time would cease to be and a new age would begin, the dead would rise from their tombs. The terror is that by the emptiness of the tomb this new age seems to have already dawned. God has acted in his world. The world as we know it has ceased to exist. Their reaction is trembling and terror, to run away, as if from an earthquake zone. So Mark's account remains open-ended to the future.

An earthquake is exactly what Matthew describes, presumably while the women were still on their way to the tomb (and in Matthew there is no worry about the size of the stone; they have no intention of anointing the three-day-old body, but are simply coming to fulfil the Jewish custom of mourning at the grave). The startling difference is in the reaction of the women: no more terror, but their fear is mixed with joy. Instead of fleeing, they set off to obey instructions by delivering the message to the disciples.

While they are on their way, Matthew adds the account, given more fully by John, of the first meeting with Jesus, a further increase of joy and peace. They recognize him, grasp his feet and do him reverence, just as did Mary Magdalen in John. By reiterating the angel's message, Jesus prepares for Matthew's final scene of mission to all nations on the mountain in Galilee.

Luke is always more concerned with facts and evidence, so he at last stresses the fact of the empty tomb by adding that the women could not find the body of the Lord Jesus, and that they were nonplussed about it until two men in flashing raiment (Luke doubles the number given by Mark and Matthew, perhaps because two witnesses are needed in a court of law) stood over them and explained. The men also give them a pocket version of the Christian *kerygma*, or proclamation, explaining that the death and resurrection of Christ were destined to happen as they did, presumably in fulfilment of scripture. This is the model for all future Christian proclamation, as will be seen in the story of the journey to Emmaus and in Acts.

Luke too has an extra little piece of tradition, found elsewhere only in John—the abortive visit of Peter to the tomb. Peter is always full of sudden enthusiasms, and he rushes off to the tomb as soon as he hears the news. He sees the grave-clothes but remains simply uncomprehending, utterly puzzled. In John, he is then contrasted with the beloved disciple: Peter sees but does not understand, while the beloved disciple's love for the Lord leads him immediately to understanding. In Luke, it will need the gift of the Holy Spirit to give Peter and the Church an understanding of these great events.

HW

EASTER DAY

YEAR A

Acts 10:34–43

At this pivotal moment of the reception of the first Gentile into the Christian community, Peter gives the nucleus of the Christian message to which the

Twelve are witnesses. In all the speeches of the Acts of the Apostles, the same pattern of *kerygma* is followed: witness to Jesus' baptism, ministry in Galilee and Jerusalem, ending with his death and resurrection to new life, testified by certain distinct witnesses. Basically the same outline appears already in the ancient piece of tradition offered by Paul in 1 Corinthians 15:3–5.

Thus the first witness is founded not so much on the empty tomb, for this is merely negative evidence that Jesus is no longer dead. Rather it is the evidence of life, for God has thereby appointed him judge. As the end of the speech shows, it is an odd sort of judgment, not a judgment of condemnation but one of forgiveness. There is another oddity about Jesus' judgment in John 5: the Father has given all judgment to the Son, but the Son judges no one. This theme runs through all the apostolic preaching, that the only necessary quality is repentance. The risen Lord accepts the self-judgment of sinfulness and exercises the divine power of forgiveness.

Jeremiah 31:1–6

In the darkest days of the threat to Jerusalem from the approach of the armies of Babylon, the prophet Jeremiah proclaims this ecstatic poem of the joy of a bride setting out for her wedding feast. It builds on two earlier moments in the Bible, and looks forward to a third.

The first moment is in the desert of the exodus. While Moses was communing with God on the mountain of Sinai, the people reneged on their pledge to Yahweh by worshipping the golden calf. But it was then that Yahweh revealed the meaning of his Name, in a passage which echoes down scripture: 'God of tenderness and compassion, slow to anger, rich in faithful love and constancy, maintaining his faithful love to thousands' (Exodus 34:6–7, NJB).

The second moment is when the prophet Hosea saw that his unquenchable, passionate love for his faithless wife was an image of God's own love for Israel, which no desertion could extinguish.

The third moment is the wedding feast of the Lamb, the climax and conclusion of the whole of scripture, the joyful final chapter of the book of Revelation, when John sees the Bride, the Church or the people of God, coming down from heaven adorned as a bride for her husband.

Colossians 3:1–4

The lesson of Romans 6 (read at the Easter Vigil) was that by baptism the Christian is plunged into Christ's death and so shares his life: we have died with Christ and will share his resurrection. The later letter to the Colossians is marked by a development from this, the awareness that the Christian already shares in Christ's resurrection, but this life is hidden with Christ in God and has yet to be revealed. It means that the Christian already shares in the divine life and is transformed by it. We are no longer earthlings, consumed by earthly concerns and worries, but 'our citizenship is in heaven' (Philippians 3:20). The rough and tumble of ordinary daily living is no longer our chief concern.

We must not make the mistake made by the Corinthian Christians to whom Paul wrote. They assumed that they had already received the Spirit in such a way that they no longer needed to be conformed any further to the pattern of Christ's resurrection. We know only too well that we are still transitory, weak and corruptible. But the seed of divine power, glory and incorruptibility is already there.

John 20:1–18

This Gospel passage consists of two recognition scenes, where the risen Lord is recognized by those who love him. Each of them comes in a much shorter version in other Gospels, the first in Luke, the second in Matthew.

In the first scene, the disciple whom Jesus loved does not have a chance to greet the Lord, but recognizes the meaning of the empty tomb and comes to belief, while Peter fails to understand. The beloved disciple stands for every disciple whom Jesus loves. This is why he remains unnamed. He is close to Jesus at the eucharist. At the cross, he is the one disciple present and with Jesus' mother is designated the first community of the saved ('Woman, here is your son; son, here is your mother', John 19:26–27). Now his love enables him to see the meaning of the empty tomb. In the final scene of the Gospel, at the lakeside in Galilee, he is the guarantor of the gospel tradition, who is to 'remain until I come'. These are the tasks of the disciple whom Jesus loves.

The second scene is memorable for Mary's affectionate recognition of the risen Lord, and her intimate acknowledgment of him as 'Rabbuni' ('my Master'), with the mysterious announcement of his exaltation to the Father.

Matthew 28:1–10

See comment on this passage under 'Easter Vigil'.

HW

YEAR B

Isaiah 25:6–9

The triumph of God cannot be fully expressed or contained by the changes of history. This is a vision of permanence, of dreams lastingly realized, never to be dashed or disappointed again. Against the scenes of ruin, want and confusion that run through chapter 24, these are pictures of mercy beyond judgment, and life out of death.

There are provision and gladness, rich food and heady wine, contented bodies and joyful hearts. The air is clean and open. The dark clouds of death are blown away. Grief evaporates, tears are dried, heads can be lifted in confidence to look into the face of God.

The invitation list is long and full. This is a broad hope, for 'all peoples, all nations'. A worldwide company will celebrate 'on this mountain' (vv. 6–7). The hilltop city of Jerusalem will be a magnet to draw the world, a place where yearning and longing turn into gladness. Israel, 'his people', will find that her 'rebuke is taken away', that her slight and slighted profile among the nations is gloriously transformed (v. 8). She had guarded faith through dark times. One day her long winter of waiting will end. The springtime of salvation will come (v. 9), and the nations will gather to its coming.

1 Corinthians 15:1–11

Paul is not trying to prove the resurrection. He appeals to it, as something believed and preached throughout the early Church (v. 11). Easter is a primary element in Christian faith (v. 3), a fixed landmark for reorienting the wayward and headstrong church in Corinth.

Easter is basic, at the heart of Christianity. The twofold gospel, of cross and resurrection (vv. 3–4), of pardon and promise, remains the centre of our good news, a message to stabilize and to save (vv. 1–2).

Easter fulfils ancient hopes: 'in accordance with the scriptures' (v. 4). Has Paul particular passages in mind—perhaps Isaiah 25? Or is he hearing in the whole Old Testament that God's power and love transcend even death? Easter fleshes that hope into life.

Easter is for unlikely people. Peter (v. 5; Cephas is his Aramaic name) had denied Jesus. James was Jesus' brother—involved, it seems, in the family's scepticism (Mark 3:21). Paul, who had persecuted the Church, was dragged into the Kingdom, like a child born without proper gestation (v. 8; Acts 9:1–22).

Easter was not a select and secret occasion. Many different people saw Jesus. The faith of the early Church rested on a broad base of witness. Easter still unites Christians. It belongs to and claims us all.

Mark 16:1-8

Is this all that Mark meant to write about the resurrection? No one knows. Has something been lost, from after verse 8? Possibly. Do verses 9–20 come from Mark? Probably not; we think they were added later, enlarging this account with material from other Gospels.

Yet the sheer brevity of this resurrection account communicates a sense of mystery. Awe and strangeness surround the empty tomb. The first impression Easter makes is to disturb and dismay: this is something we cannot fathom; it confounds all normal experience.

The women had waited to watch him die, and followed to see the burial (15:40, 47). Anointing would be a last act of devotion. Even that would depend on shifting the stone (16:3). Still, faith does what it can—and God does more. The women were caught by surprise, drawn suddenly into unearthly visions and hopes. We read of astonishment, trembling and amazement. Then the scene and the Gospel close abruptly, in fearful haste and silence.

Yet Jesus 'goes ahead into Galilee', leading his people as a shepherd (v. 7; cf. 14:27–28), to the place where he had first gathered them, and spoken of the Kingdom in all its freshness and power (1:14–15). The strangeness is laden with promise. The silent, empty grave speaks of the fullness of life.

JP

YEAR C

Isaiah 65:17-25

The earlier part of this chapter describes the rebellion of God's people and the disaster they bring upon themselves. Here the writer bursts into a great hymn that sets out God's continuing purpose to bring in a new heaven and a new earth (v. 17), the promise of restoration, forgiveness, and harmony for human society and the whole created universe. The picture is very earthy—rooted in home, houses, land tended and harvested, fulfilment in work and long life. But Isaiah knew, as we know, that this promise is never going to be completely fulfilled on earth. God's love contains both judgment and mercy and the requirements of both will, in the end, be met.

The resurrection signifies that the battle against evil is won and the new Kingdom has come. But the final victory is still awaited. The complete fulfilment of verses 19–23 will only come about at the end of time. Meanwhile we are called to do all we can to start the process, to respond to the sound of weeping and the cries of distress. When we pray, 'Your will be done on earth as in heaven' we are promising to act to bring about the new heaven and earth, and the certainty of the resurrection makes it possible.

1 Corinthians 15:19–26

The letter to the Corinthians deals with a number of problems that had arisen in the Church. Some denied the resurrection of the dead. This may have arisen from a Greek dualism that divided the physical from the spiritual, saying that the body was not important, but the soul was. This led in practice to an arrogance about spiritual gifts and the ignoring of physical sins.

Paul emphasizes the crucial importance of the resurrection of Jesus as a historical and physical fact, whatever the nature of his risen body.

- Without the resurrection, his death cannot save us and we are still unforgiven, still dead 'in Adam' (v. 22).
- Without the resurrection, there is no guarantee that we too shall rise and put on new bodies (v. 42), with all that that means in terms of individual recognizable survival after death.
- Without the resurrection, death still has the victory.
- Without the resurrection, all the great biblical promises that justice will in the end be done, that those who have served him and suffered will be vindicated, cannot be fulfilled.
- Without the resurrection, without the empty tomb, without the risen Lord who is recognizable and who eats and drinks with his friends, there is no Christian faith.

Luke 24:1–12

These events are fitted into the framework of the week. Like creation, the work of Jesus ends on the sixth day; there is rest on the seventh and then a new age begins 'on the first day' of the new covenant (v. 1).

'Why do you look for the living among the dead?' (v. 5). No one else has returned with a resurrection body. The dead lay in other tombs around them. But he is the firstfruits, as Paul describes him in 1 Corinthians 15:23, and when he comes, those who belong to him will be made alive.

The women are the first witnesses of the greatest event in history. The angels heralded his birth and announced his rising from the dead. Neither the women nor Jesus' own remembered words, nor Old Testament hints, would convince the disciples. Any other event with the kind of document-ary authenticity we have here would be accepted by most thoughtful people. But this is too big, too impossible, too unique to be believed on evidence alone. We seize the truth of it by faith and then seek to understand. We too can sympathize with the perplexity of the women and the disciples (v. 11).

MK

OLD TESTAMENT READINGS
FOR SUNDAYS IN EASTERTIDE

YEAR A

These readings are largely passages chosen for the Easter Vigil. There they provided a continuous and developing story of the history of salvation and the preparation for the resurrection and baptism. In this Eastertide selection, the order is different, largely to reflect the theme of the other readings of each Sunday.

Second Sunday: Exodus 14:10–31; 15:20–21

See the fourth reading at the Easter Vigil. This reading gives an opportunity to reflect on the baptismal theme of salvation or rescue by passing through the water. The writers of the early Church always saw the crossing of the sea as a figure of baptism.

Third Sunday: Zephaniah 3:14–20

See the eighth reading at the Easter Vigil. This reading offers a prophecy of the re-establishment of Jerusalem as the centre of salvation, which may be seen to be fulfilled in the conversions recounted in the appointed reading of Acts.

Fourth, Fifth and Sixth Sundays: Genesis 7:1—9:17

See the second reading at the Easter Vigil. The theme of the three readings of Eastertide is clearly God's care to save human beings from their wickedness, a purification by water which is a foretaste of the washing by water in baptism. The symbolism of the dove returning may also be the origin of the depiction of the Spirit of God in the form of a dove (as at Jesus' baptism); this has additional point in the preparation for Pentecost. The extended reading of the whole story demonstrates its importance in that it was handed down in two different oral traditions, each of which is preserved. For example, one tradition allows seven pairs of the clean animals into the ark, while the other allows only 'one pair of all that was alive'. There were in fact several stories of a disastrous flood as a way of wiping out sin, in the Babylonian as in other traditions. The biblical authors use such a story to express the doctrines of the universality of God's power, God's inability to tolerate moral corruption, God's choice and tenderness and protection of those who strive to observe the divine commandments, the permanence of God's alliance with human beings.

Seventh Sunday: Ezekiel 36:24–28

See the sixth reading at the Easter Vigil. The reading prepares for the coming of the Spirit at Pentecost, the opening of hearts to receive the Spirit anew.

HW

YEAR B

Second Sunday: Exodus 14:10–31; 15:20–21

Two plans have come into collision: God's promise to rescue the Israelites from slavery (3:17), and Pharaoh's determination to keep them (14:5). It seems that Pharaoh must win; he has the big battalions on his side (vv. 9–10). Israel sinks into fear (vv. 11–12). Yet from verse 14, 'The Lord will fight for you', Pharaoh becomes a mere pawn in God's strategy. He has overreached his power. God first baffles him (vv. 19–20), then as he races after his prey, all his fighting strength becomes a mere deadweight (v. 25).

Our account explains the event in two ways—a strong east wind (v. 21), and the hand of God (v. 16). This is both a natural (if unusual) occurrence and an act of God; it is the creator who redeems. So Israel is led through, from fear of man (v. 10) to fear of God (v. 31), from despair to awe. The women of Israel, whose earlier intervention had been critical (1:15—2:10), now sing glad songs (15:20–21), that will be chorused through generations to come. Out of the waters are born faith and praise.

Slaves have been set free. An era of injustice is over. A new world is ahead. God has brought his people out of futility, to see (14:13), remember and trust his saving power.

Third Sunday: Zephaniah 3:14–20

This is a resounding song of salvation, a carnival celebration that God is king. He has triumphed and brought his people security and joy. Their enemies are gone, and God stands among them (v. 15). Who, then, is this God?

* **God is king** (v. 15). He is leader and ruler, heart of his people's life, guide and strength, wisdom and care.

- **God is warrior** (v. 17). His power and anger have confronted danger, oppression and hatred. He stands over his people like a protective shield.
- **God is lover**, passionate and shouting for joy (v. 17), his heart lifted by the worship and faith of his people. When heaven rejoices (Luke 15:7), it is God's voice that leads the song.
- **God is healer**, binding up the broken-hearted, gathering the scattered, wiping away his people's tears, and ending their disgrace (vv. 18–20; cf. Psalm 147:2–3).

Our experience may rarely reflect the grandeur and gladness of these triumphant words. The grey dawning of mundane reality may summon us too often from the bright dreams of faith. Yet we are Easter people. For Christians, the surest reality of all is joy and triumph, life out of death, a resurrection to scatter all our tears. God's morning will be bright indeed, and his joy and light shall reign for ever.

Fourth Sunday: Genesis 7:1–5, 11–18; 8:6–18; 9:8–13

The whole story of the flood runs from 6:5 to 9:17. Our selection follows Noah and his family as they enter the ark and experience the crashing power of the rain that floats them away from all normal security. We share their tension and longing as the flood gradually recedes, and look with them at the rainbow of God's faithfulness.

This story arises from judgment (6:5–13), and ends in grace. God does not abandon the world he has made. The compassion that preserves Noah and his family will preserve nature itself. This family is God's bridge across the flood, carrying life to the other side. As they start anew, God promises to nourish and uphold the world they settle, 'every living creature... for all future generations' (8:22; 9:10–12).

What is the rainbow? Is it a bow of war, now laid aside, as witness that God's judgment on sin will never again be worked out through cataclysmic natural disaster? It is surely the light of sunshine after rain, grace beyond wrath. It signals hope, and reminds the people of God to cherish the world God graciously gives; to steward its gifts; and, even when all seems ungodly (6:12), to go on believing in the covenant faithfulness of God.

Fifth Sunday: Genesis 22:1–18

This story defies all sense and instinct. The emotional tension becomes almost unbearable, and even when this is resolved we recoil from the thought of what might have been. It denies the natural love of a father (let alone that of the absent and presumably unknowing mother). It ignores the grace that had crowned their old age with a child (17:15–19; 21:1–7). It surely erases the prospect of descendants to come, and blessing for the world (12:2–3). Abraham and Sarah have lived for an unseen future (12:1–3); now their very lifeblood is being taken away. What possible meaning is here?

- **God was testing Abraham** (v. 1). He passed the test (vv. 16–18; cf. James 2:21). Faith is still essential, if the promise is to be sustained. He and his children must obey God whatever it costs; only so will they have blessing to offer the world.
- **God provides** (v. 14), however near to the limits of our own fortitude and insight he brings us.

Yet this dreadful story reaches ahead, hinting that God himself must save by the death of a Son (John 3:16; Romans 8:32), and hinting too that death will be followed by resurrection. For the God Abraham has trusted is the God who raises the dead (Hebrews 11:17–19).

Sixth Sunday: Isaiah 55:1–11

Isaiah chapters 40—55 promise return from exile for Jews in Babylon in the sixth century BC. The message throughout is of homecoming (e.g. 52:11; 55:12–13). This chapter revels in the reliability of God's word: it has been given, it will surely be fulfilled; there will be restoration, and there is hope.

The offer of food and drink—'Come!'—is a summons to listen (vv. 1–2). We are nourished by what our ears hear and our minds digest: hope energizes us; without promise we weary. God's words are heavy with promise. We may not know his plans and thoughts; no more can we read the clouds in the sky. Yet the rain that falls will surely feed us, as God nourishes all who trust his word (vv. 8–11). So let sceptics listen and sinners learn (vv. 6–7). Israel will flourish again, as God's covenant Kingdom, desire of the nations and magnet for the world (vv. 3–5).

Israel did come out of exile. But fuller day would dawn when her true King came (Luke 1:32): his word would prosper like seed after rain (Mark 4:3–9, 26–29); his gospel would gather the Gentiles. Then indeed the Church would say 'Come!' and call the nations home to the joy and love of God. Promises, like seed, can flourish long after they are sown.

Seventh Sunday: Ezekiel 36:24–28

The Jews to whom Ezekiel spoke were a broken people—deported, humbled, dismayed. Yet, he tells them, tragedy will not be God's last word. The tide will turn. God's honour is at stake, and he will rescue his people (v. 23).

- There will be a return to the land, where Israel had worshipped God through many centuries (v. 24).
- 'Clean water' is a symbol of pardon, the rinsing away of defiling memories and old guilt (v. 25).
- Inner renewal, a remaking of lives from within, will prevent the repetition of past errors. As God changes human hearts from stubbornness to sensitivity, then thoughts and desires are transformed. When God himself animates their spirits, the people's conduct will alter and their lives reflect his will (vv. 26–27).
- So Israel's bond with God will be forged afresh. She will belong once again. This will be a truly new start (v. 28).

The promises were first realized in the return from exile. Later Ezekiel's 'water and spirit' pointed to the gospel renewal that Jesus brought (John 3:5). But these verses reach even further, still offering genuine spiritual renewal, however badly we have neglected our faith. This is an invitation to people who have drifted away from God, to begin again, at Pentecost.

JP

YEAR C

Second Sunday: Exodus 14:10–31; 15:20–21

It is impossible to over-emphasize the centrality and importance of this narrative. It is the defining story for Judaism, and is the defining interpretative story for Christianity as well. Human suffering caused by injustice and the immoral use of power are dealt with decisively and with planning and forethought by God. Those who cannot help themselves are rescued by the Lord whom even the wind and waves obey, although they have little faith in him or in his chosen leader (14:10–12). Those who are sure of their power and their right to conquer and enslave are engulfed in the same waters (v. 28). This story becomes the defining moment for the new nation. It is repeated over and over again; they are to obey his laws because he brought them out of the land of Egypt, the constant refrain in the books of the Law (Exodus 20:2). The Passover provides the symbolism for the new covenant of rescue for the helpless (Luke 22:14–20, for example).

Chapter 15 records the consequent rejoicing, ending with Miriam and the women. Now they could be sure of salvation and the sure hand of God for the future. But the narrative goes on and records the ups and downs of a people whose memory was always too short (Psalm 106:6–15).

Third Sunday: Zephaniah 3:14–20

Zephaniah's short prophecy echoes many of the other prophets in his warning of coming destruction, not only on Judah's neighbours, Philistia, Cush and Assyria, but also on Judah and Jerusalem. He emphasizes the coming great day of the Lord. His particular targets are those with wealth and power, in 1:8 (princes and king's sons), in 1:11 (merchants and traders), and in 1:13 (those with wealth, houses and vineyards). In chapter 3 he speaks against the officials, the rulers, prophets and priests. It is those who are haughty and proud (3:11) who will be removed, not the meek and humble (3:12). Then with verse 14 the prophet looks beyond the corruption, the idolatry (1:4–5), beyond the great day of judgment to the day of restoration. This restoration involves forgiveness (v. 15); joyous worship (v. 14); justice (v. 19a); care of the handicapped and refugee (v. 19b); and vindication (v. 19c).

His people today are given, first, a strong sense of the purposes of God working out through history, however hard it is to live in one particular moment; second, an underlying trust that it will work out in the end; and third, the assurance that we are loved both with a lover's love, and with a motherly love through it all (v. 17).

Fourth Sunday: Genesis 7:1–5, 11–18; 8:6–18; 9:8–13

Themes to be picked up include:

- **Rescue from judgment**: This is a rescue from the physical consequences of moral danger; a double rescue. The pattern of this is recalled in the Exodus escape from the judgment that fell on Egypt, passing through the waters of the Reed Sea, as well as in the greater rescue made possible by Christ's death. Peter sees the water through which Noah passed to a new life as a symbol of baptism—a rescue from judgment (1 Peter 3:20–21).
- **Obedience in faith**: Noah obeys (7:5) and the writer of Hebrews commends him for this (Hebrews 11:7).
- **Windows of opportunity**: In 7:4 God gives Noah seven days, but there will be a closure; judgment is not postponed for ever. There is plenty of warning for him and for us. But in our journey of faith we often have to wait for the right moment to move on and out (8:6–14).
- **Covenant of promise**: This covenant is with all creation including Noah and his family. The rainbow (9:13) comes with sun and rain, judgment and mercy; and the 'never again' is echoed in Isaiah 62:8 and Revelation 21.

Fifth Sunday: Genesis 22:1–18

This story of Abraham and Isaac is not easy. Many would ask whether, if God is good, it is possible for him to test someone by asking them to do something that is bad. It is often difficult to read the stories of the Bible without bringing to them our very different cultural and social attitudes. Abraham lived before the Law, emerging almost on his own from the worship of other gods. All round him there were cults and religious practices that sometimes involved human sacrifice. He has to learn that this is not the way.

How much does Abraham trust the God who promised him descendants? Does he have enough faith to give up his most precious possession? He learns that faith and obedience are rewarded by the promise of future blessing; that God himself provides the substitutionary sacrifice and that humans never sacrifice humans.

The echoes of this story are strong in the story of the death and resurrection of Jesus—the only begotten son given as a sacrifice; all the promises of future blessing (Isaac and his descendants, or forgiveness and salvation) hanging on one person's death, and on one person's faith and obedience.

Sixth Sunday: Ezekiel 37:1–14

This familiar passage is in two parts, vision and explanation. The vision is about the 'whole house of Israel' (v. 11) and is therefore more than usually applicable to the 'whole house of God', the Church. With the rate of loss from the UK church overall probably going from ten per cent in the 1980s to twenty per cent in the 1990s, 'Our bones are dried up and our hope is lost' (v. 11) is a cry we can legitimately make. There are several hopeful pointers here.

- There is an interesting relationship between the prophet and the Lord: the prophet is directly involved in the bringing to life of the bones by being made to see and understand the true state of affairs (v. 1), being challenged (v. 3), being told to tell the bones in faith that they would become flesh again (v. 7), and then being told to pray to the Spirit to bring the living breath of God into them.
- What is the role and nature of the breath, wind, spirit, all translating the one word *ruach* (*pneuma* in the Septuagint)? What is a spirit-filled church? What is a dead church? Churches (that is, individual fellowships) are often described in these terms. How can we relate this vision to the Church?

Seventh Sunday: Ezekiel 36:24–28

The context of these verses is almost more important than the verses themselves. The promises here seem to require little effort on the part of Israel. Yes, the Israelites need to be cleansed from all their impurities and from their idols (v. 25), but it will happen, along with restoration, rescue, return from exile, a fresh start with 'transplants' (v. 26), because the Spirit will 'make' (v. 27) them obey the laws. Rebellion is ruled out! Heritage and self-respect are restored.

But verses 22–24 point out that this will be done not for their sake, but in order that the name of the Lord will be honoured, which they have failed to do; and that surrounding nations will see that the Lord is God, in which they have also failed. Verses 31–32 emphasize again that it is not for their sake; one purpose is that they will at last see what they have done and be shamed into self-loathing and repentance.

Israel's responsibility as the people of God was to be the kind of fellowship that demonstrated both God's full character and his way of salvation to the surrounding nations. That responsibility has been transferred to the Church. Do we let down his name and reputation before our neighbours and the world?

MK

THE SECOND SUNDAY OF EASTER

YEAR A

The New Testament readings for Eastertide form a carefully controlled series. The readings from the Acts of the Apostles outline the beginnings and development of the first Christian community, the model church of Jerusalem. The second reading (and the second reading is virtually always from an apostolic letter, anyway) is taken from the first letter of Peter, which is widely thought to be based on a baptismal catechesis, and so is especially suitable for this time when baptism is in our thoughts, both from the newly baptized of Easter and from the fresh beginnings of Christianity itself.

Acts 2:14a, 22–32

One of the most important additions to our knowledge provided by the Dead Sea Scrolls of Qumran is to see how Jews at the time of Jesus interpreted the scriptures. It consisted largely of taking a text of scripture and applying it to present-day events. This is precisely what Peter is doing in this speech of his at Pentecost. First he takes a passage from Joel to explain what is meant by the outpouring of the Spirit, and in this passage he takes a long passage from Psalm 16 to explain the meaning of the resurrection. The chief emphasis is that God's Holy One could not be separated from him and 'see corruption'. Christ's resurrection is the firstfruits and pledge of the resurrection of the Christian. As in Psalm 16, the new life for the Christian too consists in the inexpressible joy of God's presence.

1 Peter 1:3–9

Paul's letters begin with a thanksgiving to God for the faith and perseverance of his correspondents. This letter begins with a blessing on God for the new birth into the living hope of the resurrection of believers. It may seem odd to bless God: does not God rather bless his creatures? In fact, in the Bible blessings flow in both directions. Frequently, as in the Beatitudes in Matthew's Sermon on the Mount, classes of human beings are declared blessed for certain qualities. In the Godward direction, too, God is blessed by such personalities as Abraham and David as a form of thanks and recognition of benefits conferred. God is blessed as the source of all blessings. He is recognized as exalted, separate and above all created things, able and generous to lavish good things on those who give themselves to him.

John 20:19–31

Of these two appearances of the risen Christ, the first is perhaps the most joyful of all the appearances. There is no trace of doubt or fear, simply peace and joy. In the Johannine story it is the moment of the founding of the Church, for the Spirit is the life-principle of the Church. During his ministry, and especially in the discourses after the last supper, Jesus had promised the Spirit of the Father or his Spirit, to guide his disciples into all truth and to be their Advocate or Paraclete. His death on the cross had been described with typical Johannine ambiguity as, 'He gave over his spirit' (or 'Spirit'?) Now he breathes the Spirit on them to empower them with authority in the forgiveness of sin.

The second appearance makes the perfect conclusion of the Gospel (chapter 21 is an epilogue). Thomas' confession of Jesus as 'my Lord and my God' is the only full acknowledgment of Jesus' divinity by anyone in the Gospel. It arches over to join up with the opening, 'The Word was God', to bracket the whole Gospel as a declaration of the divinity of Christ.

HW

165

Year B

Acts 4:32–35

The Church in the early chapters of Acts received its power at Pentecost—that is clear. But it received its message at Easter. The apostles were witnesses: they had known the Lord Jesus before his crucifixion, and met him after his return from the grave. Throughout these weeks and months, their preaching finds its focal point in telling of the risen Jesus (4:33; also 2:32; 3:15; 5:30–32).

These early believers showed a profound and loving commitment to one another, expressed most remarkably in their sharing of material goods. There may be influence from existing Jewish customs of poor relief, and from the marginal Essene group, with which the earliest Christians had some contact. But there is surely a more direct connection to the common life of Jesus and his disciples, their common purse and his concern for the poor. The new wine of the Spirit's coming released a joyful mood of generosity in this growing fellowship. However short-lived this initial phase turned out to be (and we find few traces of such wholesale sharing later in the New Testament), it is a potent reminder that Christians are members of one body in Christ, committed to practical concern for each other's material needs.

1 John 1:1—2:2

This opening passage of the Epistle declares a double purpose: to bind the church in fellowship, through reaffirming the roots and origins of their faith (1:1–4); and to steer them away from sin (2:1). The Christian life is about believing and doing, faith and action. Either is unbalanced without the other.

The shared memory of the Christian Church, our family heritage as Christian company, is that Jesus, the eternal Son of God, took human flesh. He was truly 'from the beginning' (1:1), bearing in himself the eternal life of God. Yet he was also a person whom men and women had seen and touched. Our faith comes from there. Telling this message cements our fellowship.

Fellowship with Jesus has practical implications. For a Christian to ignore sin is a pretence (vv. 6, 8, 10). To 'walk in the light' (v. 7) means a serious endeavour to follow and copy God's own light, the life of Jesus. It also means an honesty about ourselves: in God's light we recognize and confess our failures. Then we discover the depth of God's forgiveness, in the cross of Jesus (1:7, 9; 2:1–2). Our 'horizontal' fellowship with one another is confirmed (1:7), our commitment to holy living renewed (1:9), and we are given a message to share with the world (2:2).

John 20:19–31

The risen Jesus is described as palpably physical—with wounds, and breath, and an invitation to touch—but he is not limited by walls and locks. Compare Luke 24:16, 31; John 21:4: there is a new freedom and mystery about him. He comes now to a fearful company, with words of peace and a gladdening presence (vv. 19–21). He sends them to continue his work, to shape the world's knowledge of right and wrong, with the inspiration of his Holy Spirit among them (vv. 22–23).

Thomas had not been there. Never a natural optimist (cf. 11:16; 14:5), he would not share his friends' belief unless he too could see and touch. Then, given the opportunity to touch, it seems that he did not take it (20:27–28). Sight was enough to create confidence and worship. So Thomas' faith brings the Gospel narrative full circle: Jesus, the Word who was God (1:1), is proclaimed as 'Lord and God' in the faith of his Church. Yet this moment cannot remain. For long years God was known without being seen (1:18), and now that Jesus has made him known, the time is coming again when faith must be sustained without sight (20:29). This is why John's Gospel was written. It records Jesus' signs, to lead those who have not seen him themselves into faith and life (20:31).

(See the Feast of St Thomas, 3 July, for further comment on this passage.)

JP

YEAR C

Acts 5:27–32

The six Sunday readings in Acts form snapshots of the dramatic change that the Holy Spirit brought as the Church grew and spread out to the whole of the known world.

Linked here are *power* and *obedience*. The enormous spiritual power that the Holy Spirit was giving the disciples is illustrated by earlier events in this chapter. Whatever might happen, their certainty and assurance could not have been higher. In obedience, they were preaching in the temple from dawn. Obedience to God comes first, whatever the consequences. Peter finishes by saying that God gives the Holy Spirit to those who obey him (v. 32).

The gospel they were preaching was about repentance and the forgiveness of sins. The offer was for all, including Israel and the Sanhedrin. Does the high priest, who does not name Jesus, remember that the people called his blood down on themselves and their children (Matthew 27:25)? Although he *had* to die, that did not mean that those who made sure he was executed were not still in some part responsible for his death. There is also a wider guilt of human sin in which we all bear a part. Jews and Christians, as well as everyone else, are guilty in this sense—one no more than the other.

Revelation 1:4–8

Readings from Revelation are set for the six Sundays after Easter, bringing the triumphant assurance of the resurrection to bear on the trials of the early Church. From Patmos, as a prisoner of Rome, John launches into this dramatic vision of the history of heaven and earth, in which he particularly lambasts Rome and her empire. His first aim is to encourage and empower small groups of Christians who struggle in a hostile and persecuting society. Here in the prologue to the seven letters to seven churches, John emphasizes the following.

- **God**: Echoing the unchanging I AM, he is the one who was, is and is to come, the Alpha and Omega, covering all time and eternity, totally almighty, who already knows what will happen in the end, whatever humans try to do.
- **The gospel**: Jesus Christ, who is both man, highest of earthly kings, firstborn from the dead, and God, coming on the clouds so that all shall see him. He loves us and washes away our sin with his blood.
- **The Church**: Echoing Exodus 19:6, the fellowships of scattered believers are a kingdom of priests, carrying all the covenant promises and worldwide mission of the chosen people of God.

John 20:19–31

There are a number of contrasts here. The disciples are understandably afraid behind locked doors on the evening of the first day. But a week later (v. 26) they are still there. Jesus comes and three times speaks of peace, breathes the Spirit into them and commissions them: they are *sent*. Sent as he has been sent—to anyone and everyone—possibly to suffering and death —to the proclamation of a gospel of forgiveness, and judgment (v. 23)—to triumph and resurrection in the end. Later the full power of that breathing and sending will begin to show itself, exploding from Acts 2 on, a transformation which begins here in the locked room.

Jesus seems to be dealing with their perplexity and fear, dealing with them as individuals—Thomas, and then Peter in the next chapter. Thomas' battle with belief is a familiar one. This one unique event—did it really happen? Thomas is forced into making a dramatic declaration, 'My Lord and My God' (v. 28). He says this to the man who bears the scars of his humanity, the physical marks of redemption: the Almighty is the crucified one.

Verses 30 and 31 are John's mission statement. Those who believe although they cannot see (v. 29) now can read and hear (v. 31).

MK

The Third Sunday of Easter

Year A

Acts 2:14a, 36–41

The response to Peter's speech at Pentecost is repentance, leading to conversion and discipleship. The author stresses the overwhelming power of Peter's speech by the large number who respond immediately. Throughout his Gospel, Luke stresses that there is no discipleship without the admission of sin which is repentance. Before Peter is called on the lake he confesses, 'Go away from me, Lord, for I am a sinful man!' (Luke 5:8). Before Zacchaeus entertains Jesus in his house he admits his sin (Luke 19:8). Before the prodigal son returns home, he acknowledges his folly (Luke 15:18). Before the good thief is promised paradise, he contrasts Jesus' condition with his own just punishment (Luke 23:41). So the first step towards discipleship is always admission of the need to be saved. Otherwise, why turn to Jesus?

Baptism is both in the name of Jesus and into the name of Jesus. In Acts, disciples are described as 'those who call upon the Lord Jesus'; but 'name' means also 'company' so that baptism is into the company or society of Jesus. It is entering a group called by his name and invoking his name, who place their salvation in that name.

1 Peter 1:17–23

This passage, like many others in 1 Peter, is full of the symbolism of baptism, with terms such as 'ransom', 'purified', 'new birth'. Eastertide is a moment for considering not only the baptism of the newly baptized but also our own less recent but freshly renewed baptismal commitment. Two images of baptism particularly deserve reflection.

Baptism is equated with the ransom of a slave. In Greco-Roman society, slaves abounded and had no rights, being liable to death or punishment entirely at the whim of their master. They could be ransomed and set free by the payment of a sum of money either to their master, or even by their master to a temple. It is from such a depersonalized state that Christ has ransomed those who turn to him in baptism, and the price is the blood of Christ.

The covenant by which Israel was made God's people was sealed by the blood of a sacrifice, but 'the blood of the covenant' referred also to the blood shed at circumcision, the moment of entry into the covenant. Instead of this blood, entry into the new covenant is sealed by the precious blood of Christ. Thus in both these images of baptism the blood of Christ is central.

Luke 24:13–35

The story of the meeting of the disciples on the road to Emmaus is a sort of model of the Christian apostolate, or of coming to faith. It is a typical Lukan story, with entry, dialogue and exit. But, more than this, it is beautifully told, with concentric balance: it begins and ends in Jerusalem; the disciples are conversing as Jesus arrives and as he leaves; their first reaction is failure to recognize him, their last to acknowledge him. Within this framework, the conversion of the two disciples occurs in two phases. The first is instruction. The stranger shows how the final events of Jesus' life were destined and foretold in the scriptures. Christian instruction must start from the scriptures and be an explanation of them. The second phase of conversion is the breaking of bread: it is in this eucharistic meal that their eyes are opened and they really encounter Christ, see Christ for what he truly is. Just so, in the parallel scene in Acts of the conversion of the Ethiopian official (Acts 8:26–40), the unknown messenger appears, instruction from the scriptures leads on to the sacrament of baptism, and then the messenger disappears.

HW

YEAR B

Acts 3:12–19

A lame man had suddenly been given new health and energy (3:6–10). Peter explained that the power and glory of Jesus were at work—not absent in resurrection, but accessible and active through the faith of his Church.

Peter draws on Israel's Old Testament heritage. The God who has done this is 'the God of Abraham, Isaac and Jacob' (v. 13), the God known at the burning bush (Exodus 3), who brought Israel out of Egypt. The Lord Jesus who has been raised is the Servant glorified by God (v. 13), the wounded redeemer of Isaiah 52:13—53:12. Scripture was fulfilled not only in the resurrection, but also in the suffering and death of Jesus.

So Jerusalem, the city where Jesus had been denied and killed, should look on the resurrection as an amnesty from God. The people had been involved, along with their rulers (Luke 23:13), but God was ready to pardon their ignorance (Luke 23:34; Acts 3:17, 19). Easter gave them a window of opportunity. As often with important choices, there were angry responses (4:2; 8:1), from people antagonized by the apostles' claims. Yet in time there were many in Jerusalem who believed this message, and joined the Church (21:20).

1 John 3:1–7

This passage is about Christian identity, hope and behaviour: who we are, what we look forward to, and how that affects our living.

Christians are a people loved, drawn into the fellowship that God shares with his Son Jesus. We are God's children, but that is a secret identity for the moment. We live by the name of Jesus but are not recognized by that name. John expects that, for the world did not acknowledge Jesus either (v. 1).

Yet John writes of a bright hope, that the Church will one day see Jesus. There will be a coming together of the Lord and his followers. All the uncertainty and anonymity will recede into the background, 'for we will see him as he is' (v. 2).

That prospect ought to influence Christian behaviour. The life in us must come out, in pure and upright conduct (vv. 3, 7). John's stark perspective on sin and righteousness (v. 6) disturbs some readers; we know that we are not entirely clear of sin. The best explanation is that we 'cannot avoid the fact of sin, but we can avoid its practice' (S. Smalley). Sin may impose its company upon us, but it has no claim on our hospitality. It is a nuisance, but should not become a guest.

Luke 24:36b–48

Two followers of Jesus came breathless from Emmaus, with a tale of meeting Jesus on the road (vv. 33–35). Suddenly he was there again, standing among his friends, in Jerusalem. His mysterious presence at Emmaus, first incognito then vanishing at the very moment of recognition (vv. 16, 31), contrasts with the repeated invitations here to test that this is indeed Jesus, solid and physical (vv. 39–43).

The disciples struggled to believe, at first for sheer dread (v. 37), then amid the joyful fear that this could scarcely be real (v. 41). To shape and strengthen their faith, Jesus reminded them of teaching he had given long before, drawing from the ancient scriptures prophecies of his death and resurrection (vv. 44–46). Soon would come mission—the offer to the world of a new way of living. The friends who witnessed his risen presence would have a vital role in telling this gospel (vv. 47–49).

There are resonances with other passages in the New Testament. The way that Jesus presents himself matches John 20:19–20 closely—quite probably the same occasion. The taking of bread and fish (vv. 30 and 42–43) recalls the feeding of a crowd (9:15–17). Jesus' digest of the Old Testament is reflected in Paul's short summary of the Church's preaching (1 Corinthians 15:3–4).

JP

YEAR C

Acts 9:1–6 [7–20]

The importance of Paul's conversion is underlined by the detailed length of the account, which is told three times in Acts—this time and twice more in Paul's own first-person testimonies (Acts 22 and 26). Luke is emphasizing that Paul can legitimately claim apostle status beside the others, partly because, as we see in Paul's letters and other incidents in Acts, he is challenged on this issue. His conversion contains elements that are important for all Christians.

- He has a **personal encounter** with the risen Lord.
- He is **humbled**; he approaches Damascus in self-righteous assurance that he is doing the will of God in seeking to imprison the Christians, with serv-ants who will obey his orders; he arrives stumbling and blinded, led by those he had commanded and facing the enormity of what he had done.
- He is **restored and forgiven**; a brave man, Ananias, comes and imparts God's healing, the gift of the Holy Spirit and baptism.
- He is **called to lifelong service**; in verses 15 and 16 God reveals this to Ananias, but Ananias passes on this calling to Paul (Acts 22:14).
- He is **brought into fellowship** with other believers.

Revelation 5:11–14

Revelation describes the spiritual realities of heaven which lie behind all the turmoil of earth groaning in captivity to Satan. We too see the battles, the famines and plagues, the persecution of God's people, but John sees them on a wider canvas as the fall-out of the mighty battle between the forces of heaven and the forces of evil. However, the war has already been won; the blood of the Lamb has ransomed the saints and he has the keys to the final victory. The imagery comes from Old Testament writings, Ezekiel and Daniel, for example. It is full of symbol and metaphor which require careful reading.

In this picture of heaven, unimaginable numbers of spiritual beings are praising with 'full voice' (v. 12). At the centre of their praise is the slaughtered Lamb. The sacrificial systems of Old Testament worship, the blood on the lintels before the Exodus, together with the helplessness and vulnerability of a lamb, combine in a picture of 'meekness and majesty, manhood and deity' (G. Kendrick). Just as the sun is still shining behind the clouds of the darkest day, so even in the turmoil of a world where evil still has force, this is heaven now. The risen Lord is reigning.

John 21:1–19

This passage focuses on Peter, a leader still, initiating the fishing trip, leaping out of the boat to go to Jesus, leaping back in again to drag the net ashore, and then facing his commissioning and interrogation. The incident recalls Luke 5:1–11. Jesus again teaches the professionals how to fish, and forces a response of worship from Peter.

Entering this passage imaginatively brings us face to face with the Lord— compassionate, caring, the risen Lord of glory—who, as the early morning mists melt away, makes a fire and cooks breakfast for his overjoyed but overwhelmed (v. 12) disciples.

The reinstatement of Peter is repeated three times; suggesting echoes of the denials. Somehow these men are still clinging to Jesus' physical presence, but between this commissioning and Peter's sermon at Pentecost and predicted martyr's death has to come full reliance on the power of the Holy Spirit and their full assurance that the living Christ is with them for ever and everywhere.

Sheep and shepherding metaphors abound in scripture—Ezekiel 34, Psalm 23, the lost sheep of Luke 15, Jesus as the shepherd in John 10, and Peter's first letter. New Testament usage usually carries implicit references back to the Old, and is illuminated by an understanding of this process.

MK

THE FOURTH SUNDAY OF EASTER

YEAR A

Acts 2:42–47

It is almost as though the author is here painting a picture, not of what the community was like, but of what every Christian community should be like. At several stages in the story of the Jerusalem community, the narrative is interrupted to give a picture of the life of this first community, a model for all Christian communities. One characteristic always mentioned in these summaries is prayer, the constant prayer and praise in common; this punctuates the story, and is summed up in 'the breaking of bread', the eucharist (v. 42). Another characteristic is the brotherhood or fellowship. This is expressed especially in ownership of all goods in common and the distribution to each member according to need (vv. 44–45). The material side is, however, only an expression of the sharing of the gospel and its benefits and of a much more profound unity in the Spirit, since all Christians form one family, indeed one body of Christ, in the Spirit. A third characteristic is the respect and awe in which they are held, and the signs and wonders which they work, on the model of the signs and wonders worked by Jesus himself during his ministry (v. 43). The Christian community continues in the Spirit to live out the life and presence of Christ which he lived on earth.

1 Peter 2:19–25

One of the puzzles of the history of Christian morality is the length of time—many centuries—for which Christianity accepted without question the institution of slavery. It was possible to accept people on one level as brothers and sisters, and on another to see them deprived of every basic right. This very fact can, however, also be inspiring in that it shows that there is always room for a deeper understanding of the Christian mystery.

The solution put forward here by 1 Peter is that already suggested by the persecutions of the disciples of the Jerusalem community in Acts—participation in the innocent sufferings of Christ. The writer strengthens his teaching by allusion to the Song of the Suffering Servant of the Lord (Isaiah 53:9), which we heard during Holy Week. The first Christians rejoiced to share in the sufferings of Christ, as Paul joyfully accepted to 'partake of his sufferings by being moulded to the pattern of his death' (Philippians 3:10, NJB). As in the signs and wonders mentioned in Acts, so in physical suffering, the Christian community continues to live out the life of Christ in the world.

The reading also finally introduces the theme of the good shepherd.

John 10:1–10

Each year of the three cycles of Gospel readings has a reading about Jesus as the good shepherd on the fourth Sunday of Eastertide. It is therefore often designated 'Good Shepherd Sunday'.

Sheep are such silly, mutton-headed creatures that in any pastoral society the shepherd is the image of loving care for the naturally unlovable. It may be a different matter with white, woolly lambs, but sheep have an incredible capacity for rushing the wrong way, straight into danger. The rocky, craggy ravines in the Holy Land make the perils all the more extreme. In the Old Testament, God is frequently presented as the devoted shepherd of his people Israel, delegating his care to the human shepherds of his people, and especially to 'my servant David'. In the New Testament, and especially in John's Gospel, Jesus succeeds to many of the titles previously reserved for God: 'I am the light of the world... the way, the truth and life'. These are some of the ways in which Jesus is shown to be the incarnate God. Among these, the role of 'Shepherd' has perhaps a special place, for Jesus 'had compassion for them, because they were like sheep without a shepherd (Mark 6:34).

HW

YEAR B

Acts 4:5–12

The healing of a disabled man (3:1–10) led to the arrest of Peter and John (4:1–3). The religious leaders in Jerusalem wanted to investigate (vv. 5–7). Miracles were suspect among the Jews, for possible occult associations— and it seemed that the trouble started by Jesus had not ended.

As Jesus promised (Luke 21:13–15), the Holy Spirit comes to help Christians under trial, so that Peter is able to speak powerfully to the court (v. 8). His theme is the risen Jesus.

- Jesus is the reason for the lame man's 'resurrection' (the word 'raise' is used in 3:7) to fitness and strength (v. 10).
- Jesus is the rejected stone of Psalm 118:22, who has now become the cornerstone of God's purposes (v. 11). This ancient psalm had been quoted in the passion of Jesus (Luke 19:38; 20:17), and was used with conviction by the early Christians (cf. 1 Peter 2:4).
- Jesus is the one through whom God's saving power is known; the unique invitation of Isaiah 45:21–22 is now reissued in his name (v. 12). The word 'salvation' means both physical healing and spiritual wholeness, health out of weakness and new hope for a wayward people (2:40).

All this, for the earliest Christians, belonged to the message of Easter.

1 John 3:16–24

Love is a primary characteristic of Christian life, a sign that faith is genuine (v. 14). Hatred is always destructive and sterile (v. 15; cf. Matthew 5:21–22). The Christian family is called to something very different—to practical, observant and sacrificial love, a fellowship of open eyes, open hearts and open hands (vv. 16–18). The inspiration and pattern for our loving is the death of Jesus: as he 'laid down his life' for us (cf. John 10:11, 15), so we are committed to living for others (v. 16).

Love is a basic test of Christian faith, one we can apply to ourselves. It shows the life of Christ within us. The barometer of our spiritual feelings is notoriously unreliable, but God sees the whole orientation of our living, far more clearly than we do (vv. 19–20). Two central realities determine the quality of our Christianity (v. 23): what we believe about Jesus (explained in chapter 4); and how we love his people. Those who love, then, will grow in fellowship with God (v. 21), will develop a prayer life that reflects and discovers God's will (v. 22), and will experience the presence of the Holy Spirit (v. 24). Love is at the heart of our faith: we must learn early to love, and grow constantly in our loving, for here is the life of Christ.

John 10:11–18

Shepherding involved care and oversight, nurture and protection. God was Israel's true shepherd (Psalms 23:1; 80:1), and David had been their great shepherd king. As 'good shepherd', Jesus now assumes the royal mantle of David, the leader under God—but he leads in his own distinctive way. Like much in John's Gospel, these verses point forward also to Jesus' love for his Church.

Jesus' close knowledge of his flock matches his intimate relationship with the Father (vv. 14–15; cf. 17:25–26). He is a shepherd commissioned, not leading for himself, but for God.

Jesus' commitment is absolute, steadfast to death. His dying will be a pastoral act, for the welfare of his sheep (vv. 11, 15). It will be voluntary, accepted rather than imposed. Yet it will be an act of obedience, the culmination of his commission from God. And it will not be final, but a genuine death out of which his life will be restored to him (vv. 17–18).

Jesus' vision is broad: an enlarged flock will be gathered as one (v. 16). Caiaphas' unknowing prophecy about 'one man dying for... the dispersed children of God' (11:50, 52) echoes this verse. From Jesus' death will come an increased and extended Israel, as the crucified shepherd draws the nations to himself (12:32).

JP

Year C

Acts 9:36–43

Peter brings a dead woman back to life. This is such a straightforward story that it invites a simple retelling, bringing out the points that Luke makes—Tabitha's devoted life of good deeds; the obvious effects the death has had on the local church. Peter seems to copy Jesus bringing Jairus' daughter back to life (Mark 5:38–42), sending the mourners away and using almost the same words, *Tabitha koum*, instead of *Talitha koum*. (He also copies Jesus with the paralysed man just before this—Acts 9:32–34.) This act confirms the gospel, many become believers and Peter stays on in Joppa with the growing church (vv. 42–43), reaffirmed and ready for the next great step of faith.

How do we react to stories of the dead coming back to life? Can we believe that Jesus did it but wonder whether Peter really did? We have to work out an explanation of miracles that happened then and seem not to happen now. Is it a matter of lack of faith? Or is it that God sends miracles when they have a wider purpose—encouraging the fledgling church and establishing new believers? Above all, the promise is that even though we die, in Jesus we shall be made alive.

Revelation 7:9–17

Here is the vision of heaven that John sends to the struggling churches of Asia Minor. What a contrast to their fellowships, generally small and unnoticed, until the unwelcome notice of harassment and persecution! There is an unnumbered multitude, clean washed and dressed in white, praising God and the Lamb with all the angels of heaven (v. 9). There are several important points.

- Despite the huge numbers, John does not see 'cloned', disembodied souls, but groups recognizable by their ethnic origins. Will the new heaven and new earth contain all the riches of human culture in all its different forms, music, language and poetry?
- These are the redeemed, clothed in the white robes of salvation through the blood of the Lamb, the only clothes for heaven (Matthew 22:11–12). 'For this reason' they are before the throne of God (v. 15).
- They have emerged from the ordeal of life on earth. The death and resurrection of Christ have not cocooned and kept them from the difficulties of life, but have given them the promise of final victory. Hunger, thirst, scorching heat and tears are all gone (v. 16).

John 10:22–30

This winter solstice feast recalled the cleansing of the temple by Judas Maccabeus after its desecration by foreign conquerors (1 Maccabees 4). John may simply be alerting us to the time of year or may be hinting that this nationalistic feast is the background to demands for proof of Jesus' credentials as the Messiah (v. 24).

This Gospel is written to answer the question, 'Who is Christ?' The truth is declared in the first chapter (1:10–12) and demonstrated and worked through to 20:31 (see Easter 2). As a conquered people living under pagan rulers, the Jews had strong hopes in a Messiah sent from God to restore the glory of the chosen people, as Judas Maccabeus had done. Jesus will not allow them to push him into such a role. He has already faced that temptation in the wilderness and will do so again when he is taunted to come down from the cross.

Verse 31 shows that their question is not a straightforward one, but aimed at catching him out. They are not prepared to listen, but those who do listen are promised abundant life and permanent security because behind him is the power of the Father, to whom he is united (v. 30). This is truth or blasphemy.

MK

THE FIFTH SUNDAY OF EASTER

YEAR A

Acts 7:55–60

This is the last incident in the series of readings about the model community at Jerusalem. It is important that one reading on persecution should be included, for persecution is never absent from Christianity, whether the quieter persecution of strain and mockery or the more overt persecution of bloodshed. These are some of the ways in which the life of the Church mirrors and continues the life of its Master. This persecution is the occasion of the spread of the Christian community beyond Jerusalem—as Tertullian said, the blood of martyrs is the seed of the Church.

In the case of Stephen's martyrdom, the similarity to Jesus' is particularly clear. Just as Jesus at his trial declared that the high priest would see the Son of Man seated at the right hand of the Power and coming on the clouds of heaven, so too Stephen declares to the high priest that he sees the Son of Man standing at the right hand of God (v. 56). As, in Luke's account, Jesus forgives his killers and commends his spirit into the hands of his Father, so Stephen commends his spirit into the hands of the Lord Jesus (v. 59).

1 Peter 2:2–10

The reading circles round two ideas, a living stone, keystone, cornerstone, foundation-stone, and a chosen race which is a kingdom of priests, the successor to the chosen race created on Sinai. The two ideas come together in the image of a house, a new temple, of which Christians are the living stones. The author is able to press into service the quotation from Isaiah about the stone which the builders rejected, which has become the cornerstone, namely Christ (v. 6; Isaiah 28:16).

It is remarkable that in the New Testament Christ is called a priest in the letter to the Hebrews, but that, apart from this, the expression is not at all used of individuals. However, the Christian people as a whole are here described as a holy priesthood, the expression used of the people of God on Sinai. This holy priesthood is to offer 'spiritual sacrifices acceptable to God through Jesus Christ'. In later Judaism, the sacrifice of prayer and praise had increasingly taken pride of place over the animal sacrifices, and the end of the reading shows these 'spiritual sacrifices' to be the praises of God.

John 14:1–14

On this Sunday and the next, the Gospel readings begin to prepare for the ascension, that definitive moment of parting, after which Jesus is no more physically with his disciples. These words are spoken as part of the discourse after the last supper, but it is quite clear that the speaker is in fact already the risen Christ, or at least Jesus speaking in the power of the risen Christ. He leaves his disciples with the promise that they 'will do greater works than these' (v. 12). The physical presence of Christ is, in a way, a limitation. The presence of the Spirit of Christ, in whose power the disciples will act, is freed from bodily and physical limitations.

On the other hand, the departing Christ remains for ever the way, the truth and life. He is the means and the goal. He is the way because the faithful disciple will perform the works which he does, following the way he has traced out. He is the truth and life because he is one with the Father who is the source of all being and of life itself.

HW

YEAR B

Acts 8:26–40

The second quarter of the book of Acts, chapters 8—12, gives a flavour of the lively and widespread evangelism that followed the scattering of the Jerusalem church (8:1). Here an encounter on an isolated desert road turns a seeker for truth into an ambassador for Christ.

This Ethiopian had approached the gospel himself, for he had been drawn to worship Israel's God, had made a pilgrim journey to Jerusalem and begun to explore the scriptures. He needed Philip's insight, however, to make the connection between the suffering figure of Isaiah 53 and the Passion of Jesus. Hearing the gospel, he enthusiastically accepted Christian baptism. Then Philip, opportunist for God, is sent on his way, and—before the storyline of Acts turns north and west—the first Gentile convert continues his journey into the heart of Africa. 'Ethiopia' corresponds roughly to present-day northern Sudan.

This man was certainly one of the first black Christians. He would represent Christ in a highly responsible political post. His distant origins, and his physical malformation (if 'eunuch' is to be taken literally; it might simply denote 'courtier') witness to the new inclusiveness of the gospel, in fulfilment of Isaiah 56:3–7.

1 John 4:7–21

Two cardinal signs of Christian life were mentioned in 3:23—belief and love. The matter of belief is taken up again in 4:1–3, and love in 4:7–12.

Love begins in God, and is a sign of the life God plants within us (vv. 7–8). Christ's incarnation and crucifixion were God's love-gift to us, a sacrifice for our sins 'that we might live' (v. 9). A Christian life, nourished by faith in Jesus, is richly supplied with love. As we give that love out, God's own life dwells in us (v. 12). We know and show God by loving one another.

Verses 13–16 outline again the essential marks of fellowship with God. The Spirit comes, to teach us that Jesus has come from God (vv. 13–14; cf. 4:1–3). This faith in Jesus draws on the life and love of God, and that love shapes our relationships (vv. 15–16). The Spirit informs belief; belief energizes love. Then love looks forward and outward: forward in confidence, no longer afraid of God, or of God's judgment (vv. 17–19); and outward, to the Christian brothers and sisters whom we love for Christ's sake (vv. 20–21).

This sort of love, at large in the Church, will always reach further than the Christian fold. It will shape approachable and caring Christian character, and commend Christ to people outside.

John 15:1–8

The farewell discourses (John 14—17) look forward to Church life in the period beyond the ascension. Today's passage emphasizes that a Christian's relationship with Jesus should be productive.

In the Old Testament, Israel is likened to a vine (e.g. Psalm 80:8–16)— although the image is often used negatively, pointing to judgment for unfaithfulness. Here Jesus adopts the symbol for himself, as the 'genuine vine', and speaks of the possibility of a fruitful life with God. The Christian's bond with Jesus is a union of two lives: ours joined and dependent upon his; his nourishing and infusing ours. Only so can the life of Christ bear fruit in the Christian (v. 4).

Outside that relationship, or if it is disdained and neglected, there is only barrenness and destruction (vv. 4, 6). Even within it there will be constructive discipline, the pruning that is a mark of care and purpose (v. 2; cf. Hebrews 12:6). The disciples, as Jesus speaks, have been made ready by his teaching to take up this relationship (v. 3). As they go on, their desires will merge with his, their prayers will reflect his purposes (v. 7), and God will be honoured by their living (v. 8). Christian discipleship is shaped by the realism of painful growth, and by the inward and transforming power of Christ.

JP

Year C

Acts 11:1–18

Moving out to the Gentiles was a crucial and significant historical turning point. Jerusalem (Acts 2—7), Judea and Samaria (Acts 8) and the ends of the earth were the concentric circles of witness commanded by the ascending Lord in Acts 1:8. Crucially the Church had to decide whether converts had to become Jews who added Christian discipleship to Jewish law-keeping, or whether Gentiles simply moved straight into Christian fellowship without becoming Jews first. The Council of Jerusalem finally settled the question (Acts 15), although the issue went on making waves for a long time.

Peter relates his vision, which has already been described in Acts 10. Like Paul's conversion, Luke is emphasizing its importance. Nothing is now unclean; all those kinds of regulations have gone. No one is ever again excluded by the old rules. The Holy Spirit fell upon them (v. 15) just as it had on the believers in Jerusalem in Acts 2. For Peter, the combination of a vision and command from God, as well as the Lord's preparation of Cornelius and his authentication by the Holy Spirit, left no room for any doubt that this was the way forward.

Revelation 21:1–6

Much of John's imagery comes from Isaiah—a new heaven and earth (65:17); the bride (62:4—5) and the end of mourning (61:3). Again (see Revelation reading for Easter 4) we have the promise of a redeemed earth, replacing the earth that has passed away (v. 1). Is it this that Paul is speaking about in Romans 8:18–21?

Christians have often asked when this will happen. Can we read the signs of the times and work out a chronology for the remaining life of this earth? Some confusion arises because we forget that time is part of the created physics of the universe; God, heaven and the visions of John are outside time. Some think that the end of history coincides with the moment we die, as we leap forward out of time to the new heaven and the new earth. Others think that we sleep until we are raised to be with Christ on the last day.

The water of life in verse 6 is repeated several times in Revelation, culminating in the river of the water of life flowing from the throne of God in 22:1. There are echoes of Eden, of Isaiah 55:1, and of Jesus and the woman at the well (John 4)—a powerful symbol in a desert land. 209

John 13:31–35

John chapters 13 to 17 contain the distillation of Jesus' discourses to his disciples at the end of his life. The themes that run through this section are Jesus' departure and his return to his Father, the disciples' inability to understand and the promise of the Spirit's illumination later.

Two words stand out here—glory/being glorified and love. Both are given a new meaning. There is a jumble of tenses, but the amazing claim is that the glory of God appears in the Son, the divine glory in human form, in humility, death and suffering. This is the glory of the cross. We preach Christ crucified, a stumbling block and a foolishness, but to those whom God has called, the power of God and the wisdom of God (1 Corinthians 1:23–24). Humans do not easily see glory in humility. Isaiah 49:3 echoes the idea of splendour in servanthood.

Of course, all would see that we were his disciples if we really loved as he has loved us (v. 34). Perhaps we glimpse a love like this most clearly in the best relationships between parents and their small children—the love that loves to the end, that nourishes and comforts, but which also trains and disciplines, and will go on loving sacrificially even where there is rejection and disobedience.

MK

THE SIXTH SUNDAY OF EASTER

YEAR A

Acts 17:22–31

This reading is an apt preparation for Pentecost, contributing to the readings from Acts a certain universalism, both because it is the only reading from Acts this year which moves beyond Jerusalem into the wider world, and because it seeks to persuade that knowledge of God is available to all people.

The speech of Paul before the council of the Areopagus is one of the most polished literary pieces in the New Testament, enriched not only with a quotation from the classical poet Aratus (and a clever play on the Athenian custom of dedicating altars to a god whose name was not known) but also with multiple allusions to Stoicism, the popular philosophy of the time. Its purpose is to demonstrate that a certain knowledge of God is possible by natural means and natural philosophy—as Paul maintains also in the first chapter of Romans. Building on the Jewish refusal to allow any images of God, Paul argues that without the concept of a god not contained by the universe, but creator of it, the universe simply does not make sense. This leads on to the noble doctrine of the universal presence of God. It is when Paul introduces the strange doctrine of resurrection from the dead that he is laughed out of court.

1 Peter 3:13–22

The fascinating element about this reading is the ancient Christian profession of faith which it contains. First the author exhorts his readers to stick by their faith despite persecution, but with courtesy and a clear conscience, that is, avoiding excess and stubbornness ('it is better to suffer for doing good... than to suffer for doing evil', v. 17). Then he gives the example of Christ's suffering, its saving effect and his vindication. Here the rhythmical and rhetorical style suggests that he is using a set-piece. It is a passage which has given rise to the presence in the Creeds of the often-misunderstood statement, 'he descended into hell'. Exactly who are these 'spirits in prison' to whom Christ preached is not clear. Are they the 'sons of God' whose sexual intercourse with women seems to have been the immediate provocation of the flood (Genesis 6:1–5)? At any rate, it evokes the picture of Christ saving those who had long been waiting under duress.

In this letter, where baptism is so important, the thought turns again to three vital elements in baptism—the external washing with water, the pledge of a good conscience which the washing expresses, and its effectiveness through the resurrection of Christ.

John 14:15–21

As Jesus' own departure approaches, he speaks four times in the discourses after the last supper about the Paraclete. A 'paraclete' is literally someone 'called to the side', an advocate who protects and defends. This originally occurred in a legal sense, a counsel for the defence, but here it is used more widely. The presence of the Paraclete whom Jesus will send, or whom his Father will send, will substitute for himself. It will lead the disciples into all truth, the fuller understanding of all that Jesus has said and done. It will constitute, so to speak, the presence of Christ when Christ is absent. It will be an invisible presence which gives to the Church the life of Christ ('I live, and you also will live', v. 19), acknowledged only by the eyes of faith, and will bind believers to Christ and to the Father.

These sayings are an attempt to express the continuing presence of Christ by his Spirit in his Church. This gives Christianity confidence down the ages—despite the multiple human faults which impede and frustrate the effectiveness of the Paraclete—that Christ's empowering and enlightening Spirit will never fail.

HW

Year B

Acts 10:44–48

This is a formative moment in Church history: a group of Gentiles, in the Jewish heartland, are received into Christian fellowship. From now on, the Church is irrevocably a mixed and international company. This is a Gentile Pentecost. To the amazement of Jewish onlookers (v. 45), the Spirit is given to a Gentile household 'as it had upon us at the beginning' (11:15).

For Cornelius, this experience crowned a longer process of spiritual discovery. He was a 'righteous Gentile', hungry for the reality he saw in Israel's faith (10:2). God stirred him to send for a Christian preacher (10:4–6, 30–33), and simultaneously prompted Simon Peter to carry the gospel across the ancient chasm between Jew and Gentile (10:9–29). Then as Peter preached, word and Spirit—the story of Jesus and the life of Jesus— met in the hearts of the hearers.

They were baptized, the flowing water witnessing outwardly to the life-giving presence of God poured within them. Then the days they spent with

Peter (v. 48) would consolidate both their understanding of the gospel and their sense of belonging to the Church.

Righteous deeds and gospel words, Spirit and sacrament, faith and fellowship—Cornelius and his household would never be the same again. Nor would the Church.

1 John 5:1–6

This section draws together themes that run right through the epistle. Love is a sign of God's life within (4:7); belief is a second touchstone (5:1). Anyone who believes in Jesus as God's Son is drawn into that same relationship—'born of God'. Love for the Father and love for his children go together; if we love one, we shall love the other too. Christian love runs in two dimensions—upward to God, outward to brothers and sisters (vv. 1–2).

John's church had experienced tense relations with outsiders (3:13; cf. John 15:18; 17:14). So John writes of 'conquering the world' (v. 4). When Christians face opposition, we may respond with gentleness, persistent faith and mutual care. That is a genuine victory, sustaining our spirits under pressure and offering a genuine alternative to anger and harshness. Faith in Jesus makes such a victory possible, indeed natural (v. 5).

For Jesus came by the water of his baptism, and the blood of his cross (v. 6). There he received the Spirit (John 1:31–34), and gave the Spirit (John 16:7). When water and blood are remembered in Christian sacraments, the Holy Spirit testifies to the servant life and loving death of God's Son. A church nourished by this faith is equipped to live Christ's life.

John 15:9–17

As verses 1–8 describe the productivity of the Church's relationship with Christ, these later verses stress the intimacy and warmth of that bond. Jesus had spoken earlier of his own love as pattern for the Church (13:34–35). That love is grounded in the Father (v. 9) and handed on by Jesus, supremely in his death (v. 13), which is source and model for the Church's life (v. 12).

The disciples are 'friends' of Jesus, for he tells them openly of his work and the Father's purpose (v. 15). Their obedience will arise not only from demand or necessity, but as a natural outflow of friendship (v. 14), a response to his loving choice (v. 16). That obedience will be the 'fruit' spoken of earlier, both expressing and sustaining their life in Christ (v. 10). His choice of them will be reciprocated, as they both copy his love (v. 17) and live in its embrace (v. 11).

So fruitfulness is grounded in the intimate and costly love of Jesus. His legacy to his followers is his peace (14:27), his love (15:9) and his joy (15:11)—unparalleled peace (14:27), sacrificial love (15:13) and ineradicable joy (16:22), to sustain the Church in a hostile world (15:18), that the fruit they bear may last, and their lives draw richly on God's power (15:16).

(See the Feast of St Matthias, 14 May, for further comment on these verses from John 15.)

JP

YEAR C

Acts 16:9–15

This gives an insight into Paul's journeys, the way he travelled, how he decided where to go and what he did when he arrived at a particular place. Notice the change from 'they' to 'we' in verse 10. Did Luke join Paul, Silas and Timothy at this point? Paul is prevented twice from going in a certain direction (vv. 6–7) and then he has a positive push (v. 9) in a dream/vision. How did the Holy Spirit prevent him? It could have been illness, some inner sense, a physical or natural factor, roads being blocked, bad weather, or a word of prophecy from a fellow believer. But then when he retells his vision he and his companions 'conclude' that they should leave for Macedonia, having pondered the vision in fellowship. For us, as for them, guidance may come in a number of ways from the Lord, but all of us have to check it out with others to make sure we are not being led astray.

They head for the leading city and search out, as before, the synagogue (v. 13). Perhaps there wasn't one in Philippi, because they then have to find the group of worshippers. This church begins with the women, and the first convert is a business woman who runs her own household. How refreshing!

Revelation 21:10, 22—22:5

Heaven is described in the startling image of the perfect city. Cities are so much a human artefact and so often full of some of the worst aspects of human society, and yet that is where most humans live and where there is huge potential for relationships of all kinds. John attempts to describe its perfection in terms of a perfect cube, over 1000 miles high, wide and deep, made of gold so pure that it looks like glass, and precious stones (21:11–21). Again the links with Old Testament imagery are strong, from Ezekiel (40:2; 28:13) to Isaiah (60:11–14; 54:11–12).

There is no temple because God is present everywhere in the city with everyone in it (v. 22). There is no external light because the light of God's presence is enough (v. 23). The doors are open to all; it is for all people, all nations and kings, Jew and Gentile, but only those who are written in the Lamb's book of life. The city is not for those whose sins are unforgiven and who do not turn away from evil. Repentance is the way into the new Jerusalem.

John 14:23–29

'How can you reveal yourself to us and not to everyone else?' Jesus responds to a question in verse 22 and sums up in simple terms the nature of Christian discipleship. Are they still caught up in the expectation of some demonstration of power that leaves no one in any doubt? Jesus has faced this way of making believers in the temptation to throw himself down from the temple and in the repeated demands for signs, and will face it again on the cross, in the taunts to save himself. But what he wants is our trust and love (v. 23) and, because of that love, our obedience. When we respond to him in love and repentance, then we hear what he says, and the Holy Spirit (v. 26) begins the process we call sanctification as he transforms us, reminding us of the teaching we should obey and filling us with all peace in believing. This is the peace that transcends all understanding and keeps us unafraid and untroubled, whatever happens in the world. But he is not going to compel us with his power to accept all this. We are free to walk away. Those whose eyes of understanding are not open will not see his glory.

John 5:1–9

Jesus asks a surprising question—'Do you want to be made well?' (v. 6). Can we know whether anything lies behind it? Is the man hiding behind his disability? Is there any significance in their later encounter in the temple when Jesus finds him and tells him not to sin any more (5:14)? Was his disability linked to some specific factor in his life? Healing, repentance and turning away from sin do have a cost and are not always comfortable.

It is interesting to contrast what we know of this man with the man born blind, in chapter 9. The man born blind grew to understand who Jesus was, and stood firmly on his side when challenged by the authorities. This lame man does not know who Jesus is, and when he finds out his name he immediately reports him to the authorities (5:15) who he knows are angry at the Sabbath healing. The healing here, as elsewhere, raises some important issues about a topic that still divides Christians. He heals sometimes because they ask or pray; sometimes when they have faith and are repentant;

sometimes one out of many as in this incident (v. 3); sometimes all those who come to him. What does it mean to be healed and whole? This lame man had been healed and could walk again, but verses 14 and 15 seem to suggest that he was still at risk and his 'wholeness' had not yet gone far enough.

MK

ASCENSION DAY

YEARS A, B, C

Acts 1:1–11

The beginnings of the Church arise out of the completion of Jesus' earthly ministry, the commissioning of the apostles and the sending of the Holy Spirit.

'Now above the sky he's King,' we sing. The ascension marks the point when Jesus ends his time on earth and 'ascends' to his Father's throne (Hebrews 12:2; Philippians 2:9). He is 'taken up' and the disciples stand there looking up into the sky (v. 11). Of course this does not mean that heaven and the throne of God are literally above in the sky. Height and depth, up and down, have always been metaphors for greater and lesser degrees of honour and glory, and this must have been clear to the disciples then as it is to us now.

The disciples are commissioned. 'Are you going to restore Israel now?' they ask (v. 6). Jesus' answer is to tell them that *they* are going to bring about the Kingdom of God. It is their job, in the power of the Holy Spirit. And as they stand there staring up, the messengers come to tell them to get on with it. He will come back, but meanwhile they have a task to fulfil as witnesses to the ends of the earth. This is our task still.

Daniel 7:9–14

Daniel works in Babylon, a captive and an exile. The people of God are dispersed, their land conquered, the temple and all its religious practices gone. Daniel, faithful to God even in this situation, is given visions that speak both of hope and restoration, and of mighty empires and wicked tyrants. He sees beyond the turbulent history of his time to the eternal throne of the Ancient of Days. The imagery is repeated elsewhere (Ezekiel 1 has fire and wheels; Psalm 51 and Isaiah 1:18 have the whiteness of snow;

God's book appears in Exodus 32:32 and Malachi 3:16). The scene is set for judgment—the court sits and the books are opened (v. 10). Swiftly the 'beasts' are dealt with.

Much has been written about the significance of verse 13. The clouds of heaven are most frequently associated with the divine presence, but here the emphasis is on the humanity of the one who comes in clouds, approaches the central throne and is given all the power and glory, as well as the worship of the peoples of earth. It is one like a son of man whose Kingdom will never end. These words are taken up by Jesus (Matthew 24:15–31) and in Revelation (vv. 20 and 22). The ascension is understood in the light of them.

Ephesians 1:15–23

This letter is about 'being church' together, directing the church at Ephesus to grow in grace and knowledge, in wisdom and enlightenment, not as individuals but as a fellowship with the organic life of a body (1:23).

- They began in faith and love (v. 15); now they need to go on maturing and growing in Christian discipleship. This needs to be emphasized. There is a tendency for churchgoers, adult Christians, to assume that their understanding of their faith is complete with confirmation, just as leaving school means finishing learning. But full discipleship means beginning a life of learning that is essential for growing in grace.
- The resources available to us are rich and overflowing—wisdom, revelation and enlightenment (v. 17–18) so that we know the hope, the calling, the riches of his glorious inheritance, his incomparably great power, his mighty resurrection strength. But how are these mediated to us? What kind of learning processes are in place in local churches? Are we able to share with each other what we have learnt?
- The glory of this trinitarian vision of God (v. 17)—glorious Father, Spirit of wisdom, and Christ seated at his right hand in the heavenly realms— is reminiscent of Daniel's vision, the Lord of the universe who fills everything in every way.

Luke 24:44–53

Luke ends his Gospel with a brief summary of the ascension, with which he then begins Acts. Before this passage the disciples are described as startled and terrified (24:37), frightened and doubting, joyful but disbelieving. Jesus then brings order and explanation.

He shows them that the scriptures, which they have known all along, are the sufficient basis for an understanding of all that has happened

(vv. 44–45). Their religious thinking has been turned upside down, but now he reasserts the authority of scripture for them. They have a basis for new biblical theology, the New Testament understood by reference to the Old.

He explains the immediate traumatic past and then moves on to give them purpose and the promise of power for the future (v. 49). They have a task to perform and the authority and indwelling power to do it. Now they are to proclaim the gospel of repentance and forgiveness through the name of Jesus to the whole world.

Our task is to proclaim the same gospel, based on the same scriptures, with the same authority through the same Spirit. We must not let these be undermined, whether it is by a weak universalism, a liberal cynicism towards scriptural authority, or dilution of the Trinity and the uniqueness of Christ.

MK

THE SEVENTH SUNDAY OF EASTER

YEAR A

Acts 1:6–14

After the stories of the early Church at Jerusalem recounted during Eastertide, we return to the period before the coming of the Spirit. The ascension recounted here, and traditionally celebrated on the previous Thursday, exactly forty days after the resurrection, marks the end of the period in which the risen Christ has been preparing the disciples for their mission by his appearances. Similarly Israel was prepared for its mission by forty years in the desert, Elijah by forty days on Mount Horeb, and Jesus himself by the forty days of testing in the desert. The ascension itself is reminiscent of the assumption of Elijah, who went up to heaven in a fiery chariot, leaving a double share of his spirit to his successor, Elisha, who would then carry on his work. Just so, the disciples are to return to Jerusalem, where they will receive the Spirit of Jesus for their task of proclaiming his good news as his witnesses and so will carry on his task.

Jesus (according to Luke's account) prepares for all the important moments of his life by prayer. He is at prayer at the baptism, before the choice of the Twelve, at the transfiguration, before the Passion. So the disciples as they await the coming of the Spirit are 'with one heart... joined constantly in prayer' (v. 14, NJB).

1 Peter 4:12–14; 5:6–11

The final reading from the first letter of Peter, which has accompanied us during the whole of Eastertide, fixes firmly on the persecution that believers can expect, and on the strength and support that God will provide. This is also an immediate preparation for the coming of the Spirit at Pentecost. It is a reminder that persecution and martyrdom are constant factors in the Christian Church, however unexpected in an age of peace and tranquillity. This was not confined to the persecutions of the catacombs and the Roman Empire. Whoever, a few years previously, would have expected the 'testing by fire' demanded of the martyrs at the Reformation, or this century in Russia, Germany, China or many countries in Africa? Paul himself, writing to the Corinthians and defending his right to exercise authority in the Church, uses his sufferings for Christ as a proof of his standing: he is the suffering servant of Christ, as Christ is the Suffering Servant of the Lord. If the Church were not persecuted, there would even be something wrong—a weakness of the stance in opposition to the standards of the world and the 'roaring lion' of this passage, who looks for someone to devour (5:8).

John 17:1–11

This passage begins the final section of Jesus' discourse after the last supper, immediately before his Passion. Yet its transfer to the situation immediately before the coming of the Spirit at Pentecost is not unfitting. In this great prayer (often called 'the High-Priestly Prayer') Jesus prays that God may be glorified by the completion of his work on earth. This work is the revelation of God's love and so the gift of eternal life.

Jesus is surely speaking, as so often in John, on two levels. On the one level Jesus' love for the Father, and the Father's love for Jesus and for his creation, are fully revealed by the act of perfect union in his obedience to the Father on the Cross. The solemnity of the prayer is increased because Jesus' 'hour' has come at last, the hour of his glorification, when he is to be 'lifted up' or 'exalted', the combined moment of his Passion and resurrection. On a second level it is already the Risen Christ speaking ('I have glorified you on earth by finishing the work that you gave me to do'), praying to the Father for the disciples he leaves to carry on his work and that of the Father.

HW

Year B

Acts 1:15–17, 21–26

We hear of a resurrection appearance to some five hundred Christians at one time (1 Corinthians 15:6). Presumably that was in Galilee, for it was a smaller company (v. 15) who waited in Jerusalem. The ascension was now past (vv. 9–12), and they were earnest in prayer (v. 14) in anticipation of important work. When the Spirit came among them, as Jesus had promised, they would begin their testimony in the city and to the nation (v. 8).

Completing the apostolic circle would represent a new spiritual leadership within Israel—twelve apostles for the twelve tribes. The twelve would be reckoned 'witnesses of the resurrection' (v. 22), a distinctive role for a particular era in history. They had been with Jesus throughout his ministry, and had met him risen from death. They could proclaim, credibly and authentically, the resurrection of Jesus. Throughout Acts, the designation 'witness' applies almost exclusively to this group.

The selection of the twelfth apostle, then, depended on long association with Jesus (v. 22). The final choice between two suitable candidates was taken in prayer and by casting lots (vv. 23–26). This method sustained the conviction that the Lord himself must choose (cf. 1:2). No doubt it also avoided an invidious dilemma; the opportunities ahead must not be hampered by favouritism and envy.

(See the Feast of St Matthias, 14 May, for further comment.)

1 John 5:9–13

This epistle announces its aims early (1:3; 2:1) but, like John's Gospel (20:31), it summarizes its purpose at the end. The repeated emphases on belief and on love have been designed to nurture the readers in the eternal life of Jesus Christ (v. 13). The whole letter is written to assure and confirm them in the essentials of Christian living, that they may be confident in faith and hope.

'God's testimony' (v. 9) surely means the Spirit's witness to the life and death of Jesus (see last Sunday's comment on v. 6). That testimony divides people. Those who believe have the Spirit's witness within them; their own heart becomes an echo-chamber for the voice of God (cf. Romans 8:15–16). Those who reject the testimony about Jesus, who find no great value in his human life and ugly death, are declining the promise and offer God makes them (v. 10). For this is how God's grace comes; this is the channel of his love. To see this and turn aside is to turn aside from the life of God (vv. 11–12).

A church that grasps the love of God in Jesus will indeed be changed, both in the generosity of its behaviour and in the solidity of its hope. Its love will be warm and its assurance clear. That was John's aim in writing this letter.

John 17:6–19

This central section of Jesus' 'high-priestly prayer' is a prayer for the disciples whom he has gathered and who will continue his work on earth. They have heard and heeded his word (vv. 6–8; cf. 6:68–69), and realize that he is sent by God. They have become a distinct community within the world (v. 9). Now they are sent into the world as Jesus was sent (v. 18), with purpose, to do God's work. There may be controversy and pain of the kind he encountered (v. 14); they do not belong and will not always be popular (v. 16).

So he prays for them, for their unity and joy (vv. 11, 13). He guarded them while he was with them—with one exception only, and even this in fulfilment of prophecy (v. 12)—and he prays that they may still be protected (v. 15). He requests not their complete detachment from the world, but their separation from evil (this word could mean either 'evil' or 'the evil one') as they live within it (v. 15). The Church must be involved in its surroundings but different, distinctively committed to God and to godly living.

So Jesus commits himself deliberately to God's will and purpose—to the cross, the next morning—by which his friends will be made holy for the challenges ahead (v. 19).

JP

YEAR C

Acts 16:16–34

If this slave girl was the next convert, then we have a woman at the other end of the social and ethnic scale from Lydia (see comment on the Sixth Sunday of Easter, Year C).

Perhaps the most powerful message today in these verses is that everyone needs to hear the gospel, 'believe on the Lord Jesus' (v. 31) and be saved— the God-fearing middle-class woman, the exploited girl practising cultic magic and horoscopes, and the decent, law-abiding jailer.

What happens to Paul and Silas has a modern ring about it. The slave owners, whose anger arises from economic loss, appeal to ethnic prejudice and anti-Semitism (v. 20) and then make political capital out of the mob violence they have incited. The magistrates fear public disorder, and Paul and Silas, battered and bleeding, end up shackled in a dark cell (v. 24).

This exciting and vivid story ends with another convert taking his household into the new church (v. 34). I wonder how many of the prisoners, having listened to the testimony of Paul and Silas' prayers and songs, also joined. The jailer washes their wounds, and they 'wash' him and his household in baptism.

Revelation 22:12–14, 16–17, 20–21

'It is I, Jesus, who sent my angel to you with this testimony for the churches' (v. 16). The book began with letters to seven specific churches, and ends with visions of the redeemed, the Church, praising God around the throne of heaven. The harried, despised groups of Christians to whom John was writing needed to know that the victory had been won and that their future was certain and glorious.

The gospel of redemption is clearly spelled out here.

- Jesus the Lamb is on the throne, crucified, risen and ascended.
- Only through the salvation wrought by his death on the cross can anyone be part of this praising multitude. Those who exclude themselves from this salvation are excluded from the city (v. 15).
- He is coming back as the Alpha and Omega (v. 13), the root and descendant of David (v. 16), the fulfilment of the Old Testament, the Christ who is God.

It is interesting that today's designated reading omits verses 15, 18 and 19. Perhaps this needs to be reviewed in the light of verse 19! The love of God which offers forgiveness has also to warn of judgment where that offer is spurned. Love and justice cannot be separated.

John 17:20–26

John talks of the unity of Father and Son with believers and their unity with each other (v. 21). Jesus is praying that they may know such horizontal and vertical unity. Jesus reveals the character of God to believers and they in this unity as church fellowships reveal the character of God to the world around them.

All the metaphors of the New Testament that describe the Church—the vine, the body, the temple built stone by stone—are metaphors of unity and organic life. In these pictures the Church is to reveal the unity of glory and love that comes from this relationship with God in Trinity. Just as Israel of old was intended to model God's character and reveal him to the nations, so the Church lives out the life of love in unity and thus demonstrates the irresistibly attractive character of her Lord. Our challenge is to face the credibility gap between this prayer of Jesus and the reality of the past two thousand years. However, as the promise of the Spirit's illumination is also part of the discourse of these final chapters, we are invited to seek the Spirit's help in facing our responsibility to be the kind of believers that are being described here.

MK

DAY OF PENTECOST

YEAR A

Acts 2:1–21

The coming of the Spirit at Pentecost marks the birth of the Church and the beginning of its activity, just as (in Luke's Gospel) the coming of the Spirit on Jesus at his baptism marked the beginning of his ministry. After the days since the ascension, when the Twelve seemed to hold their breath in anticipation, the activity of the Spirit in the Church springs into action. The significance of the event is explained by Peter with reference to Joel: it is the pouring out of the Spirit on all humanity, promised for the last times of the world, the beginning of salvation for all who call on the name of the Lord.

The event as recounted is full of symbolism. The violent wind is of course the wind of the Spirit ('spirit' and 'wind' are the same word in Greek and Hebrew), and the tongues of fire probably indicates the gift of languages. It also links to the post-biblical story of the coming of the Spirit on the elders with Moses in the desert (Numbers 11:25). Pilgrims did indeed flock to Jerusalem for the festival from all over the Diaspora, and the unpronounce-able list of names (vv. 9–11) may be taken from an astronomical catalogue indicating every part of the known world, indicating the worldwide mission of the Church.

Numbers 11:24–30

The scene of the coming of the spirit of God upon the elders of Israel is the immediate preparation for the coming of the Spirit of God upon the elders of the new people of God at Pentecost. In some contemporary re-tellings of the story, the spirit of God came down in the form of tongues of fire. Luke must

195

have modelled his narration to bring out the similarity. The cloud symbolizes the presence of God which enables the elders to prophesy. Peter's speech at Pentecost explains the significance of the event: the Spirit is poured out for all people.

Here it is obvious that prophecy is regarded in its primary sense, not simply as foretelling the future but as speaking the mind of God. The prophet is one who sees things as God sees them, and the message is often uncomfortable. Indeed, it is precisely because the message is uncomfortable that we need to hear it. We do not like to look God in the eye. This is the task of the leaders of the Church, to shake us out of our comfortable half-truths and the subterfuges by which we disguise to ourselves the real demands of our Christian vocation.

1 Corinthians 12:3b–13

There is no doubt that in the early Church there were manifestations of the Spirit rare in later Christendom. Have we lost our fervour, or become more dependent on human manifestations of authority, or simply different?

However, the independence and unpredictability of these gifts formed problems for Paul at Corinth, so that he stresses that such gifts have value only in so far as they contribute to building up the Church as a whole. So even the humdrum, unspectacular gifts like motherhood and care of the disabled (if these may be called unspectacular) are important, especially as they contribute to the whole Church. They may well be more important than spectacular manifestations like speaking in tongues. Each member of the Christian community has a part to play (the eye of the body is not the ear), and the gift of the Spirit to each has its own unique contribution to make. Just as the life-principle of any human being has diverse manifestations (seeing, smelling, digesting, growing, loving, lamenting), so the Spirit which is the life-principle of the Church needs for the health of the body to manifest itself in various ways.

John 20:19–23

The Gospel of John, which has no account of the ascension, shows Jesus breathing the Spirit on his disciples, seemingly on the very day of the resurrection—also in the upper room, as in the account in Acts, but on a different day. More important than the timing is the explanation that goes with it. As Jesus breathes the Spirit on his disciples he sends them out as his representatives, giving them his authority (vv. 22–23).

In Judaism there was a clear set of rules for envoys. The envoy has the same authority as his principal—even to appointing his own envoys—and deserves the same respect and obedience. An insult to the envoy is an insult to the principal. The envoy does his principal's task and then reports back to the principal. In John's Gospel, Jesus' relationship to his Father is described in just these terms. So when he sends his envoys 'as the Father has sent me' (v. 21), he is giving them his own divine authority. This is repeated in the second saying (v. 23); again in Judaism, the power to bind and to loose includes all authority, the extremes standing for everything in between. Such authority invested in the Church does not, of course, give individual ministers the right to be petty dictators.

(See also comment on the Second Sunday of Easter, Year A.)

John 7:37–39

The festival of Tabernacles was the festival of water, when Israel prayed for the autumn rains, bringing the water which would cleanse the country after the long, dry summer, restore life to the earth and bring fertility to the crops. In the arid country of Palestine, the rains are vital to life. The Bible teems with lyrical passages celebrating the refreshing, rejuvenating, healing properties of the rains. Each day of the festival, a vessel of water was brought from the single spring which bubbled up (and still does) to give Jerusalem its water supply. On the final day of the festival, Jesus invites all to find true life not in the transitory water but in himself. The life that he offers is eternal.

It is valuable that two different understandings of this text have enriched the Christian tradition: either Jesus is the source of the water of life, or the believer is the source of that water. Both are true, for Jesus is the ultimate source, but the believer too must be a source of life from whom the water of eternal life flows, refreshing and renewing. The Christian cannot hoard or hide away the gift of life.

HW

YEAR B

Ezekiel 37:1–14

Ezekiel's prophecies are graphic, sometimes even bizarre. He saw visions that defy and confound normal perception. So his message speaks for a God whose actions confound regular expectations, and whose grace remains alive when all reasonable prospects have perished. The compelling images of chapter 37 underline the promise of 36:27: God will indeed put his Spirit within Israel.

Dry bones speak of despair, disintegration and decay, the ruined community life and deflated hopes of Israel's exile. The ensuing scene is of new creation, as the nation's life is raised from the dust and suffused with life (cf. Genesis 2:7). The four winds make Israel purposeful and strong again (vv. 9–10). God summons the creative breath of the whole earth, to bring the nation home and restore her confidence in him (v. 14).

The vision has spoken to Jews and to Christians of the future resurrection of the dead. But at Pentecost it tells of God's enlivening wind, that can reshape and reanimate broken hopes, of the promise that the defeated shall rise in strength and the scattered be gathered in power. When we hear, 'Can these bones live?' we can sometimes only say, 'Lord, you know' (v. 3). The God of Pentecost can say, 'You shall live, and... you shall know' (v. 14).

Romans 8:22–27

Pentecost celebrates the Spirit, not because the Spirit takes our troubles away but because the Spirit enters a damaged world and hurting hearts, to share and bear the trouble with us.

Creation groans (v. 22) in frustration at its present misery and pain, in the creative longing (the word means 'birthpangs') to see the new life that God will give. Christians groan too (v. 23), possessing the Spirit as the first decisive instalment of God's life within us, yet—by the Spirit's very presence—made sharply aware of hopes not yet fulfilled. We are not fully redeemed; we are mortal, creatures of time and dust, and we long for the physical experience of Christ's resurrection that will seal and complete our place in God's family. Salvation comes in stages. We wait patiently for what we do not see (vv. 24–25).

In the meantime, our prayers are often halting and frail. The Spirit bridges the gap from our ignorance to the love and wisdom of God, not filling us with divine eloquence but taking up our frustration and our groaning (as in v. 22) into the mind and purpose of God. Pentecost is a festival of hope, a day of praise to God, by whose Spirit our longings shall be turned into life, and our weakness into worship.

John 15:26–27; 16:4b–15

Jesus calls the Holy Spirit 'the Paraclete' (v. 26). That means 'called alongside' —a person who supports another in crisis or difficulty. John 15:26 mentions briefly how the Spirit helps Christians; 16:5–15 explains this more fully.

- The Spirit is sent by Jesus from the Father. He has been called 'the presence of Jesus in the absence of Jesus'. The disciples grieve at the prospect of Jesus leaving them, but they will not be truly alone for long (16:5–7).

- The Spirit deals in truth. He will teach the Church. 'He will speak whatever he hears... he will take what is mine', and will help Christians to develop and apply faithfully the teaching of Jesus (16:12–15). This makes better sense of the text than to suppose that large and unknown realms of truth are reserved for future disclosure.
- He will witness about Jesus. This is the language of the law-court. Much of that witness will be acutely adversarial, leading the world to right understanding of moral and spiritual issues (vv. 8–11).

'You also are to testify' (15:27): the Church, living the life of Jesus and telling his story, is not working alone but can trust the Spirit's power, that our influence and example in the world will count for God.

JP

YEAR C

Genesis 11:1–9

This story touches on the question of how the Lord works in human affairs. Here we have a focus on collective social action, not on individual relationships with God. Language is one crucial factor in social and political life, uniting and dividing. With religion, race, geography and ancestry it plays a part in defining ethnicity, the definition of one group over and against others. Were these people beginning the path to the sins of Noah's day that ended in the judgment of the flood? God had promised not to do that again, so instead he preempts the need by frustrating their ambitions (v. 6).

Were they seeking to disobey the injunction to fill the earth—to stay in one place and avoid the challenge and task God had given them? Were they seeking security in national identity, in grandiose schemes and utopian visions? The message of the New Testament is that those who seek God and his righteousness belong together in a fellowship that is universal and bridges all divides of class, race, gender and ethnicity. Babel is redeemed at Pentecost, not by restoring a single language but through a miraculous affirmation of difference, which delights in variety while being united in faith.

Romans 8:14–17

This passage describes the relationship of the believer with God, both Father and Son, and the role of the Spirit in that relationship. Basically, when we respond to God we are led by his Spirit and we become his children.

We are children—sons, of course, were the heirs, the true and complete inheritors from fathers; so in a society which was, almost without exception, socially patriarchal, the word 'sons' carried more fully the meaning of our status than 'children'. We become children when we trust and repent—by adoption, so that we are chosen and given an inheritance we did not obtain by natural birth (John 1:12–13). We are then joint heirs with Christ to all the riches of the Triune God (v. 17).

We are free—we do not obey, nor are we filial, out of fear or compulsion. We are not slaves (v. 15). The relationship with the father is with the best kind of loving father—better than the best of human father/child relationships.

We live the life of loved children—the life of the Spirit—a holy life (v. 12–13), in filial prayer (v. 15b), reassured and affirmed by the Spirit (v. 16), as heirs sharing in Christ's suffering and in the end sharing his glory.

John 14:8–17 [25–27]

The disciples don't understand these final discourses, but the crucial point in verses 25–27 is that all will be revealed and brought to remembrance when the Holy Spirit comes. The disciples here are very much dependent on Jesus' practical and personally present leadership. In one sense, they do not *have* to understand at this point. We can see just how far the Holy Spirit will bring them, in understanding and in leadership of the Church, as we look back on the growth of the early Church and all that they taught and wrote.

So the message to Philip is that recalling all that Jesus said and did is enough to know the eternal Father. Theological interpretation and understanding is a work of the Holy Spirit, especially where it happens in the learning community of the Church. The world knows nothing of this kind of truth (v. 17). Later the disciples will be saying to each other, 'Of course, now I understand.'

What is Jesus promising in verse 12? Not constant miracle-working for his followers, nor the ability to achieve anything—stop the traffic, stop the tide. The crucial words 'in my name' and 'that the Son may bring glory to the Father' place parameters around our own limited understanding of what we and others need for our own good.

MK

TRINITY SUNDAY

YEAR A

Isaiah 40:12–17, 27–31

The conception of God which runs through the sayings of Isaiah of Jerusalem is determined by the opening vision in Isaiah 6. God is 'the Holy One of Israel'. There is a sense of awe and reverence, almost of fear, before God, and certainly an overwhelming sense of human unworthiness and inadequacy in the presence of God. The second part of Isaiah (chs. 40—55, including today's reading) goes further, reflecting the confrontation of Israel with the polytheistic deities of Babylon, and the consequent confident assertion of the overall power and majesty of Yahweh, creator of the world.

Trinity Sunday is the celebration of God as such, and this reading celebrates the mystery of God in creation, all three Persons being involved. Traditionally in the Wisdom Literature, God creates through divine wisdom, which is the figure of God at work in the world, somehow independent yet totally dependent on God, the 'untarnished mirror of God's active power' (Wisdom 7:26). In the New Testament, Christ is seen to be the power and the wisdom of God. Similarly in this reading, the Spirit of Yahweh features as involved in the act of creation, more closely linked to Yahweh than any external counsellor could be. In the creation, then, God may already be seen as Trinity.

2 Corinthians 13:11–13

The Trinity comes most clearly to view in Paul, in that he can never talk about the Son without talking about the Father, and never about either of them without talking about the Spirit, equally the Spirit of God and the Spirit of Christ. The later doctrine of the Trinity is but a response to the challenge of these multiple sayings which characterize the relationships in diverse ways. However, seldom does Paul speak so succinctly of Christ, God and the Spirit as in this conclusion of the second letter to the Corinthians.

There is no prying into the interior life of the Godhead, and here Paul is writing primarily about human sanctification, rather than delineating relationships within the divinity. There is a long way to go before Chalcedon. However, in this reading it is already clear that 'the God of love and peace' is the initiator of this sanctification, just as in creation God is the source of all. The power and responsibility belong to God. The 'grace' of the Lord Jesus Christ could more fully be translated the 'generosity' or 'favour', and he is the agent of the generous love through whom the redemption occurs. The Spirit is the bond of union and the agent of sanctification, binding human beings to God.

Matthew 28:16–20

By the time this passage came to be written, the trinitarian liturgical formula must have been in use for baptism. It must have developed very swiftly after the resurrection. But the Trinity is already present in this final scene of the Gospel by allusion, even without the trinitarian baptismal formula.

The disciples come to Jesus and do reverence to him as to a divine figure (though some hesitate, as in all the post-resurrection stories). Then Jesus issues his mission charge as the Son of Man and more. In the book of Daniel, a mysterious Son of Man comes to the Ancient of Days and receives from him all authority and power on earth (Daniel 7:13–14). The authority of the risen Christ outdoes this, for all authority in heaven has been given to him, as well as on earth. Also divine is the authority behind his commands: as Moses taught the commands of God on the mountain, so Jesus commands his disciples to keep not the commands of God, but his own commands, 'everything that I have commanded you' (v. 20); he teaches, therefore, with divine authority.

We cannot, admittedly, see the Spirit in this passage, but the roots of the Trinity are already there in the risen Christ acting in the power and authority of God.

HW

YEAR B

Isaiah 6:1–8

Earth and heaven fuse together in Isaiah's vision. In the temple, perhaps even during a service, he is overpowered with the immediacy of the One he worships. The presence of God so fills the temple that the air rustles with angels and the ground trembles. Hymns and incense seem to gather the worship of earth into the greater and purer praise of heaven (v. 4). God himself is scarcely described: only the outer edges of his glory can be told (cf. Exodus 33:18–23); yet even here is grandeur that humbles and awes the prophet. Who is he, to serve and speak for splendour and majesty such as this (v. 5)?

Then comes a purging fiery touch. Isaiah is pardoned, his impure and sullied speech burned clean by God (vv. 6–7). The angel voice sets him free, to offer for service, and to speak of God to others (v. 8).

Why read this text on Trinity Sunday? Because of the threefold 'holy' (v. 3)? Because God says 'us' (v. 8)? Surely also that here we see God in majesty, in mercy and in mission: the glory of heaven, the pardon of the gospel, and the sending of the Church are glimpsed in this vision of God, now known by Christians as Father, Son and Holy Spirit.

Romans 8:12–17

How we live—what we confront, and how we handle it—is a thoroughly practical matter. Some Christians reckon the doctrine of the Trinity remote and theoretical. Yet Paul connects them here: Christian experience is woven into the very nature of God.

- **We live under tension**—beckoned by the selfish, indulgent and stubborn side of human nature that Paul calls 'flesh'; and invited by God's Spirit to live so that 'fleshly' habits and traits may wither. Two pressures, two paths, two very different prospects (vv. 12–13).
- **We belong to a family.** Those whom the Spirit leads are God's children (v. 14); the life he shapes within us comes from God. The Spirit does not bind and crush our freedom, but releases us into the security and care of close and strong relationship. We call God 'Father' (vv. 15–16).
- **We follow a pattern.** Knowing God as 'Father', we enter the relationship he shares with Jesus. Jesus was the prototype of all Christian experience. Suffering and struggle, hope and glory, present tension and final triumph, are patterned in his cross and resurrection (v. 17).

Led by the Spirit, in the love of Father and the life of the Son—we encounter God, the Holy Trinity, in our daily life.

John 3:1–17

Perhaps aptly for Trinity Sunday, this passage is laden with mystery and potential misunderstanding. A mature man must be born all over again (vv. 4–6). The Spirit comes like wind, invisible until he has passed by, then untraceable as he travels on (v. 8). Heavenly things will be revealed, and the learning of earth cannot take them in (v. 10). What purpose is here?

- **A purpose of love** (v. 16), as God sends his Son to save the world (v. 17).
- **A purpose that reaches far back into time**, as the promises of Ezekiel 36 and 37, 'water and Spirit… life-giving wind', are activated afresh (vv. 5, 8).
- **A purpose that connects heaven and earth**, as Jesus brings the life and wisdom of the world above (v. 13).

- **A purpose that stoops low,** for the 'lifting up of the Son of Man' (v. 14) is the degradation of the cross; here is healing for a world wounded by the ancient serpent (cf. Numbers 21:9; Genesis 3). Here is wisdom that the world cannot grasp (1 Corinthians 1:18–24).

In the sending of the Son to die (vv. 14–17), in the breath of the Spirit of life (vv. 6–8), God's Kingdom comes (vv. 3, 5). The 'night' of the world (v. 2) is drawn into the light of God (vv. 19–21). In the loving purpose of Father, Son and Spirit is eternal life (v. 16).

JP

YEAR C

Proverbs 8:1–4, 22–31

This chapter on wisdom has sometimes been seen as an implicit reference to the Trinity. However, the passage arises more probably from the Hebrew tendency to avoid theoretical language for ideas, seeking instead practical ways of expressing abstract concepts. Wisdom in the Old Testament sometimes refers simply to human knowledge and skill, but more often refers to the rational perfect understanding of God. Those who seek to serve him need to pray for such wisdom, although acquiring it will take a lifetime.

Discernment, understanding, righteousness, truth and discretion are included. Verses 1–4 point out that everyone can hear because wisdom is not hidden in holy places but is available in the highways, beside the city gates. It is part of God's common grace to all and is exercised in part by those who do not know him. However, the invitation is to fear the Lord, which is the beginning of wisdom (Psalm 111:10, Micah 6:9) and is more precious than rubies. The personification of verses 22–31 should not be pushed too far (cf. Proverbs 3:19–20). But there are echoes of these verses in the first chapter of John's Gospel and in Colossians 1:15–17; 2:3. Verses 32–36 should not be omitted. There are those who turn their backs on wisdom and the wisdom-giver.

Romans 5:1–5

Paul outlines the blessings enjoyed by him and all others who have been justified by faith. They invite thoughtful meditation on the implications of these blessings for our daily walk with God.

- We have peace with God (v. 1).
- We have gained access to him, and 'stand' in grace (v. 2).

- We rejoice in the hope of glory (v. 2).
- We rejoice in our sufferings, which are ours because we are his. (The word for 'suffering' in verse 3 is the same one that Jesus uses in John 16:33 ['persecution'] and probably means not so much the trials of life that come to all, but more specifically the tribulation of opposition and persecution.)
- We are not disappointed (v. 5).
- We have his love poured into our hearts (v. 5).
- We have been given the Holy Spirit (v. 5).

Love, joy, peace, faith, hope, love—in this short passage we are promised these gifts of the Holy Spirit, whatever happens to us. Perseverance and character (the maturity of someone who has been tested and has passed the test) contain the fruit of the Spirit that is listed in Galatians 5:22–23: patience, self-control and faithfulness, as well as kindness, goodness and gentleness.

John 16:12–15

Jesus, the man, briefly sums up the eternal relationship of the Father and Son—'all that belongs to the Father is mine'. Familiarity takes away the astounding and shocking nature of these words, written by monotheists who knew Jesus as a real human being and yet recorded these amazing claims. Two important points arise.
- The Trinity—much has been written on the crucial importance of the Trinity in exploring the nature of the love of God. If the oneness of God is over-emphasized, then God's love cannot be expressed unless he creates something to love. However, if God is characterized as self-giving, interactive, interpersonal love in his very nature, then we have a way to understand humans as primarily relational and communal, in the image of God. Interactive, self-giving love is part of the oneness of God, Father, Son and Holy Spirit.
- There can be no other definition of God. This interactive, loving, Trinitarian God cannot also be described in other contradictory ways. There is no way we can accept other gods, or other definitions, 'co-existing' alongside the one true living God. Jesus Christ is the exact imprint of God's being (Hebrews 1:3, Colossians 1:15), the one and only, unique revelation of God who is love.

MK

DAY OF THANKSGIVING FOR HOLY COMMUNION

(CORPUS CHRISTI)

EUCHARIST

Genesis 14:18–20

This whole chapter of Genesis is mysterious and difficult both to date and to elucidate. Most difficult of all is Melchizedek, king of Salem. Traditionally he is regarded as a priest-king of Jerusalem. Abraham seems to acknowledge his superiority both because he accepts the blessing of Melchizedek and because he offers him tithes. So the letter to the Hebrews expounds Christ's priesthood in terms of Melchizedek's, showing that it is superior to any priesthood sprung from Abraham's and Aaron's line. Nor is any ancestry of Melchizedek mentioned; he simply appears from nowhere. Since it was a principle of Jewish exegesis at the time that what is not mentioned may be presumed not to exist, the letter also argues that the lack of mention of any ancestry of Melchizedek makes his priesthood, like Christ's, an eternal priesthood.

The celebration of the eucharist must also be a celebration of the priesthood which gives rise to it. This reading is chosen because it includes both elements. Christian tradition has always seen Melchizedek's offering of bread and wine to be a preparation for the bread and wine offered as the eucharistic gifts.

1 Corinthians 11:23–26

What is meant by the final sentence, 'proclaiming the Lord's death until he comes'? This is clearly, in Paul's mind, the central aspect of the eucharistic celebration. Failure to act worthily at the eucharist (as some of the Corinthians were in fact failing) incurs the terrible penalty of being answerable for the body and blood of the Lord. The point of the eucharist is that in some way (and Christian theologies differ about the details and the philosophical explanation), Christ's sacrifice is made effectively present again at the eucharist. The sacrifice of Calvary cannot be repeated, having occurred once and for all. So one tradition expresses it that in the eucharist Christ 'pleads his sacrifice'.

The eschatological value of the eucharist is also an important aspect:

'until he comes'. The early Christian expectation of a swift return of Christ to gather his elect is no longer so vivid in contemporary Christianity today. The apocalyptic scenario of the Lord coming on the clouds of heaven to lead a triumphal procession is seen by many scholars as imagery which requires understanding and deconstruction. Nevertheless, the hope of Christians to be fully united with the Lord remains the all-important goal, ever-present and ever to be commemorated.

(See Maundy Thursday for further comment on this passage.)

John 6:51–58

The great discourse on the bread of life is a commentary on the scriptural verse, 'He gave them bread from heaven to eat', to show that the verse is perfectly fulfilled not by the manna which Moses gave, but by the bread which the heavenly Father gives. This final section comments principally on the final words, 'to eat'.

It is one of the main themes of the Gospel of John that Jesus is the source of life, a life which is eternal. 'Living bread', like 'living water', would be expressed in Hebrew (which has few adjectives) as 'bread of life', and 'water of life'. This can also be understood, 'bread (or water) which provides or nourishes life'. Paul tells us that in his resurrection Christ became 'a life-giving spirit'. The reading gives some outline of what this life is. It is a life which is in Christ: whoever eats this bread lives in Christ, and Christ in that person (v. 56). It is a life drawn from the Father and from Christ. Whoever eats this bread and has this life will be raised up on the last day (v. 54). By eating the eucharistic bread, the believer receives Christ and in receiving Christ draws from him the eternal life which is union with and dwelling in God.

HW

PROPER FOUR

YEAR A

Genesis 6:9–22; 7:24; 8:14–19 (Continuous)

See the Second Reading at the Easter Vigil or the Old Testament reading for the Fourth Sunday in Eastertide for comment on this passage.

Deuteronomy 11:18–21, 26–28 (Related)

In Orthodox Judaism, these words are understood literally, so that the central text of Deuteronomy, 'Hear, O Israel...' (Deuteronomy 6:4–9), written very small, is worn on the hands and the forehead and is fixed in a little box to the doorposts. Although this may not be the original intention of the instructions, it functions as a pressing and ever-present reminder of the Law, prominent in prayer and in every Jewish household. It is also an act of love and devotion, for the Law is God's gift of himself to his people, to which they respond in love and gratitude. Through the Law, God reveals himself and his nature. By revealing how his people are to behave, God shows his own nature, just as the rules laid down for a family reveal the nature of that family and its legislator. It reveals also how Israel may keep close to God and be his special people. So obedience to God's Law is no chore, but is rather a pleasure and a delight. The observance and the clinging to God is in itself a blessing, just as failure to observe and so turning one's back on God is in itself a curse.

Romans 1:16–17; 3:22b–28 [29–31]

This first of several readings from Romans over successive Sundays gives us the two key passages at the beginning of the letter. The letter is all about the 'justice' of God. This is a peculiar sort of justice, unlike justice in the normal sense of the term. Normally 'justice' means getting our rights or our due punishment in accordance with law. But God's justice is not like that. It is rather in accordance with God's own nature as revealed in his promises. God's 'justice' can be paired with his 'salvation' or with his 'forgiveness'— 'in your justice put my sins behind your back', an odd appeal to any human judge. By his 'justice' God is true to the promises of protection which he made to Abraham, and to his revelation of himself in Sinai as a God of forgiveness and mercy. Faith, like the faith of Abraham, consists simply in hanging on to this, trusting in this forgiveness and mercy, in the knowledge that any human claim or power is futile for salvation.

The act by which salvation is won for human beings is Jesus' sacrifice for reconciliation. He is the sacrifice of which the animal-sacrifice on the Day of Atonement is the foreshadowing.

Matthew 7:21–29

The Sermon on the Mount concludes with two contrasting images, the house built on rock or on sand, the last in a series of pairs of images, the narrow gate and the broad road, the sound tree and the rotten tree being the most recent.

Before that, we return to the real nub of the contrast, those who say to Jesus, 'Lord, Lord!' and those who actually do the will of the Father. Doing the will of the Father is what the whole Sermon is about. The prayer 'Thy will be done' forms the very centre of the Sermon, the centre of the Lord's Prayer which is the centre of the Sermon. It is to be echoed in practice by Jesus at that most difficult of turning-points, the agony in the garden, when he prays, 'Thy will, not mine, be done'. Matthew's morality is not merely good and ethical behaviour; it is Christocentric, joining Christ in seeking the will of his Father.

The other limb of the contrast, saying 'Lord, Lord!', is made all the more alarming because 'those who call on the name of the Lord' is in the Acts of the Apostles the very definition of a Christian. This is not enough.

HW

YEAR B

1 Samuel 3:1–10 [11–20] (Continuous)

While many Old Testament prophets tell of being called, the emphasis on youth is rarely as pronounced as this (cf. Jeremiah 1:4–8). This was a new experience for Samuel, part of his maturing knowledge of God (v. 7)—though scarcely part of any programmed education in faith. Children will sometimes show profound religious insight, and occasionally sense the beckoning of a life's vocation. Adults should listen, learn and support, but we may not set the pace for their acquaintance with God. Only God can do that.

Yet this was Samuel's summons to lifelong work, the inauguration of a major prophetic ministry. The word of the Lord had been rare (v. 1), and through Samuel it became recognized and regular (vv. 19–20). Once again Israel would be open to God.

The story confirms the coming change of religious leadership. Eli is exhausted, and can barely discern true signs of renewal (1:13–17; 3:8). He has remonstrated helplessly against his sons' corruption and greed (2:22–25), and warning has already come of judgment ahead (2:27–36). Now the relationship of master and apprentice is inverted. Samuel hears the word (3:11–14), and Eli can only listen (vv. 16–18). Credit, then, that Eli nurtures and acknowledges the ministry which will replace and eclipse his own.

Deuteronomy 5:12–15 (Related)

The Ten Commandments are claims of love, laid by God on the people he brought out of Egypt (v. 6). The sabbath command is the longest of these ten. Several aspects claim our attention as Christians:

- Sabbath was a holy day, claimed and devoted for God (v. 12). God is Lord of all time; his people deliberately acknowledge that lordship every seventh day.
- Sabbath was a day of rest (vv. 13–14). Work is good; it is right to seek useful work and do it well. But work should not claim all our days. If we choose to work seven days a week, is this healthy, and is that work becoming an idol?
- Sabbath was a day for letting neighbours, and even animals, rest (vv. 14). What demands does our lifestyle place on other people?
- Sabbath was a day of thanksgiving for redemption, a day for remembering the exodus, which had made Israel a nation (v. 15). Similarly, the Christian Sunday recalls the resurrection of Jesus, the great act of salvation that inaugurated our faith.

The details of how all this applies today are matters on which many individual Christians make up their own minds amid some complex social pressures. All the more reason for thoughtful preaching on the issue.

2 Corinthians 4:5–12

Paul describes working for Christ in three paradoxical ways.

- **The power of God.** Resources are given from outside. Christ's authority makes Paul a servant (v. 5). God's light shines through him, as borrowed light (v. 6). Paul may be recalling the bright light of his conversion (Acts 22:6). He surely refers also to the first light of creation (Genesis 1:3). For Christian life is indeed a new creation, a coming into a new world (2 Corinthians 5:17). When the light of the gospel shines in fragile lives, the mismatch of content and container shows that the real vitality is from God (v. 7).
- **The pressures of experience.** Paul has sustained rough and painful knocks, but has never been utterly broken (vv. 8–9). God's strength within has enabled him to withstand the hurts and press on.
- **The picture of resurrection.** The stresses are like a constant bearing of the cross. Yet the cross is a thing of life. It leads to resurrection. A strange chemistry has been at work in Paul's sufferings, and the people he serves have discovered that Jesus is alive (vv. 10–12).

For Paul, the pattern of Christ's cross has been infectious: his experiences have been costly and hurtful for him, but life-giving for others. This is often how serious Christian work is done.

Mark 2:23—3:6

Two short paragraphs, two clashes, over one issue: what is allowed on the sabbath? Both grain-plucking and healing were reckoned as work. What right had Jesus and his friends to carry on like this?

A detailed legal answer might have been possible, setting the restriction of Exodus 34:21 within the context of Deuteronomy 23:25. But Jesus raises broader issues.

His first response (2:25–26) recalls 1 Samuel 21:1–9. As God's anointed king fleeing for his life, David had pressing needs, which overrode certain ceremonial sensitivities. Jesus, Israel's new Messiah, also has a vital mission and task. He and his men should not be hindered as they go about it. Religious laws should serve his mission, not vice versa.

In the second incident, the focus is on mercy (3:2–5). Why postpone a man's release from his disability? But there is an irony in the telling. The men who oppose sabbath mercy are themselves capable of sabbath malice (3:6). 'Is it lawful… to save life or to kill?' (v. 4).

The whole message is encapsulated in 2:27–28. The sabbath was created for the sake of humanity, not vice versa. So Jesus, himself God's true humanity, interprets its demands and claims. Whatever serves his cause hallows the sabbath.

JP

YEAR C

1 Kings 18:20–21 [22–29] 30–39 (Continuous)

The narrative books of the Old Testament need careful handling. They are history, but history used for the purposes of teaching the way of God. Elijah is a powerful figure, whose return, prophesied by Malachi (4:5–6), is re-called when John the Baptist comes (Matthew 17:11–13). He challenges kings (and queens) as John will do, putting his life at risk.

The story of Elijah and the prophets of Baal is very powerful. Its dark pagan aspects seem very far from the world of the twenty-first century. But Elijah is challenging the forces that are opposed to the truth of God. In today's world there are those in the establishment of government, media and even religion who oppose his truth. This is especially so in the exercise of lawless power by ruling élites (1 Kings 21). He is challenging the rulers, but the people also waver and say nothing (v. 21); they have already committed themselves by joining in the worship of Baal.

How far is the Church willing and able to challenge the anti-Christian forces in society? When toleration and acceptance of all sorts of lifestyles is a virtue, what role is there for an Elijah, uncompromising and belligerent in his defence of the truth? Is he 'a man just like us'? (James 5:17).

1 Kings 8:22–23, 41–43 (Related)

'Solomon in all his glory...' The magnificent temple is complete. Solomon is secure as king and under him the kingdom will reach its farthest extent (4:20–21). He stands before the leaders of the people in front of the altar and prays. Yet the seeds of his falling away are already there. He has already secured his throne in ways that are not quite honourable. He is still sacrificing in the high places (3:3), his alliances have brought him foreign pagan wives (3:1), he lives in great splendour (4:22), his gifts are exceptional (4:29–34), all of which are sowing the seeds of pride, self-assurance and apostasy. By chapter 11 the Lord has withdrawn his favour.

In his prayer, Solomon expresses a sophisticated theology—God does not dwell in the temple. He is far too almighty and beyond human containing for that. He hears the prayers of his people from heaven which they address 'towards' the temple (v. 30). Solomon starts by reminding God that he keeps his promises to those who 'continue wholeheartedly in your way' (v. 23). The reader knows that the king is already compromised.

Verses 41–43 echo the powerful Old Testament theme that Israel is there to show God to the nations and to attract outsiders to worship him.

Galatians 1:1–12

The meaning of this letter is not immediately apparent, nor are its implications for today straightforward. Paul writes passionately about his own authority to proclaim the true gospel over against others who want to change it, about the social implications of justification by faith, and about the relationship between Judaism and Christianity.

Immediately in the first verses of greeting, he asserts that he is an apostle, in the limited sense of those who were commissioned directly by Christ and were also witnesses of his resurrection. He was not a 'deputy' apostle sent by the original leaders of the Judean church (v. 16–17). His preaching therefore has authority and others cannot add to it. He moves straight into a strong rebuke (v. 6) and gives solemn warning that tampering with the gospel will have awful consequences (v. 9). The gospel is outlined in verses 3–4: Jesus Christ's death on the cross makes possible our rescue from sin, giving us the Father's grace and peace. There is no other way of salvation.

The implication of verses 10–12 is that this good news is a direct revelation from God, and Paul is aware of the temptation to adapt or reconstruct it in order to make it more palatable to others.

Luke 7:1–10

The readings from Luke over the next eight Sundays provide a number of snapshots of Jesus' words and acts. They give examples of the themes of Luke's Gospel: firstly that the gospel is for everyone; anyone can be saved— Gentiles, women, the poor, outcasts, as well as privileged leaders. Second, Jesus is the Saviour of the world, and the Healer, the Greek word for 'save' also meaning 'heal'.

This story focuses on the centurion, a Gentile soldier in the service of Herod. Despite the loading of resentment against him in a Jewish society, he has become respected and accepted. He has made the effort to understand the culture and the faith to the extent that he has built a synagogue (v. 5), and the Jewish elders are willing to take his message to the Lord. Moreover, he trusts Jesus' power and authority to heal.

He is a man of sensitivity, humility and compassion. Whether the man who is ill is a servant or actually a slave, he is going to some lengths to find healing. Nor does he expect Jesus to come at his beck and call; maybe he is sensitive to the defilement involved in entering a Gentile house and in coming too close to a dead body. Jesus reacts with surprise at the faith of this man (v. 9).

MK

PROPER 5

YEAR A

Genesis 12:1–9 (Continuous)

The call of Abraham is one of the turning-points of history, the beginning of the history of revelation and salvation. It is particularly suitable that it should be paired with the reading from the letter to the Romans which takes the promises there made to Abraham as its vital backing.

It is a stark and daunting story. Abraham is called by a powerful Some-one, who promises him total protection and championship. This is the first appearance of the God of Abraham in human history, and Abraham knows nothing about this God except what he hears there: 'I will bless you, and make your name great, so that you will be a blessing' (v. 2). Abraham

seems to have come from a situation where the moon was the chief god-
dess. But, trusting only in the promise from this unknown God, Abraham
forsakes his comfortable homeland and household to become one of a
thousand faceless nomads wandering the deserts on the edge of civilization
in search of a new land promised to him. He is old and lacks family to
support him in his old age. He has no experience of the reliability or
trustworthiness of this God who calls him. Such is the unbounded extent
of his faith and trust.

Hosea 5:15—6:6 (Related)

The Hebrew concept of love has a tenacity all its own. Love is stronger than
death. It is more absolute. It never yields. On Sinai, God declares to Moses
that his name means tenderness and compassion, faithful love and forgiveness, generation after generation. God's love and fidelity, echoes Hosea, are
as certain as the dawn, as gentle and as healing as the spring rain (v. 3). So
love as evanescent as the morning mist, which disappears into nothing at
the first warming rays of the sun, is no love at all (v. 4). The prophet Hosea
was seared by the infidelity of his wife, by her constant flirtations and
desertions. His own love was constant, steady and unyielding; he would
never give up. The inspiration he received was that his love mirrored that of
God for his wavering, faithless people. He proclaimed his message at a time
when Israel was masking its infidelity by sacrifices which were no expression
of real devotion or commitment. They were mere ritual, backed only by a
materialistic preoccupation with wealth and luxury achieved by injustice
and contempt for the needy. Hosea's demand for love rather than sacrifice
prepares for Jesus' similar demand in the gospel.

Romans 4:13–25

In Galatians and Romans, Paul is arguing that Jewish observances are
useless. The hope of Judaism is founded on the promises of God to
Abraham, not on the legal observances which came with the Law. Judaism
is still vitally important to Paul, but Paul in effect redefines what Judaism
consists in. The circumcision group was maintaining that true Jews, the real
heirs of Abra-ham, are defined as those who obey the Law. Paul replies that
the Law did not exist in Abraham's time, and that his heirs are only those
who follow him in faith. The promise is a free gift, not earned, and the only
attitude to it is pure and unconditional trust that God will fulfil his
promises. This trusting faith is the attitude which characterizes our deepest
human relationships, a rich relationship to spouse or parents or family

members, a calm trust and confidence which nothing will shake. Only God is more trustworthy than any human being.

Our faith, however, is different from Abraham's, since we know—beyond Abraham—that God's promise included raising Jesus from the dead. So that is part of the object of our faith.

Matthew 9:9–13, 18–26

The two incidents of this passage in the Gospel have little in common; it is best to discuss them separately. The first shows Jesus' attitude to the Jewish Law. While not so extreme as Paul, who sees no advantage at all in observing the Law now that Jesus has fully accomplished it by his sacrifice on the cross, Jesus was constantly upsetting the conventions by insisting that the Law was only a means, and that observance of the Law was not an end in itself. As long as there was a desire for God, as long as there was love, he would respond to that yearning, knowing that most human beings are sick and imperfect. The doctor needs only the merest breath of life to give limitless care to a patient.

The second story, or rather pair of stories interwoven, shows Jesus' response to those who put their trust in him. Both cases are irremediable: the ruler's daughter is already dead (Mark calls him 'Jairus', makes him a synagogue-president, and leaves the daughter merely 'terminally ill' when he comes to Jesus) and the woman's complaint is described as incurable, but they put absolute trust in Jesus' power and will to heal.

HW

YEAR B

1 Samuel 8:4–11 [12–15] 16–20 [11:14–15] (Continuous)

Questions of power, of how it is assigned and how it is wielded, have no very tidy solutions, even in a community of faith. Anarchy is generally chaotic (Judges 17:6; 21:25). The powerful personality of a prophetic ruler can do great things—while he remains active (1 Samuel 7:15—8:1). Hereditary leadership is readily identified, but not always worthily exercised (8:1–3). So Israel wishes to be 'like other nations' (8:5, 20).

Yet they are supposed to be a nation apart (Exodus 19:4–6; Deuteronomy 7:6–8). This perverse itch to conform constitutes a rejection of the Lord (8:7). Quite apart from that, royal leadership brings its own problems. 'Monarchy... lives by... confiscation and concentration' (W. Brueggemann). The king's standing army (vv. 11–12) and lavish lifestyle (v. 13), his courtiers and friends (vv. 14–15), and his own sheer greed (vv. 16–17), will place a major burden on economic and social life. The royal tithe will parody what belongs to God (vv. 15, 17; cf. Deuteronomy 14:22); royal demands will be irresistible, even to prayer (v. 18). If the people choose, they must live with their choice.

God's voice, coming through Samuel, seems ambiguous. God resents this ambition; yet he can live with it and will even guide the choice of a king. His love for Israel does not depend entirely on hers for him.

Genesis 3:8–15 (Related)

There are several possible responses to being found out. One is hiding (v. 8). Sin regularly makes us want to avoid God. We feel exposed; our innocence has gone. Another common reaction is to blame someone else (v. 12): 'You gave me the woman, she gave me the fruit. I was only the last in a long chain of causation, which leads well away from me—in fact, right back to God.' A third, slightly more honest, is to acknowledge our own susceptibility to deception (v. 13). We are easily conned, taken in by the superficial, sensual and sophisticated, not pausing often enough to think about boundaries and warnings.

Excuses are transparent. God knows where we hide, and is merciful enough to seek us out (v. 9). Blame is not very convincing: there is still 'I ate it' to explain away; we weaken our human relationships if we never accept responsibility for our actions. Our moral frailty is reason for permanent vigilance: we can always be tripped up; simply to recognize this offers some protection. But bigger steps towards recovering the situation can only be taken in the company of Jesus (Mark 3:35). Of course, he too caused people to reach for excuses, and for reasons not to listen (Mark 3:22).

2 Corinthians 4:13—5:1

This passage is about resurrection. Paul has already written (vv. 10–12) about resurrection spreading outwards from him. From his own experience of suffering, he was able to share the life of Jesus with other people (v. 15).

Resurrection was also happening inside him, every day. Battered on the outside, he was sustained and renewed by the life of God within (vv. 16–18). This short paragraph contains three important contrasts:
- **Outer and inner** (v. 16): bodily weakness and spiritual renewal can often go together.
- **Temporary and permanent** (v. 17): the glories of heaven endure; the griefs of earth end.
- **Visible and invisible** (v. 18): there are important realities that the eye cannot see (Hebrews 11:27).

Resurrection was waiting ahead of him. When the process of outward decay finally ran its course, Paul's 'earthly tent' would be 'dismantled'—as must happen to us all. Then this fragile human body will not simply be abandoned, but will be replaced by 'a house not made with hands, eternal in the heavens' (5:1). Death will look like a victory for outward decay. In fact it will complete the process of inner renewal. The new life God gives will be solid and enduring, physical as well as spiritual, a time when friends will be gathered in the nearer presence of Jesus (4:14).

Mark 3:20–35

Two stories interlink—an enquiry from Jesus' family (vv. 20–21, 31–35), and a clash with scribes (vv. 22–30). They illuminate each other and raise sharp questions.

- **Is Jesus mad, or possessed?** (vv. 21–22). How does he tackle the forces of evil? Has he made a pact with the devil? He is not mad. His power to tackle evil in other people's lives comes because he has faced and overcome it himself (vv. 23, 27; cf. 1:13).
- **How does Jesus build community?** By blood relationship alone, or has he another way? What happens when people respond adversely? He invites people to gather around his teaching and mission, and tells them of God's will. Those who obey become his new family (vv. 33–35). Lifestyle shapes community, sometimes more strongly than blood ties.

Unity too is important: a divided house will surely collapse (vv. 24–26). So Israel's division against her Messiah is ominous and potentially catastrophic. If people recognize the work of God's Holy Spirit in Jesus, but refuse to acknowledge it, they set themselves decisively against God. There is no way home from this sort of position, other than retreat (vv. 28–30).

Sensitive Christians may be greatly troubled by 3:29. But eternal sin only shows itself if we persist. Sin that ends in repentance is not eternal.

JP

YEAR C

1 Kings 17:8–16 [17–24] (Continuous)

Elijah bursts upon the scene with no introduction in 17:1. The sorry tale of idolatrous kings is interrupted by his sudden appearance face to face with Ahab, the worst of the lot, announcing the drought. Elijah then flees to be especially cared for in ways that again reaffirm the supremacy of Israel's God.

The big events, the political stage, the annals of history would not include this one man, camped out by a desert brook, but Elijah knows that the Creator of the universe is working through him and not through the dissolute kings of Israel.

As the drought takes hold, God tells Elijah to move on (v. 9), but not just anywhere. He goes to the heartland of Baal, to Sidon, the homeland of Jezebel (16:31). Here he finds a woman who acknowledges the living God, whose heart has already been prepared (v. 9), but who is also struggling with famine and drought. Elijah asks her to take a great step of faith, to trust that the food will be there, and even to feed him ahead of her own son (v. 13). Elijah is encouraged, not just by the miracle for this insignificant foreign household, but by her faith.

1 Kings 17:17–24 (Related)

Elijah has been staying with the widow of Sidon, where he and her family have been eating miraculously in the midst of drought (v. 16). This is what the Lord had said would happen. Many people would sympathize with the sense of shock they felt when her son died. Such an event cuts into our confidence in the loving care of God. Both the widow and Elijah see God as being responsible for the situation (vv. 18, 20). She, fatalistically, sees the death as punishment for sin, suggesting that Elijah is the mediator of this, but Elijah does not accept the finality of it, and turns to prayer (v. 20). Will God answer him? He does, and one Sidonian woman is brought to faith in God (v. 24), In addition, one lonely and courageous prophet is affirmed and encouraged before moving on to greater and more dangerous challenges.

This incident is the culmination of the building up and strengthening of Elijah for the contest with the prophets of Baal (Proper 4). It is worth tracing the progression through this chapter, from Elijah's passive acceptance of God's miraculous nurture (v. 6) to his powerful prayer, claiming God's intervention (v. 21).

Galatians 1:11–24

Paul's account of his zealous attempts to stamp out the early Christian fellowships occurs several times. He mentions it here to establish his credentials as an apostle to whom Christ has been revealed, set apart and called by God and not commissioned by nor subordinate to anyone. He intervenes in an argument between Jewish Christians, some of whom want to ensure that Gentiles 'become Jews' before they become Christians. He may be implying that preoccupation with Jewish law-keeping, rather than living in the grace of God, can lead to this kind of fanaticism. He turned from Judaism to Christ, as they seem to be turning from Christ back to Judaism (although, of course, he never ceased to think and speak of himself as a Jew.) He points out (2:9) that the leaders of the Judean church are behind him.

Paul's conversion and calling to preach to the Gentiles are in many ways unique, but as Christians we should be able to look back and recall our own story of being called by God 'from birth' (v. 15). We too may have had a time of rebellion and open opposition to Christianity and the Church, and we too may have been encouraged and supported by other Christians. Sometimes it is important to tell these stories.

Luke 7:11–17

From an example of privilege (Proper 4), we turn to an example of poverty. Widows were particularly vulnerable, especially with no sons to support them. From the Saviour who can heal, we turn to the Saviour who conquers death. Jesus raised the dead on three recorded occasions—Lazarus in John's Gospel, Jairus' daughter in Mark and Luke and the widow's son here.

The scene has a dramatic power. Jesus, his disciples and a large crowd are funnelling into the town gate, meeting another crowd, the widow and the stretcher carrying her dead son, coming out (v. 12). Jesus reacts to her grief and perhaps also to the wider implications of her social position. He acts in two ways. He speaks to her in an ordinary human way, and then goes up to the dead body and touches it (v. 14). The strong taboos, the ritual defilement that this involved, make this a heart-stopping and dramatic moment for that crowd. No wonder they stood still.

But the context for this passage shows that on its own such a miracle is not enough. The awed reaction of the crowd—perhaps remembering Elijah's raising of a widow's son from the dead—and the exciting news that spreads like wildfire are temporary, and even those with a stronger sense that God is fulfilling his plans have doubts (v. 18–19).

MK

PROPER 6

YEAR A

Genesis 18:1–15 [21:1–7] (Continuous)

The visitors shimmer between three and one throughout the story. When it is single (and Abraham always uses the singular form of address), this One is obviously God, which has inevitably led the Fathers of the Church to see in this story a sort of premonition of the Trinity. It is a story of delightful oriental courtesy and hospitality, offered with elaborate formality. Abraham receives his reward for this hospitality in the form of a son, the fulfilment of the promise made to him by God.

Several details of the story revolve round the name Isaac, which is etymologically related to the verb 'smile', 'play' or 'laugh'. In the literature of the time, such names normally include the name of God ('El') and so constitute a sort of blessing, so originally the full name would have been 'Yitzhaq-El' which means 'May God smile [on him]'. Later, however, the divine name fell away, and various details were attached to different people: in this story, Sarah laughs in doubt (and is ashamed and afraid before her visitor) (v. 12). In the previous chapter, Abraham laughs at God's promise that he will have a child (17:17). At the naming of Isaac after his birth, two etymologies with 'laugh' are given, and finally Ishmael 'plays' with Isaac (20:9).

Exodus 19:2–8a (Related)

God leads Moses and his group of escaped slaves into the awesome desert of Sinai. There the utterly arid terrain, waterless sand and massive, towering rocks, devoid of any trace of earth or vegetation, themselves speak of the majesty of God. Here God would form a people for himself, would give them an experience of himself, described in terms of earthquake, thunder and lightning, which would knit them to himself for all time. They were to be a holy people, that is, set apart and sharing in the holiness of God himself. The Law would show them what that holiness required, for they must behave in a special way if they were to be a people set apart to be God's personal possession. 'Be holy as I am holy' is the constant refrain of the Law. They must treat one another, and especially the stranger and unfortunate among them, as God treated them. They were to be a unique people, without any earthly king, for God would be their King. This was a covenant voluntarily entered into, offered by God and accepted with free choice by the elders and the people, who, at the end of the reading of the Law, bound themselves by oath to obey it.

Romans 5:1–8

It is not easy to understand the message of the letter to the Romans when one receives only a few verses progressively each Sunday, as we are doing currently. Last Sunday's passage was devoted to Abraham as an example of faith, and this Sunday's returns behind that to link up with the passage of the previous Sunday about Christ's death. Here Paul dwells on the amazing fact that Christ was prepared to die even for sinners still in their sins. He explains the effectiveness of Christ's death on two levels. On one level he uses the sacrificial language of the Old Testament, explaining Christ's death in terms of the sacrifice of reconciliation on the great annual Day of Atonement (3:25), his blood fulfilling what the victim's blood could never accomplish. On another level (5:12–20) he sees Christ's sacrifice in terms of obedience: his obedience to the Father undoes the disobedience of Adam. As Adam led the human race into the way of sin, so Christ leads renewed humanity into the way of obedience, enabling us to become adopted sons of God.

Trusting purely in Christ's fulfilment of God's demands, Christian hope opens the way for the love of God to be poured out by the Holy Spirit, and so inspires to the hard task of perseverance.

Matthew 9:35—10:8 [9–23]

Jesus' pity for the crowds, like sheep without a shepherd, is a hint that he is the Shepherd of Israel. In the Old Testament, God was known as the Shepherd of Israel, so to give this title to Jesus is an indication of his divinity. Following this, in Matthew's Gospel it is clear that the Twelve are chosen as the twelve foundation-stones of the new Israel. Their mission is confined to Israel and they are not to go into Gentile territory. Matthew is the most Jewish of the Gospels, written for a community of Christians drawn from Judaism, and still observing the Jewish good works and the Jewish Law—but in a new way, the way of Christ, according to the principle, 'What I want is love, not sacrifice'.

The Gospel of Mark also makes it clear that Jesus' own mission had little to do with Gentiles. He meets Gentiles only on one or two occasions (the Syro-Phoenician woman whose daughter he cures, and possibly the Gerasene demoniac). But it is significant that the first human being to confess Jesus as 'Son of God' is the Gentile centurion at the crucifixion: the death and resurrection of Jesus is the start of the Church's mission to the Gentiles.

HW

Year B

1 Samuel 15:34—16:13 (Continuous)

As Saul's career and personality gradually wither, David's prospects will open into flower. This episode at Bethlehem is the seed of growth and guidance ahead. It gives the coming chapters a theological context: God is stirring, in the choice and emergence of David.

Samuel's grief at Saul's demise is understandable, even compassionate—but his moods and movements must focus on the future (15:34—16:1). Anointing a new king when the post is presently filled is a dangerous ploy (v. 2). Indeed the quest is not only perilous, but puzzling, when Samuel can find no inner conviction about any of the assembled candidates (vv. 6–10). Israel has a tall king already; a different kind of quality is needed this time (v. 7; cf. 9:2;10:23–24). David is the youngest of his family, yet his outward appearance suggests energy and inner strength. 'This is the one' whom God has sent Samuel to find (v. 12).

So Israel will have a shepherd king, who will know that leadership involves nurture, even sacrificial care (v. 11). The new heir is anointed among his brothers—which should secure their recognition, even if it is spiced with envy. The Holy Spirit comes to him, not breezing through, but breathing steadily within (v. 13). Public acknowledgment will come later. For the moment, the seed is well sown.

Ezekiel 17:22–24 (Related)

Most of Ezekiel 17 is devoted to a parable about a cedar and a vine (vv. 1–10), along with explanation and interpretation (vv. 11–21). The trees are the nation of Judah and her king, caught between two world powers: she is Babylon's vassal (v. 6), and has called on Egyptian help to shake herself free (v. 7).

This policy of rebellion will ruin her (vv. 16–21). Then God, who has judged her, will renew her again. He will pluck and plant a twig from the highest branch (v. 22), a royal leader for Israel. Under this Messiah her life will flourish, her growth be strong, and many birds find shelter in her shade. Then 'all the trees' (v. 24), all the nations of the world, will know that the God of Israel deals in sovereign and unexpected ways, to judge and to heal, to lift up and to lay low.

Ezekiel's picture appears to be taken up by Jesus in Mark 4:32. The details differ, yet with one thrust in common. From an era of defeat and duplicity, Ezekiel looked forward to days of hope, to trustworthy and solid growth, and extending blessing. Similarly, Jesus encouraged his disciples to look beyond the limitations and confrontations of their own day, at the startling potential that God's Kingdom holds.

2 Corinthians 5:6–10 [11–13] 14–17

Paul has written of unseen reality, the risen life of Christ, which touches the Christian now, and waits ahead to embrace us finally and fully (4:16–18).

The future prospect gives courage. When experiences stress and distress us (4:8–9), they are not God's last word. There is another world, another environment, to which we presently belong—though at a distance—and in which we shall ultimately be at home (5:6–8).

Some people fear that this hope makes Christians casual and complacent. Not so for Paul. He looks on the prospect of meeting God as a stimulus to serious commitment. He wants his whole life to please God, so that when his deeds are weighed, they will be seen as good (vv. 9–10). For him, judgment and security go together (1 Corinthians 3:10–15).

Indeed the gospel makes the earth a richer and worthier place. Christ's death and resurrection inspire us to live for him, as a response to his love (vv. 14–15). Paul now looks at everyone in the light of what Jesus has done: those who know Jesus have come already into a new world (v. 17). They are new people. Outward appearances, human perceptions, say so little about what we are and could become.

Motives for Christian service—hope, judgment, love, lives made new in Christ.

Mark 4:26–34

The parable of the sower, earlier in this chapter, showed the piecemeal—even apparently erratic—progress of God's Kingdom. These two small parables balance and complement that impression, as they revel in the sure outcome of the work God has begun.

Like seed, the Kingdom of God holds its own potential for growth and maturity (vv. 26–29). We watch its progress, but do not force its growth, nor shape the details of its development. Not that God's work always advances without our involvement. Jesus was not advocating lazy or casual discipleship. Yet the Kingdom has its own life. There is a God-given inevitability about this crop. There will be a consummation. The seed of God's word will accomplish the purpose for which it is sent (cf. Isaiah 55:10–11).

The second parable is about scale, the contrast between small beginnings and a grand destiny, with room for incomers from far and wide (vv. 30–32). God's Kingdom, begun in Jesus, will surpass the scope of rational expectation and measurement.

Parables were given to the crowds, explanations to the disciples (vv. 33–34). Understanding and following need to march in step. Confidence in the ultimate success of God's Kingdom is easier to understand when you are involved.

JP

YEAR C

1 Kings 21:1–10 [11–14] 15–21a (Continuous)

The story of Naboth's vineyard illustrates the disobedience of the people of God throughout the Old Testament. Ahab is both a member of that people, with an individual responsibility to keep the covenant made at Sinai, and at the same time a leader with responsibility to ensure that his subjects as a whole keep the covenant.

He has already broken the first and second commandment by his idolatry, and the third and fourth in consequence. He has broken the fifth by not honouring his kingly forbears and the throne he has inherited. In this story he begins by coveting and moves on, through his wife, to bearing false testimony, murder and theft.

As king, he allows himself, sullen and angry, to be guided by his Phoenician wife, who aggressively seeks to impose her pagan views and convinces him that being king puts him above the law. He subverts and betrays his subordinates, forcing them to sin for him. With echoes of Macbeth and Lady Macbeth, and with many examples of lawless warlords in our world today, this appalling behaviour of those with power happens all the time. The challenge is to be like Elijah and to confront with the truth: 'You will not get away with it. Judgment will come in the end.'

2 Samuel 11:26—12:10, 13–15 (Related)

There is much in this passage that echoes and reiterates the lessons of Naboth's vineyard (the 'Continuous' reading for today). A terrible abuse of power, breaking obvious commandments—here adultery and murder; a prophet fearing for his life, but willing to obey the Lord and challenge a powerful ruler. Nathan's brilliant story is so effective.

- Psalm 51 helps us to enter into David's deeply penitent heart. How does this compare with Ahab's reaction at the end of 1 Kings 21?
- Because of David's repentance, the dire consequences are softened in some ways (vv. 10–14). Again there are interesting comparisons with the prophet's words of doom to Ahab.
- However we react to God's part in the sickness and death of the baby, it is clear that we frequently reap terrible consequences when we betray those we love, break our promises of commitment, and want things (and people) we cannot and should not have. However repentant we are, however much we put right what we have done as far as we are able, we may have to bear the consequences for the rest of our lives.

Galatians 2:15–21

Justification is crucial to an understanding of the gospel. Paul is using a legal metaphor to point out that God declares a person innocent, whatever their standing. The post-Reformation emphasis on personal conversion has led this doctrine of justification by faith to give rise to a strongly individualistic 'inner separateness' in the Christian's relationship with God. However, Paul is not dealing with the relationship between a holy God and an individual sinner so much as the ethnic and social divisions within the covenant people of God. Gentiles were sinners because they were not part of the covenant people. But since all Christians—both Jewish and Gentile—are justified in the same way, then justification by faith has social implications for churches. All are equal.

The law was a means to an end—it showed up sin. Now dead to sin and the law, we live to Christ who loves us, but that does not mean we are above the law and go on sinning. 'Absolutely not!' (v. 17). Verses 20 and 21 resound with Paul's passionate gratitude to the Son of God who loved him and gave himself for him. The only possible response is to crucify self and live for him. Any attempt to live by the law diminishes the gift of grace.

Luke 7:36—8:3

As well as fulfilling Luke's purpose in disclosing Jesus as the Saviour of the world, these texts also give us Jesus as a model for relationships—simple points, such as his immediate willingness to go to the centurion's house (Proper 4), his practical compassion for the widow in word and deed (Proper 5) and, here, his sensitive and compassionate handling of the forgiven woman, in a situation that could have led to her humiliation.

The story deals with the relationship between sin and forgiveness. Little sense of sin will mean a superficial sense of being forgiven. A sense of self-righteousness will lead to judgmentalism towards others and a failure to grasp the enormity and cost of forgiveness. If we excuse and explain away sin, then we do not allow the overwhelming forgiveness of God to be accepted and experienced as has happened to this woman. Simon has treated Jesus discourteously and cannot understand what has happened. There is less hope of his finding forgiveness in Christ.

The women of 8:1–3 give an interesting insight into Jesus' attitude to women. It seems unlikely that travelling teachers of the time usually had women as disciples, who supported the enterprise from their own resources.

MK

PROPER 7

YEAR A

Genesis 21:8–21 (Continuous)

The weaning of the miracle child Isaac, indicating that he has survived his vulnerable infancy and is ready to take his place in the world, is truly a time for rejoicing (v. 8). But the presence of Ishmael reminds Abraham and Sarah of their previous attempt to defeat childlessness by using Hagar as a surrogate mother (v. 9). In the light of the birth of Isaac, that attempt becomes an embarrassment, and Ishmael a threat (v. 10); and so, despite Abraham's reluctance, Ishmael and his mother Hagar have to go (vv. 10–14). But as Ishmael's name declares, 'God hears' their cries for help (v. 17); divine care protects the poorly used pair in the desert (v. 19), and later makes Ishmael the founder of a great nation (v. 18; see Genesis 25:12–18).

Waiting for the fulfilment of God's promise is never easy, and we are prone to try to force it before it is due; but fulfilment achieved in that way is second best. Letting go of what we ourselves have engineered in the light of the true fulfilment is also difficult; but it must be done, to underline our complete dependence on God for the fulfilment of the divine will. The final reassurance is that the divine mercy can turn even mistaken attempts to force the promise into good.

Jeremiah 20:7–13 (Related)

The opposition and isolation that Jesus' followers would experience in the name of their Lord was nothing new. Dating from some six hundred years earlier, the prophecy of Jeremiah expresses just such feelings of isolation, even despair, in the heart of a man who felt compelled to speak out in the name of God but who was rejected by his hearers because of his harsh message.

The features of this intensely vivid meditation are threefold. First, there is the imperative to serve, closely intertwined with the cost of such service (vv. 7–8). The two go hand-in-hand, and it is impossible to obey the first without experiencing the second; but for those who are truly called by God, it is equally impossible to avoid the second by disobeying the first (v. 9). Also the cost, like the call, is extremely personal, and can involve the loss not only of possessions but also of friends, self-esteem and dignity (vv. 7, 10). But the third element is the assurance that, despite all the heartbreak, those who are called by the Lord to serve will be vindicated by divine power, and those who opposed them will be brought down (vv. 11–13). This, the foundational truth, is what makes it possible to carry on.

Romans 6:1b–11

Paul here deals with a misconception about the nature of the gospel, namely that the free availability of forgiveness either engenders a lack of moral responsibility or demands an abundance of sin in order to be shown to its best effect (v. 1). However, this is certainly not the case; the whole point of the forgiveness available through the death and resurrection of Christ is to allow sin to be eliminated, not multiplied (vv. 2, 6). God's grace in Christ is not a licence to sin but a means of making and keeping the faithful free from sin (v. 4), and the notion that the best way to experience God's grace is to continue in sin amounts to nothing more than the kind of legalism that the grace is intended to do away with. God's grace is just that, gracious, and cannot be manipulated by those who think that it will automatically be shown to them whenever they sin. In any case, those who are truly united with Christ will be unable to continue in sin in this fashion, because through his death, sin's hold over them has been broken, and with his resurrection they have been renewed to live life as God intended (vv. 5, 8, 11).

Matthew 10:24–39

Those who think that they are in for an enthusiastic reception when they preach the gospel need to be realistic. They can expect no better reception than Jesus himself received, which was certainly not always positive (vv. 24–25). But fear of opposition on a human level is no reason to give up, because behind the message there is a greater reality than the merely human reality, and that greater reality remains constant, no matter what happens on the human level (vv. 28–33).

The divine reality behind the message acts as a double encouragement to be faithful, because not only does it express itself in care for those who are faithful (vv. 29–31), it will bring retribution on those who deny it (v. 33). In fact, the reality is such that it must take precedence over all other commitments, and even the natural ties of blood and family which, under normal circumstances, are so pressing must be subordinated to it (vv. 35–37). The relationship and duty to Christ have priority over every other relationship and duty, and are to be expressed in embracing the way of hardship, even of death, which Jesus embraced (vv. 38–39), in the knowledge that this is the only way of proving and experiencing that ultimate divine reality—life.

DR

YEAR B

1 Samuel 17:[1a, 4–11, 19–23] 32–49 (Continuous)

This contest confounds all the pundits and predictions (v. 33). David defies the inequalities of stature, experience and equipment, fells his opponent, and Israel wins the battle (vv. 48–54). His resolve is calm and clear, his fighting method spectacularly unconventional. One believer, plus God, can lower any obstacle; faith moves mountains. Is that all?

That is certainly part of the message. David is portrayed as a religious man, concerned, like so many in the Old Testament, for God's honour in the eyes of the nations (v. 46). As he and Goliath come into shouting distance, the Philistine reaches for an oath, and David for faith (vv. 43–47); trust and arrogance are not identical. Trust in the Lord is a mighty weapon, however tight the corner.

None the less, David knows what he is doing. He 'cannot be turned into an armadillo at the drop of a helmet' (R.P. Gordon), and declines the royal armour (vv. 38–39). Yet from the moment he picks up the stones (v. 40), it is obvious that he has a plan, based on hard experience, which has itself been a training ground for faith (vv. 34–37). Times of crisis often call on both faith and gifts. We serve God best as we nurture them together, letting them teach one another in the school of experience.

1 Samuel 17:57—18:5, 10–16 (Alternative Continuous)

Triumph can lead into trouble: it must be handled with care. The victory over Goliath offers David friendship and fame. It also draws him deep into the royal court, into a disturbing environment of pride and danger.

Jonathan appears an honourable and humble man, bold (14:1–15) and gracious. Subsequently, perhaps even already, he senses the way the wind of succession is blowing (23:17). He is Saul's natural heir, but these generous gifts to David look like a symbolic act of abdication (18:4). More than this, there is an immediate personal warmth between the two men, a partnership of kindred spirits drawn together by a complex and difficult destiny.

All the nice girls love a soldier (18:6–9), but the praises of Israel's women only make Saul angry (18:11). He looks at everything through the mists of his own instability (16:14; 18:10), yet he has discerned with great clarity the secret of who will succeed him (15:28; 18:8). From now on his actions will mingle madness and cunning, in a paranoid and protracted attempt to stave off the inevitable. Attempted murder (v. 11), military command (v. 13), David rides it all and advances in popularity. Jealousy is an awful thing, a turbulent, stormy sea, compared with the simpler wrath of Goliath.

Job 38:1–11 (Related)

Job has ached to understand his suffering. He has longed for God to stand before him (31:35), but when God does appear no reasons are offered. Job never does find out the cause of his troubles, not even when the book ends. He must live by faith. This meeting with God is encounter, not explanation.

For God points to the limits of Job's knowledge. There is a vast array of God's craftsmanship, of whose formation and sustenance Job knows nothing—Orion, the ox and the ostrich, for example (38:31; 39:9–18). God built the earth on a stable base, and conducted the joyful praise of creation, long before Job was there (vv. 4–7). God brought the sea to birth like a child from the womb, cherished and nurtured it as it came into the world, and controlled it in the firmness of love (vv. 8–11). He speaks from the storm (v. 1), but even the storms are subject to him.

This tour of God's lively works turns out to be a loving, revealing experience (42:5). It draws Job nearer to God—to unexplained and unexplaining mystery, but to mystery he can trust. Sometimes, when rational argument will not reach our need, the power of God in creation can show us his face.

2 Corinthians 6:1–13

The beginning and end of this reading shape an appeal from Paul that the Corinthians respond readily and wholeheartedly to the message of reconciliation and hope in Jesus, which he has outlined in the previous chapter. He links himself to Jesus: 'working together with him'. His own ministry extends the influence of Christ's cross and resurrection (v. 1). The Old Testament chapter quoted speaks also of God's Servant as light to the nations (v. 2; cf. Isaiah 49:6, 8). Paul is spreading the light of Christ; he urges that the Corinthians accept it.

To support his appeal, Paul writes of his ministry (vv. 3–10). This long catalogue divides into shorter lists: the troubles Paul puts up with—the nouns are consistently plural (vv. 4–5); the integrity of his behaviour (vv. 6–7); the varying fortunes and reactions he encounters (v. 8a); and the stark contrasts between the ways people judge him and the realities of his spiritual life and influence (vv. 8b–10).

We too may be entering times when Christianity will be widely despised, even pitied. What commends the gospel will not be the social prominence of those who follow and represent Christ, but the resilience, integrity, and inner worth of our lives—our inner peace amid the storms. That sort of lifestyle is itself a powerful appeal (v. 11).

Mark 4:35–41

Who, then, is this? For Jews, the sea was a place of chaos and disorder, turbulent and intractable. When the earth was formless and void, God's Holy Spirit moved across the waters, to bring life and goodness into being (Genesis 1:2ff). Only God could still raging waters, settle their threats and deliver his fearful people (Psalms 65:7; 89:9; 107:23–30). When Jesus silences a stormy wind, and calms wild waves, then the power of God is at work. Jesus brings order and peace to the world of nature, as he does to human bodies and minds (Mark 5). There is an echo here of God's creative touch, and a glimpse of a time when danger, destruction and death will be no more (Revelation 21:1).

Tradition has thought of the boat as Christ's Church, battered and fearful amid turbulent times, yet always secure and protected in the company of Jesus.

More personally, the disciples would remember that night. It was their realm, their boat, their trade, and they had been reduced to panic. Then Jesus controlled the situation and restored it: suddenly they were encompassed by majestic calm. Even the realm of life we know best, he understands. It is often in storms that we recognize him most truly.

JP

YEAR C

1 Kings 19:1–4 [5–7] 8–15a (Continuous)

'Go back the way you came,' God tells Elijah (v. 15, NIV). Fleeing for his life from Jezebel's fury, afraid and lonely, with a strong sense of failure, his contest with the prophets of Baal seems to have had little effect. Jezebel still swears by the gods he thought he had discredited (v. 2).

He retreats far south (without any sense of guidance?) Eventually the Lord will tell him to go back. He divests himself of all human company and seeks the desert. He has had enough (cf. Jonah 1:1–3). He turns to the Lord again, in the desert, in a goodbye prayer, and falls asleep (v. 4). Gently he is brought back to the point where he knows he has to go on.

The forty days and forty nights through the desert echoes both Moses with God on Sinai (Exodus 24:18) and Jesus tempted (Matthew 4:1–2). Elijah arrives at Mount Horeb (another name for Sinai), the place where the covenant was sealed, the Ten Commandments given (Exodus 19; 33:22).

The theophany of Exodus 19 is reversed. The dense cloud, thunder and lightning and earthquake give way, for Elijah, to the soft whisper of the one who has fed and watered this reluctant and depressed man, saying, 'Go back the way you came' (v. 15).

Isaiah 65:1–9 (Related)

Isaiah puts passion and desperation into the words of God. His plan to open his arms to the Gentiles, to welcome into his Kingdom all the peoples of the earth (v. 1), should have come about through the witness and shining obedience of his own chosen nation. In contrast, they who already have a revelation and a covenant with the living God pursue their own idolatry and paganism. They imagine themselves so holy that instead of inviting all to participate with them in the worship of God, they tell people to keep away (v. 5).

But although this day he is holding out his hand to them, there will come a day when judgment will be meted out, though not on them all (v. 8). There is always a remnant, just as Elijah found when God told him of the others who had been faithful (1 Kings 19:18), who will inherit the promises of God. Paul comments on this in Romans 11:5. There is still a divide between religious arrogance which is sure that it knows the truth and the humble seeking for the truth of God.

Galatians 3:23–29

The nub of Paul's rebuke to the Galatians is that the Jewish Christians had accepted that they had been justified by faith in Christ. Therefore, by implication they had admitted that Jewish law and practice could not make them right with God. However, they still wanted Gentiles to become Jews and accept the burden of the law as a preliminary to becoming Christian. They were saying that more had to be done than simply having faith in Christ. In addition they were implying that Jews and Gentiles were not equal, that being Jewish was better than not being Jewish. They denied their equality before God and created two classes of Christians within their fellowships.

If there is no difference between Jew and Gentile and all can come to God in Christ and be justified, then all the practical outworkings of their lives together must demonstrate this. Paul's statement in 3:28 is pivotal. If we are all clothed with Christ equally, then there are no divisions of class, gender or race. The barriers have been broken down, but not just in theological theory. Our relationships in our fellowships should demonstrate this equality. Paul battles to convince the Galatians that this must be so between Jews and Gentiles. The battle to make this so for our ethnic and racial, class and gender divisions goes on.

Luke 8:26–39

Jesus has dealt with the dying and dead, the guilty and the self-righteous; now he deals with evil possession (and in the previous verses with the power of a storm). For the Church in many parts of the world, such possession is part of common experience, but in the rational West it is more difficult for people to accept this cause of behaviour. But mental illness and severe psychotic disturbance can lead to such disturbed behaviour, to self-destruction and to physical attacks on others in some tragic cases. Healing, where possible, will come usually from the God-given sources of medicine and psychiatry, but there are pointers here to a contribution from Christians and the Christian community. These include prayer, of course, but also a concern that shows in the recognition of the worth of every human being, however afflicted, so that their needs are considered and their rights are respected, even where the protection of others may lead to their being constrained.

Jesus Christ has all power and authority, even over the evil forces of our world. But he exercises that power and authority in compassion and love for each person individually. Those who call themselves Christians should learn boldness as well as compassion from this.

MK

PROPER 8

YEAR A

Genesis 22:1–14 (Continuous)

In this most dramatic turn of events, having dismissed his firstborn son through whom he originally hoped to fulfil the promise of progeny, Abraham is now commanded by God to take and sacrifice the miracle child Isaac (vv. 1–2), thereby leaving him once again childless and hopeless. But such is his devotion and faith in God that he willingly and sincerely goes to the brink of slaying the child (vv. 9–10), in the belief that God can work a miracle even in this situation (v. 8). At the last moment, Abraham's hand is stayed by God, and a ram replaces Isaac as the sacrifice offered on the altar (vv. 11–13).

There seem to be two ways in which to read this troubling and morally ambiguous story: either God is a God who demands complete loyalty and so is entitled to require absolutely anything of Abraham, as is indicated by Abraham's unquestioning obedience to the command (v. 3); or Abraham's offering arises out of an admirable but misplaced sense of devotion. God is not really interested in having the child Isaac as a sacrifice, even though Abraham thinks God is, and so this is the story of Abraham's correction. The interesting thing is that the two interpretations are not necessarily contradictory.

Jeremiah 28:5–9 (Related)

It is all very well to say that those who come in the name of the Lord should be received along with their messages, but it can sometimes be very difficult to tell who has been sent and who has not. This exchange between the prophets Hananiah and Jeremiah is a good example of the kind of tensions that can arise when two people both claim to have messages from God but the messages contradict each other. The situation is complicated by the fact that Hananiah is telling the people what they want to hear (v. 6), but Jeremiah is not. In the end, Jeremiah offers two ways of helping to make things clearer. The first is to look to the past (v. 8): is this in line with what we know of the prophetic messages that have come true before? But this is not the complete answer, because of course God is always free to do new things. So the only real way of finding out who is right is to look to the future (v. 9): the prophet sent by God is the one whose words eventually come true. Wise faith and patience are what, in the end, make the difference, for messenger and recipients alike.

Romans 6:12–23

In urging his audience to submit themselves to God and to the power of righteousness (vv. 12–13), Paul recognizes the potential objection that to do so is to relinquish one's freedom; but he counters the objection by arguing that there is no such thing as absolute freedom. We are slaves of whatever we give ourselves over to, whether sin or God (v. 16), and the alternative to being a slave of God is to be a slave of sin, which is certainly not the same thing as being free. In addition, comparing the results of being a slave to sin with the results of being a slave to God offers a strong incentive to become a slave of God, because whereas slavery to sin results in death, slavery to God results in eternal life (vv. 20–22). The terms in which Paul expresses the outcome of each state of slavery are a succinct summary of the difference between the two: the *wages* of sin is death, but the *free gift* of God is eternal life (v. 23). With sin, you get what you deserve; with God, you get what you don't deserve. What better illustration could there be of the contrast between the legalism that accompanies sin, and the workings of divine grace?

Matthew 10:40–42

In the conclusion to these instructions about mission, Jesus once again affirms the ultimate reality behind what the disciples are being commissioned to do. Whilst in some ways it is a commonplace to say that rejecting or accepting a messenger is the equivalent of rejecting or accepting the one from whom the messenger has come, the significant point in this instance is the weight of the commission with which the messengers travel. They are messengers not only of Christ but of the God from whom Christ is inseparable (v. 40), and so reactions to them are effectively reactions to that God. This is a reassurance for them, and a very serious encouragement to persevere, even in the face of the opposition and personal sacrifice that they will have to endure, because their task is one of such gravity.

The same overtones of encouragement and warning are present for those who are in the position of receiving the messengers: receiving them on account of their commission cannot fail to bring its reward (vv. 41–42), but the unspoken implication is that failure to receive them is an act of rejection which has dangerous consequences. After all, it is rejection of the one who can destroy both body and soul in hell (Matthew 10:28).

DR

YEAR B

2 Samuel 1:1, 17–27 (Continuous)

A heavy defeat against the Philistines has claimed the lives of Saul and Jonathan (1 Samuel 31). David could have grasped this moment of political opportunity, and moved quickly to take advantage. Yet his first act is to command and lead public grief (v. 17). The poem reads as a genuine outpouring of sorrow, a bitter lament for tragedy, ruin and loss.

The men who died were skilful and brave, committed and strong in battle (v. 22). Father and son died together (v. 23). A reign that brought Israel success and prosperity is over (v. 24). David has lost a dear and staunch friend (v. 26). For valour and comradeship, for history and human love, let Israel weep.

We sometimes tend to speak the best truth as a memorial, rather than the whole truth. Saul and Jonathan had not always been close (1 Samuel 20:30). The blessings of Saul's reign might have been greater had he himself been a wiser and better man. Yet the best truth is the stuff for grief, for this is the truth of what might have been, the gap between the potential God gave and the emptiness of its ending. Weeping reflects worth and reverence; only someone who weeps for the past can be well trusted with the future (2 Samuel 2:1).

Lamentations 3:23–33 (Related)

These songs tell of the desperate hurt and bitter grief that followed the fall of Jerusalem in 587BC. Many had died, and survival was a wretched struggle for those who remained (4:4–10). The nation's sin had been a factor in bringing this situation about (1:8, 20–22). Yet it seemed that God himself had turned against his own people (2:1–8). In chapter 3, faith looks for light.

God's mercy is not ended, by sin, judgment or disaster. He intends to start again, in compassion and goodness (vv. 22–24). So his people may wait for the tide to turn. Suffering may have crushed people into silence, but silence is space that mercy can enter (vv. 25–30). God is consistent and caring. Present events are not typical of his dealings or desires (vv. 31–33; cf. Isaiah 54:7). Wait, hope, seek and trust.

This is not tidy theology; it is faith rising to its feet after a heavy blow, 'struck down, but not destroyed' (2 Corinthians 4:9). A preacher must deal sensitively with this material: for one thing, suffering cannot always be traced to sin. Yet Christians who suffer may be helped by hearing the faith of Lamentations: 'We may have lost everything, but God has not lost us. There will be a future; there will be a morning.'

2 Corinthians 8:7–15

Paul is collecting money among his Gentile congregations for the Christian church in Jerusalem. In chapters 8 and 9 he encourages the Corinthians to play their part in this, and offers several pieces of guidance.

Why should Christians give?

- As an expression of the spiritual wealth we have received (v. 7). Healthy Christian life balances inflow and outflow, the blessings that come to us and our willingness to give.
- Because other Christians are giving (v. 8). We need not copy for copying's sake, but we may rightly be encouraged and motivated by the actions of others. That helps to prove the genuineness of our own love.
- As a response to the love of Christ, his willing acceptance of the ordinariness of human life and the abject poverty of the cross, to bring us the wealth of God's love (v. 9).

How should Christians give?

- With the loving determination that converts good intentions into good deeds (vv. 10–11).
- With the confidence that God measures our giving against our resources. He does not ask for what we have not got (v. 12).
- With the purpose of sharing, to help others who have less than we do (v. 13), and without any embarrassment when the time comes for others to give to us (v. 14).

Mark 5:21–43

One story is nested within another (cf. 3:20–35, four weeks ago); we see each character more clearly in comparison with her neighbour. 'Twelve years' (vv. 25, 42) hints at connections to be explored.

The girl, born into love, in the heart of community life (vv. 22–23), is set to die in adolescence, her potential for adult life never realized, whereas the sick woman has a miserable adult existence—she appears an isolated and fearful figure, pushed to the margins of society.

Both stories feature secrecy and publicity, but very differently. The woman's secretive touch leads to Jesus' openly pronouncing her healed (vv. 30–34); let the town, that surely knows of her affliction, know it has ceased. With the girl's parents, who are public people, Jesus acts in seclusion and privacy (v. 40); the outcome will be evident enough before long.

Jesus moves on (vv. 34, 38; 6:1), leaving two lives released into hope. The unnamed 'daughter' (vv. 23, 35) will become a woman, with a mature identity of her own. The woman with no family has become again a 'Daughter'

(v. 34), restored to belonging, joined afresh to the family that is Israel.

Bodily healing always affects more than our body. Full human wholeness includes faith, relationships, and the capacity to fulfil the future for which God made us.

JP

YEAR C

2 Kings 2:1–2, 6–14 (Continuous)

It seems likely that Elijah's main role in combating the worship of Baal finished at the end of 1 Kings 19, where God tells him that the future battle will take place after he has handed over his mantle to Elisha. In this passage it is difficult to work out what is happening, but it seems that Elijah is still reluctant to anoint Elisha properly. Everyone knows that Elisha is going to be the man of God from 'today' (v. 3), but Elijah draws out the process. He tries to leave him behind (vv. 6–7), but finally acknowledges the transfer of God's power and disappears mysteriously from the scene.

This 'handing over' relationship is echoed in others, for example Moses and Joshua (Elisha and Joshua are similar names, meaning 'God saves', and 'the Lord saves'). As in Joshua's case, the miracle of the parting of the waters encourages and affirms. It is similar to John the Baptist's early relationship with Jesus. Maybe one lesson for leaders lies in Elijah's flawed response to his calling as a prophet—his unwillingness to see himself as only part of God's plan and to hand over to others. We can compare this with John the Baptist, also unsure about his greater cousin (Luke 7:20), but willing to acknowledge his own lesser role (Luke 3:16).

1 Kings 19:15–16, 19–21 (Related)

Echoing John the Baptist, Elijah is now told to prepare the way for God's plans in others, rather than being personally, actively and spectacularly involved in them himself. He is told to appoint two kings and a prophet to succeed him (v. 15–16). There is no record that he did the first two anointings. The plan to defeat Baal idolatry in Israel is now political and military, not the direct and miraculous challenge of chapter 18.

Those who truly keep the faith are a minority. That is certainly so in Western Europe at the turn of the millennium. Continuing decline means that well under ten per cent have any commitment to the Church of God. How to live as an increasingly misunderstood minority is an important issue for church relationships and structures.

Elisha's call (vv. 19, 21) echoes the call of the disciples in the Gospels (Matthew 4:18–22). He is working when it comes; he gives up his employment and makes a total break with his past life—he leaves his 'nets'. 'May I say goodbye?' Elisha asks. Elijah's reply is somewhat enigmatic (v. 20). Is he saying that he does not mind what Elisha does? Does the prophet still resist being replaced?

Elisha throws a party, kisses his parents and with youthful enthusiasm follows Elijah.

Galatians 5:1, 13–25

What kind of freedom is Paul talking about (v. 1)? Not, of course, the freedom to do what we like (v. 13). He frees us and we spend the rest of our lives following him. We do not have to earn salvation by obeying the law, which is slavery (3:3). We cannot earn God's blessing by trying to be good; we try to be good as a response to God's blessing. The law was a means to an end; it governed the covenant life of the people of God, to tell them what being holy meant and to unite them under the law. Now, free grace in Christ brings us into the covenant people, and our response is to be holy and to be one with each other. We live by the Spirit and are led by the Spirit. The law will play its part by helping us to understand what following him in love and service require. By forcing new Gentile Christians to work to keep the law, the Jewish Christians were bringing them into bondage and not fulfilling the law of love towards neighbour (v. 14–15).

There are laws against some of the sins in the list (v. 19–21), and many of them surface in the average church. Laws cannot 'order' the fruit of verses 22–23; the only command here is to 'keep in step with the Spirit' (v. 25).

Luke 9:51–62

Luke 9:51 marks a turning point in the Gospel narrative. Generally speaking, there is a change from Jesus' actions to his teaching. There is more direct confrontation with the authorities and he resolutely sets out for Jerusalem (v. 51). The popular exciting days of miracles and crowds fade and harder lessons have to be learnt.

Jesus begins to walk his long and difficult path to death. The little party is not welcomed for the night on their journey (v. 53). Did they expect to be? Did they have previous contacts there? Rejection and suspicion, dislike of those who, by going to worship in Jerusalem, imply that the Samaritans' beliefs are wrong may all be factors in this, but Jesus rebukes those who want a simple and contemptuous revenge (v. 54–55). These kinds of rejecting responses will grow. This may be the Christian path for many faithful disciples.

Following Jesus is not easy and involves sacrifices and conflicts of priorities. Compare this with Luke 14:25–34. One offers to follow him, and is warned of the hardships. Another is called to follow and wants to be a part-time disciple. Jesus is warning against facile, unassessed enthusiasm, and half-hearted, foot-in-both-camps, partial commitment. The Church of today, and sometimes the same kind of people, show both tendencies.

MK

PROPER 9

YEAR A

Genesis 24:34–38, 42–49, 58–67 (Continuous)

Isaac, the miracle child, bearer of the promise, has now become a man, and if the promise is to continue to be fulfilled he needs a wife and children of his own. So Abraham sends his servant to find a wife for Isaac from among Abraham's own family (vv. 37–38). That way, there is no risk that Isaac will be drawn away from his destiny as part of the new nation to be founded under God, by being swallowed up in the race and religion of the surrounding indigenous peoples.

With the help of God, the servant is spectacularly successful. He asks for a sign (vv. 40–42), which is not a miracle in itself but which speaks of the woman's character, and which, through the discernment granted by faith, indicates the one who is destined to be Isaac's wife. Rebekah herself is open to the course of events and, seeing that she will become part of a household that enjoys God's blessing (v. 35), is willing to go with the servant and become the wife of an unknown husband (vv. 58–67).

Both Rebekah and the servant show a commendable readiness to trust themselves to the God-ordained providence which they can see is at work in what appear to be everyday events.

Zechariah 9:9–12 (Related)

Spoken at a time when the Jews were an occupied people with no king of their own, these lines describe a glorious future for them in terms of God's restoration of the kingdom of Israel. Several significant features of that kingdom are to be restored. *The king* (v. 9) is God's own representative among the people; *Jerusalem* (v. 9) is God's own city and chosen dwelling place; and *the covenant* (v. 11) is the solemn binding relationship between people and God.

But what is pictured here is more than just a restoration. It is a declaration of the utter faithfulness of God, whose covenant, once made, is for ever. It is also a redefinition of the former glory. The worldwide kingship is based not on conquest which has to be maintained, but on peace; and the peace is assured not by a build-up of weapons to give security against attack and frighten off the enemy, but by the destruction of weapons (v. 10). Even the king's own triumph is expressed not by riding a war-horse but by riding on a donkey (v. 9), and at the same time as being victorious he is humble (v. 9). This is a vision of the perfect expression of God's will, a foretaste of the Kingdom of heaven.

Romans 7:15–25a

The situation in which Paul finds himself, of being unable to do what he knows is right (vv. 15, 18–19), is one that most people have experienced at some time. It might be described as a state of 'Jekyll and Hyde righteousness', whereby the knowledge of and the desire for goodness are there but the inability to put that knowledge and desire into practice means that the person remains unrighteous. As in many other areas of life, actions speak louder than words, and if the knowledge of what is good or the desire for it do not mean that a person actually does what is good, then the person cannot be regarded as 'good'. This is evidently the problem with the Law: it can give knowledge of what is good, and indeed it is good in itself (v. 16), but it cannot overcome the power of sin sufficiently to motivate a person to do what is good (vv. 22–23), and so it is unable to make anyone good.

This is where the power of Christ comes in. For Paul, it is the element that cures the Jekyll and Hyde syndrome by enabling him to do the good he really wants to do (vv. 24–25a); and as such, it is the element that enables him to be true to himself.

Matthew 11:16–19, 25–30

It seems that nothing is good enough for some people: neither the asceticism of John the Baptist nor the feasting of Jesus appeals to them, and all they can do is criticize (vv. 18–19). The problem is that they are too set in their own self-righteous, religious ways to be able to recognize the things of God which present themselves in other ways. This is a dangerous state to be in, because it puts reverence for the forms of religious expression in the place of understanding and response to the religious message. But those who are not bound by this preoccupation with form can hear and respond to the content of the message, however and wherever it comes to them. Thus, the things of God are hidden from the wise but revealed to the simple (v. 25).

The same idea is continued in Jesus' saying about his easy yoke (vv. 28–30), which is prefaced by a claim to his heavenly authority so as to undergird its revolutionary nature (v. 27). What he demands is at once easier and harder; it is not a 'formal' yoke of specific, legalistic, religious requirements, but a yoke of commitment to him, pure and simple. Remember, though, that the yoke may also turn out to be a cross.

DR

YEAR B

2 Samuel 5:1–5, 9–10 (Continuous)

David had taken power in Hebron, near his own home in southern Palestine (2:1–4), and had reigned there for seven years. Now the tribes of the north seek a union, under his rule. Their appeal recognizes social and kinship links, his proven record as a leader in Israel, and his earlier call by God (v. 2).

David then takes the city of Jerusalem, to adopt as his capital (vv. 6–10). It is neutral territory, between the southern tribes and the north, belonging to neither. The references to fortification and expanding influence round off the story of David's rise (vv. 9–10). This is the destination towards which the narrative has moved, ever since David was anointed (1 Samuel 16:13). He has finally and fully come to power. All that remains is to exercise it!

David's name became a slogan for royal leadership in Israel for centuries to come, and was one theological motif against which Jesus' ministry was understood, by himself and others. The theme of solidarity—'flesh and blood' (v. 2)—is taken up in this connection (e.g. Hebrews 2:14–18). The image of the shepherd (v. 2), as a leader vigilant and selfless for the welfare of his flock, has also shaped Christian thought—an ideal realized more fully in Jesus than in any Old Testament king (e.g. John 10:11–18).

Ezekiel 2:1–5 (Related)

Rarely was a preacher called to a less attractive ministry. Ezekiel has just fallen to his face in reverence (1:28), as a strange and glorious vision unfolded before him. He understands that God is glorious and majestic. Then God raises him to his feet (v. 1). The Spirit comes that he may be receptive to God's word (v. 2), and he is assigned a fearful and bitter task.

This is a general commission to Ezekiel's prophetic future. No particular message is given at this point. No single incident has prompted the appraisal of Israel that he hears. The people in general, past and present, are perverse and pig-headed, stubborn in manner and will (vv. 3, 4). Yet their resistance is not the ultimate and dominant factor in the situation. God's purpose will control the course of events.

The commission is threefold. 'I am sending... you shall say... they shall know' (vv. 4–5). Ezekiel's word will impress even on these hard hearts that a messenger of God has been among them. The people will be reminded, surely and unavoidably, that they live within range of God's wisdom and concern. Tough commission indeed, but not fruitless or useless. Faithful service counts, even in places we would not expect. God sees to that.

2 Corinthians 12:2–10

Paul's readers may wonder about his spiritual experiences. He hints at memorable spiritual highs (vv. 2–6; verse 6 is the clue that he refers to himself). Yet he will not dwell on these, for three reasons:

* Visions are difficult to communicate. The most splendid things about God cannot be told (vv. 2–4).
* People might be more impressed by such talk than his conduct or preaching really warranted (v. 6).
* God had not wanted Paul to live with a permanent sense of spiritual uplift. The uplifting experience was followed by a troublesome and persistent difficulty, a 'thorn in the flesh' (v. 7). As Paul wrestled with this, he discovered a fuller and more satisfying awareness of God's grace and power. The very weakness became a channel for Christ's power (v. 9).

Nobody knows what 'the thorn' was, although there have been many intelligent guesses! It is clear that something evil in itself, 'a messenger of Satan' (v. 7), can be used by God for good.

This passage helps us to put our varied Christian experiences in perspective. God may graciously lift us up to exuberant joy and mysterious awareness of his majesty and love. Yet deeper and longer-lasting Christian growth may result when our sufferings open us to the grace of Christ.

Mark 6:1–13

The episode in Nazareth has been seen as a turning point in Mark's Gospel. The disparaging reception given Jesus in his home town raises dark suspicions of greater rejections ahead. Faith, such a potent element of previous stories (5:34, 36), is now discouragingly sparse and there are few opportunities for healing signs (6:5–6). Jesus has a greater mission than simply to make bodies whole: his healings are signs of a wider grace, and where the message of the Kingdom is ignored, the signs themselves will be of little value. Familiarity breeds, if not exactly contempt, certainly lack of expectancy.

The disciples' mission, by contrast, yields good results. They were called to 'be with him, and to be sent out' (3:14). They have followed and watched. Now is the time for them to represent Jesus. They make no elaborate material preparations for their journey, but depend on God for daily needs (vv. 8–9). Like Jesus, they do not try to force doors that close against them (v. 11). Yet there is vigour in the account of their travels (vv. 12–13). The fresh witness of new believers can often make a potent impression for Christ. Cynical responses may reveal much more about some hearers than about the messengers (v. 11).

JP

YEAR C

2 Kings 5:1–14 (Continuous)

Wise, thoughtful caring from the lowly, and proud assumptions from the strong, are contrasting features in this story. The young slave girl, far from home, showing concern and not bitter revenge (vv. 2–3), the slave-servants of Naaman who seek his good and reason with him (v. 13), contrast with the actions of the powerful.

Naaman is valiant and highly regarded; he is also rich and expects to buy what he wants immediately. He is used to being obeyed and frightens the life out of the king of Israel who, in the uneasy truce between Israel and Aram, wonders whether this is a trick to renew the war (v. 7).

The story underlines how God works. He is sovereign and in charge; he is not at the beck and call of anyone, not even one of his own prophets. He has given the victory to Aram under Naaman. He gives healing when he chooses and not even the king of Israel can do that. Elisha knows that only God can do this. By distancing himself from the healing process (v. 10), he makes sure that Naaman will not think that he is simply a miracle worker but will acknowledge the God of Israel. 'Now I know that there is no God in all the world except in Israel' (v. 15).

Isaiah 66:10–14 (Related)

Jerusalem is a constant theme in the Bible, as an actual city, as the people of God, as the place where God dwells, and as heaven. We can journey through the Bible, seeing the capital of the kings, the holy city of the psalms, the heavenly Jerusalem of Revelation. (This city is still with us today, holy for Jews, Christians and Muslims, still being built up layer on layer after nearly five thousand years.)

The prophet speaks to those who love her, to all who have prayed for the peace of Jerusalem (Psalm 122:6), that is, to those who seek God's Kingdom and long for the fulfilment of his promises. The richness of the language of comfort is startling and arresting. The Bible in other places puts the words of a husband and bridegroom into the mouth of God speaking to his people, but here, just as earthy and human, is a picture of a mothered baby, dandled and breastfed, the 'mother' changing from Jerusalem, God's beloved people, to God himself in verse 13. Hosea spoke too of the mothering love of God (Hosea 11) but in the end no human analogy is rich and deep enough to describe the love of God.

Galatians 6:[1–6] 7–16

After the practical exhortations in verses 1–6, Paul turns again to the burning issue of this letter. His language could not be stronger as he confronts those who would re-introduce Jewish practices and Jewish law as a necessary requirement for Gentile believers. He questions their motives, suggesting that it is to avoid the scandal of the cross. If they are outwardly conforming to respectable Jewish synagogue society, they will not be persecuted for being Christians. But none of them can obey the law; it has been superseded and subverted by the cross of Christ, which can be our only plea and boast, and which ends for ever our reliance on anything else for salvation and for pleasing God. Through the cross we are a new creation, and all past systems for pleasing God are swept away, even for the Jews (v. 16).

The cross frees us from the curse of the law and the supervision of the law, so that we can live for God. The Spirit reproduces in us the character of Jesus as we serve one another in love and thus fulfil the ultimate moral standard of the law. We sow to please the Spirit and thus inherit eternal life (v. 8). There is only one other way to live, as a slave to the sinful nature, and that sowing reaps destruction (v. 8).

Luke 10:1–11, 16–20

Acts 1:8 and Matthew 28:19 record the sending out of the disciples and, by implication, all those disciples through the ages and across the world. Aspects of this 'sending out' come in this passage.

- They are heralds of Jesus and the Kingdom of God, bringing healing (vv. 1, 9).
- They have a challenging task since there are too few labourers, but they are to go and pray for more (v. 2).
- They are to live simply and depend on others, not too proud to accept food and shelter in return for a message of infinite value (vv. 4, 7, 8).
- They are to be single-minded and not to waste time in casual relationships that do not lead anywhere (vv. 4, 10).
- They are not to worry about their comfort, their food (vv. 7–8) or the danger (vv. 3, 19).
- If people do not listen, then they are simply to move on, leaving the judgments to God (vv. 10–12).

Jesus reminds them that this simple and practical work is part of a bigger and more violent battle. Rejection of them is rejection of him (v. 16). Their success means defeat for the power of evil (vv. 18–19). Jesus knows that the victory is assured in the end, but the disciples' own success or failure should not take away their joy at belonging to God for ever (v. 20).

MK

PROPER 10

YEAR A

Genesis 25:19–34 (Continuous)

Isaac now has the wife appointed for him by God, but she is barren (v. 21); and yet together they are heirs of the promise of descendants made to Abraham. So once again they depend for its continued fulfilment entirely on God, as Isaac prays for offspring for Rebekah and the Lord grants his prayer.

The struggles of the children in Rebekah's womb (v. 22), the explanatory oracle (v. 23) and the narrative of their birth (vv. 24–26) are a foretaste of what is to come: the normal order of things is to be overturned, for the elder will serve the younger. Barrenness, followed by the birth of two sons and the preferring of the younger over the elder, a pattern already seen in the narrative of Abraham and Sarah, is entirely contrary to all natural expectations, and emphasizes the workings of the divine in the course of events. The contrasting descriptions of the grown men (v. 27) add to the irony: surely a strong hunter would prevail over a stay-at-home mother's boy? But the crass and worldly Esau despises his status and right as the elder son and potential promise-bearer (vv. 29–34), and is eventually cut out of the line of promise in favour of the unlikely Jacob, who is a deceiver but also a God-wrestler (Genesis 32:24–28; see Proper 13).

Isaiah 55:10–13 (Related)

These lines from Isaiah picture the word of God in a similar fashion to that of the parable of the sower. Although here the word is the rain that makes the ground fertile rather than being the seed that grows (vv. 10–11), there is the same sense of the word producing fruit and thereby achieving the purposes of God. The reason for this is the nature of the divine word. Not only is it a vital, active, effective word, like the God from whom it proceeds, but the lack of distinction in Hebrew thought between a word and a deed means that God's word, once spoken, is as good as done. To speak and name something is to call it into reality, as is evidenced on a divine scale by the creation story, and so for God to speak something is to guarantee its fulfilment.

The second half of the passage describes more closely the result of the divine word, and gives a picture of Israel's redemption which shows the whole of nature in harmony with God's will (vv. 12–13). The singing hills, clapping trees and flourishing cypress and myrtle speak of an interconnected creation in which the correct relationship between God and people is a vital factor.

Romans 8:1–11

The chapter begins with an exclamation of thanks to the God who has broken the bonds of slavery to sin and death which were such a problem in the previous chapters (1—2). God's condemnation of sin in the flesh, through the death of Christ on the cross, means that those who believe are enabled by the Spirit to be everything that the Law was intended to make them but could not because it was corrupted by sinful flesh (vv. 3–4). The contrast between flesh and Spirit expresses the new kind of life that is available to those in Christ; instead of human life being an end in itself, leading only to death, it becomes the route to something else of lasting significance (vv. 5–6). This change in orientation can only be realized by the inward renewal brought about by the Spirit, which leads to the transformation of the individual's life (vv. 9–10). Without such inward renewal there is no such transformed life (vv. 7–8), and this is the difference between Law and Spirit—the Law tells people what to do but does not empower them to do it, but the Spirit's power transforms lives and, by making them righteous, now gives both body and soul life for ever (vv. 10–11).

Matthew 13:1–9, 18–23

This whole chapter is the centrepiece of Matthew's Gospel, and consists of a series of parables about the Kingdom of heaven. A number of the parables, like this one, compare the Kingdom to organic, growing things, and this is surely no accident. The Kingdom is not something lifeless which has to be erected, but it has its own mysterious life-force, like that in growing things. Such a comparison gives the lie to the idea of an instantaneous kingdom, because the very concept of growth implies a period of waiting and maturing before the final outcome is known.

The parable of the sower depicts the rather untidy spread of the Kingdom in terms of a person flinging seed in all directions (vv. 3–9). Some of the seed finds suitable ground in which to grow, but other seed is inevitably trampled or eaten or scorched or choked. The indiscriminate nature of the sowing process seems extremely wasteful, but it reflects the indiscriminate nature of the Kingdom. It is impossible to tell who will receive the word of God and who will not (vv. 18–23), but the word is for everyone, and must therefore be distributed to everyone, regardless of the fact that some will not respond.

DR

YEAR B

2 Samuel 6:1–5, 12b–19 (Continuous)

David now journeys to bring the principal emblem of Israel's worship to his new capital. The ark was a symbol of heritage, faith and unity, and had been in temporary accommodation for about a generation (6:3; 1 Samuel 7:1). The move to bring it to Jerusalem is surely politically astute. It will establish the city as a focal point of national faith, as well as the base from which David rules. None the less, the venture seems also to be an act of serious devotion to the Lord, and is recalled as such in Psalm 132.

The pause in proceedings recorded in 6:6–12a underlines the awesome holiness of Israel's God, but also suggests that he is ready to bless. Signs of his presence are not to be treated lightly, but it is safe and right to continue. So the ark comes to Jerusalem, with lavish extravagance of every kind, sacrifice and dancing, music and feasting. The sense is of benediction and completeness (vv. 17–19).

The greatest occasions in worship deserve wholehearted celebration. God's presence rightly evokes visible joy and thankful love. Yet there is a note of caution and reverence implied in verses 6–9. Worship must enhance —not diminish—the sense of God's greatness among us. Then it is worship indeed.

Amos 7:7–15 (Related)

The original wording of some verses is difficult to ascertain, but the general sense is clear. Amos has a vision of God's judgment against Israel, against her people, priests and king (vv. 7–9). This sort of prophetic warning is totally unwelcome at the royal shrine. So Amaziah, as a good guardian of state religion, tries to silence Amos.

A report to the king (vv. 10–11) covers Amaziah's own back, and may bring some strong-arm support. Amaziah does not consider whether Amos might be right; he merely complains of his nuisance value. Then he tries to send Amos away. After all, he does not fit. He is a southerner from Judah in the northern kingdom of Israel, and a rough country boy in a royal shrine (vv. 12–13).

Amos knows perfectly well where he comes from, and what he is doing. He was impelled by God, taken out of the fields and into the spiritual frontline (vv. 14–15). His only credentials are his call from God, the commitment that holds him to that call, and the gifts that give his ministry substance. Faithful ministry is often painful. God's word is not always palatable and popular. A preacher should have a tender heart—also a thick skin.

Ephesians 1:3–14

Ephesians spreads a grand and sweeping vision, setting the love and purpose of God against the whole expanse of space and time, and focusing that loving purpose upon the Church. The opening panorama traces God's choice from the beginning (vv. 3–6), his gracious and deliberate intention that Christ's people live holy and irreproachable lives (v. 4). At the centre of the plan is the costly death of Jesus Christ, by which God's ancient and abundant grace is given to his people (vv. 7–8). Then the design opens wide, to gather all creation into the headship and wholeness of Christ (vv. 9–10). Christians live within this hope, called to bring praise to God through their living, and sustained by the Holy Spirit, who is foretaste and assurance of richer blessing to come (vv. 11–14).

These words offered confidence to a fragile church. God, whose grandeur and glory surpass all limits of measure and language, draws ordinary and humble believers into a gracious cosmic plan. Christian living is no trivial matter, but part of a majestic purpose. Let the readers not feel overshadowed by a dominant pagan culture, for they are braced and embraced by God's supreme power. Let their Christian perspective not become introverted— they are a people for God's praise and holy purpose.

Mark 6:14–29

The successes of the Twelve prompt curious enquiries about Jesus. Then the story following draws the reader's attention to the acute cost of discipleship. For John the Baptist is alike enough to Jesus to be compared and confused with him (vv. 14, 16). John suffered and was killed for his preaching (v. 18). What will be ahead for Jesus and those who work with him?

Herod Antipas appears a pathetic character. Imprisoning John, he is himself arrested, perplexed and fascinated by the prophet's teaching. He has silenced public criticism of his illegal marriage, but he cannot quieten his private unease (vv. 18–20). Then confronted by Herodias' sly request (vv. 22–25), he lacks the spine—or sense, or sobriety—to follow his better instincts (vv. 26–28; cf. 15:15). Finally he is a man haunted, fearful to have tangled with power greater than his own (vv. 14, 16).

And John? He is the faithful forerunner of Jesus, bearing his suffering without losing faith or purpose (v. 20). His execution 'prepares the way' (1:3) for the greater passion ahead. When 6:14f is echoed in 8:28, we shall realize that another death is in view.

Is suffering for the gospel a regular part of Christian living? Not necessarily, and we do not seek it—but aspiring disciples must not shirk the possibility (8:34–38).

JP

YEAR C

Amos 7:7–17 (Continuous)

Amos is given a number of snapshot pictures, omens for Israel. At the beginning of this passage the Lord holds a plumb-line. Already Amos has seen locusts and fire, and his cry for mercy from such destructive judgments has been answered (vv. 1–6).

A plumb-line is held against a wall to show that the wall is straight, true and upright (v. 7). The judgment of God's standards cannot be put aside. His laws and his character do not change, and whatever way human societies and bent cultures go, there is only one plumb-line. Our lives, personally, nationally and as churches, are judged by God's plumb-line, which cannot change.

The consequences of judgment cannot be sidestepped. Amaziah and Jeraboam try to deny the inbuilt 'providence' of sin's consequences. They hide from the word of the Lord, which they know. Those who know the plumb-line's meaning but still ignore it have a huge responsibility. The 'plumb-line' approach to individual and social life today is not popular. Yet there is an urgent need for the courage of Amos, who challenges the power of those in charge, the influence of cultural and social trends, with standards that are ignored at our peril. The Lord's words (v. 17) do not only speak of judgment, but also of consequences.

Deuteronomy 30:9–14 (Related)

Throughout the ancient Near East, small groups of people, conquered or seeking aid, would make a treaty with a superior power which would give them protection in return for legal obligations. Many examples of these treaties have been recovered. Such a treaty identified the parties, recalled the circumstances, set out the terms and the enforcement, indicated the benefits, or blessings, as well as the penalties, or cursings, and made provision for review. Sections of the books of the Law form the same pattern. Here we have the promise of blessing if the Law is kept. Verse 9 has a 'return to Eden' ring about it—God's blessing expressed in the prospering of the land.

History, both in the Old Testament and subsequently, suggests that the Law is never kept, God is only partially obeyed and the blessing of social and economic well-being is also only partially and occasionally enjoyed. But history is also open-ended. In one sense this passage says that it is in our hands. We can change things; we can avoid the cursing. Obedience does not require heights of understanding (v. 12), nor great struggle (v. 13); it is not impossibly idealistic, impractical nor unachievable. The choice is ours; the command is God's (vv. 15–16).

Colossians 1:1–14

The two readings from the first chapter of Colossians (Proper 10 and 11) can both be summarized by three headings:

- Where Christians once were
- Where they now stand
- How they must go on

These emerge from a prayer of thanksgiving and petition by Paul for the Colossian church, into which he sweeps immediately after the customary greeting. (Compare the beginning of Galatians, where greeting is followed by rebuke—Proper 4.) The ministry and preaching of Paul, Timothy and of Epaphras have resulted in the establishment of this church.

Growth is what Paul is praying about—the process of sanctification, a life-long, fruit-bearing obedience. Particularly important in this very corporate message is that they grow together in action, loving each other, bearing fruit in every good work. They must also grow together in knowledge (Paul uses words such as understanding, learning, hearing, wisdom). It is this knowledge of his will, leading to right action, that is pleasing to God. The implications of this passage must be that individual churches have to find structures to facilitate relationships between Christians that make such growth, such intimacy and such corporate learning actually happen.

Luke 10:23–37

This parable is so familiar that it is almost impossible to recapture the original shocking impact. 'Good Samaritan' is a name for someone who does good deeds. For the original hearers it meant a member of a despised ethnic minority. Some of the significant points are:
- People sometimes hide battles of the heart behind difficult questions and theological argument. Jesus turned the question round so that the challenge could not be avoided.
- Anybody who seeks to love their neighbour has to be prepared to have plans disrupted and resources diverted.
- Anyone who takes on a commitment has to be prepared to see it through, and make it possible for others to help without presuming on their generosity.
- You could earn eternal life by loving God and others perfectly, but...
- 'What must I do?' suggests one bold action. 'Do this' means go on and on doing it.
- Involvement does not end. The Samaritan could have gone on to set up a hostel for travellers, found out why there were robbers in the hills and pressed for land reform and work for the unemployed!
- Finally, Jesus is giving the word 'neighbour' the widest possible meaning—that is, anyone. There are no distinctions at all between

human beings when it comes to being neighbourly. Our personal preferences, ethnic or otherwise, are irrelevant.

MK

PROPER 11

YEAR A

Genesis 28:10–19a (Continuous)

The rivalry between Jacob and Esau (fuelled by Rebekah) has come to a head, and Jacob is on his way to his mother's relatives, ostensibly to find himself a wife but in actual fact to avoid the wrath of Esau who has sworn to kill him (Genesis 27:41—28:2). Stopping for the night somewhere along the way, Jacob receives a vision from God which designates him as the new bearer of the promise (vv. 11–15).

The most remarkable thing about this vision is its timing. Jacob has just deceived his father and brother for his own ends (Genesis 27:1–40), and will continue in his deceitful ways for several years to come; and quite apart from his apparent moral degradation, if he is to be the bearer of the promise he must not only find a wife but first save his own skin from the marauding Esau. The expression of the promise therefore comes at the time when it seems least likely to be fulfilled, once again turning the focus from human circumstances on to the divine power and purpose which both define and defy those circumstances.

The whole vision, and Jacob's startled response to it (vv. 16–19a), sums up the unexpectedness of the encounter with God in terms of both time and place.

Isaiah 44:6–8 (Related)

This passage is a clear declaration of the uniqueness of God. At the time when it was written, the people of Israel were in exile in Babylon, undergoing great heart-searching to try to understand why their God had failed to protect them and their land against the invasion of the Babylonians. Was it because the Babylonian gods were more powerful than their own God? And what was to become of them now that they were in exile? The prophet answers their concerns in resounding fashion. There are no gods more powerful than the Lord, because there are no other gods (v. 6); neither other human beings nor the gods of Babylon are anything like the Lord (v. 7). This one and only God was there before everything else existed and will remain when everything else has gone (v. 6).

The proof of God's unique status is in the fact that God alone has been able to give accurate prophecies of what was to come, because God was the one who was bringing it about (vv. 7b–8). In the light of such a declaration, the exiled and demoralized people need not be afraid, because their God is well and truly in control, regardless of what has happened to them and where they are.

Romans 8:12–25

Despite his declaration that Christians have life because of the work of the Spirit in them (vv. 12–13), Paul recognizes that there is a further stage in the process of salvation, whereby not only Christians but the whole of the created order will be released for ever from the effects of sin and death (vv. 19–23). The gift of life in Christ and the Spirit of sonship which makes Christians into children of God (vv. 14–16) are only the beginning of this process of salvation; but they are the guarantee that the final salvation will come (vv. 17–23). There will inevitably be difficulties and suffering to go through—after all, Christ's own route to glory was via suffering and, as fellow heirs of Christ, believers can expect nothing different (v. 17). But the down-payment of the Spirit which enables believers to call upon God as their Father gives the certainty that there will be a glorious final resolution (vv. 15–17).

It is in this context that Paul speaks about hope. Hope is not about wishing for something that does not exist. It is the result of the promise which is guaranteed by the down-payment of the Spirit (vv. 23–24), and it is this promise with its guarantee that enables believers to face with patience whatever comes their way (v. 25).

Matthew 13:24–30, 36–43

The parable of the weeds is another picture of the 'organic kingdom' which emphasizes the need for patience in the face of growth and development. This time, though, there are a number of other elements introduced into the basic picture of the Kingdom as a field of wheat. There is a much stronger sense here of the presence of evil alongside even the good seed (vv. 26, 38–39), and of the clear attempts of the forces of evil to disrupt the grow-ing process (vv. 25, 28). The parable also has a much more pronounced eschatological element than the parable of the sower, in that it sees a definite time of harvest when the good and the bad will be sorted out and the good saved but the bad destroyed (vv. 30, 40–43).

The overall message seems to be that evil will attempt to thwart the Kingdom's development, but it will not in the end succeed; God will determine a time of harvest when the two are finally separated. Our part is to live with both the good and the evil, and not to attempt any pre-harvest judgments as to which is which, because the two can so closely resemble each other that God alone is fit to discriminate between them.

DR

YEAR B

2 Samuel 7:1–14a (Continuous)

David considers building God a house in which to live, a permanent place of worship. Why does the Lord reject what seems to be a laudable attempt to honour him? In fact, what appears to be a rejection turns out to be a profound and marvellous promise.

God does not need David to build him a house. But this is not because he wants nothing to do with David. As God says, he has faithfully guided and protected both David and his people. His response makes it clear that this loving faithfulness will continue. He turns David's suggestion on its head by saying that he, the Lord, will establish a 'house' for David (v. 11): his dynasty will be established for ever. For Christians, this promise has been fulfilled definitively in the kingship of Jesus Christ, the true Son of David.

This passage shows us the abundant and loving faithfulness of God. It also has important things to say about our relationship with him. Being his children (v. 14) means our attitude should be one not of presumption, but of trusting obedience and reliance on his faithful love, both now and for the future.

Jeremiah 23:1–6 (Related)

In today's Gospel reading, Jesus sees the crowds as 'like sheep without a shepherd', in need of true leadership. This echoes several Old Testament prophecies, including Jeremiah 23.

The shepherds of verses 1—2 are sinful kings who have brought disaster on Judah. They are described in more detail in the previous chapter. Yet human sin can never defeat the triumph of God, and he will redeem his people in the end (vv. 3–4). At the end of a century marked as no other by the terrible consequences of evil leadership, this message of future hope is extremely relevant to our generation.

Then Jeremiah looks forward to a particular king who will be a true descendant of David and therefore heir to the promises in 2 Samuel 7 (see today's 'Continuous' Old Testament reading). He will be more than just a good king; he will be 'the Lord our righteousness'.

For Christians, this prophecy is fulfilled in Jesus, the good shepherd and rightful king. He is not only righteous himself, but becomes our righteousness (1 Corinthians 1:30). What a contrast between the humble, loving kingship of the Jesus of today's Gospel readings and the violent, unjust oppresssion exercised by the kings criticized by Jeremiah.

Ephesians 2:11–22

This is a magnificent description of the effect of the cross on the future of humanity. Paul explains what God's plan to bring all things together in Christ (1:10) means for the ancient division between Jew and Gentile.

Previously, Gentiles (who made up most of the first readers of this letter) had been in a terrible position: outside the covenant, without hope, without God (vv. 11–13). But the cross has changed all that. Jesus' death has removed at a stroke both the hostile division between Jew and Gentile (v. 14) and the commandments and regulations which had excluded Gentiles from the people of God (v. 15).

Yet God is doing much more than bringing Jews and Gentiles together. He is creating a new humanity which is radically different from both groups, and open to all. The cross means peace between believers and peace with God, in a community where God himself now dwells (v. 22).

So this passage states the reality of our unity in Christ. It also urges us to work in the power of the Spirit, both to break down social and ethnic barriers within the Church, and to encourage those currently outside God's people to become part of his new creation.

Mark 6:30–34, 53–56

These two scenes from Jesus' ministry speak volumes about the love of God and the human response to it.

Jesus is clearly a deeply attractive character. His compassion (v. 34: Mark uses a very strong word, implying powerful emotion), the authority of his teaching (v. 34) and his power to heal (v. 56) draw huge crowds, determined to be with him. To an extent they recognize their needs and have clear ideas about how Jesus will meet them; they hurry to bring the sick to be healed (vv. 53–56). But in other ways they are simply helpless, 'like sheep without a shepherd', a reference back to Old Testament imagery of the leaderless people of Israel (see especially Jeremiah 23:1–6—today's 'Related' Old Testament reading—and Ezekiel 34).

Yet Jesus ministers to every need, touching every part of people's lives— accepting them, teaching them, healing them. His ministry is not only 'spiritual': the feeding of the five thousand is sandwiched between these two passages, and he brings physical wholeness to the sick. Neither is it only to individuals: he is the true shepherd of the people (v. 34), and his arrival at Gennesaret prompts the whole community to work together to bring the sick to be healed.

MG

YEAR C

Amos 8:1–12 (Continuous)

One Old Testament theme is that God in his mercy patiently waits for his people to repent and turn to him, so that he can forgive and restore, delaying over and over again the doom they are bringing on themselves (2 Peter 3:9). But judgment will come. Verse 3 has a terrible ring to it. Many scenes of the twentieth-century world come to mind. The sins of humanity bring destruction down on those guilty and responsible as well as those who are not.

The judgment comes not just for individual sin but for structural and institutional evil—for idolatry (7:9), breaking the first commandment to love God; and also for the systematic breaking of the second, to love one's neighbour. Greed, commercial exploitation, obsession with material wealth, cheating and injustice for the poor are listed. The sins of Amos' time, a world of small-scale agricultural societies, pale before the sins of today, where exploitation, greed, the exercise of power and environmental destruction are literally threatening the apocalyptic doom of verses 9–12.

Does the search for the word of the Lord (v. 12) echo the kind of spiritual searching which looks anywhere but to the living God and his revelation in Jesus Christ?

Genesis 18:1–10a (Related)

The three visitors stand in the sun. They are not knocking or asking for hospitality. But it is siesta time and when Abraham sees them he leaps up, begs them to rest and to stay, refresh themselves and have a meal. Hastily the household—Sarah and servants—prepare a sumptuous meal and Abraham stands and waits on the visitors.

The reader knows from the beginning that this is the Lord, but Abraham may only be doing his duty as a host—his form of address in verse 3 simply courtesy—until the end of the meal when the promise of a son, the promise of a miracle that can only come from God, is voiced by one of the guests. The Lord deals gently with this elderly couple and appears in the guise of ordinary visitors. As the story moves on in this encounter, especially to verses 16–33, it is not clear how the three visitors and the Lord are differentiated. Some have suggested a picture of the Trinity. Orthodox iconography has traditionally used the image of Abraham's visitors. The fifteenth-century icon by Andrey Rublev is a popular one.

The command to be hospitable is repeated frequently in the Bible and the rewards are sometimes just as unexpected (Hebrews 13:1–2; 1 Peter 4:9).

Colossians 1:15–28

This astounding and audacious theological poem places the highest Christological statement as early, probably, as the mid 50s AD. That is, only twenty years after the crucifixion, Paul is saying that in Jesus Christ God has revealed himself as the Creator and Redeemer of all, that Jesus is the full, final and complete human expression of the nature of God, that reconciliation and new life are only found in Christ.

Verses 21–23 remind the Colossians that they and 'every creature under heaven' need to hear and receive the gospel, because all are alienated from God and all need to be reconciled and to continue in faith. The word translated 'mind' in verse 21 includes all human processes of thought and ways of understanding. We are used to the idea that our emotions and personalities are awry, fallen and distorted, but we need to be reminded that the fall affects our rational intelligence as well. Not even the greatest genius, the most brilliant scholar, can totally 'think straight'.

Paul sees his sufferings in spreading the gospel in some sense as an extension of Christ's sufferings to bring redemption. This could connect with Jesus' command that disciples take up the cross. Nothing, however, can compare with the glory of 'Christ in you, the hope of glory' (v. 27).

Luke 10:38–42

A small human incident, understandable in any age, with a message for everyone.

What are our priorities? Do we fuss about tidiness, order, ceremony and laying the table correctly, and lose sight of what hospitality is really about? Do we fail to listen properly to our spouses, our children, because we are preoccupied with serving them and feeding them? Are we willing to give up our plans and structures to give our full attention to other people?

Do we give enough time to prayer and thoughtful reflection on our faith and our Lord? Do we feel that prayer and Bible study have to be done as quickly as possible in order to get on with the busy important things? This incident has much to say to 21st-century Christians!

This is one of several incidents that point to Jesus' radical attitude to women: women were not usually counted as disciples, as pupils of Jewish rabbi teachers. Martha's role as housekeeper and cook would be far more culturally acceptable. The 'one thing' of verse 42 could mean the words of the Lord, one thing at a time, or even that bread and cheese will do!

MK

PROPER 12

YEAR A

Genesis 29:15–28 (Continuous)

Jacob finds his way safely to his mother's brother, Laban, where he gets a taste of his own medicine: having agreed to serve Laban for seven years in return for the hand of Laban's daughter Rachel in marriage (vv. 18–20), Jacob finds that he has been given her elder sister Leah instead (vv. 21–25). Jacob himself might have evaded the normal expectation that seniority gives priority among siblings, but he cannot assume that that will always be the case regardless of others' rights. Indeed, in a culture where a woman's failure to find a husband was a desperate state of affairs, Laban's insistence on his daughter's rights of seniority protects Leah against being overlooked for her more attractive younger sister and secures her future.

In this situation of trickery, though, the first hint of a redeeming feature in Jacob's character comes through, because he loves Rachel so much that he is prepared to go along with the scheming Laban and serve for another seven years in order to have her too (vv. 26–30). With Jacob's acquisition of not one but two wives of Abrahamic extract, the promise of descendants is now ready to be abundantly fulfilled. The unlikely Jacob is indeed the promise-bearer.

1 Kings 3:5–12 (Related)

The story of Solomon's dream at Gibeon and his request for the wisdom which has become legendary is a good illustration of someone who knows what are the most important things in life. The newly established King Solomon is given the opportunity to ask from God whatever he wants (v. 5), which is both a test and a temptation for him. But he realizes that it is not the circumstances in which his kingship is exercised (wealth, long life, freedom from enemies, v. 11) that will enable him to be true to his vocation as king of Israel, but the ability to tell the difference between good and evil and therefore to govern the people in accordance with God's will (v. 9). In making this request, Solomon acknowledges not only that he is indebted to God for having gained the kingship at all, but that he is dependent on God's power in order to retain it.

The readiness with which God grants Solomon's request (vv. 10–12), together with the promise in the following verses to give Solomon the material benefits he did not ask for (v. 13), is reminiscent of Jesus' saying that if his followers give first place to the Kingdom of God, all their other needs will be supplied (Matthew 6:33).

Romans 8:26–39

The end of chapter 8 is spent in drawing out the consequences of the salvation which was outlined in the first part of the chapter. The presence of the Spirit with believers enables communication between them and God on a level beyond words, even beyond knowledge (vv. 26–27), and the promise of final salvation as guaranteed by the Spirit means that there is absolute certainty about the love of God even in the face of the most terrible tribulations of human circumstances (vv. 28, 35–36). Indeed, not only is God ever present with those who are believers, but for them God's purpose is being furthered even in the midst of such tribulations (vv. 28, 37). This is an affirmation of the power of God, which is not defeated or frustrated, whatever the outward appearance may be.

Paul draws two closing conclusions. First, the evil things that Christians suffer in their lives are not to be interpreted as punishment from God for their sins, because God, through Christ, in love, has already dealt with their sins, so there is no more need for punishment (vv. 31–36). Second, the overarching, conquering power of the love of God is affirmed in words which make clear Paul's conviction that this love is ultimately the power that rules the universe (vv. 37–39).

Matthew 13:31–33, 44–52

Three groups of parables here emphasize three different aspects of the Kingdom of heaven. First, the parables of the **mustard seed** (vv. 31–32) and the **yeast** (v. 33) continue the theme of the 'organic' kingdom which grows rather than being constructed. Both illustrate the miraculous aspect of this growth, in that it starts from very small beginnings but eventually develops into something many times larger. Never underestimate the power of small beginnings which are endued with Kingdom life!

The parables of the **treasure in the field** (v. 44) and the **pearl of great price** (vv. 45–46) then illustrate the value of the Kingdom; those who find the Kingdom do not think twice about getting rid of everything else they have in order to be able to possess it, such is its value. The Kingdom is costly, but well worth the sacrifice.

Finally, the parable of the **drag-net** (vv. 47–50) illustrates what might be called the consummation of the Kingdom. In a way reminiscent of the parable of the weeds, it promises a final reckoning when the good will be sorted from the bad that has got mixed in with it along the way (vv. 48–50). Hence, the inevitability of evil is illustrated, as is the assurance that evil will not finally prevail.

DR

YEAR B

2 Samuel 11:1–15 (Continuous)

David is enjoying great military victories with God's help (v. 1). Yet he allows himself to give in to temptation. Our guard is often at its lowest in successful times. David commits adultery with Bathsheba, who presumably had little choice in the matter. The king is not only sinning but also abusing his power.

The story underlines the insidious nature of evil. David gets entangled deeper and deeper as he tries to cover up his wrongdoing. This kind of situation is a familiar one to many of us; but for David, the consequences were appalling. The irony is that he is driven by a desire to preserve his outward respectability, but the pursuit of this goal blinds him to the terrible evil he is perpetrating.

David has behaved dishonourably, and his first ploy relies on Uriah also being prepared to act dishonourably (vv. 6–13). When this plan fails, David hatches a far worse plot which will result in the needless deaths not only of Uriah but of other soldiers as well (v. 15).

We underestimate sin at our peril. Setting our face against God's standards brings dangers for us and for others. What began with David's wrong exercise of power was to end in personal tragedy.

2 Kings 4:42–44 (Related)

This incident demonstrates the saving power of God, exercised through his servant Elisha. Notice the parallels with the role played by Jesus in the feeding of the five thousand.

First, just as Jesus showed concern for the hunger of the crowd, so Elisha has compassion on the company of prophets, without food in a time of famine.

Second, Elisha, the prophet of God, demonstrates his authority, ordering the bread to be set before the people and relaying God's statement that there will indeed be enough to eat; similarly, Jesus takes charge on the mountainside.

Third, the details in John's account echo the Elisha story more closely than in the other Gospels (only John mentions that the loaves are made from barley and only John includes the boy with the bread and fish, using the same word as the Greek Old Testament uses for Elisha's servant in 2 Kings 4). The implication is that one greater than Elisha is here, just as, later in John 6, Jesus claims to be superior to Moses.

So reading this episode alongside the feeding of the five thousand underlines both the unchanging generosity of God (common to both incidents) and at the same time the uniqueness of Jesus' ministry.

Ephesians 3:14–21

This wonderful prayer closes the first half of Ephesians with a climax of praise, before detailed instructions for right living begin in chapter 4. As it both summarizes the first half of the letter and looks forward to the second half, the focus in the prayer is constantly shifting between the big picture (the greatness of God's love) and the life of the believer within that big picture.

God the Father of humanity, our creator and redeemer, has glorious riches with which to bless us (vv. 14–16). Paul then narrows the focus, praying that God will specifically strengthen the Ephesians through his Spirit as they seek to live out their life of faith (vv. 16–17). The love of Christ is simply amazing and cannot be grasped, yet Paul still prays specifically that the Ephesians will know Christ's love in their lives and be rooted and grounded in it (vv. 18–19). God is able to do far more than we can ever imagine, yet his power is actually at work within us (vv. 20–21).

So the prayer holds together on the one hand the tremendous scope of God's love in action, and on the other hand, his intimate involvement in every detail of our lives.

John 6:1–21

The feeding of the multitude shows the sheer generosity of God's grace. Jesus provides unconditionally and abundantly. The timing (v. 4) is highly significant, anticipating Jesus' death at Passover time the following year; the cross is the place where the abundant grace of God is supremely demonstrated.

Yet Jesus accepts the boy's bread and fish—also freely given, but totally inadequate for the task. Jesus uses our weak offerings in remarkable ways, despite our struggle to muster faith in return (vv. 7–9). So our relationship with God is grounded in love: his wonderful, sacrificial, all-sufficient love, and our faltering response as we learn trust and loving obedience. (This message is reinforced in verses 16–21, where the disciples learn that their efforts are inadequate without the loving intervention of Jesus.)

Jesus therefore rejects alternative relationships based not on love but on manipulation or violence. The crowd are preoccupied with Jesus' material provision of bread, at the expense of the real message of the miracle, for which Jesus later rebukes them (vv. 26–27). This in turn leads them to seek to make Jesus king by force (v. 15), which he also rejects. Love and selflessness are to characterize our dealings both with God and with each other.

MG

YEAR C

Hosea 1:2–10 (Continuous)

While Amos, the other prophet to the northern kingdom, tells the people they have broken God's law, Hosea shows how they have broken God's heart. The data is not there to answer our questions about this shocking story. It appears to be a record of actual events, but the focus is on how these events disclose Israel's sin.

The image of prostitution (v. 2) is controversial, now that we are aware of the complex social factors involved. But in ancient Israel, the connection is with the fertility cults of Baal. It speaks both of the failure to be faithful, and of the failure to trust God to provide. As with sex, so with worship. What should be given in love, freely, in the context of covenant faithfulness, has been used for gain, with anyone or anything that will pay the price. God's judgment is just.

The place of compromise, Jezreel, will be the place of judgment (vv. 4–5), a symmetry echoed in Romans 1:18–19. The comment about bloodshed is a condemnation of Jehu's 'reform' (2 Kings 9–10); this alternative view to the one in Kings demonstrates the Old Testament's ambivalence about the politics of kingship, because the temptation is always to trust in human resources, not God's (v. 7, a theme repeated in Isaiah 30:15–16 and Zechariah 4:6). God's judgment is real.

But the future is open, not closed (v. 10; see also 2:23 and 1 Peter 2:10). There is always hope, since the goal of judgment is repentance. As on the cross, 'where wrath and mercy meet' (Graham Kendrick), the place of judgment becomes the place of restoration. God's judgment is full of mercy.

Genesis 18:20–32 (Related)
After meeting at the oaks of Mamre, God makes his plans known to Abraham in a remarkable act of condescension ('Shall I hide...?' v. 17).

Between the sentence of judgment on Sodom (v. 20) and its execution (19:24) there is an intrusion of grace. Here, Abraham pleads for the righteous, and so reverses the assumption that the sinful few can bring judgment on the many, instead seeing that the sinful many can be saved by the few righteous—perhaps even that one can save all (Isaiah 53; Romans 5:15–17).

But the ground of Abraham's appeal is the character and holiness of God ('Far be it from you...', v. 25). As he risks bringing his heartfelt question in prayer-encounter, he meets not a capricious tyrant but one who is truly God—constrained by compassion (Hosea 11:8–9), more concerned with saving a few than destroying the wicked and ready to intervene in free graciousness to break apart the bond of indictment and punishment. Through this opening, Lot escapes (19:12–16).

Abraham stands here as the bearer of God's promise of new possibilities —the one chosen, blessed and charged by God (vv. 18–19). As inheritors of that promise and descendants of Abraham (Romans 4; Galatians 3:7), we stand in the same place of grace in a world under judgment, and plead for that world as we await the revealing of God's Kingdom.

Colossians 2:6–15 [16–19]
Paul introduces himself and his message (ch. 1) and then appeals to the Colossians to grow in Christian maturity. There are close parallels here with verses in Ephesians, Romans and Galatians.

To receive Christ (v. 6) is less a decision than a way of life—living in the movement from what we were to what we will be. In a dense interweaving of images and metaphors, Paul characterizes this movement in five ways:
• From *emptiness* to *fullness* of life in Christ's own fullness (v. 10).

- From the *uncircumcision* of life lived according to our own selfish desires ('flesh') in common with the rest of humanity to spiritual *circumcision* which marks us out as God's distinctive people (vv. 11, 13).
- From *death*, the destiny of all who sin, to resurrection *life*, following the pattern of Jesus (v. 13).
- From *condemnation* to *acquittal*, as Christ bears our sin on the cross (v. 14).
- From *captivity* to *freedom* from every force or way of thinking that would enslave us (vv. 8, 15).

All this is to be received (v. 6) as a gift—so that our lives overflow with thanks (*eucharistia*, v. 7) in response to God's grace (*charis*).

Luke 11:1–13

In Luke 10 we learnt that Jesus' disciples minister with power (vv. 1–20), obey the commandments (vv. 25–28), show radical compassion (vv. 29–37) and attend to the teaching of Jesus (vv. 38–42). Here we learn that their prayer is modelled on that of Jesus, as he is the pattern for our relating to God (1 Corinthians 11:1; 15:20).

To whom should we pray? To a loving Father, who knows our needs, and delights to respond with good things (vv. 2, 11–12). Jesus' addressing of God as 'Abba' was both characteristic and distinctive, a relationship of intimacy for all who are in Christ (Romans 8:15–17).

How should we pray? With simplicity—the Lord's Prayer has a rhythmic simplicity that survives the process of translation—with directness (vv. 3–4), and with persistence, knowing that God longs to do us good even while we wait for an answer (vv. 5–8).

Why should we pray? The primary concern, that God's will be done, is not in conflict with making known our needs. 'Daily bread' can mean 'bread for the coming day' when the Kingdom will finally be consummated. And our greatest need is for spiritual resources to live the Kingdom life (v. 13). God's promise to answer is central to the restoration of his people (Jeremiah 29:14).

Discipleship means being concerned with his Kingdom, relying on his power, and desiring above all to see his glory made known.

IP

PROPER 13

YEAR A

Genesis 32:22–31 (Continuous)

Once again, Jacob has a life-changing close encounter with God. In the time since the last such encounter, he has acquired flocks, herds, servants, two wives, eleven sons and a daughter, and he is on his way back to Canaan. But again, the fulfilment of the promise is threatened—Esau, whom Jacob cheated out of a blessing from their father, is coming to meet him, and Jacob fears that Esau may kill them all (Genesis 32:6–8).

No wonder that when Jacob is faced with the mysterious nocturnal wrestler and recognizes the presence of God, even when the being injures him he refuses to let go until he has extracted a blessing (vv. 24–26), thereby securing the promise again. The blessing involves changing Jacob's name to Israel as a recognition of his metamorphosis from the deceiver who steals blessings from people to the struggler who wins them from God (vv. 27–28); he now has a name to live up to instead of one to live down (or down to). It also involves a debilitating injury (v. 31), which serves to remind him that all of his human vitality, and therefore his position as bearer of the promise, depends upon God. As long as he lives by that awareness, the promise will be secure.

Isaiah 55:1–5 (Related)

The notion of Israel as the vehicle of salvation to the whole world has its roots in passages such as this one, where clear hints are given of how God's dealings with Israel will affect the wider world. Here, continuing the tradition of God's love for and faithfulness to the Davidic kings, the people are invited to enter into a covenant relationship with the Lord (v. 3) which will not only give them the true fulfilment that money cannot buy (vv. 1–2), but will endow them with such glory that the whole world will be scrambling to be associated with them (v. 5). Although the prophet does not say that the rest of the world will be saved because of Israel, there is certainly the sense that the effects of God's loving plan and the result of Israel's obedient response to the divine summons will be much wider than those who are involved in it could ever imagine. Their obedience means that God's glory can be displayed to the whole world, and this is the first step down the road to salvation for all. The world needs to learn what God can do, and marvel, before it is ready to be invited to share in the glory.

Romans 9:1–5

Here Paul sets out the tragically ironical position of his people the Jews, to whom all the privileges of divine revelation and promise have been given (vv. 4–5), but who are apparently now in a state of condemnation by God for their failure to recognize in Christ the fulfilment of the promise made to them (v. 3). The implied contrast here between Paul's kinsfolk by race and his spiritual brothers and sisters in Christ (v. 3), as well as his talk of the Messiah 'in human terms' (v. 5), gives a clue about how this has happened. Paul's kinsfolk seem to have regarded what are essentially preparatory measures as an end in themselves rather than as a means to an end. They have become bogged down in the physical requirements and have missed the spiritual content to which the physical requirements should point, which is why they failed to recognize the very one they were looking for. The result is that despite being the vehicle through which God's plan of salvation was made known to the world (vv. 4–5), they cannot themselves benefit from it until they recognize its fulfilment in Christ. This is a sobering thought, which the Church as the new Israel would do well to ponder.

Matthew 14:13–21

The feeding of the five thousand is one of the best-known miracles of Jesus. It is reminiscent of a similar miracle performed by the prophet Elisha (2 Kings 4:42–44), but more dramatic because Jesus feeds far more people with far less food (vv. 17–21). However, like the miracles performed by Elisha, the miracle here serves as a prophetic sign, verifying Jesus' credentials as a man of God and validating his preaching ministry. Actions without words are ambivalent, and words without actions lack validation. But when actions and words go together, the actions are interpreted by the words which are in turn validated by the actions.

However, the feeding of the multitude is more than a *prophetic* sign. It is also a foretaste of the messianic banquet, the great festal celebration at the end of time when the Messiah has come, evil has been defeated and all human need has been met. In that sense, therefore, it can be regarded as a *messianic* sign, especially as it is so much more dramatic than the equivalent 'prophetic' miracle worked by Elisha.

Finally, the miracle illustrates the very practical concern for human welfare which must accompany any genuine preaching of the word of God.

DR

YEAR B

2 Samuel 11:26—12:13a (Continuous)

God now faces David with the consequences of Uriah's murder (from last week's reading). If David thought he could keep his sin from God, he was wrong (v. 27). As David's deception unravels, key characteristics of God come to the fore.

First, God's holiness. The parable delivered through Nathan (vv. 1–6) is a powerful indictment of injustice. David instinctively attacks the rich man's behaviour. Yet does the vehemence of his reaction (v. 5) betray an emerging sense of his own guilt, which he is projecting on to the villain of the story?

Second, God's judgment (vv. 7–12) is uncompromising. David's hypocrisy and guilt are laid bare, together with the long-term consequences for the relationships within his family (see ch. 13 onwards). The judgment throws David's sin into even sharper relief by stressing the blessings he had received from God.

Third, God's mercy (v. 13). David at last comes to his senses and realizes what he has done. He will have to live with the consequences of his actions, but God in his mercy enables him to make a fresh start. See the deep expression of repentance combined with trust in the mercy of God in Psalm 51, set for today, and traditionally associated with this story.

Exodus 16:2–4, 9–15 (Related)

The story of the manna from heaven is referred to several times in the New Testament, nowhere more profoundly than in Jesus' bread of life discourse in John 6 (see today's Gospel reading), so it is illuminating to compare and contrast the two passages.

Whereas the manna in the wilderness provided merely material nourishment, the bread of life offered by Jesus provides spiritual nourishment and eternal life (John 6:49, 58).

However, the story of the manna is not just an inferior precursor of the ministry of Jesus. It has its own significance as a key example of God's provision for his people at a time of great need. And the story serves to counterbalance an over-spiritualized reading of John 6. Yes, the bread of life is of ultimate importance for each human being, and Jesus criticizes those who are out merely to fill their stomachs. But God is also concerned for his people's physical well-being: witness the feeding of the five thousand in John 6:1–21. So, by extension, the provision of manna shows God's profound involvement in issues of justice in this world (he was, after all, leading his people out of slavery), not merely in some unseen spiritual realm.

Ephesians 4:1–16

Paul gives an exciting and invigorating call to the Church to live and grow in the service of God. Taking this passage seriously will shake us out of the complacency, disunity and dullness which can threaten so much church life.

First, Paul reminds us of the unity we share as Christians. We are all called to witness to the love of Christ in the way we treat each other (vv. 1–2). This is both a challenge to Christians (all churches need to learn from it) and a sign to the world (what could be more distinctive than living genuinely and radically by the principles outlined here?) Thankfully, the Church is not left to demonstrate this unity on its own: the unity we have is founded on the unity of God himself (vv. 4–6), and his sovereignty, love and peace.

Second, this unity does not mean static uniformity, but dynamic diversity as Christ equips us for his service, and the Church grows in unity and maturity. Specific gifts are mentioned (v. 11) and these callings must be encouraged. Yet all God's people work together as the body of Christ (v. 12). We are all gifted by Christ, and we are all his ministers!

John 6:24–35

Is our God too small? In this conversation with the crowd, Jesus tackles two distortions of what true faith in God should be—distortions which are still with us.

The first distortion is to see God merely as the supplier of material needs, rather than the giver of eternal life (vv. 26–27). We might feel safe from the temptation to regard Jesus merely as a provider of our daily bread. But what about the tendency for our prayer to lapse into mere lists of requests?

The second distortion is to see God as the supplier of miracles to order (v. 30). The crowd demand a sign to enable them to believe. Yet they have already seen miracles and have not believed. Still more 'proofs' will not help (see Jesus' ironic comment at 4:48).

In contrast, true faith is not merely driven by response to outward signs, important though these can be, but is rather commitment to the person of Jesus (v. 29). Ironically, the crowd still fail to see (v. 34) that the gift of God in Jesus is greater than any material gift could be (v. 35) and is bringing a far greater miracle than they could imagine—the salvation of the world (v. 33).

MG

YEAR C

Hosea 11:1–11 (Continuous)

God's self-disclosure here reaches a level of tenderness and power unmatched anywhere else in the Old Testament. It challenges our view of:

- **God.** He is not passive and remote but actively calls people into relationship with himself (v. 1). As in the garden of Eden (Genesis 3:9) and in the ministry of Jesus (Matthew 11:28), so he calls today (Revelation 3:20). He is concerned less with law than with love, showing the greatest tenderness of human relations—yet transforming and surpassing it (vv. 3–4). What human father shows such passion, patience and persistence?
- **Ourselves.** Small as Israel was, soon to be swallowed up by the great powers (v. 5), destined to repeat the slavery of the past ('Egypt', v. 5), doomed to annihilation (Admah, Zeboiim, v. 8; Deuteronomy 29:23)— it was the object of God's love (v. 8b), the one in whom he delighted to show his tenderness. Torn between self-sufficiency and hopelessness, we recall our dependence on him—it is his fingers we grasp in our faltering steps to maturity (v. 3). We are ever the objects of his compassion.
- **Others.** Those within the covenant community are similarly objects of tenderness. Those outside are the ones over whom God still agonizes. Jesus, taking up the story of Israel in himself (Matthew 2:15), stretched his arms wide on the cross in the recoil of compassion from wrath (vv. 8–9).

Ecclesiastes 1:2, 12–14; 2:18–23 (Related)

The authority of any biblical text derives from its place within the biblical narrative. These verses are not doctrine to be believed but wise reflection to be pondered in the context of the wider biblical picture.

The sum total of all life is less than a breath (v. 2), reflects the Teacher. It is insubstantial, ephemeral, nothingness. This contrasts with the Old Testament sense of God's glory, *kabod*, which literally means 'weight' or 'substance.'

In particular, all our efforts in work are futile. Work itself is unsatisfactory (1:13), the results count for nothing (1:14), and we cannot even enjoy what we have done as it passes to others once we die (2:18).

In creation we are given a high vision of work (Genesis 1:28) as the means by which we exercise dominion over the world as God's stewards. And we live in hope that God will more than restore this vision in new heavens and a new earth (Isaiah 65:17–25), where work will not be futile, and each person will enjoy the fruit of their labours.

Yet strung between these is the experience of futility, both inside and outside the community of faith. God's transforming vision does not trivialize or simplify this experience, but takes it seriously and works through it.

Colossians 3:1–11

What does the new life Christ has brought us through the cross (2:13) look like? It involves:

- **Looking up** (vv. 1–4). God's future has broken through into the present through the cross and resurrection. Christians are already living in this future (v. 1a), even though it has yet to be fully revealed (v. 4). This does not mean being 'other-worldly' and of no earthly use, but living as citizens of heaven on earth, in the reality of Christ's authority and reign (vv. 1–2). We are to be what we will become in Christ.
- **Putting down** (vv. 5–7; cf. Romans 6:11; 8:13). This world's habit of putting the self and its desires (v. 5) at centre stage will not survive into God's future where we now belong. So we must let go of them—put them down in the veterinary sense of the word. They belong to the past (v. 7), so let's make them history!
- **Taking off** (vv. 8–11). This world's attitude to others (vv. 8–9) is based on division, deceit and defensiveness. But Christ's death has broken down the dividing wall of hostility (Ephesians 2:14) and made real the oneness of humankind through his presence (v. 11; cf. Galatians 3:28).

All this comes as an act of will, but not by the power of will. It is brought about by a sovereign act of new creation (v. 11a).

Luke 12:13–21

Jesus' line of teaching is diverted by a request for arbitration (v. 13). He refuses, ostensibly because he is not a trained rabbi and so is unqualified (v. 14). But the implication is that he has a more important mission than to administer avarice.

Greed is insidious. It creeps in seemingly uninvited, and must be guarded against (v. 15). In ancient Israel, the promise of God's blessing leading to prosperity (Deuteronomy 28:1–14; Job 42:10–17) had been corrupted so that all prosperity was seen as a sign of God's blessing. In the modern West, the triumph of material prosperity has fooled us into believing that consumerism is the superior ideology, and that those with more and better things that they do not need ('abundance' or perhaps 'superfluity', v. 15) are better or more worthy people. Greed, we are told, is the motive power of progress.

270

But real life is life with God. Do we invest as much thought, planning, creativity and resourcefulness in our spiritual life as in our barns—our cars and clothes, holidays and houses (v. 18)?

As his possessions possess him, the man's world shrinks until his own comfort completely fills his horizons (v. 19). The needs of others and the worship of God fail even to register on the periphery. But mortality brings reality, and his true state is revealed (v. 20).

Are we wise or foolish investors (v. 21)?

IP

PROPER 14

YEAR A

Genesis 37:1–4, 12–28 (Continuous)

Jacob's experiences of sibling rivalry are duplicated among his own sons by Jacob's favouring of Joseph (v. 3), his youngest son but one, whose birth to the beloved Rachel ended her barrenness (Genesis 30:22–24). Once again the same factors appear: the child born to the barren mother epitomizes divine intervention, and the rules of seniority are disregarded in his favour. This time, however, it all seems to go badly wrong, because Jacob's favouring of Joseph, as well as Joseph's remarkable dreams, excite the hostility of the other brothers (vv. 4–8), and they hatch a plot to get rid of him (vv. 19–20).

There is a certain irony in the mention of the Ishmaelites as those to whom Joseph is sold by his brothers (vv. 25, 27–28); they are supposedly the descendants of the son of Abraham who was cast out by his father, and they now help to ferry another outcast of the patriarchal line to his destiny, a destiny which at present is quite unknown. The one glimmer of hope is that Joseph is not dead. Even though the brothers think they have seen the last of him, he has the signs of God's hand on his life, and they may all live to be surprised.

1 Kings 19:9–18 (Related)

Elijah is in rather a precarious situation. Having defeated and slaughtered the prophets of Baal in a contest on Mount Carmel (1 Kings 18:20–40), he now has the wrath of Jezebel to contend with (1 Kings 19:1–2), who has threatened to do the same to Elijah. Overcome with fear and self-pity, he flees into the wilderness to Horeb (another name for Sinai) (1 Kings 19:3, 8), where he encounters God, but not in the traditional modes of storm and fire that Moses and the Israelites had experienced on Sinai. This time there is a new revelation, for God is in the whispering voice that the stormy phenomena would have hidden (vv. 11–12). The voice not only renews Elijah's prophetic commission (vv. 15–16), it tells him that there are another seven thousand in Israel who are still faithful to the Lord (v. 18).

It is very easy in the midst of the storm to despair and lose sight of reality; in fact, that is probably the chief danger. But at the centre of the storm there is the whisper of reassurance that speaks of One in control who is more powerful than the storm, and who can give the necessary courage to go on, by refreshing and renewing the vision of those who are faithful.

Romans 10:5–15

There are two clear messages here about salvation in Christ. The first is that it is a universal gift, and not something confined to one particular group of people (vv. 11–13). Before the coming of Christ, the Jews were the ones who received the revelation of God's purposes, including the Law (v. 5), and so were traditionally the ones to benefit from the divine mercy. Now, however, there is no distinction between the Jews and the rest of the human race in this respect. Salvation is not a matter of perfect human observance of the Law, something which is impossible anyway; hence, the possibility of salvation is not confined to those who received the Law. On the contrary, salvation is the gift of God, and everyone who believes sincerely and proclaims openly that Jesus is the risen Lord will be saved (vv. 6–10), regardless of whether or not they belong to the traditional religious grouping.

The theme of open confession of Jesus as Lord is taken up in the second part of the passage, where it is God's will that those who have already believed should preach and spread the good news about Jesus in order that this design of universal salvation can be realized (vv. 14–15).

Matthew 14:22–33

The miracle of Jesus walking on the water is redolent with theological overtones. The strong wind and the beating waves (v. 24) represent the powers of chaos which were subdued into orderliness at creation but which are always ready to burst out again. Humans on their own are liable to be overwhelmed when this happens, but not the Creator who did and still does subdue the chaos. When Jesus makes his way unharmed through the storm, walking on the water (v. 25), he demonstrates the power of the

Creator to prevail in the face of chaos; his action is therefore an implicit claim about his identity, as are perhaps his words 'It is I', which could also be translated 'I am' (see Proper 17, Exodus 3:13–14). Peter's initial enthusiasm to get out of the boat and walk through the storm towards Jesus, followed by his terror at the waves and his near submersion (vv. 28–30), are an apposite comment on the dangers of enthusiastic love accompanied by insufficient faith. It is not the waves in themselves that cause Peter to sink, but his fear of them. Given that the passage speaks of trusting oneself to the unassailable power of the Creator even when the storm is not calmed, the lesson is clear.

DR

YEAR B

2 Samuel 18:5–9, 15, 31–33 (Continuous)

The train of events set in motion by David's sins of adultery and murder (11:1—12:13a) now reaches a climax. Nathan warned David that his family would be cursed with violence and that calamity would come upon him (12:10–11). The rebellion by Absalom fulfils this prophecy.

David presents a tragic figure. He is torn throughout between the need to defend his throne and his deep love for his wayward son (vv. 5, 33). His suffering is intensified by the realization that he is himself to blame for much of what has happened. His own sin and his failure to discipline Absalom earlier have both contributed to the tragedy. So the news of his army's victory leaves David confused and wretched (vv. 31–33). His understandable remorse over the death of Absalom appears to outweigh any gratitude either to his troops or to God for the victory.

This is a harsh and violent story, from which few people emerge with credit. Yet God remains in ultimate control, no matter how appalling the circumstances. He delivers David from his enemies (v. 31); even nature seems to help (vv. 8–9). So amid all the desperate consequences of human sin, there are still reasons for hope.

1 Kings 19:4–8 (Related)

After the astonishing experience of the contest with the prophets of Baal on Mount Carmel, Elijah is brought down to earth by Jezebel's threats against him. As a result, he flees in terror, abandoning the land of Israel (travelling beyond Beersheba) and apparently giving up the ministry to which God had called him, so depressed has he become (v. 4). For those of us prone to swinging between spiritual highs and lows, the knowledge that a great servant of God experienced this is somewhat reassuring!

The response of God in sending an angel with food and drink is gracious and beautifully compassionate. This reminds us of the sustaining reality of God's presence even in dark times when it is hard to distinguish it. The nourishment Elijah receives from heaven appears to have a special quality which enables his extraordinary journey to Horeb, where he will encounter the still, small voice of God and be commissioned once again for God's work (vv. 12–18). So there is a link between being nourished by God and growing in acceptance of his will, just as in today's Gospel reading. If we need encouragement to seek sustenance from God in Bible reading and prayer, here it is.

Ephesians 4:25—5:2

The first half of Ephesians explains how the Church fits into God's overall plan of salvation. Then chapter 4 lays down principles about the unity of the Church (4:1–16) and the need for Christians to live a new life in Christ, putting off the old self and putting on the new (4:22–24). Now Paul gets right down to brass tacks: how does this work out in practice?

The list of instructions shows how the principles of unity and love in the Church should affect the way we behave. Lying, unjustified anger, and stealing, all of which undermine fellowship with each other, are condemned. The everyday nature of these sins makes the passage all the more challenging. Unity and love must be real not just in principle, not just in our overall priorities, but in the detail of our daily relationships.

God enables us to live in his light, of course. The security of knowing we are loved by God our Father helps us to love others in turn (5:1). Christ's sacrificial love is an example for us to follow (5:2). The Holy Spirit lives in us as the guarantee of our redemption (4:30), empowering us to live lives pleasing to God.

John 6:35, 41–51

'I am the bread of life' is the first of the seven famous 'I am' sayings of Jesus in this Gospel—sayings which make fundamental claims about his relationship to God and which bring into sharp focus the implications of accepting or rejecting his message. As the bread of life, Jesus is the one who nourishes us, the one on whom we are to depend for everlasting life.

Notice what Jesus says about this offer of divine love and sustenance. On the one hand, the offer is made to those whom God chooses (vv. 37, 44).

274

On the other hand, this is balanced by stress on our responsibility to come to God through Christ (vv. 35, 45; see also 5:40).

Understanding the relationship between God's sovereign choice and free human response is not easy! But Jesus offers us help, recalling Isaiah's prophecy that in the restored Jerusalem, 'they will all be taught by God' (v. 45; Isaiah 54:13). The promise is now applied to the new community which trusts in Jesus. Through his Spirit, God teaches us and gives us insight so that our will becomes more attuned to his (cf. 16:12–15 and Jeremiah 31:31–34); his choice and our response work in harmony.

MG

YEAR C

Isaiah 1:1, 10–20 (Continuous)

The vision of Isaiah reveals the truth about God's people with a stinging indictment of their worship.

- **Bad news and good news.** The people are (shockingly) compared with Sodom and Gomorrah (v. 10), a byword for both sin and judgment. Their worship is an offence to God as long as there is no reform of lifestyle. But this is because God's holiness concerns every aspect life, in particular honesty, justice and concern for the poor (v. 17; cf. Leviticus 19:34).
- **Form and content.** Ritual and lifestyle were equal concerns of the Torah ('teaching', v. 10b). Worship consisting of one and not the other is an affront to a God who is One (Deuteronomy 6:4, a central confession of Israel's faith). Rites and wrongs (v. 13b) do not mix! The blood of bulls cannot hide murderous intent (v. 15b); washing with water is no substitute for holiness of life (v. 16). Sunday and Monday belong together.
- **Cleansing and worship.** The people are put on trial (v. 18)—but suddenly God is not only accuser but acquitter! What God offers in cleansing always precedes anything we can offer in worship ('Therefore... offer...' Romans 12:1). Even the Law (whose blessings and curses from Deuteronomy 28–30 are echoed in verses 19–20) came as a gift, the initiative of a gracious God who rescued his people.

Genesis 15:1–6 (Related)

After the first word of promise and Abraham's obedience to it (12:1–4), we find him living by the truth of God's provision (14:23).

Afresh comes the word of **promise** (v. 1). It is based on relationship with God, but with tangible rewards (the land, v. 18). Yet this reward is not a *quid pro quo*, a wage earned, but a gift of grace. Trusting is not the cause of fulfilment, and yet only those who hope can receive it—which is the paradox of faith.

In response comes Abraham's word of **protest** (vv. 2–3): what use is land without an heir? Faith is not a peaceful, pious acceptance, but a hard-fought and deeply argued conviction. God's promise comes against the situation of barrenness, but those who live by faith have to live with barrenness until the promise is fulfilled.

Against this comes God's 'But...', his **restatement of promise** (v. 4). There are no new facts here, no proof, but in the stars a sign (cf. for example, John 2:11): 'This have I done; this will I do.' God stands with Abraham and gives not a formula but his personal pledge. And the promise of the stars is not obscured by the earthbound lights of human effort.

The new response is one of **acceptance** (v. 6). God has not used persuasion but revelation, and for Abraham he is no longer a theory but 'a voice around which his life is organized' (Walter Brueggemann, *Interpretation* Commentary, John Knox Press, p. 144). From the closed present he stands open to God's future, a future that finds its fulfilment in Christ.

Hebrews 11:1–3, 8–16

'We walk by faith, not by sight' (2 Corinthians 5:7).

Faith gives confidence (v. 1). Our sight misleads us, since appearances are deceptive. The world is not always as it seems. But faith opens our eyes to God's promise of how things will be (v. 9). Faith is not a leap in the dark, but a leap into the light of God's future (vv. 10, 12).

Faith leads to action (v. 8). What we believe about the world will determine how we act, and how we act reveals what we believe. The confidence of faith enables us to take the risk of costly obedience, following in the footsteps of Abraham. Faith is not about jumping to conclusions, but about coming to the conclusion to jump.

Faith makes us different. Where many are uncertain about the world we live in, we know by faith that it is God's good world over which he still reigns (v. 3). Where many are comfortable with their world, we are always dissatisfied, because we know that God has a better plan in which we will be at home (v. 14). And yet we delight in the foretaste that we have had of the coming Kingdom (v. 13).

Faith is the hallmark of those who are citizens of heaven's outpost here on earth (v. 16).

Anxiety about material needs is pointless because life is about more important things (12:23), because God has promised to provide (12:24) and because it achieves nothing (12:25). The same is true of our concern for the Kingdom (v. 32). When we look at ourselves ('little flock'), we are given to fear (or perhaps false confidence). But when we focus on God's generosity, we are liberated to live in that generosity (v. 33).

Our desires often determine our actions, but the converse is also true. If we simply act according to God's promise ('sell... give... make...') then our desires will be shaped by this—our hearts *will* be where we have invested our lives (v. 34). Accumulating treasure on earth makes us self-centred, but working for treasure in heaven makes us other-centred.

This treasure is inflation-proof, there is no commission to pay, no unscrupulous middle-man selling us the wrong policy, and the value of our investment can only go up.

Living in the 'in-between' era before Jesus' return (v. 36), our actions must be shaped by the future to come. The master comes to our lives as he will come to the world (vv. 36–37; cf. Revelation 3:20)—as a friend in the day for those who are ready (John 11:9; 1 John 1:7) but as a thief in the night for those who are not, in unexpected ways (v. 39, 'breaks in' through the clay walls rather than the door) as well as at an unexpected time (see also 1 Thessalonians 5:2, 4; 2 Peter 3:10; Revelation 3:3; 16:15).

IP

PROPER 15

YEAR A

Genesis 45:1–15 (Continuous)

The contrast between Joseph the stripped and bedraggled youth, sold as a slave, and Joseph the head of all Egypt could hardly be more startling. Now the real reason for the brothers' failure to kill Joseph becomes apparent: in killing him they would have cut off their own chances of surviving the famine, and that would have invalidated the promise to Abraham. So God transmuted their death sentence on Joseph into an exile, thereby enabling their evil intentions to be transformed into good and safeguarding the promise (vv. 5–8). Joseph's gift of dreaming and interpreting dreams, which so angered his brothers, turns out to be what secures their survival; it was Joseph's interpretation of Pharaoh's dream, to warn of the seven-year famine, that was instrumental in getting him to his authoritative position, thereby equipping him to provide for his whole family (v. 11; see Genesis 41:25–36).

The power of God knows no geographical boundaries, manipulating events in Egypt as well as in Canaan and involving other races in fulfilling the promise to Abraham's kin. Discerning the hand of God in the events (as well as their prosperous outcome) enables Joseph to be reunited with his brothers without recrimination, although not before an understandable test of their sincerity (Genesis 44).

Isaiah 56:1, 6–8 (Related)

In all three of the other readings for today, there can be discerned the theme of other races being used for the benefit of God's chosen people, either to further God's purposes for Israel or as a kind of lesson or example to unfaithful Israel. Here, however, there appears a more direct appreciation of other races for their own sake, and an invitation to them to be accepted along with Israel, on the same terms as Israel (vv. 6–7). This, of course, flows partly from rejecting the gods of other nations as unreal and declaring that there is only one true God (Isaiah 44:6–8); if humans are to worship any god, it must be this one. But what is remarkable is the generosity of the offer of acceptance. It would be conceivable to have a kind of holy hierarchy whereby Israelites had pride of place and everyone else was a second-class citizen of heaven. Here, however, there is no such hierarchy; anyone who does the will of God, Israelite or not, is acceptable in the divine presence, on the holy mountain, in the temple itself. In the people of God as constituted by God, there is no room for holy huddles. God accepts the 'foreigner'; so must we.

Romans 11:1–2a, 29–32

It might be thought from Paul's comments that the Jews' failure to acknowledge Christ has resulted in God abandoning them in favour of non-Jews. But his own position as a Jew and an apostle of the gospel is proof enough that Jews are no more rejected than anyone else (vv. 1–2a). God is still in control of the process of salvation, and the Jews still have a place in it (v. 29). Even though things apparently have not gone according to plan, there is no need to despair, because God can put even the disappointments to good use. The Jews' initial failure to acknowledge Christ means that the Gentiles have been given the opportunity of salvation (v. 30); and the Gentiles' response in faith will eventually result in the Jews too being convinced of the truth of the gospel (v. 31).

Ultimately, what has happened is a breaking down of the division between Jews and Gentiles. All have been put on the same level in the eyes of God (v. 32): the Jews are being disobedient as the Gentiles were previously, and the Gentiles are receiving the mercy of God as the Jews had done previously. Likewise, all will share the sole means of salvation—the mercy of God in Christ.

Matthew 15:[10–20] 21–28

These two passages serve to compare and contrast the attitudes to Jesus of the religious groups among his own people and a Gentile woman who is a complete outsider in Jewish terms. The critical attitude of the Pharisees towards Jesus and his disciples over their lack of observance of a minor issue of ritual purity (15:1–2), and their offence at his retort that moral impurity is what really defiles people (vv. 10–12), are contrasted strongly with the faith in Jesus of the Gentile woman who is prepared to plead with him until he heals her daughter (vv. 22–28). As well as emphasizing the contrast between the cynical, self-righteous Pharisees and the believing woman, the juxtaposition illustrates the lesson that Jesus gives to his disciples in the first part. It is not the external observances which in the end determine purity and impurity and therefore elicit the blessing of God; rather, it is the inward faith and preparedness to honour God from the heart. In that sense, the Gentile woman, who is certainly not 'clean' or 'pure' in the way that the Pharisees would understand, is more pure than they are, and is the one who ultimately receives the blessing.

DR

Year B

1 Kings 2:10–12; 3:3–14 (Continuous)

Solomon succeeds his father David, and his reign begins well.

First, Solomon has a right perspective. He acknowledges God's faithfulness to his father (3:6). He recognizes his own weakness (v. 7): notice how he describes himself as a little child, even though he was about forty at his accession (11:42; 14:21).

Second, Solomon has right priorities. He asks (v. 9) for a 'discerning heart' (NIV) or 'understanding mind' (NRSV) so that he may rule wisely. His concern is to serve God and others, not himself.

Third, Solomon's request pleases God—so much so that God grants his request for wisdom (see 3:16–28) and adds the blessings of wealth and lifelong honour as well, even though Solomon had not asked for these (v. 13). God's desire is always to bless us in ways beyond our imagining.

Despite this good start, Solomon was later to turn away from God, under the influence of foreign wives; this led God to divide the kingdom after his death (11:1–13). His marriage to an Egyptian (3:1) is an early indication of what was to come. Even when things go well and our relationship with God is close, we are open to temptation, and need God's help to resist it.

Proverbs 9:1–6 (Related)

The personification of Wisdom as the creative power of God is an important theme in Proverbs. It is also seen as one of the roots of the idea of Christ as the *Logos*, the creative Word of God, characteristic of John's Gospel.

Three gifts of God are evident in this passage—gifts which emerge also in Jesus' teaching in today's Gospel reading.

Wisdom offers generous hospitality (vv. 2, 5; cf. John 6:53–56). The image of a banquet provided by God is a vivid one which recurs often in scripture. God takes the initiative, offering blessing on a grand scale to all who are prepared to admit their need of him.

Wisdom offers understanding (v. 6; cf. John 6:45). God does not expect mere blind obedience; rather, through his Spirit, our minds are illuminated so that we become willing partners in his purposes.

Wisdom offers life (vv. 6, 10–11; cf. John 6:51, 53–54, 57–58). The stark choice between wisdom and folly in Proverbs is portrayed as a matter of life and death (cf. Proverbs 9:13–18), calling to mind the challenge in John to make a decision for or against Jesus—except that in John, the life on offer is explicitly everlasting.

Ephesians 5:15–20

The whole of this part of Ephesians is a 'wake-up call' to the Church, to live the distinctive, committed life God wants us to live in an indifferent or hostile world.

Here, the emphasis is on living in the wisdom of God, not the folly of the world. Paul makes the point with a threefold exhortation. First, we are to use our time wisely to serve God, in a sinful age (v. 16). Second, we are to live wisely by gaining a practical understanding of what God's will for us is (v. 17). Third (v. 18), being filled with the Spirit, the bringer of wisdom (cf. John 16:13), is contrasted with the folly of drunkenness (cf. Proverbs 23:31–35).

Being filled with the wisdom of the Holy Spirit manifests itself in our worship (vv. 19–20). Our praise of God shows the world that our commitment is to God's will and his wisdom. In turn, our worship of God reinforces our relationship with him, binding us more closely to him, individually and as his Church. Notice that the worship is corporate, demonstrating the unity which is such a theme of Ephesians, and reflecting the trinitarian community of God himself, Father (v. 20), Son (v. 20) and Spirit (v. 18).

John 6:51–58

We have arrived at the climax of Jesus' teaching about himself as the bread of life, and these verses place that teaching firmly in the context of Jesus' work on the cross. The tone is set in verse 51, where Jesus says he will give his flesh for the life of the world, perhaps echoing the description of the Suffering Servant in Isaiah 53.

Commentaries will document the debates about these verses. Some see them as a clear reference to the eucharist. Others see them as a metaphor describing the believer's relationship with Jesus (for example, verse 54 looks like a metaphorical restatement of verse 40). In a way, both interpretations are right, and combine to provide a wide-ranging message, pulling chapter 6 together and also pointing beyond it.

The chapter describes the believer's dependence on Jesus. The feeding miracle is one picture of this. References to the eucharist are another such picture (this passage therefore helps to put Holy Communion in context and explain its significance). Neither picture is an end in itself. They both point further: back to the person of Jesus, his sacrificial love (epitomized by his death) and the need for a faithful response to that love.

MG

Year C

Isaiah 5:1–7 (Continuous)

This parable is full of rhythm and poetry, and appears to be the basis for Jesus' parable of the vineyard in Mark 12.

At first, it looks to be an oracle of unremitting judgment. God has laboured over the vineyard of Judah with great care, doing everything necessary to grow, protect and bring to fruit what he had planted. He had patiently waited for the time when the first grapes would appear. And the result? Wild grapes—literally 'stinking things' (v. 2)—good for nothing. Judah's sin was like a bad smell in the nostrils of God.

Jesus' version of the parable has the religious leaders as tenants, and the prophets as emissaries for the owner whom the tenants mistreat. Finally, after the tenants kill the owner's son, the owner himself comes in judgment. Yet paradoxically Jesus represented God's own visitation (Luke 19:44) and through the judgment of the cross comes the hope of forgiveness.

And so we see that the parable here is actually the story of a lover (v. 1). God's plan is for his people to be fruitful (4:2) and through judgment will come hope (4:4). The exodus reality of God's covenant presence will be restored (4:5) and his glory will shelter all who come to Zion (4:6; Psalm 121:5–6).

This hope cannot annihilate the reality of the sinful present—but neither can the sinful present suppress the future hope.

Jeremiah 23:23–29 (Related)

This is a difficult passage, but it points to the heart of Jeremiah's message—the character and reality of God.

- **God is free.** God is 'far off' in the sense that he cannot be claimed and domesticated, even by those loyal to the heart of institutionalized worship, the temple (see Jeremiah 7:4). He cannot be fooled or deceived (v. 24, echoing Genesis 22:14, literally 'the God who sees'; see also Isaiah 44:18). No one can use God to claim for themselves a privileged position.
- **God is other.** The truth about God comes by revelation of his character ('name', v. 27). Dreams were a popular means of divination at the time, but are here rejected (as in Deuteronomy 13:1–2 and Zechariah 10:2) as unreliable, as they come from the mind of the individual. But God's word (v. 28)—spoken or acted, then written (Jeremiah 36:4)—comes from beyond, and hence leads to a morality distinct from those around (v. 14). In pointing to God's truth, we must always point beyond ourselves.
- **God's word endures.** In the conflict of truth claims arising from the rival versions of reality, the truth of God's word prevails. It breaks open and brings judgment and change (v. 29).

In Jesus, the free God shares our boundedness, the God who is other draws near, and the unchanging God touches our mutability—and yet, as Trinity, he does this without compromising who he is.

Hebrews 11:29—12:2

This passage continues the litany of faith begun in 11:1.

Faith is closely related to obedience (vv. 29–31; cf. John 14:15). Believing in God is not a casual hobby, but leads to radical obedience even when that appears to be foolish—when was the last time you marched round a city blowing trumpets?

Faith is something of an adventure (vv. 32–38). The last thing you could say about the stories summarized here is that they are dull!

Faith anticipates the full revelation (vv. 39–40). Though we have had a glorious taste of God's Kingdom, we still strain on tiptoes to see the full truth of what God has done (Romans 8:23).

Faith is shared (12:1). As we embark on the journey of faith, we join a great crowd of pilgrims on the same road. We are not on this journey alone but are surrounded, in front, behind, to the left and to the right with fellow travellers.

Faith enables us to break through the barriers of human limitation as we step into the world of God's possibilities, following the pattern of Jesus (12:2).

Luke 12:49–56

In these two sections, not clearly connected with the preceding passage or each other, Jesus throws down two distinct challenges:

• **'Not what you were expecting!'** The paradox of Jesus' ministry was that he was what people were expecting in some ways (Luke 7:22) but not in others (Luke 7:39). The Messiah was expected to bring peace (Isaiah 9:6; Luke 1:79) but he also brings judgment ('fire', v. 49; cf. 1 Kings 18); he brings reconciliation within families (Micah 7:6, contrast Malachi 4:6 and Luke 1:17) but he also brings division (v. 53).

Family division is a feature of Jesus' ministry because loyalty to him transcends all human ties (Luke 14:26; Mark 10:29). Discipleship involves a new pattern of allegiance (Luke 8:21). Though Jesus inaugurates the new age, and with it the power for reconciliation, relationships fracture across the divide between new age and old. The call to follow itself threatens judgment (John 3:19), a paradox most clearly seen in the cross (his 'baptism', v. 50).

• **'Not what you were looking for!'** Peasants who lived on the land knew how to predict the weather. Clouds from the west of Palestine came over the Mediterranean and so brought rain (v. 54); wind from the south came across the desert and so brought the heat (v. 55). When we use our abilities in other aspects of our life and not in exploring Jesus and discipleship, we are merely play-acting (the literal meaning of 'hypocrites', v. 56)—a dangerous game in the light of the choice between reconciliation and judgment.

IP

PROPER 16

YEAR A

Exodus 1:8—2:10 (Continuous)

The promise of progeny to Abraham has been fulfilled, and the descendants of his grandson Israel have multiplied beyond all imagining (Exodus 1:7). But they are not yet a nation, nor do they have their own land, and these are also elements of the promise. And now a new threat emerges: a Pharaoh who is ignorant of how Egypt had prospered under Joseph, and who attempts to trap the descendants of Joseph in Egypt as landless slaves (1:8–11). However, oppression results only in the miraculous increase of the Israelite population (1:12), as if to mock Pharaoh's attempts to subdue this budding nation and defeat the promise.

Pharaoh turns to more drastic measures (1:15–16), but he reckons without the defiance of the midwives who fear a far greater God than Pharaoh and whose courageous actions force a change of plan (1:17–22). Pharaoh also reckons without the courage of the woman who hides her baby son and then casts him adrift on the Nile (2:1–4); and finally, he reckons without the divine irony which causes his own daughter to adopt the Hebrew child who is later to become his downfall (2:5–10). Hence, the seeds of Pharaoh's destruction are sown by the actions of the most powerless, which are blessed and prospered by the Most Powerful.

Isaiah 51:1–6 (Related)

In a situation of disheartenment, with their city conquered, their temple in ruins and themselves in exile, the people of Israel badly need reassurance. This the prophet sets out to provide by reminding his hearers of the faithfulness and power of God. Abraham was an old man with a barren wife when God called him and promised to make him a nation, and the promise was duly fulfilled (v. 2). Neither has the promise been forgotten, and the God who built the nation in the first place is more than capable and willing to rebuild it now. The same power that was displayed in the creation of the world will be displayed again in the redemption of Israel, so that redemption becomes re-creation, a new start, with a new Eden for the people to inhabit (v. 3).

God's power is also at work among the nations of the world in order to bring about the deliverance of Israel (vv. 4–5), and the certainty and everlasting nature of that deliverance are emphasized by comparison with the created order (v. 6). There is nothing in creation that can disrupt God's plan because, unlike its Creator, it will all perish, no matter how firm and solid it might seem at the moment.

Romans 12:1–8

Salvation in Christ is not just a set of doctrines. If it is genuine, it has outward and observable consequences; and just as belief in the heart has to be backed up by spoken confession of the name of Jesus, the experience of true salvation will affect the way believers live their lives (v. 1). Paul therefore spends most of the rest of the letter explaining how Christians are to live in the light of the salvation which he has just described in such detail. Just as, in chapter 8, those who are in the flesh cannot please God (8:8), so here it is necessary not to be conformed to this world but to be transformed by a renewed mind in order to live out the divine will (v. 2).

The instructions that Paul gives are designed to enable the believers to fulfil their heavenly potential in the context of the realities of this world. One of the most striking characteristics of this new life in Christ is its corporate dimension. The use of 'body' language (vv. 4–5) emphasizes the interconnectedness of those who are in Christ, and all the gifts mentioned (vv. 6–8) are those which benefit others. There is no room for mere performers in the body of Christ!

Matthew 16:13–20

Jesus' ministry is now well established, and it is time to find out what the reaction to him has been, both among the people (v. 13) and among his own disciples (v. 15). The various attempts made by the crowds to identify him all have in common that they regard Jesus as a prophet (v. 14). The mention of Elijah implies that some have a sense of the time of the Messiah drawing near, because Elijah was expected to return as the forerunner of the Messiah (cf. Malachi 4:5), but the identification of Jesus as a prophet shows that the crowds are looking beyond Jesus for their Messiah to someone else who has not yet come. Their understanding is flawed; they know enough to realize that Jesus is a man of God, as the prophets were, but they do not have the discernment to be any more exact about their identification.

By contrast, Peter recognizes precisely who Jesus is (v. 16), and knows that he and his companions need look no further because the Messiah is there with them. That recognition speaks of a real openness to the things of God, and it is rewarded with both blessing and responsibility, as Jesus proclaims Peter the foundation stone of the Church (vv. 17–19).

DR

YEAR B

1 Kings 8 [1, 6, 10–11] 22–30, 41–43 (Continuous)

Solomon's great prayer at the dedication of the temple is testimony to the amazing faithfulness of God, which is expressed in a series of ever-widening concentric circles.

Solomon moves almost straightaway to his most pressing concern, God's promises to the house of David (vv. 24–26). So Solomon is trusting in the faithfulness of God close to home, in the commitment God has made to his family.

Then the picture widens, as Solomon calls upon God to answer prayers that both he and the rest of Israel will raise to him (v. 30), with a particular focus on the need for God's forgiveness.

Verses 41–43 widen the picture further, as Solomon asks that foreigners might receive mercy when they pray towards the temple, 'so that all the peoples of the earth may know your name'. This is a marvellous expression of hope in the mercy of God for all nations.

From a Christian perspective, we might add that although the house of David ultimately forfeited God's promises, and the temple was destroyed, God remains faithful. Jesus, great David's greater Son, declared himself to be the true temple, and offers the forgiveness of God more widely and comprehensively than even Solomon imagined.

Joshua 24:1–2a, 14–18 (Related)

Towards the end of his life, Joshua pleads with the people of Israel to make a double commitment: to serve God totally and faithfully (v. 14) and to reject all other gods (v. 15). Making and keeping this double commitment is what it means to be truly the people of God.

This is a free choice. Joshua has outlined the way God has protected and fought for Israel (vv. 3–13). So the people are to weigh up the choice for themselves and make an informed decision (v. 15). It is open to them to reject the Lord. Ultimately, despite their protestations here, the people do reject the Lord and judgment comes upon Israel. During that whole tragic story, this renewal of the covenant by a united and (apparently) faithful nation at Shechem stands as a yardstick against which the people may judge themselves.

The call of God to human beings to make a free choice to respond totally and faithfully to his protective love is a constant feature of scripture. In the Gospel reading, Jesus (who bears the Greek form of the name Joshua, meaning 'Yahweh is salvation') calls his disciples to the same choice. Today we still face that choice.

Ephesians 6:10–20

As Ephesians draws to a close, the camera pulls out to show the daily lives of the believers in a cosmic context. Their struggles in seeking to do God's will and resist temptation are part of a much bigger conflict with hostile spiritual forces. Whether today we understand the forces ranged against us as spiritual beings or as the sheer power of human sin, this is a real battle. Every Christian must fight in it, using the 'armour of God', the protection which God provides and on which we are to rely in trust and self-discipline.

Ephesians is realistic about the challenge we face. Yet the struggle is not between two equal powers. God's ultimate victory is assured (1:20–22). In the words of Gus Marwieh, an African evangelist, 'The devil he got a right to fight, but he ain't got no right to win.' Therefore the Church can face the fight with confidence, proclaiming the gospel entrusted to it (vv. 19–20).

If anyone is uncomfortable with so much military imagery, it might help to remember the context. The struggle is all part of God's marvellous plan to restore peace and justice to the cosmos by bringing all things under Christ (1:10).

John 6:56–69

Jesus' teaching in chapter 6 is extremely challenging (v. 60). Many of those who had been following him are scandalized by his claims about himself, and perhaps by the idea of eating his flesh and drinking his blood. Far from backing off, Jesus then heightens the challenge by suggesting that he might subsequently ascend 'to where he was before' (v. 62). For John, Jesus' glorious return to his Father is inextricably, and paradoxically, linked with his being 'lifted up' on the cross. But is the idea of a humiliated, crucified Messiah a blasphemous scandal or the supreme focus of faith? The way the suggestion in verse 62 is left unanswered is deliberate: each person in the crowd and every subsequent reader of the Gospel must fill in their own response to the challenge of Jesus.

John shows us two ways of responding to that challenge. Many disciples find Jesus' teaching unpalatable and drift away (v. 66). Another will subsequently betray him (v. 64). In contrast, Peter makes a moving and committed confession of faith in Jesus (vv. 68–69). John always describes this choice in stark terms: do we accept Jesus and his offer of eternal life, or do we reject him? There is no halfway house.

MG

YEAR C

Jeremiah 1:4–10 (Continuous)

This wonderfully evocative description of Jeremiah's call makes clear three truths about God's call to us.

- **It is God's initiative** (vv. 4–5). Throughout the book of Jeremiah, the word of the Lord simply 'comes' to him. It is not conjured up or persuaded out of God—it simply comes as a gift. God's knowing beforehand (v. 5) is not about his controlling our lives but about his loving plan for us to know him and enjoy him for ever (Romans 8:30; Ephesians 1:11). His consecration of us is a gift to be received (Romans 3:24); it is his decision before ever it is ours.
- **It is God's vision** (vv. 6–8). Jeremiah's protest has a parallel in Isaiah 6 and Exodus 3—4: 'I am not up to the job!' But God's vision is much larger than the vision of those he has called (cf. Isaiah 55:9), and he is able to accomplish far more than we can imagine (Ephesians 3:20).
- **It is God's equipping** (vv. 9, 10). Again like Isaiah, Jeremiah experiences God's touch that empowers him to fulfil God's call. 'God's work done in God's way will never lack God's resources' (William Carey). 'Apart from me, you can do nothing,' said Jesus (John 15:5)—but by God's grace, ordinary people can do extraordinary things.

Isaiah 58:9b–14 (Related)

The returning exiles complain about God's lack of response to their prayer (58:3), probably around the time when the rebuilding of Jerusalem is making very slow progress (see Nehemiah 1).

God's reply is that if they want to experience spiritual reality, they must engage with spiritual reality. At the moment, the basis of their worship is self-interest—what they can get out of others and God (vv. 4–5). He calls them to a new kind of fasting—fasting from apathy, complacency and self-interest (vv. 6, 7, 13). This will affect:

- relations with the poor ('the hungry... the poor... the naked', v. 7)
- relations within the community ('your own kin', v. 7; 'the yoke from among you', v. 9)
- relationship with God ('the holy day of the Lord', v. 13).

Each section (vv. 6–9a, 9b–12, 13–14) has a command and a promise ('If... then...'). This is not quite that the promise is conditional, in the sense that it has to be earned. But as with the pattern of Deuteronomy 28, there are blessings that follow on from obedience. In this case, allowing the reality of God to permeate all of life will result in knowing the reality of God's presence. True worship is not about opening prayer books before God, but opening our lives to him. Have we allowed the grace of God to transform us?

The call to reform is a call to return to the truths of the past. The concern for the poor echoes, for example, Deuteronomy 15:7–11; verse 8b recalls the exodus presence of God; verse 13 refers to the fourth commandment. But it is also a call into the future (v. 12; cf. v. 8a with Luke 1:78).

Hebrews 12:18–29
This passage is sometimes used to show the contrast or discontinuity between the first and the new covenant. But to Jewish Christians tempted to return to their pre-Christian practice and belief, what is key is the continuity: God is a God of covenant (v. 24) who speaks (vv. 19, 25), the judge of all (v. 23; Genesis 18:25) and a consuming fire (v. 29).

The contrast is not between two different goals, but between the journey and the destination, between the interim and the ultimate. Sinai was God's supreme revelation of himself in the Old Testament, and the prophets are frequently redolent with exodus themes. But the physical cannot contain the reality of God, and everywhere in the Old Testament there is an expectation of something more, most pregnantly in the texts of exile and return (v. 26b, quoting Haggai 2:6).

This 'something more' has been revealed in Jesus: what was unbearable (v. 19) is now bearable, and what was unapproachable (v. 20) is now gloriously accessible (10:20) because God the judge (v. 23) is also mediator (v. 24a). The sacrifices of condemnation have been taken up in the sacrifice of forgiveness (v. 24b). We have now come to Mount Zion, not Mount Sinai—the city of God (v. 22) rather than the temporary resting place, permanent reality rather than passing ephemera (vv. 27–28). Those who went before in the first covenant find their completion, with us, in this spiritual reality (v. 23; 11:40).

If we have known God's faithfulness in the past, it is the same in the present. If we honour God with our ritual, we must honour him in our lives.

Luke 13:10–17

The first half of chapter 13 contains material unique to Luke, but the theme of this story is a common one in Jesus' ministry (Matthew 12:11; Mark 3:4; Luke 6:9; 14:5).

The woman's 'spirit' of infirmity (v. 11, RSV) should be understood loosely; there is no sense in which this healing is an exorcism. Jesus' response to her, of pronouncing healing as he lays hands on her (vv. 12–13), is spontaneous—one of simple compassion.

Then comes the dispute. The point of difference does not centre on the power to heal (v. 14b). Nor is it the importance or value of the Law; Jesus replies (v. 15) in terms of the Law, which in scribal debate allowed animals to be tethered and watered. The central question is whether the Law is being used as an instrument of condemnation or as an instrument of grace.

Those using it to condemn are 'hypocrites' (v. 15), masquerading as agents of a gracious God while they are really nothing of the sort. While Jesus' action demonstrates compassion, highlights his power to heal and bears the fruit of God being praised (v. 13), their actions show none of these. Perhaps the synagogue leader knows this; he cannot bring himself to rebuke Jesus directly (v. 14).

There are many areas of contemporary discussion—Sunday trading, homosexuality, remarriage of divorcees, parenting—where the same question applies. The 'laws' in question may be right, but how are they being used?

This is (significantly?) the last time in Luke that Jesus teaches in a synagogue.

IP

PROPER 17

YEAR A

Exodus 3:1–15 (Continuous)

Pharaoh does not know of Joseph and his God (Exodus 1:8), the people may have forgotten their God (v. 13), and even Moses seems unsure of who it is who is speaking to him from the burning bush (v. 13). But God is far from being forgetful of the people of Israel or deaf to their cries. After all, there is a promise to fulfil, which has been honoured thus far for Abraham, Isaac and Jacob, and is now due to be honoured for their descendants.

Moses' commission marks the beginning of a more active style of divine intervention, as opposed to the hiddenness of destiny behind the events of the previous two chapters. In this context, the revelation of the divine name (vv. 14–15) is important, if enigmatic; it conceals as much as it reveals, because God is whatever God chooses to be at any given time, ever old and ever new, constantly existing, comprehensible only through experience and certainly not to be encapsulated in or tied down by a single definition. The message of this name to Moses is, 'If you want to know who I am, then come with me and watch how I deal with the Egyptians!'

Jeremiah 15:15–21 (Related)

The theme of the cost of true service can be seen in this passage (linking most notably with the Gospel reading for today). Receiving the call of God on one's life can be an extremely uncomfortable experience; once the call is recognized, there may well be an initial sense of joy (v. 16), which gives the motivation to pursue it, but that often gives way to great pain and distress, leading to the sense of having been deceived or even abandoned by the God who issued the call (vv. 17–18). The reasons for this distress are varied: it may be that others refuse to recognize the call, or oppose it, or even that what the call is about causes distress to the one who has to fulfil it. In Jeremiah's case, all three elements seem to be present. His eyes are opened to the sins of his people and to God's imminent punishment, and he is told to declare it. The message not only grieves the prophet himself, it arouses opposition and hatred in those to whom it is addressed, resulting in his feeling rejected and abandoned by all, including God. But God does not abandon those who are called, and the assurance is that perseverance, even in the face of opposition, will lead to vindication (vv. 19–21).

Romans 12:9–21

This list of ethical imperatives can be summed up by verse 21: overcome evil with good. This is precisely what God has done in Christ, and so for Christians to embody this same approach is a genuine indicator of their transformation by inward renewal. It is notable that these are very positive instructions. The transformation brought about by salvation is not demonstrated merely by what is not done, but by what is actually done. Paul does not forbid something without giving something positive to do instead (vv. 9, 11, 16, 17, 21).

Generally speaking, the instructions start with how to behave towards 'friends' (vv. 9, 13, 16), and move towards the more difficult question of how to treat those who are 'enemies' (vv. 14, 17–21). It is in this second area that evil is most clearly overcome with good, where blessing is returned for persecution in the hope of redeeming the enemy (vv. 14, 20–21).

The hint of God's eventual judgment provides a context for this Christian behaviour (v. 19). Even if repaying evil with good has no immediate redemptive effect upon the enemy, Christians who do it overcome evil with good within themselves and can therefore stand secure in the judgment, while the unrepentant enemy will be suitably repaid by the ultimate Power of Good.

Matthew 16:21–28

Although there have been hints in the narrative before now, concerning Jesus's eventual fate, it is not until the disciples have recognized him for who he is that he starts to talk openly about it (v. 21)—much to the horror of Peter, who, having declared Jesus the Son of the Living God, cannot comprehend that this is what Messiahship means (v. 22). But just as Moses' 'I Am' would not be tied down to preconceived definitions of deity, the Son of 'I Am' refuses to let himself be bound by traditional triumphalistic notions of Messiahship (v. 23). The unorthodoxy of this Messiah is such that he has to prove himself and be recognized as Messiah before he dare speak openly about his death, because otherwise he would have no credibility. However, once he has proved himself, he can lead his disciples on from the known to the unknown and thereby expand their comprehension of the things of God (vv. 24–28).

In the context of Jesus' discussion of his own death, his earlier words about those who follow him taking up their cross and losing their life in order to save it (Matthew 10:38–39) have a new seriousness. Discipleship is certainly not for the faint-hearted; but it will be rewarded.

DR

YEAR B

Song of Solomon 2:8–13 (Continuous)

This is one of the most beautiful parts of a beautiful book. The depth of the relationship between the lovers is reflected in the vivid description, the sense of oneness with creation, and the overwhelming feeling of joy.

The Song of Solomon is a collection of love songs, which might originally have been performed at marriage festivals. They celebrate human love frankly and exuberantly. For some, this has been a source of embarrassment, and attempts were made (and still are made) to explain the text allegorically, as a picture of the love between Yahweh and Israel and, later, between Christ and the Church.

But this is to miss the point. For one thing, erotic love between a man and a woman in the context of lifelong commitment is a gift from God, not an embarrassment! More generally, the fact that the Song of Solomon is in the canon of scripture at all underlines that we should not seek to divide our lives between areas where God is relevant and areas where he is not. God is God of the whole of human existence, not just church services. So our relationship with him provides the context for all our other relationships.

Deuteronomy 4:1–2, 6–9 (Related)

The people are about to enter the promised land. In chapters 1—3, Moses has reminded them of the ways in which God has delivered them in the past. The people are called to obey God's law as a response to what he has done for them. The call to obedience is partly for the sake of the people's ongoing relationship with God, and consequently their future life in the promised land, which will depend on their loyalty to God (v. 1). It is also for the sake of surrounding nations, who will recognize the goodness of the laws God has given (v. 6).

As Christians, we are called to the same obedience in response to the salvation God has provided through Jesus. And as this passage suggests, others will notice how we live. Positively, Christlike lives are the single most effective witness to the world. Negatively, Christians are under constant scrutiny from others, who are particularly sensitive to any hint of hypocrisy. The relationship God wants with his people is an intimate one (v. 7), involving all aspects of our lives, and based on mutual love. Are we doing enough to pass on this challenging but profoundly hopeful message to our children (v. 9)?

James 1:17–27

In this passage are two verses which underpin the whole of James' argument. In verse 18, James states that Christians have been saved by God to act as his witnesses, holy and dedicated to him like the firstfruits of the harvest (Numbers 18:12). In verse 22, James (always intensely practical) stresses that to be God's witnesses we must 'be doers of the word and not merely hearers' (v. 22). Merely hearing the word is as superficial as glancing in a mirror. It is the dedicated reflection of God's purposes in our lives which will please him (cf. Luke 11:28; Romans 2:13).

So our personal relationship with God cannot be divided from our outward actions. God demands a revolution in our hearts, as we allow his word to grow in us (v. 21). In turn, the word of truth in us should be reflected in the way we speak (vv. 19, 26). And God's initiative in saving us (v. 18) should be reflected in our practical help for the weak (v. 27). Christianity is not just a matter of believing the right things, nor just a matter of trying to do good: it is both of these, and James shows us how and why.

Mark 7:1–8, 14–15, 21–23

The Jewish religious leaders criticize Jesus for allowing his disciples to neglect some of the purification rituals demanded by oral traditions which had been handed down alongside the written law of the Old Testament. Ideas of ceremonial washing began with the highest of motives, relating to dedication to holy living. The problem, as Jesus pointed out, was that they could become a hypocritical illusion to mask sinfulness (v. 7) or even a substitute for God's law, the very thing they were supposed to reinforce (v. 8).

So Jesus calls us back to the fundamentals of our relationship with God, which shows itself in the attitudes which characterize us inwardly and which manifest themselves in how we behave. Obeying God involves a radical commitment affecting our whole life.

It would be a serious mistake, however, to interpret Jesus' words as merely an attack on tradition, tempting as this might be for those of us from branches of the Church which set less obvious store by ceremony. We all rely heavily on tradition, whether or not we acknowledge this explicitly. The challenge is to keep tradition in perspective, so that it does not hinder a living relationship with God, but rather reinforces it.

MG

YEAR C

Jeremiah 2:4–13 (Continuous)

This passage has an ominous tone to it, with its resonances of a law court accusation. God is, it appears, suing for divorce from his bride, his people. But the content of the accusation reveals God to be the great giver. He offers:
- **A relationship of intimacy.** The words describing Yahweh's relationship with his people are words of intimacy: 'devotion', 'love', 'following'

(v. 2). Far from being aloof, he has journeyed with his people in bad times as well as good (v. 6).

- **A place of abundance** (v. 7). Even if Israel's wealth could not compare with other nations for much of her national life, the promise of a land 'flowing with milk and honey' (Exodus 3:8) indicated God's abundant provision.
- **A source of refreshment** (v. 13). One can survive weeks or even months without food, but without water death comes swiftly.

Though God's grace cannot be earned, there is a cost involved in receiving it. To receive these gifts requires:
- **Following his ways** (vv. 2, 5). As in a marriage relationship, we become like the one we choose as a partner ('worthless… worthless', v. 5). To walk in intimacy means a life of holiness (v. 3).
- **Femembering his story** (vv. 6–7). If we forget what God has done, we will fail to understand what he has in store for us.
- **Depending on his provision** (v. 13). Building our own cisterns is hard work, hazardous, and a poor alternative to the freshness of springs.

Luke 14:1, 7–14; Proverbs 25:6–7 (Related)

- **Seeing:** Jesus and his opponents both scrutinize each other (Luke 14:1, 7) but there are two ways of looking—at the outward and superficial, or at the inward and true. At a banquet, it is common sense to realize that you do not know who will be the guest of most honour until all have arrived (Luke 14:8; cf. Proverbs 25:6–7). Similarly, it is God who knows who is greatest in the Kingdom; it is hidden from human eyes, but will be revealed at the end in a surprising eschatological reversal (Luke 14:11). God is no respecter of persons (1 Peter 1:17; literally 'he does not look on the face'); his loving gaze refuses to be misled by outward appearances ('love is colour-blind'), a sharp challenge to our image-dominated era.
- **Honouring:** We can take honour for ourselves, in which case it will not last (Luke 14:9), or we can receive it as a gift, which requires patient waiting (Luke 14:10). The hiddenness of the truth stands against any institutionalization of Kingdom values. As we wait in this life for God's verdict to be revealed, we are simply sitting at table waiting for the feast to begin.
- **Welcoming:** How hard we find it to give without thought of reward (Luke 14:12–14)! But this mirrors God's attitude to us, and challenges the principle of reciprocity explicit in Jesus' day but still operative in

ours. The metaphorical meaning here does not dissolve the literal—a change in inner attitude leads to a change in outward behaviour.

Hebrews 13:1–8, 15–16

As in Paul's letters, having completed the more theological discussion, the writer finishes with a more practical set of injunctions—an ethical checklist.

- **Love:** Mutual love of the Christian community was all-important (1 Thessalonians 4:9; 1 John 3:16). Love among the like-minded was prized in ancient society, but the Christian distinctive is that such love flows beyond the bounds of those like us, to strangers (v. 2, with its reminiscence of Abraham in Genesis 18) and to those imprisoned and tortured (v. 3, without the suggestion of 10:33 that they are Christians).
- **Purity:** Lust and greed are seen as closely related in both Old and New Testaments, and both related to idolatry (1 Thessalonians 4:5; Colossians 3:5). The continuity of God's dealings with his people before and in Christ (see comment on Hebrews 12:18–29, Proper 16, Year C) means that the quotation from Psalm 118 remains apt.
- **Respect:** Leadership is a gift of God to his Church, and our role models (v. 7) include both those who trusted in the God of Israel and in the Lord of the Church, since the two are here identified (v. 8; cf. Psalm 102:27).
- **Worship:** True worship involves lives as well as lips (vv. 15–16), a well-worn prophetic theme (see comment on Isaiah 58:9b–14, Proper 16, Year C). As the college Ethics lecturer said to the Worship lecturer, 'I teach worship; you simply discuss ecclesiastical group dynamics.'

Communities awash with self-giving openness, moral integrity, respect and gratitude are as attractive now as they ever have been.

IP

PROPER 18

YEAR A

Exodus 12:1–14 (Continuous)

The climax of the confrontation between the forces of good and evil has come, with one final terrifying demonstration of God's unquestioned superiority over the gods of Egypt, including, of course, Pharaoh himself. The beginning of the Israelites' oppression was the slaughter of their male children (Exodus 1:22), so it is chillingly appropriate that the slaughter of Egypt's firstborn sons should mark its end (v. 12; see Exodus 4:23). The Israelites protect their lives by smearing blood, the sign of life, on their doorposts (vv. 7, 13); their salvation is at hand, and they have to be ready to seize the opportunity for freedom that will be theirs (v. 11), moving quickly and fearlessly through the inevitable chaos that will result from the dread visitation. These are the labour pains for the birth of the new nation, and the fulfilment of another segment of the promise is imminent.

Two commands are given which underline the significance of the Passover for Israel's self-understanding: the command to make the month of the Passover the first month of the year (v. 2), and therefore the marker for the beginning of the new era; and the command above all to 'remember' (v. 14). Remember how God has remembered you and, whatever happens, you need never experience the same kind of despair again.

Ezekiel 33:7–11 (Related)

These verses underline the corporate nature of responsibility for sin, in that those who know what is right must share that knowledge with others who do not. It is all too easy to dissociate oneself from those who are regarded as 'sinners', but if such dissociation means that these 'sinners' never get to know the difference between right and wrong, then those who do know, but who failed even to try to tell them the difference, are themselves also culpable (vv. 7–9). Passively accepting evil does nothing to get rid of it, and ends up by not only condemning those who are in the wrong, but also incriminating those who think that it is nothing to do with them because they themselves are in the right.

On the other hand, telling other people when they are in the wrong is not about condemning them in a high-handed fashion. When done in the name of God, the motivation for it comes from God's earnest desire to see everyone turn away from sin so that none need suffer the punishment of eternal death (v. 11). The idea, therefore, is to persuade people to abandon their sinfulness by communicating to them that desire, and not to antagonize them into continuing in sin.

Romans 13:8–14

Paul continues his ethical exhortation by explicitly stating what was implicit in chapter 12, and replacing the negatives of the Ten Commandments with the positive instruction to love one's neighbour as oneself (vv. 8–10). The command to love is not just about warm feelings but about actions, as has already been demonstrated by the previous chapter. It is interesting that Paul here refers to the Law in the context of Christian righteousness apart from the Law, thereby emphasizing the continuity between Christianity and Judaism. Active, practical love of one's neighbour is ultimately what the Law is intended to promote, so that by doing this, Christians are in effect fulfilling the demands of the Law.

Also made explicit here is the sense of an impending final consummation of God's plan of salvation (vv. 11–12a), which was only hinted at at the end of chapter 12. This gives an added urgency to the instructions, because they are to be carried out in the light of an eternity to which Christians are called and which could break through at any minute. When that happens, those who are 'asleep', that is, who have not taken it to heart or prepared themselves properly for it, will find themselves left behind.

Matthew 18:15–20

Whenever there is behaviour in the church community which does not measure up to the Christian ideal, it must be dealt with openly and honestly, not only to prevent the growth of ill-feeling and division in the community, but to protect the interests of the one who has lapsed (v. 15b). No distinction is made between deliberate and unwitting sin; the important thing is to deal with the sin as quickly and efficiently as possible, initially and ideally on a one-to-one basis (v. 15). That way, the effect of the lapse on the community, and on the sinner, is minimized, and there should certainly be none of the carping behind people's backs that is so destructive and divisive.

However, in the recognition that a single private confrontation may not be enough, provision is made for a process of increasing severity, culminating in the excommunication of the unrepentant guilty party (vv. 16–17). The picture is of an extremely egalitarian community in which members have responsibility for one another and which has the authority of Christ in its midst when making such decisions (vv. 18–19). No particular officers are mentioned as those responsible for the decision, but instead there is the assurance of Christ's presence, however small the community may be (v. 20).

DR

YEAR B

Proverbs 22:1–2, 8–9, 22–23 (Continuous)

God's concern for the plight of the poor is a consistent theme throughout the Bible, and not least in Proverbs. The Lord is the maker of rich and poor alike (v. 2). The relationship of creator to created means that God loves all people, but at the same time holds them to account for their behaviour.

So God has a special care for the poor and the oppressed (v. 22) and promises judgment on those who exploit them (vv. 8, 23). Those who reflect God's concern for the poor in practical ways will be rewarded (v. 9). The command to work for justice and to be generous givers could not be clearer.

Yet are we left with a nagging feeling that life is often less clear-cut than this? In a world where the rich seem to get richer and the poor poorer, where is the divine justice Proverbs assumes? Perhaps we are to acknowledge these proverbs as a statement of how life ought to be, acknowledge also that we live in a fallen world, but strive within it for God's justice to be upheld. After all, God's justice and judgment will definitely triumph in the end, and we shall be held accountable (Matthew 25:31–46).

Isaiah 35:4–7a (Related)

This is a magnificent picture of decisive intervention by God to transform the earth and save his people. The imagery focuses on pilgrims travelling through the desert to Jerusalem. The journey is hard (v. 3), made worse by the pilgrims' own infirmities (vv. 5–6). Yet God acts in an amazing way, bringing healing and utterly transforming the landscape.

Just as the pilgrims are assured that God will intervene to end their present suffering, so the people of God as a whole are invited to look forward to a time when the justice and salvation of God will be manifest in this world (v. 4).

Notice the very physical description of this future hope. Our hope is not for some divinely inspired escape to a purely spiritual realm, despite the way that Christian tradition has sometimes suggested this. The biblical picture of future hope is that God will transform *this* world in a remarkable way, conquering evil for good, and vindicating his people. Jesus' healing ministry (see today's Gospel reading) is a sign of God's commitment to humanity physically and spiritually—a foretaste of our resurrection. Wesley's 'O for a thousand tongues to sing', drawing on Isaiah 35, expresses vividly this connection between healing and hope.

James 2:1–10 [11–13] 14–17

James' attack on favouritism might meet with sage nodding of heads. Of course showing favour to the rich is wrong! And what about all the money our church sends to the two-thirds world? But are we really doing so well? What about the local homeless, for example? A less fashionable cause, perhaps, but exactly the kind of person James has in mind.

James sees favouring the rich over the poor—letting money do the talking—as a serious failing. It means setting ourselves up as judges in place of God, discriminating where he does not (v. 4). It means mocking the glorious humility of Christ, who left the splendour of heaven to be born on earth (v. 1). It means flagrant disregard for God's command to love our neighbour (v. 8). Should we fail to show mercy to the downtrodden, we are liable to God's judgment (vv. 12–13).

All this is part of James' campaign to get his readers to understand that faith in Christ is meaningless unless it shows in actions. That's not to say that our actions (works) save us: God does that (v. 5). But our new life in Christ must result in good works. Otherwise our faith is mere delusion (v. 17).

Mark 7:24–37

These two healing miracles show God's love breaking through barriers to meet everyone in their need.

First, Jesus heals the Syro-Phoenician woman's daughter (vv. 24–30). It was extraordinary for a Jewish teacher to have such contact with a Gentile. Although Jesus seems consciously to have limited his own ministry essentially to Jews (Matthew 15:24), he clearly assumed that his message was universally applicable (Acts 1:8), and incidents such as this one underlined that. In his love, God reaches out to all, regardless of nationality or race, and Jesus took risks in order to demonstrate this. Are we prepared to do the same?

Second, Jesus breaks through the barriers which may be caused by disability, in healing the deaf and dumb man. Jesus' cry of *ephphatha*, 'be opened', is addressed not just to the man's ears, but is also perhaps a more general exhortation to be open to the saving activity of God in his life.

The universal scope of God's love is reflected beautifully in verse 37, which both looks back to creation (Genesis 1:31: 'God saw all that he had made, and it was very good') and forward to future hope for the world, as it echoes Isaiah 35:5–6.

MG

YEAR C

Jeremiah 18:1–11 (Continuous)

This is perhaps the best-known and most evocative passage in Jeremiah. As elsewhere (1:11–14), God speaks to Jeremiah through the simple events of daily life—pottery was an essential trade in ancient Israel.

At first sight the illustration is simple: the potter is completely in control, and can work and rework the clay as he sees fit (v. 4). It is usually understood to speak of God's sovereignty. He can work with those he chooses, and can build up or pull down at will (vv. 7, 9). What he does is not to be questioned (or even comprehended?) but submitted to.

But that is not the whole story. The potter does not have absolute control over the clay; if he did, why would pots ever become misshapen? No, the character of the clay plays a crucial part. God is sovereign but he is not an autocrat. We are to be submissive, but not passive. Instead, he calls us to work with him in his moulding of us, to participate in his purposes rather than either obstinately resisting them or passively observing them.

In fact, God must be able to 'change his mind' (RSV 'repent', vv. 8, 10) if he is to be just and faithful. How could God turn a blind eye to his people's disobedience? How could he ignore those who turn to him and desire to do good? His sovereignty is a gracious one that opens the future and the possibilities for change, and not one that closes it. Only stubborn refusal can limit what God can do (v. 12).

Deuteronomy 30:15–20 (Related)

This conclusion to Moses' teaching (see 31:1) is a heartfelt appeal for obedience.

- **Obedience is about love.** The two are intertwined right at the heart of God's call to his people ('You are to love the Lord your God...' Deuteronomy 6:5). This is not about emotionalism but about a whole-life response to the reality of God ('loving... walking... observing', v. 16). It involves intimacy that is fulfilled in our following Christ (John 14:23; 1 John 5:3).
- **Obedience is about responsibility.** It involves care over discovering what God wants for us ('commandments, decrees and ordinances', v. 16). It means making a life-or-death decision (vv. 15, 18) of cosmic significance (v. 19). There is no room for a comfortable *via media* or for intellectual assent without the corresponding change of life.
- **Obedience is about response** to God's gracious initiative. His way of life was first given as a gift at Sinai and its fullness revealed in the sacrifice of Christ. God longs that all should receive this gift (John 3:16; 2 Peter 3:9). Before our choice of God lies his prior choice of us (John 15:16); his initiative always precedes our response (v. 20). He is much more ready to bless us through our obedience than we are ready to be blessed by being obedient.

Philemon 1–21

Eavesdropping on this personal note reminds us that Paul knew of no divide between the 'personal' and the 'professional'—what he expounds, he exemplifies.

- **Integrity.** This carefully crafted note introduces themes in verses 4–7 that are expanded and revisited in verses 8–21: love (vv. 5, 9); fellowship ('sharing', v. 6; 'partner' v. 17); doing good (vv. 6, 14); refreshing the heart (literally 'bowels', vv. 7, 12, 20); brotherhood (vv. 7, 20). Paul's theological convictions, expressed in prayer, shape his conversation and action.

- **Authority.** Despite his authoritative standing with Philemon (v. 8) and the personal debt owed (v. 19, presumably referring to the fact that, like Onesimus, Philemon came to faith through Paul's ministry), Paul refuses to coerce but rather seeks to invite and persuade ('appeal', v. 9), as he does in his other letters.

- **Fellowship.** The whole basis of Paul's request is the mutual participation or identification among Christians as a result of shared faith in Christ. It is this that leads to both understanding and fruitfulness (v. 6). It is this that binds people together (here, both Paul and Onesimus, v. 12, and Paul and Philemon, vv. 17, 20) to the point at which one person's debt is another's (v. 19; cf. Acts 2:44–45).

'All are bound together in a mutual bond that makes our much-prized individualism look shallow and petty' (N.T. Wright, *Colossians & Philemon*, IVP, p. 176).

Luke 14:25–33

Still on the way to Jerusalem ('travelling', v. 25; cf. 9:51; 13:22), Jesus sets out the cost of discipleship.

In a time of declining church attendance, it is strange to think of Jesus deliberately discouraging the large crowds (v. 25). In typical Jewish polemic (v. 26) he makes clear that allegiance to him must come before everything else. This is not a call to neglect these others (1 Timothy 5:8), but to let them go and trust in him—and we will receive them back with interest (Luke 18:29–30). Jesus calls us to a relationship of love, but 'love's bonds are the most enduring and the most exacting' (Adam Welch, *Jeremiah, His Time and His Work*, Blackwells, p. 183).

The only people in Palestine to carry crosses (v. 27) were those on the road to their own execution—they were 'dead men walking'. Here the call is not to take up or carry a burden, but to lay down one's life, to let go of all concerns that might get in the way of following Jesus—to let go of the good for the sake of the best. 'When Christ calls a man to follow him, he bids him come and die' (Bonhoeffer, *The Cost of Discipleship*).

Don't underestimate the cost of discipleship (v. 28). If we only go half way, we will make fools of ourselves (v. 29) and miss his goal for our lives, maturity (Ephesians 4:13). We cannot control God (v. 31) but must submit to his demands if we are to know his love—and this includes a final goodbye to our possessions (v. 33) as we acknowledge that they are to be used for his glory and not our comfort.

IP

PROPER 19

YEAR A

Exodus 14:19–31 (Continuous)

Israel may be out of Egypt, but she is not out of the woods yet. In an encore to the destruction of Passover night, God has hardened the Egyptian hearts yet again and sent Pharaoh's men chasing after the Israelites (Exodus 14:8–9). The Israelites are now trapped between the devil (Pharaoh) and the deep Red Sea. But once again, the apparently impossible situation becomes the opportunity for God's power to be decisively displayed.

In this account of the crossing of the Red Sea, there are echoes of the creation motif in Genesis 1, where the wind or Spirit of God blows across the face of the deep, and by the power of God the waters are parted to let dry land appear (Genesis 1:2, 9; Exodus 14:21). The same creative power of God which was at work then is at work now, creating a nation, fighting for the Hebrews, who are obviously powerless on their own. Even the Egyptians recognize the hand of God (v. 25), but too late, and they are overwhelmed by the returning waters (vv. 26–28).

Both the waters and the Egyptians are symbols of the forces of chaos, uncontrollable and destructive in human terms but manipulated effortlessly by God in a way that elicits awe and praise from all who see it (vv. 30–31).

Genesis 50:15–21 (Related)

This description of Joseph's response to his brothers' plea for forgiveness after the death of their father is a good illustration of the principles of forgiveness and tolerance outlined in today's Gospel reading. Joseph's brothers had tried to get rid of him, but in God's hands the effect of their actions had been quite different. Not only had Joseph himself benefited immeasurably from what had happened to him, he had been enabled to save his whole family from dying of starvation in a seven-year famine. In the light of the fact that God has shown him such mercy and favour, Joseph regards his brothers' actions too as part of the overall divine plan to provide for all of their well-being (vv. 19–20). And if God has treated their actions in this way, who is Joseph to condemn them? He refuses to take on the mantle of judge (v. 19), recognizing that, for all his high earthly status, there is only one who has the right to judge; and that One has judged with mercy.

Our treatment of others should depend not on how they treat us, but on the recognition of how God has treated us; and where God treats us with mercy and even blessing, then we too must be merciful.

Romans 14:1–12

Here Paul addresses what must be one of the thorniest questions in Christian life, that of living together in the body of Christ with those who have different ways of expressing personal devotion in terms of ritual and custom. Essentially this is a plea for tolerance, and so an extension of the love commandment cited in chapter 13. Christians should not despise each other for their individual customs, because even opposite customs such as fasting and feasting can be genuine expressions of devotion to God (vv. 2–3, 6). This is also a warning against the kind of legalism that misses the point of observances and gets bogged down in either keeping or criticizing them as if they were somehow important on their own rather than as a way of expressing something else. In the end, feasting or fasting or festivals will not in themselves make any difference to salvation in Christ (vv. 7–9). What is important is the integrity and the motivation of those who perform the customs (vv. 5–6), and God alone can be the judge of that, because it is to God alone that the observances are dedicated. Christians should not compromise themselves and violate their prime commandment of love by criticizing what is not theirs to criticize (vv. 4, 10–12).

Matthew 18:21–35

The parable of the unforgiving servant is a cautionary tale that follows on from the passage about winning back the fellow Christian who has sinned, and it underlines the necessity of repeated, full and frank forgiveness within the community (vv. 21–22). The contrast between the debt owed to the king by the servant (v. 24) and the debt owed to that servant by his fellow servant (v. 28) is so enormous as to be incomprehensible, ridiculous even, and it is clear that whereas the debt to the king could barely even begin to be repaid, that owed to the servant could well be repaid, given a little time and patience. This makes the servant's treatment of his debtor (vv. 28–30) even more reprehensible. In the end it comes down to the idea that what we owe and what we are owed are two sides of the same coin, and we cannot separate the way we ourselves have been treated by God from the way we should treat others in the light of that (vv. 32–33). The same mercy that we have received must be extended to our fellow Christians, because the mercy we have been shown is vastly greater than any mercy we shall be called upon to show.

DR

YEAR B

Proverbs 1:20–33 (Continuous)

Wisdom is described in Proverbs in a series of vivid portraits, each of which reveals something of God's guidance for right living. Here we meet Wisdom for the first time. She stands in the street, in the public squares and at the city gates, proclaiming her message to any who will hear. This is highly significant. God's wisdom is no private matter, but essential guidance for public life. The standards of his justice should govern our behaviour not merely in some isolated 'religious' realm, but in the bustle of everyday life—in our work, in our relationships, in all our dealings.

Wisdom's speech is in three parts:

- She calls to those who have no time for her (vv. 22–23). God's loving offer of guidance and right relationship with him is freely made to all (v. 23); those who reject it do so freely.
- She warns that the consequence of rejecting God's wisdom is disastrous (vv. 24–31). Divine judgment will surely follow sooner or later.
- She summarizes the stark reality of the choice facing every person (vv. 32–33). There are two ways to live: relying on self rather than God, which ends in destruction, or obeying the voice of God, which brings life.

Isaiah 50:4–9a (Related)

There has, of course, been enormous debate about the original identity of the Suffering Servant in Isaiah. But whoever Isaiah had in mind, the passages certainly remind Christian readers strongly of the mission of Jesus hundreds of years later. This Servant Song foreshadows in a striking way the teaching of Jesus in the Gospel reading about his approaching death and resurrection.

Like the Servant (v. 5), Jesus is totally committed to the will of God, and ready to lay down his life. Like the Servant (v. 6), Jesus undergoes punishment and humiliation for God's sake. Like the Servant (v. 7), Jesus presses on determinedly in God's strength, despite violent opposition. And like the Servant (vv. 8–9), Jesus knows that God will vindicate him so that his accusers' apparent triumph will be an illusion.

The words of the Servant Song are not only background to the ordeal of Jesus. They are also a sobering yet deeply encouraging reflection on what it means for anyone to dedicate one's life to the will of God, taking up one's cross. The risk of persecution, graphically described by both Isaiah and Jesus, is real; but so is the promise of vindication and deliverance by a powerful and loving God.

James 3:1–12

As part of his argument that faith must show itself in the way we behave, James now concentrates on one particular part of the body, the tongue; the power it wields and the danger it poses.

He offers us a series of striking images which make four points about the tongue. First, although it is small, it is powerful and capable of determining a person's destiny (vv. 3–4). Second, our words can be frighteningly destructive and lead to terrible, unforeseen consequences (vv. 5–6). Third, taming our tongues is not possible in our own strength (vv. 7–8)—it is just so tempting to gossip. Fourth, we are all capable of hypocrisy and double talk in what we say (vv. 9–12). As a wit once said, 'There are only two things about him I can't stand: his face!'

This is a message the Church desperately needs to hear and act on (remember that James was writing to fellow Christians—2:1). In many churches today, gossip and destructive criticism are at least as widespread as among unbelievers. Relationships are destroyed, hurts administered, ministries undermined. Yet this is often passed over when Christians think about sin. What an indictment. Verse 10 should become a personal and corporate motto.

Mark 8:27–38

This is a turning point in Mark, as Jesus begins his journey to Jerusalem and the challenges raised by his message fall more clearly into place. What do people really make of him, and what are they going to do about it?

The picture Jesus gives of what it means to follow him (vv. 34–38) is devastating in its call to radical commitment. There are no half measures. Following Jesus means giving up our whole life for him, so that we live no longer for ourselves, for our own self-interest, but for his glory. Only in this way will we be able to receive the eternal life he offers. By the same token, should we choose instead to continue trying to run our lives for ourselves, not for God, then God will grant us that dubious privilege, which will end ultimately in death. It is our choice.

Taking up our own cross is daunting but possible because Jesus has gone before us with his cross. And he stays with us through all the highs and lows of discipleship, just as Peter discovered, one moment voicing his amazing recognition of the Messiah (v. 29), the next getting things completely wrong (vv. 32–33)!

MG

YEAR C

Jeremiah 4:11–12, 22–28 (Continuous)

Jeremiah uses the image of the desert wind—often carrying with it clouds (v. 13) of choking orange sand—to warn of judgment to come. As such a wind is not good for the work of separating wheat from chaff (v. 11), so this wind of destruction will carry all before it. The army invading from the north ('Dan', v. 15) will be the agents of God's judgment.

But the result of judgment will be pregnant with symbolic significance. Step by step it will turn back the creation (light, dry land, people, birds, fruitfulness, vv. 23–26) until the earth is 'waste and void' (v. 23; Genesis 1:2). All this is because his people have turned from the intimate knowledge he called them to (v. 22a), as shown by their inability to live out covenant obedience (v. 22c). Knowledge that is the mere accumulation of information is no knowledge at all. To refuse to welcome God's creative word is to turn from life itself. God's response mirrors perfectly his people's action ('turn back', v. 28; 5:3; cf. 18:8). Where once the declaration was, 'It is very good', the verdict now is that 'it is very evil.' Such evil must eventually be answered for.

Where we turn from reality as God has ordered it, the alternative is not another ordering of reality but no ordering of reality—and eventually no reality of any sort. Yet even now, the destruction will not be total (v. 27); there is the tiniest chink of light still possible (cf. Isaiah 10:21) if we will yet turn.

Exodus 32:7–14 (Related)

This is an episode bristling with all the difficulties an Old Testament text could have: fickle people who forget in an instant (v. 4); an angry God, ready to change his mind in an instant (vv. 10, 14); revenge admired (v. 20) and violence blessed (vv. 28–29).

Yet whatever questions we bring to this text, it still asks questions of us—unless, of course, we do the easy thing and simply throw it away.

Moses had been gone a long time ('forty days', 24:18, proverbially a long stretch). The use of animal images was common in Egypt, where the people had lived for generations. They have not turned to 'other' gods as much as wished to use the calf to invoke God's presence in Moses' absence ('*These are your gods*... a festival to the *Lord*', vv. 4–5). So the *volte face* was not as dramatic as might as first appear. The sin is to refuse to worship God in the way he has ordained.

God looks to disown them ('*your* people, whom *you* brought up...' v. 7). Moses is at first stunned to silence (so God resumes in verse 9). But on hearing the threat of judgment, he implores God on the basis of God's faithful character (v. 11; as far as Moses is concerned they are still God's people) and reputation (v. 12), and in complete identification with his people (see also v. 32).

Are we shaped—for good—by our encounters with God, or does their impact fade? Are we careful not to compromise in lifestyle and worship? Do we identify wholeheartedly with the whole people of God? And are we passionate about God's reputation, not least as it is shaped by others' views of the Church?

1 Timothy 1:12–17

What appears to be a digression in the flow of the letter is actually a move to the centre of Paul's concern—the nature of the gospel. It stands in contradiction to:

- **Self-sufficiency or passive acceptance.** Paul holds together the amazing affirmation he has received (v. 12) of being made an ambassador of Christ with the damning verdict on his own actions (v. 13). His ministry is at root about being taken up in active partnership into God's purposes by his grace (cf. Colossians 1:29; Ephesians 3:20).
- **Fatalism.** Paul expresses this drastic change in his life by describing himself as being (not having been) the worst of sinners ('I am...' v. 15)—he is for ever a sinner forgiven. The one who arrested others was himself arrested by grace.
- **Self-preservation.** Familiarity can dull the shock of the central saying of

verse 15. God's own Messiah came to rescue those who failed to keep his law. God's search led him beyond his own people to include those who did not know him. The Church can therefore never be simply a self-preservation society.

• **Compromise.** God's authority as king (or emperor) of 'the ages' (that is, this age and the age to come, v. 17) stands over against all earthly powers. Those trusting in him begin now to live the 'life of the age [to come]' (the literal meaning of 'eternal life', v. 16) and so participate in its allegiance and its praises.

Luke 15:1–10

Tax collectors (v. 1), agents of Roman oppression, were perceived as enemies of the liberation of God's people. 'Sinners' is an almost technical term denoting those who do not or cannot keep the law. So Jesus' preaching of God's holy and kingly rule must have been strikingly fresh to draw both these groups habitually (v. 1). If we are giving off the aroma of Christ (2 Corinthians 2:15), are we attracting the same kind of people?

In reply to the Pharisees' complaint, Jesus pushes anthropomorphism to its limits in describing God as a sheep farmer—probably smelly from his work, and certainly looked down on in Palestinian society. At first sight his actions appear to us strange or foolish. But it is not necessary to conclude that the farmer leaves the sheep unguarded (v. 4), and laying a sheep on one's shoulders (v. 5) would be normal rural practice. The emphasis is on the persistence and then joy in the recovery of the lost.

Joy in heaven (circumlocution for God's own joy) contrasts with the rabbinical belief in God's glee at the damning of the godless, and also with any sense of God as dispassionate. The hyperbolic contrast (v. 7; cf. Luke 14:26) does not mean that God has no joy in the righteous (see Luke 1:6); the sense is rather that God is at least as committed to searching for the lost as he is to keeping the found—unless there is the ironic sense of those who think they need not repent. Jesus' mission to the 'lost sheep of Israel' (Matthew 10:6) precisely reflected his Father's heart (John 5:19).

The Pharisees unwittingly declare the truth (v. 2, cf. John 11:51): 'This fellow welcomes sinners and eats with them.' Good news indeed!

IP

PROPER 20

YEAR A

Exodus 16:2–15 (Continuous)

So much for 'remember'! Once the initial wave of enthusiasm has faded and the hard realities of desert life begin to bite, the desire for freedom turns into the desire for security and comfort (v. 3). Nostalgia clouds the view of Egypt, and those who were at one time too broken in spirit by their cruel servitude even to contemplate the possibility of escape (Exodus 6:9) now look back to those days as a golden era, far preferable to what they have now.

Being in a state of transition is one of the most difficult things to handle, especially when it is not clear when or what the end will be. The lure of the known, however bad the known might be, is for many a far more powerful force than the lure of the unknown. But there is one Known that the Israelites seem to have forgotten about. God might have led them into the harshness of the wilderness, but they have not been abandoned there; and they will know that there is a divine hand behind this plan when they see with their eyes and taste with their mouths the food that will crystallize for them in a most unexpected fashion (vv. 6–8, 11–15). 'I Am' is still being.

Jonah 3:10—4:11 (Related)

This passage is a variation on the theme of treating others in accordance with the mercy that one receives, only this time, like the parable in Matthew 20:1–16, it is a warning against being jealous of God's generosity to others. When God fails to destroy the city of Nineveh because its people repent after hearing Jonah's message to them, Jonah feels himself to have been diminished for some reason (3:10—4:3). Maybe he thinks that God has made a fool of him, either by sending him with a message of destruction and then failing to carry out the destruction, or by treating the proverbially wicked Ninevites with the same mercy as the faithful people of God. But the key is to understand the justice of God. Is it really fair to destroy a city whose people do not know right from wrong until they receive the message of God (4:11)? Not that Jonah can complain about his own treatment by God: even though he tried to escape his commission, he was treated with mercy and was not punished but restored (Jonah 1:1—3:2). In the end, both Nineveh and Jonah have been treated with the same kind of mercy that answered their particular needs, and nothing could be fairer than that.

Philippians 1:21–30

The letter to the Philippians was written by Paul when he was in prison for preaching the gospel (Philippians 1:12–14), and this context gives his words a peculiar vividness. Perhaps the most striking thought in this passage is that death, far from being an evil, is the welcome passport to complete salvation in Christ (vv. 21, 23). However, Paul realizes that while his death might benefit him, it would not benefit the Philippians, and so he is willing for it to be postponed for their sake (vv. 24–26). This is the mark of the true Christian leader, for whom personal desires must take second place to the needs of those for whom he or she has God-given responsibility.

The second thought is that suffering for the sake of the gospel is not a sign of failure but of success (vv. 29–30). As both Paul and Jesus experienced, the gospel evokes a violent reaction from those who are opposed to it because they regard it as a threat. This in itself is testimony to the power of its message, and so the Philippians should not allow themselves to be frightened away from its truth by those who are themselves afraid of it (vv. 27–28). Persecution, like death, is transformed when seen in the context of the gospel.

Matthew 20:1–16

This parable of the Kingdom is more difficult to understand than its predecessors, not least because it seems to introduce an element of unfairness into the way the Kingdom works. Is it really fair that those who worked for only an hour should be paid the same wages as those who worked all day long (vv. 9–10)? And yet the amount the first labourers received for their whole day's labour was not in itself unfair (v. 13)—it only seemed so in comparison to the generosity with which the later workers were treated (vv. 14–15). It could also be remarked that whether the labourers worked for the whole day or just an hour, their need for money to support themselves and their families was equally as great. Surely, if the later ones were effectively penalized for other employers' failure to hire them (vv. 6–7) it would be more unfair than if all the labourers were paid the same. In the end, it seems that the Kingdom is run on the basis of equal pay for equal need rather than linking rewards to earning power, so that it is not possible to work one's way to a status of superiority over others simply by having had the opportunity for longer service.

DR

Year B

Proverbs 31:10–31 (Continuous)

This famous pen-picture of the wife of noble character brings Proverbs to a close. Given the frequency of male examples in the rest of the book (the farmer, the king, the son and so on), it is significant that the book ends with a marvellous description of a woman who seems to embody wisdom. This woman exercises power and responsibility, conducting business deals as well as running the affairs of the household—a timely message for a church still struggling to come to terms with women in positions of leadership.

Some have found this a rather intimidating picture. If it is taken (wrongly) as a blueprint to which all Christian wives should measure up, it will merely produce a sense of inadequacy. Rather, three things should be remembered. First, God appreciates (of course) that none of us is perfect. Second, the kind of standards set out here are standards to which all of us, women and men, should aspire in God's strength. Third, some have suggested that rather than portraying a purely human figure, this passage actually describes the figure of Wisdom at work in the domestic context. Seen in this way, the description is not dispiriting, but wonderfully life-giving.

Jeremiah 11:18–20 (Related)

The 'Passion prediction' of Jesus in Mark 9:30–32 echoes strikingly this passage from Jeremiah.

Jeremiah has pronounced God's judgment on Judah (11:16–17), just as Jesus has pronounced judgment on the religious leaders of his day. God now reveals to Jeremiah that the people's reaction will be to plot his death, rejecting him and his message. In the Mark reading, Jesus has also received from God the Father an insight into the reaction against him. He too will be subject to a violent plot. Jeremiah remains none the less confident in the just dealings of God (v. 20a), just as Jesus is confident in his ultimate vindication by God in his resurrection. Jesus, however, unlike Jeremiah (v. 20b), does not call on God to take vengeance on his persecutors.

The inextricable link between prophetic ministry and suffering is clearly seen in the experience of Jeremiah and Jesus. Both are aware of the risks they run; both hold fast to proclaiming God's message.

This is a difficult area for the Church in the West today. How far are we genuinely prepared to take risks for the sake of the gospel? Do we consciously or otherwise dilute our message in order to avoid the risk of rejection?

James 3:13—4:3, 7–8a

James describes two kinds of wisdom. One is the wisdom from above (v. 17), which shows itself in right living and humility (v. 13). The other 'wisdom', envious self-interest which is ultimately demonic, is a grotesque parody of the first (vv. 14–15). We are open to the influence of both, and James pleads with his readers to choose wisely.

This is because both kinds of wisdom produce profound consequences for our relationships with God and with each other. Those who are open to the wisdom from above are enabled to live lives pleasing to God ('raising a harvest of righteousness') and to show peace and mercy towards others (vv. 17–18). The evil 'wisdom' distorts our relationship with God, turning prayer into fruitless attempts to manipulate him for our own ends (v. 3), and dragging our relationships with each other into discontent, quarrels and even murder (vv. 1–2)—'do unto others before they do you', as someone memorably described modern ethics.

Yet we are not left on our own to grapple with the choice between these two kinds of wisdom. We can resist the temptation to put selfish ambition before all else, by submitting to God and drawing on the strength he promises to give us (vv. 7–8a).

Mark 9:30–37

Jesus' statement about his coming death and resurrection, the second he makes in Mark (see 8:31), goes right over the disciples' heads. This is probably because they simply cannot get their minds round the idea that God's promised Messiah will suffer in this way: surely he is to be a victorious, conquering figure? Our problem with the statement may be the reverse. We are so used to the idea of Jesus' sacrifice for us on the cross that we tend to take it for granted.

Jesus calls his disciples to follow this example of servanthood, turning on its head the attitude of the Twelve, as they argue among themselves for precedence. Just as we take the cross for granted, perhaps we take Jesus' teaching here for granted as well. We might laugh at the crude debate among the disciples and think ourselves above it. But we all find more sophisticated ways of doing exactly the same thing; even within the Church, as we look to our own reputations or seek responsibilities for ourselves. We would all do well to reflect on verse 35 and its implications: 'Whoever wants to be first must be last of all and servant of all.'

MG

313

YEAR C

Jeremiah 8:18—9:1 (Continuous)

It is almost impossible to separate the voice of the prophet from the voice of God; both feel the shattering sense of grief at realizing that God's people are literally sick to death. God's anger here is almost totally subsumed in grief and sadness.

The people continue in a liturgical pretence, relying on formulae (v. 19) and timetables (v. 20). The heart of their sickness is the attempt to 'organize life around controllable objects rather than in reference to a holy subject' (v. 19c; Brueggemann, *To Pluck Up, To Tear Down*, Eerdmans, p. 89). The first place we need healing is not in sick bodies but in sinful lives that do not give God the worship we owe.

God's agony, and the agony of those close to his heart, is the heart-sickness of a betrayed lover or a yearning parent. We can put a brave face on pain we feel on our own behalf, but there is no technique for hiding the pain we feel on behalf of others.

God's final act is to grant his people's implicit request and depart from them (9:2, reflecting the language of Psalm 55:6–8), but not before he has known the betrayal in person (Psalm 55:12–14; cf. Psalm 41:9; John 13:18) and his humiliation in public (Galatians 3:1). Only then is there a place for healing beyond the walls of Jerusalem.

Amos 8:4–7 (Related)

God's judgment falls on his people (8:2) because they have trusted in another god—economic prosperity—to provide for their needs and grant them security.

The juggernaut of economism works its evil in many and various ways:
- It drives roughshod over the needs of those who cannot provide for themselves (v. 4).
- It damages God-given patterns that provide for rest and refreshment (v. 5a).
- It develops widespread corruption in trade, both in weights and measures and in terms of payment (v. 5b).
- It decrees that financial commitments be pressed home, regardless of the human cost (v. 6a; the exchange of sandals was a common way of closing a deal).
- It demands that profit is maximized in every possible way (v. 6b; contrast Leviticus 19:9; 23:22).

314

The extent to which we see these things happening in our world is the extent to which our way of life is under God's judgment, and there is darkness over the earth (v. 9). But there was another day when God remembered sin and it brought darkness at noon (Luke 23:44), so that we might dwell in the light of a new way of living under God's just and kingly rule.

1 Timothy 2:1–7

Paul begins his specific instructions to Timothy, not to set out a timeless prescription for ministry, but to reform and guard against false teaching (1:3). Of first importance come the following:

- **Prayer.** Timothy's commission is not a human task, but a continuation of God's mission. As there is only one God (v. 5), he is God over all. So there is no sphere of human activity, no form of government or secular authority (v. 2), that is beyond his rule and therefore beyond the need of prayer. This is despite the claim of God as king/emperor (1:17) that offers a prophetic critique of the system of the day.
- **Truth.** The emphasis on both personal integrity (v. 7b) and continuity with gospel truth (vv. 4, 7b)—the subjective and the objective, form and content—stands over against the false teachers and relates to the unity of God (v. 5). Paul's motivation is sincere as he fulfils the commission for which God chose him (the use of the passive indicates God's action in verse 7)—he was not self-appointed.
- **Evangelism.** The concern that all might be saved (v. 4) is central to the truth about God, and the driving force behind these first two concerns. To be seen as people of good conduct (v. 2b) is primarily a mission concern (as is made clear in 1 Thessalonians 4:11–12). Jesus' giving of himself was not only unique, it was universal (vv. 5, 6, a Hellenized version of the more Semitic Mark 10:45, which uses 'many' to mean 'all'). So everything must be done to create opportunity for and remove obstacles to the dissemination of this truth.

Luke 16:1–13

This is a problematical parable to understand—it looks as if we are being encouraged to be dishonest!

The steward was in a fix. Time was running out, and he had a problem to solve. Absentee landlords were common in Galilee, and there was a great gulf between rich and poor. With no employment rights, no social security, and perhaps little prospect of another job, the steward faced real difficulties

(v. 3). In a 'eureka' moment, he hits on a plan to use the system for his own benefit (v. 4).

There is no evidence to suggest that he is writing off unfair interest, or cancelling his own commission (vv. 5–7). In his single-minded determination and resourcefulness, he has simply beaten the system. When others do this—passing exams without revision, getting promotion without hard work, earning money from a fortuitous investment—we usually feel a mixture of pious superiority and sneaking admiration. Jesus is saying that we are to be as shrewd as them (Matthew 10:16) but motivated by something much higher than greed (v. 13).

Like the steward, we are in a fix. Time is ticking by, most people around us know nothing of God's good news, and God will want to know what we have done about it. We are to be as single-minded, resourceful and energetic as the steward in solving our problem, using every means at our disposal.

IP

Proper 21

Year A

Exodus 17:1–7 (Continuous)

This time, the issue is lack of water (v. 1), not food, but in many ways the same kind of features are present as in the manna incident (vv. 2–3; Proper 20, Year A, Exodus 16:2–15). This in itself is worthy of note, because despite the clearly miraculous provision of food which continues until the end of their wanderings, the Israelites seem unable or unwilling to reckon that the God who gives them food might also be able to give them water. But fear often blinds, and the fear of no water would be very great. This fear presents itself as an attack on Moses (v. 4), but he is, of course, only the visible representative of the one who engineered the whole plan. Moses himself has no power to give them water to drink, nor would he have had any authority to bring them out of Egypt were it not for the Lord (Exodus 3:7–12). The people might forget about the unseen dimension of this whole escapade, but Moses cannot, and it is his job not only to rely upon it at all times but also to remind the people of it constantly. Otherwise he will fail in his commission, and they will condemn themselves by their disbelieving rebellion.

Ezekiel 18:1–4, 25–32 (Related)

By contrast with some other passages where the corporate dimension of responsibility for sin is stressed (Proper 18, Year A, Matthew 18:15–20; Ezekiel 33:7–11), here the focus is clearly on the individual's responsibility. The 'down side' of the corporate dimension is that individuals can use it to evade their own very real and particular responsibility by blaming other people for what are actually their own failures. Ezekiel's contemporaries, for example, were apparently claiming that they were being punished for the sins of a previous generation (v. 2). But the message from God is that sin, whatever its cause, will be punished wherever it is found, just as righteousness will be rewarded wherever it is found (vv. 26–28). There is no pre-ordained status that will exempt people from this principle; everyone is treated equally. No one is stamped 'wicked' and therefore condemned, or stamped 'righteous' and therefore saved, without regard to their own actions. The righteous can become wicked, and the wicked righteous, depending on whether or not they do the will of God; and so the responsibility is great. But there is also real hope, because God has no desire to punish anyone and, in treating people like this, is urging them to choose the right and to live (vv. 31–32).

Philippians 2:1–13

In these verses, Paul is describing how the Philippians should live as Christians, and, in order to give them a model of the kind of humility and self-sacrifice that should characterize their life together, he incorporates what was probably a familiar piece of early Christian hymnody (vv. 5–11) into his flow of thought. In this way, Paul reminds the Philippians that doctrinal statements are not just to be recited, but they have practical implications for living the Christian life. The hymn describes how God has glorified Christ because he willingly humbled himself from a position of the highest imaginable rank to the lowest level of servitude. If Christ undertook that kind of self-humiliation, then his followers certainly must, because for none of them is the humiliation going to be anything like as great.

The ability to follow Christ's model of self-sacrifice is a matter of taking hold of what the Spirit of God has made possible for those who believe (vv. 12–13). So although believers cannot save themselves or make themselves righteous in the eyes of God, in living their lives they must none the less co-operate actively with God who is working in them and giving them both the desire and the ability to do what is right.

Matthew 21:23–32

The climax is approaching. Jesus is now in Jerusalem, having made his entry into the city to the acclaim of the crowds, and has cleansed the temple (Matthew 21:1–17). Not surprisingly, in so doing he has attracted the attention of the religious authorities—he is, after all, in their home territory—and their response to his provocative actions is to challenge his authority (v. 23). But their challenge, and therefore their authority, is undermined by their unwillingness to commit themselves in answering the question he puts to them about the baptism of John (vv. 25–27). They do not have the courage of their convictions to come down clearly on one side or the other; the impression is that they know what the answer ought to be, but they also know that in giving it they would be condemned out of their own mouths because of their failure to respond appropriately to John. So they choose to save face but lose credibility by saying that they do not know. The parable that Jesus then tells them (vv. 28–32) emphasizes what has just been brought home to them—that actions speak louder than words, and simply knowing what is right is no substitute for actually doing God's will.

DR

YEAR B

Esther 7:1–6, 9–10; 9:20–22 (Continuous)

Esther is a strange book—a great story, but feeling more like a historical romance than part of scripture. Oddly, God is mentioned nowhere in the entire text. So why is it in the Bible?

Although God is not explicitly mentioned in Esther, the downfall of Haman (7:9–10) can be seen as the outworking of divine justice, especially when Esther is seen in its wider Old Testament context. God is still at work, even when no one seems to acknowledge him explicitly.

The protection of the innocent (9:22) reminds us of God's constant care for his people, past, present and future. The establishment of a festival, Purim, celebrating the deliverance of the Jews, recalls other Jewish festivals such as Passover and the Feast of Tabernacles, which are rooted in God's redemption of his people in the exodus.

Of course, the preservation of God's chosen people from the threat of extermination has enormous resonances from our recent past. The unimaginable horror of the Holocaust has understandably led some to think that God was absent. There are no easy explanations. But might God have been there, suffering with his people in the terrible darkness, as he was also present in Esther's day?

Numbers 11:4–6, 10–16, 24–29 (Related)

Faced with discontent among the people about the monotony of a diet of manna, Moses appeals to God for help. God's response is to commission seventy elders to support Moses, and he anoints them with his Spirit (v. 25). However, the Spirit also inspires Eldad and Medad to prophesy, even though they are not among the select seventy. Moses allows them to continue, his response (v. 29) strikingly reminiscent of Paul's comment in 1 Corinthians 14:5.

The case of Eldad and Medad is reminiscent of the unknown exorcist in Mark 9:38. The Spirit goes wherever he wants (John 3:8); it is not for God's people to try to restrict him.

There are two challenges here for the contemporary Church. First, when the Spirit moves in surprising ways, is our attitude the same as that of Joshua (v. 28) and the disciples (Mark 9:38)? In other words, do we rate our own view of what is appropriate more highly than God's? Second, do we genuinely expect to see the Spirit at work outside the Church? Our attitude to those currently outside the Church will be changed for the better if we recognize that, in his love, God is already at work in their lives.

James 5:13–20

It is significant that at the end of this most practical of letters, James turns to the subject of prayer. The active and effective witness James has been arguing for will lack all purpose and power if it is not based on a prayerful relationship with God. And we are to pray at all times (cf. Ephesians 6:18), whatever our situation (v. 13).

James then writes in more detail about prayer for healing. As with other prayer, prayer for healing is to be offered in the firm hope and expectation that God will hear and answer (v. 15). But this raises problems. What about occasions when God does not heal, despite fervent and faithful prayer? The New Testament writers knew, of course, that God does not always heal (2 Corinthians 12:7–9).

This is a difficult area, but we need to hold on to the fact that it all comes back to God. James is clear that it is God who heals (v. 15), not those praying, no matter how righteous (v. 16) they might be. So we pray that God's will will be done (Matthew 6:10), knowing that if the answers are not what we would immediately choose, his will is ultimately for the best.

Mark 9:38–50

The disciples betray a misunderstanding of what it means to be a follower of Jesus, or to be 'on his side'. Their concern is whether someone is part of their little group, rather than whether that person happens to be doing the will of God. Jesus responds with a lesson in the generous values of God's Kingdom: three yardsticks of discipleship against which to measure ourselves.

First, we are to be committed to the work of God in the world, through the Holy Spirit (vv. 38–40). The Church, or one part of it, does not control the Spirit. He is constantly at work all around us and we are called to recognize that and rejoice in it.

Second, we are to be committed to our fellow believers. 'Little ones' (v. 42) might mean children, or recent converts, or simply any follower of Jesus. But our attitude to our fellow believers is to be marked by constructive and loving concern which helps their relationship with God to grow.

Third, we are to be committed to personal holiness, resisting temptation in God's strength (vv. 43–48) and living distinctive lives which make a difference to the world just as salt brings flavour to food (v. 50).

MG

YEAR C

Jeremiah 32:1–3a, 6–15 (Continuous)

On the brink of disaster, the word of the Lord comes to Jeremiah bursting with confidence and brimful of hope for the future.

There is real hardship in the siege (v. 2) and personal pressure from the questioning of the king (v. 3b) with whom Jeremiah once had common cause (see 29:3). Yet Jeremiah is still open to hear the word of the Lord (v. 6) and act on it. It is a message that makes no real sense even to Jeremiah (v. 25), and yet obedient action here precedes complete understanding. And the action is concrete and costly (vv. 9–10)—there is no weak vagueness of 'Well, I'm praying for you'!

In the midst of judgment, God continues to speak—directly (v. 6), through others (v. 8) and in symbolic action (vv. 9–10). God's word is true; both Hanamel's request (v. 8) and the burial of the world's first time capsule (v. 14) are objective touchstones which give credence to what is otherwise merely subjective. And God's word brings tangible hope as the prophetic spills over to engage with the economic and social. 'Houses and fields and vineyards' (v. 15) speak not simply of prosperity, but of relationship; the right of redemption (v. 7) was designed to keep the family inheritance together.

Jeremiah invests in God's promised future exactly when that future seems completely closed off. We must do the same—in prayer for, witness to and service of others. And in our investing we are helping to bring about precisely the future that God has promised—life in all its fullness (John 10:10).

Amos 6:1a, 4–7 (Related)

Under Omri and Jeroboam II, the northern kingdom enjoyed great economic prosperity, but the disparity between rich and poor had grown ever wider. Samaria and Jerusalem (v. 1) had become royal cities, and did not identify with the surrounding rural peasant population as did other cities—wealth had been divorced from need.

Amos' indictment of this affluent society is remarkably suggestive of a wish-list for the average citizen of Britain today:

- freedom from anxiety ('at ease', v. 1)
- security, stability and influence (v. 1b)
- quality furniture, leisure, eclectic lifestyle (v. 4; local custom was to sit on the floor)
- wining and dining (vv. 4b, 6)
- entertainment (karaoke?! v. 5)
- expensive cosmetics (v. 6)

All this luxury was at the expense of the poor, and gained through violence (v. 3). As a result, the leaders of the people would be the ones to lead them into exile (v. 7), the noise of revelry giving way to a barren silence.

The awkward thing about this reading is that it fits rather closely with the situation of the Western nations today. We claim to exercise moral leadership but live in luxury, make money through arms manufacture and control trade in such a way as to keep the poor poor.

The wish-list is sharply inverted by the coming of the Kingdom of God (see Luke 6:24–26). Real moral leadership—personal, local and national—puts a passion for justice ahead of personal indulgence and a demand for equality in place of the defence of violence.

1 Timothy 6:6–19

As elsewhere (see, for example, 2 Corinthians 11) it appears that those teaching falsely (6:3) were doing so for personal gain (6:5). But, despite what the televangelists tell us, selfish ambition and Christian ministry are like oil and water—they don't mix.

The desire for gain begins with dissatisfaction (v. 8); it is characterized by painful and fruitless suffering (v. 10); it weakens, enslaves, and is ultimately destructive. And it ends in futility, as all that is gained is swept away by death (v. 7).

By contrast, faithfulness to the teaching of Jesus begins with a decisive step of grasping the gift held out by grace (v. 12). There is a struggle (v. 12a), but it is one that is purposeful and full of hope, following as it does the example of Jesus (v. 13). Staying true to faith builds character (v. 11; cf. Galatians 5:23), leads to life (vv. 12–13), and will be affirmed at the appearance of Christ (v. 14).

In setting out the nature of these two unmixables, Paul appeals not only to the Old Testament (v. 7; cf. Job 1:21) and the teaching of Jesus (v. 8; cf., for example, Luke 12:22–32) but also common sense (v. 10, a version of a proverb in wide currency at the time).

The striking and majestic series of epithets (vv. 15–16) combines biblical and pagan titles (for example, Ezekiel 26:7; Deuteronomy 10:17) in a way reminiscent of Revelation (17:14; 19:16)—most apt in Ephesus which was a centre both of pagan religion and emperor worship.

Luke 16:19–31

This parable is not concerned with cosmic geography, nor is it a story of simple reversal or a guilt-inducing plea for generosity. Like a cartoon, it is almost comic in its portrayal of the exaggerated contrast between the two characters. Nothing could be better for the one; nothing worse for the other (vv. 19–21). Yet the clue to their destinies is there from the beginning: the rich man is nameless, whilst the poor man is Lazarus—'he whom God helps' (cf. Matthew 5:3; Luke 6:20). Its stark contrasts urge upon us two realities.

- **Inequality:** The rich are not in the first place those most blessed by God, or members of a society with the best economic and social policies, so much as those with most responsibility when faced with the ever-present challenge of responding to the poor (Deuteronomy 15:11; John 12:8; Luke 12:48). We find it too easy to put people in boxes and think that there is nothing we can or should do to change things.
- **Judgment:** There will come a time when we cannot change from one destiny to the other (v. 26)—we cannot keep waiting till tomorrow to change, since tomorrows will stop coming. The time for obedience is now.

The story of Jesus' death and resurrection has become, for our generation, equivalent to their 'Moses and the prophets' (v. 29)—a text rather than lived experience. Yet here lies the key to seeing reality as it is and responding in the light both of God's demands on us and of God's provision for us.

IP

PROPER 22

YEAR A

Exodus 20:1–4, 7–9, 12–20 (Continuous)

The Ten Commandments are the first part of the Law as a whole that the Israelites receive from God at Sinai. As such, they form a basis for everything that follows, and lay down broad guidelines for how to live as a community —in this case, as the community of God.

The commandments reflect the relative order of commitments that are demanded of the community. First and foremost is the commitment to God (vv. 1–4, 7–9). This is a commitment that involves remembering who God is, and this in turn means remembering what God has done (v. 2), because the two things are inseparable. Remembering the 'who' and 'what' of God's identity precludes attempts to minimize or control that identity by either locking it up in a static, finite image (v. 4) or using the name of God to invoke divine power for inappropriate or evil purposes (v. 7). After the commitment to God comes the commitment to family (v. 12), and then the commitment to respect of neighbours, without which no community could function (vv. 13–17).

It is notable that, in the Hebrew, the commandments are phrased in the singular, and so are an address to each individual member of the community. No one can evade the responsibilities laid down by these ten 'words' (Exodus 34:28).

Isaiah 5:1–7 (Related)

The song of the vineyard is a damning condemnation of those who have been chosen and nurtured by God but who have failed to respond appropriately to that nurture. The intense disappointment of the sour yield is underlined by the way that the one who plants the vineyard gives it every possible chance of producing the finest grapes (v. 2). The plot of land chosen is itself very fertile; the land is then dug over and all the large stones which would inhibit the chances of growth are removed. The vines are choice vines, not just any old plants, and a watchtower is built to protect them from sabotage. As the song says, there is nothing more that the owner could possibly have done to ensure a sweet yield (v. 4); so all that can be done now is to destroy the vineyard (vv. 5–6).

The privilege of being chosen for nurture in the ways of God, a nurture which is more than generous, is matched by an equally great responsibility to live up to that calling. Being chosen is no guarantee of immunity from punishment, and where evil is found among the chosen ones, it will not be tolerated indefinitely.

Philippians 3:4b–14

Humility has two dimensions. There is humility before God, whereby believers acknowledge that no one and nothing except Christ can give salvation. There is also humility towards others, which flows from the believer's attitude of humility before God, is exemplified in the attitude of Christ and is the pattern for Christian morality. Both these kinds of humility appear in Philippians. In encouraging the Philippians to live their Christian lives appropriately, Paul encourages them to adopt the attitude of humility towards others, which Christ had embodied (see comment on Philippians 2:1–13 in Proper 21, Year A). Here he describes his own attitude of humility before God, as a warning against trusting in anything else for salvation except the power of God in Christ. Paul has already humbled himself by putting aside everything that went to make up his previous status (v. 7), even though it was a religious status (vv. 4b–6), because he knows that only by so doing can he share in Christ's humiliation and thereby in his glorification (vv. 8–11). But Christ's once-for-all humiliation provided the pattern of behaviour on which believers must base their whole lives; and so, for Paul, the whole of his Christian life will be a repeated act of humiliation emphasizing his dependence on God, in order that he may finally reach the goal and be worthy of the prize (vv. 12–14).

Matthew 21:33–46

In this parable, having just accused the religious leaders of what might be called 'passive hypocrisy', that is, of pretending to be godly but failing to respond to God's message, Jesus goes on to accuse them of active opposition to the will of God. The parable is another Kingdom parable, and it is based loosely on the song of the vineyard in Isaiah 5:1–7, where the people of Israel, God's special planting, are condemned for failing to produce worthy fruit. This makes it clear that Jesus' parable is aimed at those who have traditionally regarded themselves as the people of God. However, in the present parable, the people themselves are not the vineyard, merely its tenants (v. 33), and the essence of the criticism is that, having been given the privilege of use of the vineyard, these unworthy tenants have usurped the right of ownership (vv. 38–39).

The result of their treacherous behaviour is not the destruction of the vineyard, as it is in Isaiah, but the destruction of the tenants and the letting of the vineyard to other, more worthy tenants (v. 41). In this way, the parable indicates that the Kingdom of God and the nation of Israel are not the same, and that failure of the original tenants to fulfil their obligations will not result in the Kingdom's failure but in its broadening out.

DR

YEAR B

Job 1:1; 2:1–10 (Continuous)

The opening of the book poses two deeply troubling questions.

First, the integrity of God himself is called into question. What kind of God would do all this to a good and faithful man, in response to suggestions from Satan, the heavenly accuser? How can we possibly trust or honour God if he is like this?

Second, we at least have the full picture of what is going on. Job does not. All he experiences is the despair of loss and affliction. And if anything, his faith in God, which remains intact (2:3, 10), seems to make things worse. If he believed in no god, or in a capricious god, he might despair, which would be bad enough. But how can he reconcile his experience with the existence of a loving, sovereign Creator?

This most profound book is grappling with the problem of how pain and suffering can exist in God's world. The drama of the book is a way of expressing the tragedy of this world: yes, God is sovereign, but the world is fallen, and bad things happen to good people. Reading Job will not give glib answers; but then it would not help us if it did.

Genesis 2:18–24 (Related)

Jesus' prohibition of divorce in Mark must be seen in the context of these fundamental and positive statements: Jesus refers to them explicitly. Three principles underlying marriage are clearly set out.

First, companionship and mutual support are fundamentally important. God's comment that 'it is not good for the man to be alone' (v. 18) is striking because up until now everything has been very good. His intention, expressed in the first creation account (1:28–30) is that men and women together should be stewards of his earth.

Second, the husband's bond to his wife is said to supersede the bond to his parents (v. 24). This is 'an astounding declaration in a world where filial duty was the most sacred obligation next to loyalty to God' (Gordon J.

Wenham, *Genesis 1—15*, Word Books, p. 88), emphasizing the strength of the marriage bond as God intends it.

Third, the depth of the marriage relationship is expressed in the idea of union in one flesh. This is not only a reference to sexual intercourse, the birth of children and emotional attachment: it also suggests the establishment of a new, permanent kinship between husband and wife, which is not to be broken (Mark 10:8–9).

Hebrews 1:1–4; 2:5–12

The central theme of Hebrews is that the past has given way to better things. God has revealed himself in the past, but now he has shown himself definitively in the person of Jesus Christ.

From these two passages early in the letter, we get a magnificent picture of what later generations would call the two natures of Christ: divine and human. The early date of this description makes it all the more mind-blowing.

In 1:1–4, the writer affirms the deity of Christ. He is God's supreme revelation, his Son and heir, the one through whom the universe was created, the Saviour of the world. This language might tend to wash over us; we need to recapture the sheer amazement and wonder that these characteristics and roles could be assigned to a carpenter from Nazareth.

Then, in 2:5–12, we read of the other side of Jesus—the one who became fully human for us, to make the perfect sacrifice to save us. This is a passage of tremendous hope. Jesus has shown astonishing solidarity with us in his life and death; we are now his close family. Let's take time to remind ourselves of the sheer wonder of all this.

Mark 10:2–16

Divorce and remarriage was as thorny a subject then as it is now. Perhaps that is why the Pharisees raised it with Jesus, hoping that he would say something controversial which would alienate the crowd.

He takes them back to first principles, affirming lifelong monogamy as the pattern for marriage established by God at creation (vv. 6–9). He also acknowledges the concession in the Law allowing divorce (v. 5), although he clearly sees it as a tragic necessity in the face of human sinfulness.

So what are we to make of this teaching in our culture, where divorce and remarriage are commonplace? Like Jesus (and Moses), we should recognize that there are circumstances where divorce becomes inevitable. We might find support for remarriage in Matthew 19:9. But the clear burden of Jesus' teaching here is against any divorce. It is significant that this passage is included in a block of teaching about discipleship. We badly need to rediscover the sense that as Jesus' disciples we are to live distinctive lives which witness to his values, not those of the world. Loving concern for those whose marriages fail is entirely consistent with seeking to uphold firmly and confidently the pattern Jesus also upholds.

MG

YEAR C

Lamentations 1:1–6 (Continuous)

This lament over the downfall of Jerusalem shows all the hallmarks of grief. There is loneliness, reflection on what was or might have been (v. 1), sleeplessness, tears, a sense of isolation (v. 2), restlessness, feelings of being overwhelmed (v. 3), desolation and loss of hope (v. 4) and simple exhaustion (v. 6). Though the text has been ascribed to various people or places, no doubt these things were felt most keenly by those like Jeremiah (the traditional author), now in exile and with little hope of seeing the city again.

But perhaps what is most remarkable is that this has been written at all. Although this form of writing was well known in the ancient Near East, there seems at first little theological basis for it—the destruction of Jerusalem was not only the judgment of God on his people for their sin (v. 5), it also signalled the departure of God's *shekinah* presence.

Yet the human impulse to mourn prevails, and in fact proves true; there is still hope in crying out to God (3:24). We live in a culture which prefers respectful silence to the wail of grief; perhaps we need to learn here the value of articulating our feelings of loss.

But consolation is as yet premature; the only certainties to hold on to are of the letters themselves (chapters 1 and 2 are 'acrostics', each of the 22 verses beginning with successive letters of the Hebrew alphabet). In time, the pain will give way to hope—in time.

Habakkuk 1:1–4; 2:1–4 (Related)

Paradoxically, we live in an age of instant everything, yet asking questions is often seen to be more profound than providing answers, to travel more interesting than to arrive. Habakkuk teaches us how to ask aright—not looking for instant answers or no answers but real answers.

First, he reminds us that the questions are real. If answers are given, they must be born of real engagement with the questions of this world, not least the questions arising from the claim that an all-powerful, sovereign and loving God is involved with this messy and evil world. Habakkuk wrestles with the notion that God can use the proud Babylonians (Chaldeans, v. 6) to accomplish his holy purposes.

Second, he recalls us to the stature of waiting—waiting for God, waiting with others, waiting for understanding (2:1). Travelling with questions can be a mark of patience, but only as long as there is expectation of an answer. To still desire an answer that has not come is to be profoundly vulnerable, and the refusal to keep looking marks the pride of independence.

Third, he challenges us to look for answers in relationship, supremely in relationship with God (2:4; Romans 1:17). It is those who trust in him who will find the wanting taken out of waiting, and a glimpse of glory even as they continue the journey (ch. 3).

2 Timothy 1:1–14

Paul's last extant letter is full of urgent imperatives. He appeals to Timothy to be faithful to the heritage of faith in which he has been brought up (v. 5), to make real in his present ministry what God has initiated in him in the past (v. 6), confidently to join Paul in suffering (v. 8), to keep and guard the treasure of truth that he has received (vv. 13–14; cf. Matthew 13:44).

At a personal level, Paul is aware that his time is short, and that Timothy is his successor (4:6). But the real ground of his appeal is what God has done in history and in Timothy's life.

In his mini-creed (vv. 9–10), he reminds Timothy that God has given us a wonderful gift (not because we deserved it, but out of the overflow of his grace and generosity)—a call to holy living, empowered by his Spirit present within (v. 7), in relationship with one who can be trusted with what is most precious to us (v. 12). It is no accident, nor a passing whim—God knew what he would do before even dinosaurs roamed the earth (v. 9)!

But he also reminds Timothy of the work God has done in his life (vv. 5–6). He is to treasure his personal history of God's dealings with him.

In an impersonal, changing and unreliable world, God's call to us is trustworthy and lasting. It is of both cosmic and personal significance, and it is too good, too important and too precious to be squandered.

Luke 17:5–10

This slightly baffling saying (vv. 5–6) appears unconnected with surrounding material. The question may have been instanced by the disciples' observations of Jesus' power in prayer (see Mark 9:28–29 or Luke 11:1). In contrast to their pre-occupation with *themselves* and *their* faith, Jesus points them away from the self. The mustard seed (v. 6) was proverbially small (Matthew 13:32), and the fig-mulberry traditionally known as deep-rooted; the absurdity of the example ('be planted in the sea') shows its hyperbolic nature. The focus is not on having great faith in God, but having faith in a great God. The power of prayer does not depend on the greatness of the person praying, but on the character of the God who is prayed to.

The second saying continues the theme of looking away from the self. Discipleship is not about self-aggrandizement but about self-forgetting—not self-serving but God-serving. What God does for us comes as a gift, not to be demanded or expected by right. The appropriate response to God's goodness and grace is the sacrifice of self (Romans 12:1). But this is not the same as self-loathing; though by nature we are no more than slaves, we are in fact received as friends, as brothers and sisters (John 15:15). The gift of grace stands against both the arrogance of works and the poverty of worthlessness.

IP

PROPER 23

YEAR A

Exodus 32:1–14 (Continuous)

So much for 'remember the Lord your God' and 'no graven images'! When nothing happens for some time and the leader who was their lifeline to God seems to have disappeared, the people get edgy and want a new leader and visible reassurance of gods with them (v. 1)—an understandable reaction when they are stuck in the middle of the desert with nowhere to go. They still do not have the courage of their convictions about the God who has brought them to this point. That God, though, is well aware of what they are doing (vv. 7–8). And now a new aspect of the divine character is shown —that of restraint and mercy in the face of great sin (vv. 9–14). The exodus events showed mercy and redemptive power directed at the oppressed, and punitive, destructive power directed at the oppressors, but not wrath withheld for the sake of a previous commitment.

Once again, the fulfilment of the promise to Abraham is threatened—this time by the God who gave it. But ultimately it is preserved as the divine nature remains true to itself even in the face of such blatant disobedience. God remembers, even if the people do not.

Isaiah 25:1–9 (Related)

This passage contains several ideas and themes that reappear in the New Testament. It begins by describing the character of God, praising the One whose power is displayed in overwhelming even the strongest of human constructions (v. 2) and in protecting the helpless (v. 4), a recurrent theme from Exodus to the Magnificat. Such clear demonstrations of power force everyone to recognize how marvellous God is, and elicit praise and awe from the faithful and enemies alike (vv. 1, 3). God's faithfulness is also emphasized, as is the divine control of history, in the reference to longstanding plans which have been fulfilled (v. 1).

In the light of these affirmations about God's character, the writer offers a picture of final future salvation (presumably the consummation of the longstanding plans mentioned in verse 1) in terms of an extravagant feast for all the world (v. 6), the so-called messianic banquet. This is a symbol of the joy and plenty that will abound when God's creation-wide rule is finally established in power on the earth (v. 9). The ultimate symbol of that joy and plenty is the swallowing up of death (vv. 7–8), so that for all those who have waited trustingly for God's salvation, life will be divinely abundant not only in its quality (rich, full, joyous) and its availability (for all), but in its quantity (everlasting).

Philippians 4:1–9

Paul's words to the Philippians end with sentiments that are all the more potent for being expressed from the confines of prison. The first three verses are a heartfelt plea to the Philippians not to make Paul's sacrifices worthless by reneging on their commitment to Christ or by allowing division and dissent to rupture the fellowship they enjoy. While he is not there, and once he has gone for good, they have the responsibility of passing on the message and upholding the faith, and so, having urged them to stand fast in the Lord, he gives them final instructions about how they should carry out their responsibility.

Perhaps most striking are the instructions to rejoice and not to be anxious about anything (vv. 4, 6)—easy enough to say when life is good. But it is only the response of joy and trust, whatever the circumstances, that will enable the peace of God to be experienced in a way which passes understanding because it transcends the outward circumstances (vv. 7). The exhortation to think about worthy and excellent things (v. 8) is once again a very positive piece of advice which helps to prevent negative attitudes and thereby to preserve the unity and strength of the congregation.

Matthew 22:1–14

The theme of the broadening out of the Kingdom in the face of its rejection by those for whom it was originally intended is continued in the parable of the king's wedding feast. This parable has overtones of the theme of the messianic banquet (see comment on Matthew 14:13–21, Proper 13, Year A). Whereas the parable of the vineyard (Matthew 21:33–43) emphasized the culpability of the tenants for maliciously appropriating what did not belong to them, here the criticism is of the breathtaking stupidity of those who reject the king's invitation (vv. 5–6). Surely those who were in a position to be invited would know not to refuse the king in such a cavalier fashion! But their priorities are completely wrong, and they have no sense of the value of the invitation, or of the consequences of refusal (v. 7).

As with the vineyard parable, though, the plan is bigger than those for whom it was initially intended, and so the invitation is broadened out to include all sorts of unlikely people (vv. 8–10). However, although the invitation is free for all, it is not a free-for-all: there are standards of life and conduct to maintain as an appropriate response to it (vv. 11–12; see comment on Romans 6:1b–11, Proper 7, Year A), and failure to maintain those standards is as damning as refusing the invitation in the first place (vv. 13–14).

DR

YEAR B

Job 23:1–9, 16–17 (Continuous)

This speech by Job comes from the third round of debate he has with his three friends. So many of the key questions of the book ('Is God just? What has Job done to deserve this?' and so on) have already been aired, though not answered.

Job now moves into still more profound territory. He seems now to think that theological debate of itself is inadequate. What he really craves is to meet with God, and put his case (vv. 3–7), even though this is a terrifying prospect (v. 15). Yet God is not to be found (vv. 8–9).

In a way, this is an astonishingly timeless text. This sense of the hiddenness of God and frustration in the face of alienation and suffering is often felt today. So walking this road with Job can speak to the deepest fears of believers and non-believers alike as they struggle to make sense of life.

However, in all this turmoil, Job clings to his faith, and expresses in words of terrible beauty the utter dependability of the Lord and his ultimate purposes (vv. 10–12). And therefore, for all his pain and bewilderment,

Job still sees his relationship with God as somehow holding the key to the future.

Amos 5:6–7, 10–15 (Related)

The rich man in Mark 10 claims to have kept the commandments from his youth, and seems to have one outstanding stumbling-block—the importance he attaches to his wealth, and hence his unwillingness to use his money for the benefit of the poor.

But the prophecy which God gives Amos throws the rich man's position into sharp focus. God expresses his deep concern for the poor. Justice and righteousness (v. 7) are not merely abstract concepts: rather, they are characteristics which should mark relationships within the community. Being just and righteous is inextricably linked with caring for the poor and weak.

The leaders of Israel have rejected God's justice, however, corrupting the courts and growing richer by exploiting the poor (vv. 10–11). Contrary to outward appearances, this is not the end of the story. The picture of the ultimate futility of their position (v. 11) is reminiscent of the rich man's sad exit in Mark 10:22. And God judges them with the utmost seriousness: even if they genuinely repent, they cannot blithely assume that God will relent (v. 15).

A bias to the poor is not an optional extra for God's people. It has to be built into the heart of the Church's mission.

Hebrews 4:12–16

In these few verses the writer gives us a marvellous survey of the gospel.

The word of God (God's revelation of himself to humanity) has amazing power. It penetrates every part of our lives, bringing his message of judgment to confront us and demand a response. We can hide nothing from God: our actions, our thoughts, our motives are all open to his gaze.

At one level, that is a deeply unsettling and disturbing picture—our sinful, helpless nature exposed before a holy God. But at another level, the picture brings hope, because our gracious God knows everything about us, yet still reaches out in love.

God has, of course, reached out supremely in the person of Jesus, our great high priest, who has conquered sin and bridged the gulf between God and humanity. Jesus is not some distant figure but someone who really does know what it is to be human. He knows intimately the trials and temptations of human existence, so in turning to him in our need we meet one who has been through the same pain and suffering. Through Jesus, we are able to approach God with confidence, knowing that he has saved us from judgment.

Mark 10:17–31

Does the rich man get a raw deal? He has done his best to obey the commandments, and he is seeking a deeper relationship with God. There is something attractive about his earnest desire to learn (as shown in Jesus' response to him in verse 21). Yet Jesus sets him an enormous challenge— selling all he has—when this does not seem from elsewhere in the Gospels to be a pre-condition for entering the Kingdom. Moreover, in his reflections afterwards, Jesus appears to suggest that it is downright impossible for the rich to enter the Kingdom (v. 25).

So what is Jesus getting at? In verse 15, he talks about receiving the Kingdom of God like a child. To enter the Kingdom, we must acknowledge our total dependence on God. It is not something we can achieve for ourselves. Perhaps the rich man does not yet understand this (v. 17). His possessions are ultimately more important to him than his quest to inherit eternal life. That is the point. Are we seeking God above all else, and therefore dedicated to his service (which for the rich man would have involved using his resources to benefit the poor)? Or are we prevented by other things from coming to God in total commitment?

MG

YEAR C

Jeremiah 29:1, 4–7 (Continuous)

From the first deportation of 598BC to the destruction of Jerusalem in 587BC there was considerable tension between those deported and those who remained. With whom lay God's future for the nation?

Jeremiah tells the Babylonian exiles that they will be there for the long haul (29:10), and gives two surprising words from God. First, the string of imperatives ('build... live... plant... eat...' v. 5) urges them to continue in creation and covenant fruitfulness. 'Even in displacement, Judah continues to be the people over which God's promise for the future presides with power... the suffering of exile is the matrix in which the hope of God is most powerfully and characteristically at work' (Brueggemann, *To Build, To Plant*, Eerdmans, 1991, p 30). Second, the people are to engage in a mission task of seeking the welfare (*shalom*) of their place of exile, for in its *shalom* lies their *shalom* (v. 7). Prophetic faith does not lose its political realism.

When we are in a place that feels less than God's ideal for us, we too share this exile call to fruitfulness and mutual welfare, despite our restlessness and dissatisfaction. The stature of waiting leads to a new experience of hope, which 'does not disappoint us' (Romans 5:3–5).

In fact, we share in the experience of exile as we await a city to call our own (Hebrews 13:14). As a result we also share in the paradox of recognizing the powers-that-be as both agents of God (Romans 13) and enemies of God (Revelation 13), something that will be resolved only when we are restored to our homeland, the new Jerusalem.

2 Kings 5:1–3, 7–15c (Related)

This well-told tale, with its classic characters—proud nobleman, humble maidservant, sceptical king, inscrutable prophet, greedy servant—teaches us about God's power in achieving his plan.

- **God's work is too hard for us.** The king of Israel was naturally disturbed when his more powerful neighbour expected him to do the impossible (v. 7)—a feeling we may share in the face of God's call on us. The king needed his vision of what God could do enlarged.
- **God's work is too easy for us.** Naaman wanted to do something difficult or glamorous (v. 12), as if what he had to do was the cause of his cure. We too find it easier to be busy with something of our own devising than simply to stop and wait on God. How much in our churches would cease to happen if the Spirit quietly departed?
- **God's plan does not depend on us.** Naaman is only a great commander because it is God who has given victory through him (v. 1). And despite the faithlessness of the king of Israel (v. 7), the pride of Naaman (v. 11) and the greed of Elisha's servant (v. 20), the end result is that God's name is glorified, his sovereignty now acknowledged by this foreigner (v. 15a).
- **God's plan does depend on us.** The plot hinges on the witness of a servant girl (vv. 2–3), the initial response of Naaman (v. 4), the powerful prophetic ministry of Elisha (v. 10) and the common sense of Naaman's servants (v. 13). God uses people to fulfil his plan!

The contradictions here are the ones always present when a sovereign God acts in grace.

2 Timothy 2:8–15

Paul is, at this last stage of his life, having to confront a sense of failure at several levels. He must realize by now that his long-term plan to share the gospel in Spain (Romans 15:24) will not be realized. His work in Asia Minor (Turkey) is in danger of coming to nothing, through false teaching (1 Timothy 1:3) and personal betrayal (2 Timothy 1:15). His own situation (vv. 9–10) must have seemed a stark contrast to the power of God that he preached (for example, 1 Corinthians 2:4–5; 2 Corinthians 10:4).

But central to Paul's gospel is the pattern of Jesus' death and resurrection (v. 8). For those looking for the Messiah (the Davidic king) to come, Jesus' death would have seemed God-forsaken, and his resurrection simply inexplicable. And if this pattern of public failure and hidden victory marked Jesus' life, it will mark his followers' (John 13:16). Paul anticipated neither easy triumph nor terminal failure—and neither should we.

Instead, suffering and self-forgetting now will lead to fullness of life (v. 11). Patient endurance (reflecting God's own nature, 1 Timothy 1:16) will be rewarded with eschatological glory (v. 12a). There are no short cuts in this—we cannot play games with God (v. 12b). But when the going gets tough, what matters most is not that we have grasped him, but that he has grasped us, and that he is faithful (v. 13).

To continue strong in this pattern of grace, we need to rely not on *our* words (v. 14) but on *his* word (v. 15), effective as it is no matter what our circumstances (v. 9c).

Luke 17:11–19

This narrative is full of vivid, naturalistic detail. The border with Samaria and Galilee (v. 11) would have been the natural route to Jerusalem avoiding Samaria itself (contrast the episode in John 4). Those suffering infectious skin diseases (not necessarily leprosy as we understand it) had to live on the outskirts of villages and were used to keeping their distance (v. 12). As Jesus rested in the village, he would easily have been found (v. 16).

The lepers' obedience in going to the priest (v. 14) showed real faith. The reason for going was for the priest to certify that they had been healed (Leviticus 14:3). The priest would, among other things, anoint the healed person with blood from a sacrifice of atonement and with oil to signal God's blessing and gladness (Leviticus 14:14–18)—faith and thanksgiving belong together.

But only the Samaritan demonstrates both faith and thanks (v. 16). As is characteristic of Luke's Gospel, it is the outsider who receives the full blessing; his faith 'saves' him (v. 19)—the word means much more than mere physical healing. This makes clear the nature of God's favour: it is not a right granted by virtue of who you are or where you are born, but is a gift freely given. 'Foreigner' (v. 18) was the term used on the 'keep out' signs around the inner court of the temple.

Faith is incomplete without gratitude. When we give thanks (*eucharisteo*), we put ourselves in a place of grace (*charis*) by recognizing that all we have is God's gift.

IP

PROPER 24

YEAR A

Exodus 33:12–23 (Continuous)

This episode is a kind of legitimate equivalent of the episode of the golden calf, and contrasts the maturity and understanding possessed by Moses with the fear and ignorance of the people. It seems that Moses is not exempt from the kind of doubts displayed by the people because, like them, he too wants reassurance of the presence of God with them on the journey, as well as a glimpse of the being of God (vv. 12–18). However, the people panic and turn to their own devices in order to get the reassurance they need, whereas Moses turns to the God who has brought them thus far and is therefore the only true source of reassurance. God is sympathetic to the request and the need for reassurance, and is ready to give it in appropriate ways and under appropriate circumstances. But as with the burning bush encounter, and the revelation of the name that conceals as well as reveals (see comment on Exodus 3:1–15, Proper 17, Year A), even though a glimpse of the divine presence is granted to Moses, the complete revelation can never be given to a human being (vv. 19–20). There is always an element of mystery and inscrutability about God, because the full truth is quite simply beyond human comprehension.

Isaiah 45:1–7 (Related)

These verses are a remarkable affirmation of faith in the God whose hand is over all the earth, and whose influence is so great that even those who do not acknowledge God's existence can be used to fulfil God's purposes of salvation. As far as Cyrus king of Persia was concerned, it was the god Marduk who gave him victory over the Babylonian empire, after which exiled peoples were permitted to return to their homelands. But as far as the writer of this passage is concerned, it was the Lord who was giving Cyrus the victory (vv. 1–3) so that he could send the Jews home from exile and the world would know what a powerful and faithful God they worshipped (vv. 4–7).

There are marvels and dangers here. The marvel is that God's power is not limited, nor can the divine plan be defeated, by time or space or political or religious boundaries. But the danger is that God's people can become insular and selfish because they think that God is concerned only for them. In reality, God's faithful love for them also demonstrates God's power and mercy to a world which needs to know this God, beside whom there is no other (v. 6).

1 Thessalonians 1:1–10

In the opening paragraph of this letter, generally believed to be the earliest of Paul's letters in the New Testament, what might be called the three cardinal Christian virtues make their appearance: Paul commends the Thessalonians for their faith, love and hope which are expressed in various aspects of their Christian life (v. 3). However, he immediately goes on to say that the Thessalonians have been chosen by God, and that their joyful reception of the gospel in the face of persecution was inspired by the Holy Spirit (vv. 4, 6). In other words, it is not just a matter of the Thessalonians' own excellence, but a case of God working in them to inspire such praise-worthy responses. Both divine initiative and human response are important components in any Christian endeavour, and we should never lose the sense of balance between them.

This opening paragraph ends with a reference to the Thessalonians waiting for the return of Jesus (v. 10). Paul believed that he himself might live to see Jesus return, but even though Jesus has not yet returned, the need to keep in mind the time of final reckoning and to live the Christian life in the light of eternity is as great now as it was then.

Matthew 22:15–22

The Pharisees have taken quite a lot of criticism from Jesus, and not surprisingly they are keen to get their own back (v. 15). The question about paying taxes (vv. 16–17) is their equivalent of his question to them about John the Baptist (see comment on Matthew 21:23–32, Proper 21, Year A), and is intended to force him into antagonizing either the crowds or the Romans with his reply. Jesus' answer (vv. 18–21) might appear evasive, but it actually shows how nuanced an answer must be given to what is quite a complex question. The question of loyalty to the state *vis à vis* loyalty to God is always a difficult one, and in general the New Testament writers advocate compliance with the worldly authorities, largely because they thought that with the end of the world being imminent, spiritual reform was more important than political reform. Jesus' saying is compatible with this sort of outlook, in that it implies that there is a duty to the state, which is not necessarily incompatible with one's duty to God; on the other hand, the two are not the same, and even if at times they overlap, they may also clash. In the end, it depends on the individual circumstances where the duties to God and Caesar begin and end.

DR

Year B

Job 38:1–7 [34–41] (Continuous)

Finally the moment to which the book has been building arrives. God himself speaks. But why does he take Job on a detailed tour of creation? At first sight this does not even begin to address Job's torment.

However, there is marvellous purpose in God's speech.

First, as we saw last week, Job was desperately seeking contact with God. Now God addresses Job directly (v. 1); he is no longer hidden. We should never underestimate the importance of the fact that God has chosen to reveal himself to us—supremely, of course, in Jesus.

Second, God's wide-ranging references to the design of his creation are a direct counter to Job's complaint that God is capricious (12:13–25). There *is* order in creation, and this should offer Job at least some reassurance. Notice the references to limits appointed by God in the natural world (vv. 5, 8–11). Perhaps these are a response to Job's complaint in 3:23. Yes, God does place limits on human understanding, but as part of the overall order of things.

Third, the intimate care of God for his creation (vv. 34–41) assures Job that despite apparent evidence to the contrary, God is both sovereign and loving. There is hope after all.

Isaiah 53:4–12 (Related)

This reading provides essential background to Jesus' description of himself as the Servant who gives his life as a ransom for many (Mark 10:45), and has been central to the Christian understanding of the significance of Jesus' death. The immediate context might have been the execution of a Jewish leader (some have suggested Zerubbabel), but in its theological depth the passage reflects more generally on the way God deals with humanity's sin. In the sacrificial system established in the Old Testament Law, God dealt with sin through the offering of animals. Here, the idea is developed pro-foundly, so that the willing death of an innocent person brings atonement.

Much of the Christian understanding of the death of Jesus is prefigured here:

- The Servant dies willingly for the people, bearing the punishment they deserve (vv. 4–5, 7, 11–12).
- He is innocent (vv. 7–9).
- The people recognize their sin as rebellion against God, and see the need for repentance (vv. 4–6).
- The death is in accordance with God's will, and he accepts it as atoning for the people's sin (vv. 10–12).
- As a result, many are healed (v. 5) and made righteous (v. 11).
- The Servant will be vindicated by God (vv. 10–12).

Hebrews 5:1–10

This passage develops the theme of the priesthood of Jesus, drawing comparisons and contrasts with the Aaronic priesthood established in the Old Testament.

The writer does not denigrate the high priests: they have been called by God to care for the people and to represent them before him. Notice, however, the stark contrasts between the purely human priesthood of verses 1–4 and the glorious ministry of Jesus. The priests of verses 1–4 can sympathize with their flock in their struggles with sin because they too are sinners (vv. 2–3). But the priests' own sinfulness means that their ministry cannot offer true salvation. Jesus has also lived through the trials of a human life (4:15, 5:8). The difference with Jesus is that he remained sinless and was therefore in a position to act as the perfect priest, bringing full salvation (v. 9).

Once again, the uniqueness of Jesus as both divine and human underlies the argument. Jesus stands far superior to any purely human priesthood; hence the reference to Melchizedek, that strange, almost timeless figure of Genesis 14:18–20. Yet this Jesus offers up intensely human tears (v. 7) and, by his submission to his Father's will, provides an example for us to follow (v. 9).

Mark 10:35–45

The words with which Jesus concludes this passage (v. 45) are the most important in the whole of Mark. The astonishing humility and sacrifice of Christ has far-reaching implications.

First, we can but wonder at the utterly amazing love of God, and the lengths to which he was, and is, prepared to go for our sake: 'Thou who wast rich beyond all splendour, all for love's sake becamest poor', in the words of Frank Houghton's fine hymn.

Second, for us, following the example of Jesus will also involve sacrifice. The imagery of the cup (v. 39) implies suffering (cf. 14:36), as does baptism —being plunged into the depths. The easy agreement of James and John is given too hastily.

Third, humility and service are to mark our relationships with each other (vv. 43–44), in complete contrast to the way of the world.

We might be tempted to snigger at the palpable spiritual shallowness displayed by James and John (and by the jealous reaction of the other ten). But the challenge laid down by Jesus here is just as taxing for us. How far do we *really* pattern our lives on Christ the servant? How far do our church structures mirror the picture in verses 43–44?

MG

YEAR C

Jeremiah 31:27–34 (Continuous)

God's promise of newness to the exiles (v. 31) includes aspects of continuity as well as discontinuity—God who is unchanging (Hebrews 13:8) is ever doing a new thing (Isaiah 42:9; 43:19).

As before, it is God who watches over Israel (v. 28); he is sovereign over his people. But now his will is to build and plant, not to pluck up and break down—to bring life to what is good, not death to what is evil. As before, God's love is extended to generation after generation. But now there will be a new sense of a fresh start (v. 29; cf. Exodus 34:7; Jeremiah 32:18). As before, God will lead with the cords of human kindness (v. 32; cf. Hosea 11:1–4), but now there will be a response of the heart (v. 33). As before, God reveals himself to his people, but now there is to be a radical egalitarianism in his people's understanding (v. 34).

Since we are grafted on to the root of the olive tree of Israel (Romans 11:17), we share in this 'as before' and 'but now.' As before, we live between the death of the old and the birth of the new (Romans 8:23), but now we experience that heart-knowledge of the forgiving Father (Romans 8:15; 1 John 1:9). We know both the fulfilment of Jeremiah's promise and the longing for its completeness. The exile is not over, but the end of exile has begun.

Where in our lives, in our congregations, do we need to hear God's 'As before…' and where do we need to hear his 'But now…'?

Genesis 32:22–31 (Related)

This is a most puzzling passage, shrouded in mystery. Jacob greatly fears meeting Esau whom he deceived all those years before (32:7). Unable to trounce him, unlikely to trick him, he throws himself at last on God (32:11), though a God he still hardly knows.

In the stubbornness of the years, he still refuses to submit to the divine stranger (v. 24). But this time he cannot force a blessing out of his adversary (v. 26). Instead, he is given something he did not ask for—a new name, a new destiny (v. 28). This is grace, but not as usually imagined. Jacob goes one step further—he wants to know the name, the character, of this adversary (v. 29). But he has gone too far; this will not be granted until much later (Exodus 3:14) and Jacob must make do with his blessing.

But he has changed. He now recognizes that he has had a narrow escape (v. 30). He sees that he is not master of his own destiny. He now walks with a limp; if there has been victory in his prevailing, there has also been defeat. It has been a costly blessing. And he appears to treat Esau with genuine openness and respect (ch. 33).

The God he has met has not destroyed him, but he has disarmed him. He has made him realize how small he is. He has given Jacob a new power, but also a new weakness. True encounter with God is costly, but great things come out of it, even if they are not of our own choosing.

2 Timothy 3:14—4:5

Paul's last injunctions to Timothy are united by a theme of universality. There are very wide bounds to his vision of the gospel.

Every part of scripture is breathed out by God (3:16); although the grammar of the sentence is ambiguous, in context it is clear what Paul means. As God breathed life into his first creation (Genesis 2:7) so the (Old Testament) scriptures form a vital part of establishing the new creation (2 Corinthians 5:17), pointing to faith in Christ (3:15). The false teachers don't share this assessment, but Timothy is to be quite distinct in his approach ('But as for you…' 3:14). Scripture affects *every* part of life—both understanding ('teaching… reproof') and behaviour ('correction… training')—positively and negatively, so that *every* believer should be equipped for *every*thing God has for them.

*Every*thing comes under Christ's scrutiny (4:1), so Timothy is to take *every* opportunity to proclaim the message of God's love and judgment shown in Christ (v. 2). This may not suit him or the listeners ('favourable or unfavourable') but time is short, not only because Christ will return (v. 1) but also because people will stop listening (vv. 3–4).

And Timothy is to fulfil *every* aspect of the ministry God has called him to (v. 5). He is to be ready at *every* moment ('sober'), in *every* kind of situation, good or bad ('suffering'), and take *every* opportunity to share faith.

Luke 18:1–8

This is an interesting parable, because it teaches us what God is *not*, and very often what our prayer is not.

This caricature of a judge appears to have no reason to grant the woman's request for justice after she has been wronged. He does not care what others think, and has no sense of giving an account to a higher authority. The only reason he finally relents is to have a bit of peace and quiet.

But God is not heartless, resentful or grudging when he hears our prayers. (Even if he was, we should still persist!) How do we end up thinking that he is? Perhaps through the real frustration of seemingly unanswered prayer, but more often because we forget the answers and blessings that we *have* received in the past.

If God is not like the judge, are we like the widow? Are we persistent, or is our patience soon exhausted? She was motivated by nothing other than the justice of her cause. But we are called to love God, and love is patient (1 Corinthians 13:4). As we pray, we are confronted with the truth about how we see God and the truth about ourselves, which is perhaps what makes intercessory prayer a 'purifying bath' (Richard Foster, *Prayer*).

IP

PROPER 25

YEAR A

Deuteronomy 34:1–12 (Continuous)

At long last, the journey is nearly over. Abraham's descendants have multiplied and have become a nation, constituted as such by the God who brought them out of Egypt and gave them the Law at Sinai. Now all that remains to be fulfilled is the promise of the land, which is before them, waiting to be possessed.

In what seems a rather cruelly ironical twist, Moses is allowed to see the land but not to enter it (v. 4), and he dies at the border (v. 5). According to Numbers 20:2–12, the reason for this was Moses' lack of faith when under pressure from the people, but whatever the explanation, the effect is that the people now have to make their way without him. Indeed, it seems that being without him makes them appreciate him more than they ever did when he was there, and they are prepared to follow his commands without question (v. 9). They are like children preparing to leave home; they have had their 'upbringing' in the desert, during which they have made mistakes, been punished, but hopefully grown and learned as well; and now they are ready to put into practice what they have learned. This is a moment of enormous potential, a moment of truth. How will they fare?

Leviticus 19:1–2, 15–18 (Related)

Here we have the 'love your neighbour' saying in its context in the Law. It appears in a section of Leviticus (chs. 17—26) which is known as the 'Holiness Code', because the regulations contained in it are intended to enable the people of Israel to be holy as God is holy (vv. 1–2). Holiness is about being set apart, different, distinct, and in the Law holiness is expressed in every area of life, from the way the people worship to the way they dress. Holiness is therefore also an active thing. The people's holiness does not simply consist in their having been chosen by God, it consists in their living out that holiness by keeping the regulations set down for them which tell them how to be holy.

In Leviticus 19, many of the instructions, including the command to love one's neighbour, are followed by the saying 'I am the Lord' (vv. 16, 18), as if to emphasize that in keeping them the people are coming particularly close to the heart of God, and that in these things above all, the holiness of God is demonstrated. The ultimate motivation, therefore, for loving one's neighbour is that by doing so, one is fulfilling the calling to become more like God.

1 Thessalonians 2:1–8

The themes which appear in this passage are familiar but important ones. The first theme is that of perseverance in the face of suffering. Paul reminds the Thessalonians that maltreatment in the previous town had not prevented him and his companions from declaring the gospel boldly to the Thessalonians (1—2). Such courage can only come from a deep conviction about the nature of the message and, indeed, about the nature of the One who is the source of the message. Paul and his fellow workers were able to keep going and avoid disillusionment, even in the face of hardships and scepticism, because their mission was rooted in the power of the God who is far greater than anything that human beings can devise or inflict, and to whom they knew themselves responsible.

The second theme is that of the humility of leadership. Here, too, Paul's consciousness of his responsibility before God determined the way he fulfilled his commission (vv. 3–6), as he and his companions were humble and gentle with the Thessalonians, like a nurse taking care of her children (v. 7). Their embodiment of the servant leadership of Christ in this way, living as well as preaching the gospel of equality, must have made a powerful impression.

Matthew 22:34–46

The Pharisees' final attempt to trap Jesus is no more successful than the previous ones: Jesus not only answers their question satisfactorily, he puts to them one of his own which they are unable to answer, thereby beating them at their own game. The question as to which is the greatest of the commandments (v. 36) is answered in a way that the Pharisees could not possibly disagree with, even if they wanted to (vv. 37–40): love of God—that is, commitment to doing God's will—is, after all, what they claim to live by. However, the stipulation of love for one's neighbour in addition to love of God (v. 39) indicates how closely these two elements are intertwined, as also in the Ten Commandments. The implication is that there can be no true love of God without love of neighbour, which can be construed as a dig at those who view the compassionless observance of legal minutiae as 'love of God'.

The final question about the Messiah as the son of David (vv. 42–45) is a way of claiming that Jesus himself, who has never refused the title 'son of David', is much more than a mere human being, even if that human being is of royal blood.

DR

Year B

Job 42:1–6, 10–17 (Continuous)

The epic story of Job draws to a close. Job retracts his case against God, echoing the words of God in 38:2 and acknowledging the limits of his understanding (vv. 1–6). Yet Job's acceptance of God's ordering of things results not so much from his being out-argued by God, but rather from his personal encounter with God. It is this explicit re-establishment of his relationship with God which has satisfied Job. Job's repentance (v. 6) is due to his acknowledgment of his fallen humanity in the presence of a holy God (cf. Isaiah 6:5), not an admission that his troubles have been the direct result of specific sin.

God restores Job's fortunes. Feasting (v. 11) recalls his former life (1:4). But he is twice as wealthy as before, and lives a further 140 years, twice the allotted human lifespan. Although the book of Job speaks profoundly about the everlasting God and fundamental questions of human existence, it is important that the book ends like this. The final blessings Job receives are in this world, with all its ambiguities, reaffirming that God is sovereign of this earth, not heaven only. Job is blessed graciously by God in the same place in which he suffered.

Jeremiah 31:7–9 (Related)

Jeremiah's marvellous picture of the exiles returning from Babylon provides a moving backdrop to the healing of Bartimaeus.

The ingathering of the remnant of Israel from the ends of the earth, guided and protected by the love and power of God, is a frequent theme in the prophets. Time and again, Israel is encouraged to return to the Lord who is faithful and will ultimately bring deliverance. God's salvation is for all, including the vulnerable such as the blind (like Bartimaeus), the lame, and expectant and nursing mothers. The straight path upon which the exiles now walk without stumbling is to be understood not only literally (returning confidently to their homeland), but also figuratively (walking with the Lord).

There is another side to this. The returning people are described as weeping, perhaps simply because of their ordeal, but perhaps with repentance (see vv. 18–19). Like Bartimaeus' desperate cry for mercy, this reflects dependence on God for deliverance. Notice that the relationship between God and his people is described as that between a father and his firstborn son (v. 9). Yes, Israel can be confident of God's love, shown in their rescue from exile, but with this love comes a call to obedience.

Hebrews 7:23–28

The writer to the Hebrews continues to reflect on the rich theme of the priestly ministry of Jesus. This passage gives us four pointers to the magnificent fullness of Jesus' ministry.

Jesus' priesthood is permanent because, unlike the case of purely human priests, it is not ended by death (v. 24). What might at first sight seem an obvious point actually has fundamental importance. The ministry of Jesus is simply not subject to the changes and chances of human existence. Wherever and whenever we call upon him, he is there.

Therefore, the salvation which Jesus brings is both complete and for all time (the Greek of verse 25 carries this dual meaning). We should hold to the objective reality of this great gift through the good times and the tough times.

Jesus is always praying for us (v. 25). He is praying for you at this moment. It is difficult to think of a more encouraging truth, or of a more telling example of the importance of prayer.

Because God has exalted Jesus above the heavens (v. 26), he is interceding for us in the immediate presence of God the Father. Through the priestly ministry of Jesus we shall one day join him there.

Mark 10:46–52

In the passages preceding this reading, the rich man has gone away sadly because of his inability to put Jesus before his possessions (vv. 17–22), and the disciples have demonstrated spiritual shallowness in their disputes about status (vv. 35–45). One was privileged in worldly terms, the others privileged in their close friendship of Jesus. Yet in both cases, they failed to demonstrate the humble dependence on God which is a feature of true discipleship.

Ironically, it is the blind man who now shows real perception. Unlike the others, he has no privileges. His poverty and marginal status are underlined by the reaction of the crowd, which tries to silence him (v. 48). But he knows his need and his dependence on the loving mercy of Jesus. Jesus heals him and he follows along the road: a vivid illustration of Jesus' saying in verse 31 that 'many who are first will be last, and the last first.'

So this healing is partly about reversal of expectations in the face of divine mercy. Bartimaeus' use of the messianic title 'Son of David' as Jesus heads toward his death foreshadows the clash between the new order of God's Kingdom and the political and religious establishment in Jerusalem.

MG

YEAR C

Joel 2:23–32 (Continuous)

Most likely immediately post-exilic, Joel's message is an admixture of judgment, repentance and blessings. As with other prophets, he is a 'covenant enforcement mediator' (Stuart and Fee, *How to Read the Bible for All its Worth*, SU, 1983, p. 151), and frequently cites other prophets and the law (2:13 quotes Exodus 34:6; 2:32 quotes Obadiah 1:17; 3:10, cf. Isaiah 2:4). He proclaims the coming of:

• **Renewed covenant** (vv. 23–26). The material blessings will be real enough, but their primary significance is in declaring that, following the people's repentance (2:12–17), the covenant with God is re-established (see Deuteronomy 11:13–17; Leviticus 26:3–5). A change of heart opens the doors to God's generous rule (Mark 1:15).

- **Renewed people** (vv. 27–29). The renewal of covenant leads to the restoration of God's presence (v. 27), a sharp contrast to the departure of the glory in the destruction of the temple. Open hearts to God's covenant love also means open hearts to the renewing work of his Spirit.
- **Renewed visitation** (vv. 30–32). The Day of the Lord was to be a moment of judgment and mercy—judgment on the nations (3:2) but also on Israel (1:15–16), but mercy on all who call on God's name (v. 32).

This passage 'bursts its original wrappings and leaps into the New Testament with wider and deeper significance' (L.C. Allen, *Joel, Obadiah, Jonah and Micah*, Eerdmans, 1976, p. 102). For Jesus' arrival was God's visitation (Luke 19:44); judgment and mercy met on the cross (Romans 10:13); the Spirit was poured out at Pentecost (Acts 2:16ff); and God's renewed covenant re-established with a wider Israel (Acts 10:34–35). And we await the final visitation, when the fulfilment inaugurated in Christ reaches its completion.

Jeremiah 14:7–10, 19–22 (Related)

In this simulated liturgy, Jeremiah probes the vexed question of real and superficial repentance.

There is a formal acknowledgment of the people's sin (v. 7), but this quickly returns to the real preoccupation—Israel's needs. Given the quick confession and the assumption of God's presence (v. 9), there can only be one problem—God is not doing his job (vv. 8–9)! At the end of the chapter there is the same pattern—a statement of trust (v. 22), a word of repentance (v. 20), and an appeal for God to honour his part (v. 21). But this is a desire for the gifts without desire for the giver—love of the rain without love for the rainmaker.

Israel is looking for 'cheap grace' (Bonhoeffer, *The Cost of Discipleship*). They hope that the easy liturgy will do its job. But God is looking for a change of heart, not a change of words (Hosea 6:6). While their prayer talks of steadfastness, their lives speak of wandering (v. 10).

God's forgiveness is free, but it is also costly—the price of Jesus' death. When God forgives, he does not say, 'It does not matter.' That would trivialize all the ways we hurt him, each other and his world. Instead, he says, 'It has been dealt with.'

The price of God's presence (the real question in verses 9 and 19) has already been paid. But to experience it, we need to face the cost of commitment.

2 Timothy 4:6–8, 16–18

Facing death, Paul is able to look back and see his life as a whole, and he shows us the marks of a life given to Christian ministry.

There is *loneliness* as Paul is left high and dry by the human weakness of others (v. 16). There is *sacrifice*: Paul sees all his hardship and self-giving as a drink-offering poured out (v. 6)—presumably on the sacrifice of Christ, not adding to it but sharing in it (Philippians 3:10). And there is *struggle* and *hard work* as Paul has strained with every fibre of his being to make Christ known and to build up the Church (v. 7).

But there is also a *graciousness* to those who have let him down (v. 16b), born of a *testimony* of God's lifelong faithfulness (v. 17) and power to save (v. 18; cf. Daniel 3:17–18) and a conviction that the whole enterprise is not Paul's but God's ('kingdom', v. 18). And there is great *confidence* as Paul not only looks back but looks forward to meeting face to face the one he has served (v. 8). The chapter is over, but the story has only just begun.

His ministry might be different in degree to ours, but it is a ministry which all who are Christ's share (1 Corinthians 12:4–7). Is there any more satisfying way to be able to look back on one's life? What should I be doing now that will enable me to look back and look forward with the confidence Paul has?

Luke 18:9–14

This classic parable of contrasts has a simple point that Luke sets out (v. 9) in case we were to miss it, and Jesus reinforces with a saying of eschatological reversal (v. 14).

The Pharisee practises things that we should make our goal (Matthew 23:3)—honesty, sexual morality, purity, discipline and generosity. But he wears them as badges of merit, rather than receiving them as blessings of grace. Whenever we are proud of such things rather than grateful for them, we share his blindness. These are not reasons why God should favour us, but signs that God has been good to us. Whenever we trust in our experiences, our soundness, our success rather than God's mercy, we indeed stand on our own (v. 11a).

The tax collector does not yet show the fruit of repentance (see 19:8). But he recognizes the truth of his human situation: it all depends on God's mercy, and nothing depends on his merit (v. 13).

This message of grace is crucial in our relations with those of other beliefs. To be a Christian is not to participate in a superior religious system that more effectively gains credit with God. No, it is to recognize that all we can do is to hold out empty hands and receive the gift he longs to give—his new life in Christ Jesus. As to who exactly has taken this step of trust, the truth will out in the end (v. 14).

IP

BIBLE SUNDAY

YEAR A

Nehemiah 8:1–4a [5–6] 8–12

These verses describe the reading of the book of the Law to the people of Judah by Ezra the scribe, and they depict some important principles about the reading and hearing of the word of God. First of all, hearing the word of God is properly a corporate act, because it is a word for a community, given in order to constitute a community, and not the private possession of individuals. In the narrative here, the whole community is gathered for the reading of the Law (vv. 1–3).

Second, hearing the word is for everyone: everyone was gathered, 'both men and women' (vv. 2–3), and assistance was given to enable all the people to understand (v. 8).

Third, hearing the word of God is a holy act: reading from the Law is accompanied by worship (v. 6), and according to Leviticus 23:24–25, the first day of the seventh month, on which Ezra reads the Law (v. 2), is a festival day. The choice of a holy day as the day on which to read the word of God implies that the act of reading is itself holy.

Finally, hearing (and understanding) the word of God is a joyous event: the people are to rejoice, not weep (vv. 9, 11), and they celebrate because they have understood what was read to them (v. 12).

Colossians 3:12–17

When the word of God is viewed as a corporate word, aimed at a community in order to constitute that community as the people of God, it can be seen to be full of corporate instructions. Here is an example of a set of corporate instructions about how Christians are to behave as those whom God has called into community. The kind of qualities and attitudes to be shown to each other by these fellow Christians are those that are found in Christ and have been shown to them by Christ (vv. 12–14). In order to build up the community, they are also to give pride of place to what they have learned as the gospel about Jesus (v. 16), and to be thankful (v. 15), thankful (v. 16), thankful (v. 17) because of it.

It is doubtful whether, at this time, Christian congregations would have had any written documents containing the good news about Jesus: their only scripture would have been what we call the Old Testament. But still they are to meditate on 'the word of Christ' (v. 16), on the way in which God has spoken to humankind in Jesus. How much more should we do the same, when we have a whole collection of documents about the good news of Jesus Christ!

Matthew 24:30–35

This passage reveals yet another aspect of the word of God. The passage starts with a promise of final vindication for those who are faithful to God, a time when true loyalties will be made evident and 'what is hidden made known' (vv. 30–31; see Matthew 10:26), and it then reinforces that promise with a comment on the nature of the divine word (v. 35). This is a concept which is straight out of the Old Testament. In a world where writing was the skill of the élite, verbal exchanges were much more significant than they are today. Once words were spoken, they took on a kind of existence of their own, with no distinction between the word and what it designated. As for the word of God, it was as good as done once it was spoken, just as, in Genesis 1, the world was created by God simply speaking. God's powerful speech existed before creation, and will therefore continue to exist even though everything we regard as immovable will, in the end, come to nothing (v. 35).

In the light of this, the community of God should be both reassured and warned by the word of promise that has been spoken (vv. 30–31), because it contains irrevocable truth which, having been spoken, cannot be turned back.

DR

YEAR B

Isaiah 55:1–11

In this remarkable passage, we encounter perhaps the most profound statement about God's word anywhere in the Old Testament (vv. 10–11). Isaiah combines two vivid pictures: the word of God going out from his mouth, and rain and snow coming down from heaven to water the earth. The point is that just as the rain and the snow enable plants and trees to grow, so God's word cannot fail to achieve its purpose.

Two particular characteristics of God's word stand out.

First, it is life-giving (v. 10). Those unfamiliar with the Bible might think of it as a rather arid and outdated set of rules. The reverse is true. God's word is refreshing, attractive and vital to our spiritual growth. It is to be enjoyed and treasured.

Second, it is powerful and effective (v. 11), always achieving God's purpose. This is a tremendous comfort to those who choose to obey God's word, and a warning for those who choose to resist it.

The immediate context is a call to repentance (vv. 6–7), which illustrates these two characteristics. God's word powerfully and effectively plants the seed of repentance in human hearts. In turn, it refreshes and sustains those who repent and return to God.

2 Timothy 3:14—4:5

Year after year, the Bible is *the* bestseller. Yet it often ends up gathering dust on the shelf. These verses challenge that complacency head-on, reminding us of the explosive, life-changing power of scripture.

Scripture is 'God-breathed', or 'inspired by God' (v. 16). The Bible has been described as 'God's love-letter to humanity'. It is not just writing about God, but it is actually God's own loving, powerful and totally trustworthy message to us. So if we read scripture expectantly, God will address us in remarkable ways through it.

Scripture is therefore deeply relevant to us, showing the way to salvation through Jesus (v. 15), explaining the truth and showing us how to live (v. 16). It really *is* worth reading, and not just for the purpose of accumulating knowledge. Through it, God wants to shape our lives and enable us to carry out the tasks he has planned for us.

So scripture is not to be sat on! The charge to Timothy to preach the word at all times (v. 2) underlines the urgency and relevance of thoughtful biblical witness to a fallen world. For those of us called to preach, this charge is both a command and an encouragement to proclaim God's word.

John 5:36b–47

Why should we read the Bible? What is it for? What are the basic assumptions which we should use in interpreting it? Arguing with his opponents, Jesus gets on to this ground, and it makes fascinating and challenging reading.

First, for us to experience the life-transforming power of scripture, we need to realize that the Bible constantly points away from itself to Jesus (v. 39). The person of Jesus is the key to understanding scripture.

Second, this is true not only of the New Testament but—more surprisingly—of the Old Testament also (v. 46). The books of Moses do not refer to Jesus explicitly, of course. But they deal with God's relationship with humanity, how humans have broken that relationship, and how God sets about restoring it. God's supreme revelation of himself and the salvation promised in the Old Testament come together in Jesus. So the whole of scripture is to be read in the light of Christ.

Third, the purpose of reading the Bible like this is not just to know *about* Jesus, but actually to come to *know* Jesus (v. 40). Unless our Bible reading and our preaching centre on personal relationship with Jesus in the present day, they are futile.

MG

YEAR C

Isaiah 45:22–25

As part of the message to the exiles, looking to return to Jerusalem under the edict of Cyrus, this passage echoes the refrain, 'There is no other God besides me!' (44:6, 8; 45:5, 6, 14, 18, 21).

- **God is the only rescuer** (v. 22). Babylon has fallen to Cyrus of Persia, and as 'earth's proud empires pass away' in turn, God is shown to be the one who endures. Amazingly, instead of gloating over this fall, his word is one of grace that extends the offer of salvation to the very ones who have denied him ('all the ends of the earth').
- **God is the only power** (v. 24a). As empires fall, it is clear that all earthly power is derivative from God (cf. Romans 13:1). Therefore, in the face of the forces of destruction, darkness and decay, we can turn only to him (v. 25).
- **God is the only judge** (v. 24b). Since all power comes from him, he is the only one to whom we are accountable. This liberates us from all who would enslave by asserting their authority over us. They and we have to give account to another (Romans 14:11–12).

These assertions of God's uniqueness (cf. Deuteronomy 6:4) were precisely the ones ascribed to Jesus (see Philippians 2:10–11 and compare Isaiah 44:6 with Revelation 1:17), thus (ironically) sowing the seeds of trinitarian belief. It is in Jesus that God rescues, gives power and judges.

Romans 15:1–6

Paul here summarizes his argument about the observance of festivals and food laws: the strong (who take a relaxed, 'liberal' view) should bear with the weaknesses of the weak (who continue to observe such regulations).

Our **example** in this matter is Christ himself (v. 3). But he himself was exemplary of the whole of God's working in salvation history. The weakness of the cross was a weakness felt by the psalmist—verse 3 quotes Psalm 69:10, a psalm used of Christ in John 2:17 (Psalm 69:9) and John 19:28–29 (Psalm 69:21). And it was a weakness felt by God's people in exile, in the person of the Suffering Servant—verse 1 alludes to Isaiah 53:4, 11.

Our **goal** in this matter is to be like Christ (v. 5), being of one mind (cf. Philippians 5:2), sharing the harmony that is in Christ (Galatians 3:28). But again, this is the lesson of the history of God's dealings with his people. As the God of all creation, his covenant was always bursting the bounds of national interest (Genesis 12:3; Isaiah 45:22; 49:6) so that all humanity might reflect his oneness (Deuteronomy 6:4).

So the former scriptures, whilst not our instructions, are for our instruction—not our curiosity or our scepticism (v. 4). God's acting through weakness makes us steadfast, and his achieving his purposes through this gives us the encouragement of hope (vv. 4–5).

Luke 4:16–24

Jesus' declaration of his 'Nazareth manifesto' tells us much about God's mission, about Jesus' self-understanding and about how we are to read scripture.

We are to read **typologically**—recognizing the patterns of God's dealings with people (vv. 24–27) and looking for the same in our day. No one has a monopoly on God's grace, and he is constantly delighting in blessing those who were thought to be beyond his reach.

We are to read **eschatologically**—always with the end in view. The gathering Old Testament anticipation of God's 'end-times' visitation of his people in mercy and judgment was fulfilled in the person of Jesus (v. 21; 19:44). But, while God's kingly rule has broken in, it has not been fully revealed. So there is a vital surplus of anticipation as we look forward to the renewal of the whole of creation (Romans 8:23; Revelation 21).

And we are to read **Christologically**—in the light of what God has done in Christ. This does not mean neglecting each passage's original context but it does mean reading in the wider context of the whole. If God is one (Deuteronomy 6:4), then his word must be read as one—not crudely harmonized, cutting out the awkward parts to make a smooth fit, but in surprising harmony.

Like life, the Bible has to be lived forwards, but understood backwards—
and so won't be fully understood by any of us until the end of time.

IP

DEDICATION FESTIVAL

YEAR A

1 Kings 8:22–30

The majestic sweep of Solomon's prayer at the dedication of the temple helps
us to put our life as God's people into past, present and future perspective.

Solomon looks back, giving thanks for the covenant faithfulness of God
to his father David (vv. 23–26). Dedication festivals are great opportunities
for reminding ourselves of God's faithfulness in the past, and for learning
from the commitment of those who have gone before us, responding to
God's faithfulness.

Solomon turns to the present (vv. 27–28). The temple cannot contain the
God who rules the universe but, amazingly, God is present and is listening.
Church buildings can help us to draw closer to God. But they are not ends
in themselves: their purpose is to point to a God who is lovingly and
powerfully active everywhere, ready to hear and save.

Solomon looks to the future (vv. 29–30), asking that God will hear and
answer the prayers offered towards the temple. Similarly, we need to look to
the future, asking as the Church for vision and guidance from God. Notice
that Solomon picks out forgiveness in verse 30, underlining our continuing
total dependence on the mercy and love of God.

(See Proper 16, Year B, for further comment on this passage.)

Revelation 21:9–14

John's description of the new Jerusalem is one of the most moving passages
in scripture. It is a glorious vision, in the light of which we are to understand
our present experience as the Church of God.

It is a social vision. God's ultimate purpose for his people is to live in
community, in a city, not as isolated individuals. In our church life, we need
to reflect this corporate nature of our relationship with God, acknowledging
our interdependence and encouraging the ministry of all.

God lives in the city (21:22, 22:3–4) and it is full of his glory (vv. 10–11).
In contrast, God's presence with us now is invisible. It is none the less real,

and this glimpse of life in the new Jerusalem underpins the Church's hope in God's intimate faithfulness, both now and in the future.

Although the city is a gift which comes down from heaven (v. 10), and radiates divine perfection (underlined by the twelves and multiples of twelve in its dimensions), the people of God contribute to it as well, as represented by the names of the tribes and apostles (vv. 12–14). God works creatively with his people, proclaiming his word through them and honouring their dedication to him.

Hebrews 12:18–24

When Christians gather for worship, there is more happening than meets the eye. Through two contrasting pictures, the passage explains this wider context: first, the situation of the Israelites at Mount Sinai, where God gave the Law; second, the situation of Christian believers, who are members of a wonderful heavenly city, Mount Zion (cf. Revelation 21).

The description of Sinai is awesome, with frightening darkness and noise, and although God is present, he is unapproachable. In contrast, Zion is a scene of celebration and joyful worship, where God is accessible because of the sacrifice of Jesus.

Although this heavenly city is not yet visible, it is a reality that believers can anticipate already (11:1). Membership of the city includes all believers, from the old and new covenants, on earth and in heaven (v. 23), so that the Church on earth today worships 'with angels and archangels and all the company of heaven'.

This, then, is a tremendously encouraging passage, reminding congregations that they are not isolated, but part of the huge company of believers from all times and places, with joyful access to the presence of God.

(See the alternative provision for All Saints' Day for further comment.)

Matthew 21:12–16

In Matthew's account of the cleansing of the temple, Jesus does three things which reveal something of what he thinks of the temple and how it should be run. In each case, there are important lessons for the life and role of the Church today. A dedication festival is a good opportunity to reflect on these.

Jesus' expulsion of the traders and the comments he makes (vv. 12–13) emphasize that the temple should have been fully dedicated to prayer and worship, not distracted by commercial considerations. Do the activities in our churches reflect this single-minded dedication or is our commitment to God compromised by preoccupation with material things?

Jesus heals the blind and the lame in the temple (v. 14). The decree recorded in 2 Samuel 5:8 excluded the blind and the lame from God's house, yet Jesus welcomes them and restores them. Our churches should similarly be places where people of all backgrounds feel welcome.

Jesus accepts the praises of the children, who recognize his messianic authority (vv. 15–16). Are we as clear that Jesus is at the centre of our personal and corporate life, and that we are to acknowledge his authority humbly, as children of God?

MG

YEAR B

Genesis 28:11–18

Jacob has fled, leaving his scheming mother, revengeful brother and dying father. He is alone, on the run, not knowing when, or even if, he will return. Seeking his mother's kin to find a wife, he has obtained his brother's birthright and blessing, but once his father is dead he may never be able to claim them.

- Alone at night in a rocky place, in his loneliness he finds that angels and God himself are his companions.
- With home and family far behind, he finds that the personal God of his father and grandfather is there with him.
- With no possessions and no land, he is promised both land and progeny and therefore marriage.
- Unsure of the future and of his return, he is promised both.
- With only the minimum of aims and purpose—just to find a wife—he is assured that God is working out his purposes through him and that God will not leave him until he has done all that he has promised.

Awed and afraid, he responds with all the commitment of which he is capable, but, as events will show, he still has a lot to learn.

Revelation 21:9–14

The picture of the holy city usually refers to the people of God as a community. The Church is both city and bride. Echoing the imagery of Isaiah, this is the Church, the new Jerusalem, finally arriving at the end of time, as God completes his plans and what we know of time and space is wrapped up in the final glory.

- The city is now perfect. Reflect on the part this city has played in the biblical story, finally rejecting her Messiah, and being conquered and levelled by her enemies as had happened before. Now the city is restored, redeemed and made perfect, expressed in precious jewels and perfect numbers.
- The city shines with the glory of God—in trinitarian glory, the Bride of the Lamb, seen by a revelation of the Spirit.
- It is the city of the chosen, the twelve chosen tribes and the twelve chosen apostles representing those whom God has loved and redeemed by his grace.
- The people who belong to God together are not just his servants, nor even his brothers and sisters: they are his bride. This rich imagery, coming in many parts of scripture, holds some of the most daring, passionate and compelling pictures of the love of God for us.

1 Peter 2:1–10

This passage is speaking to the Church, rather than to individuals, about the process of growth.
- Growth requires getting rid of all that hurts a fellowship (v. 1).
- Growth requires being single-minded about the things that lead to growth—there is only one kind of food (v. 2).
- Growth means growing together so that the sum of the whole—the Church—is more than the sum of the individual parts (v. 5).
- Growth means building a right relationship with Jesus Christ, who is the cornerstone of the whole building—coming to him (v. 4), not rejecting him (v. 7), worshipping God through him (vv. 5, 9), and obeying him (v. 8).

Verses 9 and 10 echo Exodus 19:6. They carry the same implications, that each individual member of the people of God has responsibility for the fulfilling of the purposes of God by his chosen body, the Church. United as one, the Church is to demonstrate the character of God in all its doings, and to witness to his grace to all the world, mediating his sacrifice and making disciples, thus incorporating others into the royal priesthood. The churches to which Peter was writing were small, harrassed and socially insignificant. The titles given in the great covenant promises of Sinai now apply to them, as they do to churches today. After mercy comes a commission: 'On your feet!'

John 10:22–29

See comment on the Fourth Sunday of Easter, Year C.

MK

YEAR C

1 Chronicles 29:6–19

These events appear to form the climax of David's reign in the eyes of the Chronicler.

The **means** of raising the collection was in the first place David's own example (vv. 2–5), with a joyful and freewill response (vv. 6, 9)—that is, over and above the normal disciplines of tithing and sacrifice that would have continued alongside.

The **motivation** for giving was a recognition of God's kingly rule (v. 11). This issued in humility, since the people were not doing God any favours or earning any merit, as it was all God's anyway (v. 14)! But it also issued in generosity; it is much easier to give when conscious of how much one has been given, and when secure in relationship with the giver rather than trusting in the gifts. Is this why we in the West find sacrificial giving so hard?

The **main aim** for the whole project was not to give security, or to glorify individual donors—they were, apart from David, anonymous. Rather, it was that the people's vision of God should be enlarged (vv. 10–13) and that they should walk in faithful obedience (vv. 17–19). This forms part of the Old Testament's ambivalence towards special places (see also 2 Chronicles 6:18). The purpose of buildings is not to draw boundaries and create limitations, but to open us to the possibilities of God. Yet this purpose was so often frustrated then as it is now.

Ephesians 2:19–22

Paul here offers us a 'saints' sandwich'—the bread and butter is belonging, and the meat of it is God's building of his people.

* **Belonging** (v. 19). Once aliens to God (v. 12), we now belong to his people and inherit his promises—the kingdom of faith is now our home country. Conversely, we have also moved from being at home in the world to being strangers in it (see 1 Peter 1:1). The Greek word for 'aliens' is the root of our word 'parochial'—we have much in common with our neighbours, but as citizens of another country. If buildings tell us that we belong here, they deceive us!

- **Building** (vv. 20–21). 'Going to church' does not mean visiting a building, but participating in that awkward and glorious process of having corners knocked off so that we fit together in Christ to become a holy meeting point of God with his world. If our fellowship looks a mess, it is because it is God's building site over which he places the sign 'Work in Progress'—if we will let him!
- **Belonging** (v. 22). As we allow ourselves to be fitted together with one another, as we align ourselves with the teaching of the apostles and prophets as recorded in scripture, and as we trust in and depend on Christ (all v. 20), then we find that the Spirit of God delights to dwell in us. The building may be the house of God's people, but it is God's people who are the house of God, a 'temple in which God is quite at home' (Eugene Peterson, *The Message*).

John 2:13–22

The temple is viewed with ambivalence throughout the Bible (see, for example, Jeremiah 7:4).

As a resting place for the ark, the first temple was a sign of God's presence, his *shekinah* glory in the midst of his people.

But here we see the temple corrupted by self-interest—the making of money from what should have been a service to enable worship (vv. 14–16) —and by an institutionalism that refused to recognize the new thing that God was doing (vv. 18–20). Self-interest and institutionalization are dangers from which we are not immune under the new covenant.

De-centring of self and de-institutionalizing of buildings can only happen through Jesus. It is Jesus' living presence that turns a building into a place where God and humanity can meet (v. 19). Only he can defy our small expectations and shatter the limitations we put on what God can do (v. 20). And it is Jesus' living presence that brings faith, hope and understanding (v. 22). For it is in Jesus that God visited his people (Luke 19:44) and it is Jesus who makes God's presence real to us by his Spirit (John 1:14, 18; 4:24; Romans 8:15–16).

All this is because of Jesus' taking on himself the death-dealing destructiveness of humanity, that in his resurrection he might make available the life-giving creativity of God (v. 19).

IP

ALL SAINTS' DAY (EUCHARIST)

YEAR A

Revelation 7:9–17

This is a wonderful description of worship in heaven, which gives a remarkable picture of the generosity of salvation offered by God in Christ. In the first place, the number of people in the crowd around the throne is countless (v. 9)—both an assurance that there is no limit on the numbers who are eligible for salvation and a reassurance that those who feel alone in their devotion to Christ are far from being so (remember, the vision is given to John who is imprisoned on an island for his faith—1:9). Second, they are from all over the world (v. 9), an indication that salvation is not limited to a few specially favoured races but is universal in its application. Third, they are all in heaven around the very throne of God (v. 9), showing that the end of salvation is indeed to enable everyone, not just a small minority, to be brought into the presence of God, where they will be enthralled in worship as God cares for them with loving tenderness.

The way of attaining salvation is also described: those who are around the throne in worship have been saved by their endurance and by the blood of the Lamb (v. 14). One is no good without the other.

1 John 3:1–3

As elsewhere in the New Testament, this passage displays the concept of a dimension to salvation which is still to come. The opening words marvel at the love shown to humans by God in allowing them the intimacy of being called children of God (v. 1). But the full implications of the title are not yet apparent, either to the eyes of the sceptical world looking on, or indeed to the eyes of God's children themselves (v. 2a). For the moment, it is very much a matter of faith, just as believing in the earthly Jesus as Son of God was also a matter of faith which many rejected (v. 1b). But these children of God are undergoing a process of transformation which will be fully revealed only when Christ appears (v. 2b). The ultimate hope is that they will become like Christ, which probably means that they will share in the glory of Christ. In the meantime, though, their faith in the God who can bring this to fulfilment is purifying them (v. 3), making them more like Christ in the way they live their lives, so that they are ready to be glorified with Christ when he finally appears. God's children must be holy, as God is holy.

Matthew 5:1–12

The so-called Beatitudes are some of the most famous sayings of Jesus. In Matthew's Gospel, they are Jesus' first recorded address to the crowds who have swarmed around him to see his miracles and hear his words (4:23–25), and they form a kind of manifesto of desirable spiritual qualities for those who aspire to be his followers. The manifesto is set in the context of a final realization of God's will on earth, as begun in Jesus, so that those who display the desired qualities will get their reward not in human terms but in that eschatological Kingdom of heaven. The qualities cited are those which resonate with aspects of God's own character or which God particularly favours. Thus, the poor in spirit (v. 3), the mourners (v. 4) and the meek (v. 5) are those who know their need of divine help, while righteousness (v. 6), mercy (v. 7), purity (v. 8) and peace (v. 9) are divine characteristics. The juxtaposition of persecution for righteousness' sake and for Jesus' sake (vv. 10–11) links the two together, and implies that to be persecuted for one is to be persecuted for the other. This is reminiscent of the thought that where help is given or refused to those in need, it is given or refused to Christ himself (Matthew 25:40, 45).

DR

YEAR B

Isaiah 25:6–9

All Saints' Day would have little meaning without hope in the ultimate triumph of God and the vindication of his people. This prophecy expresses in marvellous picture language what will happen when God finally and definitively intervenes at the end of this age, with emphasis on the corporate hope of the entire people of God.

God promises unimaginable blessings for his people, pictured in terms of a great banquet (v. 6). Notice the universal scope of the salvation God offers (all peoples, all nations, all faces); compare Jesus' parable of the wedding feast in Luke 14:15–24.

At the same time, God will remove disgrace, suffering and death from his people (vv. 7–8). The emphasis here is on the removal of death as the curse which has been the result of human disobedience down through history.

All this is God's work (v. 9), accomplished in his strength. His people are simply called to trust faithfully in his love. This is not merely a pious future hope, but the reality of God's saving power. It will only be fully manifested in the future, but it is already present. Looking back, the people acknowledge that God was with them all along (v. 9).

Revelation 21:1–6a

If today's reading from Isaiah expresses the corporate hope of God's people, Revelation 21 goes even wider than that. Here, there is magnificent hope for the entire cosmos. God's act to bring this present age to a close is seen not only in terms of his plans for his people, but in terms of his plans for the whole of time and space.

Leading up to this point, the book of Revelation has described in vivid and metaphorical language the current situation of the world. God is the almighty sovereign, but his rule is acknowledged only in heaven and in the hearts of his people on earth. Life is still marked by injustice, persecution and rebellion against God.

The sacrifice of Jesus (chs. 4—5) heralds the resolution of this conflict, and now the alienation of the world from God is finally resolved, symbolized by the city descending from heaven. God creates a new heaven and earth, where he will live face to face with his people, and where they will suffer no more.

As the people of God, we are called to proclaim the reality of this transforming work of God. He really is making all things new (v. 5).

John 11:32–44

From the corporate hope of the reading from Isaiah and the cosmic hope of Revelation, the story of the raising of Lazarus brings us to the believer's *personal* hope in Jesus, 'the resurrection and the life' (11:25).

The story is personal in the sense that it relates to one individual. It also reveals the depth of the personal commitment Jesus makes to us all. Jesus' love for Lazarus and his sisters, coupled with his anger at the suffering humans experience in a fallen world, moved him to tears. He feels just as passionately about each one of us.

The raising of Lazarus is an astounding miracle, one of the amazing signs which Jesus performs in John's Gospel to point to his authority and identity. Yet astounding though it is, it is 'only' a raising back to mortal life. Lazarus would later die, as we all must. As the people of God, we are the inheritors of an even greater miracle. Through his resurrection, Jesus has opened up the way for all who trust in him to follow, so that death is no longer the end, but merely the prelude to a new, transformed life together in the presence of God.

MG

Year C

Daniel 7:1–3, 15–18

When seen clearly, the world we live in appears a terrifying place. Convulsing in chaos ('the great sea', v. 2), it is stalked by apparitions of great power (v. 3)—people and regimes and ideologies that consume and destroy through greed, violence and brutal indifference. It can make us feel very small and vulnerable.

But above the comings and goings of such powers sits one who is unchanging, whose power and sway make these others seem transient and insignificant (vv. 9–10). And he shares this power with frail humanity (v. 14), with those conscious of their mortality and insignificance (see the use of the phrase 'son of man' in Ezekiel). The human form presented before the Ancient of Days represents God's holy people ('saints'; see the explanatory verses 18 and 27), who will continue to stand before him long after the greatest powers have been forgotten.

All this assurance is held together in Christ. It is in him that the Ancient of Days meets with humanity—the 'son of man' who accepted the suffering of the cross (see, for example, Mark 8:31) bears an uncanny resemblance to the one on the throne (Revelation 1:14–15). And it is as we follow him (our 'pioneer', Hebrews 12:2) by walking in his holiness—his gift to us by the cross—that we begin to experience the coming Kingdom of God.

Ephesians 1:11–23

This complex passage, packed with theological concepts, is held together by something profoundly simple—Paul's radically egalitarian view of the Church. All Christians ('saints', v. 1) have in Christ:

- A stake in the future (v. 11) as inheritors of all God's promises and his coming Kingdom;
- Access to the truth (v. 13a) about God's love, not mediated by a priestly caste but made available directly to them;
- A steady confidence arising from the work of the Spirit (vv. 13b–14);
- The experience of transformed relationships ('love toward all the saints', v. 15);
- Growing spiritual discernment through growth in the knowledge of God (v. 17);
- Personal grasp of God's plan for the world and the Church (v. 18);
- A demonstrable share in God's resurrection, kingdom, creative power (vv. 19–21);

- A sense of cosmic significance (vv. 22–23) that comes from being in vital communion with the one who sustains the universe.

This is an impressive inventory! Through his saints, God wants to make these things known in his world. As a little girl once said, saints are what the light shines through.

Luke 6:20–31

Jesus' words divide the world in two—'this age' and 'the age to come' of rabbinical belief (see, for example, Luke 18:30).

Luke's version of the Beatitudes (vv. 20–26) is shorter than Matthew's (Matthew 5), and appears to focus on material rather than spiritual issues. But the contrast can be over-estimated. Life is marked by both poverty and wealth, hunger and filling, tears and laughter, abuse and acclaim—dissatisfaction and satisfaction. Which we have now and which we have in eternity is up to us. If we are satisfied with what we have in this world, then that is all there will be. There comes a point where the train divides, and we have to decide which of the coaches we will make our home. One half will go no further.

But the amazing news is that Jesus' death and resurrection actually bring the new age bursting in even before the old age has passed away. His death defeats Satan, the god of this age (2 Corinthians 4:4; Revelation 12:8), deals with sin (1 Peter 2:24) and makes available to us the resurrection life of the age to come (John 11:24–25). We begin to live the life of the Kingdom even as we continue to live in the world (vv. 27–30)—life marked by radical goodness (v. 27), graciousness (vv. 28–29) and generosity (v. 30).

IP

ON 1 NOVEMBER IF THE MATERIAL ABOVE IS USED ON THE SUNDAY

Isaiah 56:3–8

For some, any mention of saints suggests exclusivity, a sort of 'holier-than-thou' attitude. Nothing could be further from the biblical picture of the people of God. A key theme of both Old and New Testaments is the need for God's people to be outward-looking, because God's love is for the whole world, not just one group.

Here, Isaiah is given a prophecy about two groups (foreigners and eunuchs) who historically were denied full access to the worshipping community of

Israel. But God is determined that such barriers should be broken down. What counts is not people's background but their commitment to serving God (v. 4). Thus it is open to everyone who loves the Lord to play a full part in worshipping him (vv. 6–7). The description of the temple as 'a house of prayer for all nations' (v. 7) reinforces this: anyone who wants to pray to God is welcome.

In celebrating our fellowship with all believers, it is crucial that we maintain this outward focus. As William Temple put it, 'The Church is the only society which exists for the benefit of non-members'. Are we committed to God's constant desire to gather more and more people into his Kingdom (v. 8)?

Hebrews 12:18–24

Christian believers are part of the great fellowship of God's people on earth and in heaven, from both old and new covenants. All members of this vast fellowship share remarkable privileges in their relationship with God. So this passage reminds us of the common heritage of believers in every age, a key theme for All Saints' Day.

Believers are described as 'the church of the firstborn' (v. 23). In other words, we are all equal heirs of the salvation God has promised. The Church is not a hierarchy where certain individuals enjoy more rights than others (contrast the reference to Esau in 12:16–17).

Believers' names are written in heaven (v. 23). See also Luke 10:20 and Revelation 21:27 for this idea. Those who trust in Christ are enrolled in membership of the heavenly city (v. 22); their salvation is completely assured.

Believers are also described as 'the spirits of righteous men made perfect' (v. 23). It is not that the saints are perfect by reason of their own achievements. Rather, the sacrifice of Jesus (v. 24) has meant that their relationship with God is now wholly restored; in that sense, they have been made perfect and counted righteous.

(See the Dedication Festival, Year A, for further comment on this passage.)

Matthew 5:1–12

At the beginning of the Sermon on the Mount, Jesus summarizes the characteristics of true disciples, their relationship with God, and the care God shows them both now and in the future.

The Beatitudes reflect the overwhelming grace of God. The faithful are promised life in the Kingdom of heaven—complete fulfilment in the presence of God. This is not something that the faithful earn by righteous living.

Rather, the reward God promises (v. 12) is freely given, out of all proportion to what we can offer him.

However, Jesus does also describe how true discipleship should respond to God's love—seeking righteousness, showing mercy, being pure in heart (that is, single-mindedly dedicated to God). Of course, Jesus himself is the supreme embodiment, and example to us, of the way of life God requires.

The Beatitudes are also realistic. Living for God is likely to bring opposition from the world (vv. 10–12). But Jesus reassures us that the problems of the present will ultimately give way to the glorious future God has promised. Indeed, as the present tenses of verses 3 and 10 suggest, believers can even now begin to experience something of what it means to live in the Kingdom.

MG

THE FOURTH SUNDAY BEFORE ADVENT

YEAR A

Themes of divine judgment dominate the run-up to Advent, but in the clamour of competing voices, whose pronouncements do you trust?

Micah 3:5–12

Declaring the purposes of God, interpreting the signs of the times—political, social, moral—from a divine perspective, announcing God's judgment and its consequences; all this and more was part of the prophet's role.

Micah's contention is that false prophets are soon spotted: the tenor of their message is dictated by their own vested interests. Injustice and oppression flourish in the land, with affluence for rulers and grinding poverty for their subjects (graphically described in verses 1–3). Yet to please their paymasters, prophets of court and temple declare 'shalom'—God's in his heaven and all's right with the world. Their adverse comments are reserved for those who do not hold the purse strings.

God's judgment will fall on all such false prophets. Micah is gripped by a burning conviction of the true justice and real power that come from God alone. He is prepared fearlessly to denounce evil wherever it is found. Political rulers are condemned for corruption, priests for bending the law to keep their job, prophets for saying what their patrons want to hear.

The complacent assumption that Yahweh's presence among them guarantees security will be shattered by foreign invasion and total devastation. Hammering home that challenge is the message of the true prophet.

1 Thessalonians 2:9—13

The integrity of the messenger guarantees the truth of the message. That is Paul's contention as he evidently faces unspecified accusations about his motives as an apostle.

Earlier in the chapter he has called God as witness to what the Thessalonians already know: he and his companions, Sylvanus and Timothy, have never in their preaching of the gospel flattered anyone or looked for personal gain and popularity. Rather they have given themselves sacrificially to their task and to their hearers.

Three aspects of the apostles' ministry are significant (and here the Thessalonians themselves can be called as witnesses):

• **Their financial integrity.** They had worked tirelessly (setting a precedent for self-supporting ministers!) so that the good news did not come with a price tag.
• **Their moral integrity.** Exemplary behaviour confirms the good news of being set free from the grip of evil.
• **Their pastoral integrity.** The good news is backed up by loving encouragement, so that the Thessalonians in their turn may live lives worthy of the gospel they embrace and of the God who has called them.

Evidently the Thessalonian Christians were convinced, for they had accepted the apostles' message as the word of God (v. 13).

Matthew 24:1—14

It's not the end of the world... or is it?

When the first temple was destroyed, it seemed as if God had deserted Israel. National life as well as religious life lay in ruins. The Jews of Jesus' day believed that the new temple, not yet completed, would be indestructible.

For the bemused disciples, gazing in admiration at the solid and imposing magnificence of the temple buildings, Jesus' forecast that it would be razed to the ground must have felt like a bucket of cold water. If he is right, it surely *will* be the end of the world!

Subdued and anxious, the disciples ask for a prophetic sign. Jesus invites them to read the signs of the times, neither leaping to conclusions nor caught unawares.

False prophets flourish in times of national and natural disaster, in the atmosphere of fear and distrust and betrayal that suffering brings. People are desperate to believe anything or anyone who promises deliverance.

Is Jesus talking about the end of the age or the destruction of the temple or both? The person of Jesus himself connects the two events. The destruction of the temple is clearly understood by the evangelist as God's punishment for a nation that has rejected Christ at his first coming. The end of the age will be the consummation of all things in Christ at his second coming.

GS

YEAR B

Deuteronomy 6:1–9

Deuteronomy 6:4–9, the *shema*, has been part of Jewish daily prayer for many centuries. This fundamental command to love God wholeheartedly is in response to what God has already done for his people in bringing them to the promised land.

Especially striking is the single-minded commitment to which the people are called:

- Israel is reminded that the Lord alone is God (v. 4). He is not one among many vying for their allegiance, but the only true God, and he therefore demands their total commitment.
- The commitment of the people is based not on fear or dry legalism, but on love (v. 5). Obedience which flows from love implies gratitude, devotion and, again, total commitment.
- Devotion to God should permeate every aspect of life, both inwardly, in the heart (the mind and emotions) and in the soul (one's very being) (vv. 5–6), and outwardly in what the people say and do (v. 7).

This call to single-minded commitment is a constant challenge to the people of God, especially when pressure to compromise is great. How far is this commitment a reality for congregations and individual Christians today? The scope and content of personal and corporate prayer life is a good indicator!

Hebrews 9:11–14

Sometimes the central truths of Christianity seem so familiar to us that we lose sight of the sheer scale of God's love for us. Here, there is a chance to reflect again on the greatness of the sacrifice Jesus has made, and to recapture a sense of wonder and joy at what he has achieved for us. Even the grace and mercy of God's covenant with Israel in the Old Testament pales in comparison.

Clear contrasts are made between the previous system of sacrifices and the death of Jesus. For example, the old sacrifices achieved outward, ceremonial purity, whereas the death of Jesus cleanses us on the inside; the old sacrifices had to be repeated regularly, whereas Jesus' death was once for all.

Although the comparison between Jesus and the Old Testament might seem a million miles from our world, there are intensely important truths here which are as relevant today as they were then. The death of Jesus provides the answer to alienation from God (Jesus is our high priest and the perfect mediator, v. 12), to guilt (cleansing our consciences, v. 14), and to futility and lack of purpose (freeing us to serve God as we were designed to do, v. 14).

Mark 12:28–34

In his famous reply to the lawyer's question, Jesus quotes the command-ment to love God with all of one's being, from Deuteronomy 6 (see above). So there is fundamental continuity between the Old Testament Law and the ministry of Jesus. But there are also new developments here which intensify the command and broaden the way we are to understand it.

First, Jesus adds to the great command to love God a further command from Leviticus 19:18 to love one's neighbour as oneself. Bringing both commands together in this way gives each a distinctive emphasis. Loving God and loving one's neighbour become inseparable. Commitment to God which does not result in love for one another is merely pious delusion (Matthew 25:44). Equally, genuine love for one's neighbour flows from response to God's love (John 13:34).

Second, the exchange with the lawyer takes place in the week before Jesus' death. Jesus' command to love God and neighbour needs to be seen in the context of the cross, the supreme demonstration of devotion to God the Father and to one's fellow human beings. Jesus himself offers us the definitive practical example of how to obey the greatest commandments.

MG

YEAR C

Isaiah 1:10–18

The vision of Isaiah reveals the truth about God's people with a stinging indictment of their worship.

- **Bad news and good news**. The people are (shockingly) compared with Sodom and Gomorrah (v. 10), a byword for both sin and judgment. Their worship is an offence to God as long as there is no reform of life-style. But this is because God's holiness concerns every aspect life, in particular honesty, justice and concern for the poor (v. 17; cf. Leviticus 19:34).

- **Form and content**. Ritual and lifestyle were equal concerns of the Torah ('teaching', v. 10b). Worship consisting of one and not the other is an affront to a God who is One (Deuteronomy 6:4, a central confession of Israel's faith). Rites and wrongs (v. 13b) do not mix! The blood of bulls cannot hide murderous intent (v. 15b); washing with water is no substitute for holiness of life (v. 16). Sunday and Monday belong together.
- **Cleansing and worship**. The people are put on trial (v. 18)—but suddenly God is not only accuser but acquitter! What God offers in cleansing always precedes anything we can offer in worship ('Therefore… offer…' Romans 12:1). Even the Law (whose blessings and curses from Deuteronomy 28–30 are echoed in verses 19–20) came as a gift, the initiative of a gracious God who rescued his people.

2 Thessalonians 1:1–12

Paul is rightly proud of the Thessalonian Christians, as they are overflowing with faith in God (v. 3a), with hope (v. 4) which holds them steadfast in the face of opposition, and with love (v. 3b) which is marking them out as a distinctive community. These are at the heart of gospel living (1 Corinthians 13:13). As he boasts of them (see 2 Corinthians 8:1), he is boasting in what the Lord has done in and for them (cf. Philippians 1:6).

Their persecution is further evidence that they are living kingdom lives (Luke 6:22; see comment under All Saints' Day, Year C). Paul's language of vengeance (vv. 6–9) will make most of us feel uncomfortable. But we must remember to read this text in the context of the whole canon of scripture, and allow it to criticize us before we criticize it.

For it teaches that sin is serious, when we are prone to be blasé; that people are responsible, when we like to blame background, genes or circumstances; and that it is God alone who punishes, when we always want to get our own back. Eternal destruction (v. 9) is the only alternative to receiving the gift of eternal life from the One who alone is the fountain of life (Psalm 36:9). And all this is declared by one who persecuted the Church but had mercy shown to him.

The hope of vindication fashions in the Thessalonians not only endurance, but a desire to be the best they can be in preparation for that day (vv. 11–12).

Luke 19:1–10

This final encounter on Jesus' journey to Jerusalem (from 9:51) is a climax in his ministry, containing the key elements of Luke's Gospel.

- **The universality of the gospel** (vv. 2–3). Zacchaeus is a *chief* tax collector, whose wealth (v. 2) indicates how much he has exploited his position and robbed others. The crowd will not let him have so much as a glimpse of Jesus (v. 3). A sinner and collaborator, dishonest and unpopular—the good news is available even to him.
- **The initiative of Jesus** (v. 5). Zacchaeus has shown curiosity (v. 4), but not much more. It is Jesus who takes the initiative (v. 5), even for those who are sons of Abraham (v. 9). But then the history of God's people was always of God's gracious and loving initiative (Deuteronomy 7:7–8).
- **The joy of the welcome** (v. 6). Zacchaeus is overwhelmed at Jesus' decision to share table-fellowship. His joy is characteristic of repentance —it is the joy of heaven (15:7)—and is in sharp contrast with the attitude of others, especially the Pharisees (e.g. 15:2, 28).
- **The change of life** (v. 8). Luke of all the Gospels is most concerned with poverty and wealth. The wealthy will miss out on God's blessing (Luke 6:24) since the good news is for the poor (Luke 4:18). Those who wish to receive the Kingdom must let go of their wealth—conversion is not complete unless it includes conversion of the wallet.

IP

THE THIRD SUNDAY BEFORE ADVENT

YEAR A

Amos 5:18–24

Hear the superficial optimism of a prosperous society: 'The Day of the Lord will simply confirm our national superiority, demonstrating that Yahweh's favour rests on us. Are we not his people?'

The prophecy of Amos reverses these expectations. The light-hearted holiday atmosphere will dissolve into trauma and dark terror. The wealth of Samaria and the Northern Kingdom rests on dishonesty and ruthless exploitation. The day of reckoning cannot be evaded and there will be no-where left to run to. Just as the fugitive from justice is congratulating himself on a narrow escape, a yet more terrifying prospect confronts him.

It is difficult to recapture the shock that Amos' next words bring. Yahweh rejects the whole panoply of Israel's worship. Festivals and sacrifices, psalmody and praise, none of it is acceptable to him. 'I take no delight in your Christmas carol services. I withdraw my presence from your eucharists.'

Yahweh is not their insurance policy, much less their property. He cannot be manipulated. He is transcendent and he is holy. Those who would find his coming a time of rejoicing must follow his paths of justice and righteousness. Amos holds out little hope of repentance for a nation whose healthy appearance masks terminal sickness.

1 Thessalonians 4:13–18

The Thessalonian Christians had confidently expected that Jesus would return in glory in their lifetime. The years passed and nothing happened. Now, some of their number are naturally growing old and dying. Will they finally despair of Christ's coming?

Paul seeks to underpin their faith:

- Jesus himself died and was raised. That is their guarantee that God's purpose is a similar resurrection for all who are in Christ. (Three times in three verses Paul refers to the dead as 'asleep'—a temporary state.)
- Christ will come in person and his coming will be unmistakable. There is no danger of missing the event.
- They will be reunited with their loved ones in the presence of their Lord.

Their hope (v. 13) rests on solid foundations. It can only be expressed in metaphors of trumpets and aerial reunions—but it is real, and a comfort in their grief.

For Paul, the 'day of the Lord' is entirely centred on Christ—his death and resurrection (v. 14), his promise of eternal life (v. 15), his coming again in glory (v. 16), being in his presence (v. 17).

Hope rests not on vague optimism but is focused on a person. The exact timing of his return becomes unimportant, because we live in daily expectation of his presence.

Matthew 25:1–13

All ten young women intend to be at the party; all ten make basic initial preparations; all ten fall wearily asleep when the bridegroom is delayed. The only difference is that the 'wise' among them have the foresight to prepare for a long wait (not unusual, with haggling over financial settlements).

The maidens (bridesmaids? family servants? neighbours?) are waiting to escort the groom in a torchlight procession as he brings his bride home. The 'lamps' were probably oil-soaked rags on a stick: yesterday's oil would largely have evaporated.

The wise maidens' sharp refusal to lend oil was not unreasonable, for the whole village would be waking up to celebrate, and the foolish did find supplies eventually. The point is to emphasize that each person has to make their own preparations for the Kingdom of heaven.

More difficult is the awful finality of the locked door. It is not enough to profess general enthusiasm for Jesus and the Kingdom. His true followers must be constantly prepared for the final encounter with their Lord.

Pray and plan as if Christ will not come in your lifetime. Live and love as though he will return tomorrow.

GS

YEAR B

Jonah 3:1–5, 10

What relationship could survive if there was no scope for a second chance? Jonah, who completely failed God when he was first sent to Nineveh, hears the word of the Lord a second time. Having initially disobeyed, he experienced God's wrath in the storm (1:12). At the same time, God's mercy was evident in the provision of the great fish (1:17), which held him in a space between life and death. Inside the fish, Jonah expressed his heartfelt repentance and marvelled at God's deliverance (2:1–9). As he emerged from the fish's belly into the light and on to the land, he experienced a kind of resurrection—a rebirth into the beginning of the rest of his life. Now the Lord speaks a second time (v. 1), giving him a second chance to live life in relationship with God and in accordance with his will.

Despite his own experience of God's wrath being mitigated by mercy, Jonah is indignant when the Ninevites have a change of heart (4:1) (just as he himself had done) and are granted a second chance. In our criticisms of others, we are equally capable of failing to allow them even a portion of the mercy that has been shown to us.

Hebrews 9:24–28

Inventors build prototypes and architects build models as a way of representing a larger, as yet ungraspable, reality. The priests of the temple believed that the temple on earth had a heavenly counterpart (9:23), so that what took place on earth also somehow took place in heaven. The temple, if you like, was a model of heaven. There is, of course, a vast difference between a model and the real thing. So the writer to the Hebrews exclaims that Jesus entered into heaven itself (v. 24)—not the miniature human version.

The priests of the temple were acting out a ritual that expressed profound truths about the absolute nature of God's holiness. However, that ritual could only ever serve as an indirect illustration of, and preparation for, the final sacrifice that would do away with sin (v. 26). Thus, the writer argues, what Jesus has done for us is as far from what the priests of the temple could do as the real thing is from a mere illustration.

Mark 1:14–20

An old poster used to ask, 'If you were on trial for being a Christian, would there be enough evidence to convict you?' In such a trial, perhaps the most telling question would be, 'How has being a Christian changed your life?' As Jesus begins his ministry, as described here by Mark, he invites radical change. Change in attitude to God (repentance and belief, v. 15) and change in lifestyle (follow me and fish for people, v. 17). It is on the evidence of the latter that a case could be made for the former having taken place.

For the first disciples, these two changes began with a radical separation from their past life. Reading of their ability to drop everything and follow Jesus fills us with some trepidation that such is also demanded of us. However, it is notable that Jesus chose his disciples, rather than their choosing him—as would have been more usual in the culture of Jesus' time—and so he accepts the responsibility to provide for them. This provision begins, in the first instance, in calling two pairs of brothers (vv. 16, 19). It is noticeable that later in the Gospel, Jesus sends the disciples out in pairs. In trying to follow Christ in the world, we shouldn't try to do anything alone; we need God's call and the support of at least one other person.

AG

YEAR C

Job 19:23–27a

Whilst arguably the best-known passage in Job (not least thanks to Handel), it is also one of the most obscure.

Job's desire for his words to be made permanent (vv. 23–24) is a cry for his innocence to be acknowledged in the here and now. To be told, 'Don't worry, things will be all right in the end' really is (to coin a cliché) just pie in the sky. When we feel we have been wronged—especially if it is by God—it somehow seems to matter that others acknowledge it.

The great logical difficulty with this passage is the idea that God will in fact be Job's redeemer (v. 25), partly because of his protestation of innocence and partly because God appears to be his enemy (vv. 6–12, 21). Yet redeemer is what God turns out to be (42:10, 12)—and that on the earth.

It is reading too much back to see Job expressing belief in bodily resurrection. But resurrection does answer the longing that Job expresses (vv. 26–27)—that we shall see God's justice triumph on a renewed earth, not in some ethereal realm of which we cannot conceive. It is just such an earthy hope that God sets before us in Christ: the heavenly city descends to earth and its light is the Lamb that was slain (Revelation 21:23).

2 Thessalonians 2:1–5, 13–17

The meaning of Paul's discussion of the antichrist is largely lost to us; Augustine in the sixth century commented that 'the meaning of this ["restraint", v. 7] completely escapes me' (City of God, XX). The antichrist figure in Revelation becomes a beast from the abyss (Revelation 11:7), identified with Roman imperial power (Revelation 13:1–2). But things are too sensitive in Thessalonica for Paul to suggest this explicitly. His emphasis is not on speculation, but on the fact that Christ's return will be public, taking unbelievers by surprise but not believers (1 Thessalonians 5:4), that he will put an end to evil (v. 8), and that times will be difficult before his return (v. 3).

How should we prepare for this? Not by arguing about times and places, but by following the Thessalonians' example. By opening their lives to the transforming power of the Spirit and letting their understanding be shaped by the truth (v. 13b), they are a model for and means of many others coming to know Christ ('firstfruits'). They are to 'keep a tight grip' (v. 15, Peterson's paraphrase in The Message) on what they have learnt from Paul and continue to live by grace. As God reached out to them and surprised them with his love, so he will continue to give them a fresh heart, invigorate their work, and enliven their speech (v. 17).

Luke 20:27–38

The Sadducees were an aristocratic priestly group, centred on the Temple, who co-operated with the Romans so as to protect their privileged position. They held that only the Torah (Pentateuch) was scripture (which they read fairly literally) and that resurrection was a later Pharisaic innovation.

In context and content, it appears that the Sadducees were not really interested in an answer, but wanted to trick Jesus in posing the problem about resurrection. The incident teaches us that:

- **Knowing scripture involves embracing relationship more than grasping facts.** In their wooden literalism, they assumed that resurrection life would be on the same terms as this life—something Jesus immediately dismisses (vv. 35–36). In Mark and Matthew, Jesus upbraids them for knowing 'neither the scripture nor the power of God'. Without the latter, we cannot have the former.
- **Jesus answers their question in terms they relate to** (v. 37). Rather than look elsewhere, or start a debate about the extent of scripture, Jesus plays on their home ground. Exodus 3:6, to which he alludes, is at the heart of the Torah. God's covenant love must transcend death, since to be 'God of' someone means to be in an active, caring relationship with them.
- **Eternal perspective is essential to moral strength.** Without the hope of resurrection life, the Sadducees were more than willing to compromise with the occupying power of Rome so as to maintain their position of influence. As a result, they disappeared completely with the destruction of the temple in AD 70.

IP

THE SECOND SUNDAY BEFORE ADVENT

YEAR A

Zephaniah 1:7, 12–18

'A day of wrath…' In Christian theology, this came to be identified with the day of judgment, of rewards and punishments. But for the prophets of the seventh century BC, the Day of Yahweh was to be the culmination of world events. Judah had languished under the oppressive rule of Assyria, paying heavy tribute, but now the prophets foresaw a whole new horizon in world politics.

Zephaniah foretells the destruction of arrogant Nineveh, but he does not spare his own countrymen: priests, courtiers, merchants who have colluded with the foreign power and spurned Yahweh as an irrelevance (vv. 4–13), all will be caught in the searchlight of his wrath. As they have sacrificed to Baal, so they themselves will become a sacrifice to Yahweh (v. 7).

This cleansing of every aspect of the nation's daily life is part of a day of cosmic warfare (cf. Joel 2:2–10) as God will come suddenly in overwhelming power. The rule of evil will be over.

It is tempting to read verses 14–17 as figurative language for the horrors of war. But this is a unique event, a day that cannot be measured, when Yahweh will show himself as he really is.

1 Thessalonians 5:1–11

The Thessalonians too are preoccupied with the Day of the Lord: when will it be? Paul's answer in some ways echoes Zephaniah: the Day of the Lord will come suddenly and it will be destructive. It will shatter false security. There will be no escape.

Paul contrasts this terrifying prospect with the position of Christian believers. 'Darkness' is a metaphorical shorthand to include every aspect of our lives that is not controlled by Christ. But Christians are in permanent spiritual daylight, so the Day of the Lord should not take them by surprise. The Christ-light in us is constantly pushing back the frontiers of darkness.

The sharpest contrast with Zephaniah, however, comes in verse 9. The prophet saw God's coming among his people only as wrath and universal destruction. The apostle knows that God's purpose is to bring salvation. But this is not a different God, or a God who has changed his mind. What has transformed the relationship of God with his people is the coming of Christ and the cross of Christ (vv. 8–9). So the Day of the Lord should be neither a source of speculation nor a prospect of fear. It is a topic of conversation among Christians, to encourage and strengthen each other's resolve in the stresses of daily life.

Matthew 25:14–30

The absent master of Jesus' parable recalls the apparently absent God of Zephaniah's oracle—but he will surely return!

The three slaves were entrusted with huge sums and clearly expected to trade. (A talent was 6000 denarii, and a denarius was equivalent to a labourer's daily wage.) The different amounts of money may represent the different gifts and abilities each disciple has, or the privileges and opportunities of the Kingdom of heaven. Being ready for the master's return means carrying out whatever responsibilities he has given us—he decides what those differing responsibilities will be.

The reward for faithful trading is not to be pensioned off with a lump sum, but to be given even greater responsibilities. Both the industrious and resourceful slaves are given an identical commendation—despite the difference in the amounts they had handled. The third slave has been gripped by fear and inertia: in 'playing safe' he secures his own downfall.

Money under the mattress does not keep pace with inflation and loses its value in real terms. Those who try to 'preserve' ways of doing theology or worship or ministry unchanged are left with devalued currency. Faith is given to be developed, spiritual understanding to be deepened, sacrificial service to be extended, opportunities for witness to be seized.

GS

YEAR B

Daniel 12:1–3

Some people have a favourite book or film that somehow encapsulates what life is about for them. Daniel was a book of vital importance to Jesus in his ministry and he used it frequently as a means of explaining his person and purpose. This passage from the final chapter of Daniel's prophecy looks forward to the pattern of final events on which all the prophets of the Old and New Testament agree. He sees a time of trial (v. 1) followed by a judgment in which the righteous are vindicated and the unrighteous are punished (vv. 1, 2). This is really a vision of table-turning where those who have been faithful under pressure have those who have been pressing down on them taken away and given a taste of the treatment they have given to others.

Pictures of judgment are often unpalatable to Western Christians. This may be because, in our riches, we are closer to the oppressors who are judged than to the oppressed who are vindicated.

Hebrews 10:11–14 [15–18] 19–25

Musicians rehearsing for the big concert or athletes rehearsing for the main event will repeat their discipline again and again on the build-up to the big day. However, these preparations are always just a shadow of the real thing. In the same way, the temple ritual (v. 11) said something vital about the seriousness of sin—that it costs life—but it was only a foreshadowing of the truly and eternally effective sacrifice.

Once that sacrifice has been made, the way is open to a new and living intimacy with God. We are like children standing at the locked palace gates and longing to go inside. When the door is opened to us, however, shyness overcomes us and we feel unable to step across the threshold into the new kingdom and new relationship that has been won for us. The writer to the Hebrews prods us across that threshold (v. 19) and encourages us to support one another in living the life of the new Kingdom and reaping its benefits. They have been won for us at the greatest cost possible, and it would be churlish not to embrace the gift wholeheartedly and with joy.

Mark 13:1–8

It is tempting for us to make Jesus' prophecy about the temple buildings (v. 2) too small. Because Jerusalem fell in AD70, we are inclined to limit the scope of his words to a simple prediction of a future event in the history of human politics. However, Jesus is not speaking about just any building, he is talking about a building that represents the nature of the relationship between God and his people. It is a building that stands for a system and an order of things. In a similar, though infinitely lesser, way, someone who predicted that the Houses of Parliament or the White House were to be completely destroyed would be saying something about the whole institution and what they represent, not just the bricks and mortar.

Jesus' prediction of the various calamities listed in these verses (vv. 7ff.) are, equally, not just random events that may be interpreted much as a soothsayer observes omens. They are instead the symptoms of an ongoing struggle between good and evil. Christ's resurrection marks a revolution in the fortunes of that battle. However, the final victory and the bringing to birth of the new creation will, Jesus predicts, necessarily generate painful birthpangs (v. 8).

AG

YEAR C

Malachi 4:1–2a

The words ring like a refrain throughout the book of 'My Messenger': 'Thus says the Lord of hosts'. It is the assurance that these are the true words of God, and that he is the one with the power to make these things happen.

The great and terrible day of the Lord (v. 5) will certainly bring judgment. For how can I deny the One who is the source of all life and still enjoy life? Yet in the certainty of this declaration, God cannot withhold mercy. Even as the day comes, God will send one who will turn people from judgment (v. 6).

Looking forward to the day of God's coming also involves looking back (v. 4). For the God who will come is the same as the God who has already visited his people. Malachi, like all the other prophets, is a 'covenant enforcement mediator' (Stuart and Fee, *How to Read the Bible for All Its Worth*, SU, 1983, p. 151). The best thing we can do to prepare to meet God is to be grounded in the truth we have already been given.

And when the day came, mercy had the upper hand. The Word bursting upon the world was God's own presence coming at the last as it had been at the first, in the fragility of a tented dwelling (John 1:14). His coming was first of all to bring life, not to take it away (John 3:16). Judgment is still to come, but even as it hangs in the air, ready to fall at the end of time (ours or the world's), God's mercy is at work (Romans 11:25).

2 Thessalonians 3:6–13

It seems that some of the Thessalonians thought that, since Christ was to return so soon, there was no longer any need to work—why not just sit it out until the end? In correcting this attitude, Paul offers insights into our priorities for Christian living:

- **Responsibilities, not rights** (vv. 7–8). Despite Jesus' teaching that it is legitimate to earn one's living from the gospel (Luke 10:7), teaching that Paul knew (1 Corinthians 9:14), and despite the example of the other apostles (1 Corinthians 9:4–5) Paul wants to go out of his way not to burden the Thessalonians with his presence. We too must ensure that open and supportive relationships do not make the subtle shift into taking advantage of one another.
- **Example, not indulgence** (vv. 9–11). Though he might have argued that he was a special case, Paul wanted to set an example to the Thessalonians as to how they themselves should live. This was part both of Paul's egalitarian attitude (among his letters, only Philippians even mentions church leaders in its opening greeting) and his readiness to let sharing the gospel override personal preferences (1 Corinthians 9:22).
- **Discipline, not demonizing** (vv. 11–15). Tempting as it might have been to exclude permanently those who disagreed with Paul, their salvation takes priority over his pride. Any distancing of the fellowship from them was for the purpose of having them restored (v. 15). Paul is at every point concerned with building God's Kingdom, not his own empire.

Luke 21:5–19

While Jesus is teaching in the temple, a comment about the splendour of the building leads into Luke's version of the 'little apocalypse'. In a dramatically changing world:

- **God is unchanging** (vv. 5–8). Even if the most magnificent symbol of God's presence is destroyed, God remains. The great danger of institutions and buildings is that we associate them so closely with God that we think their destiny and God's are intimately bound up. This is a short step from the idolatry of trusting the institution instead of God (cf. Jeremiah 7:4).

- **God is in control** (vv. 9–11). Jesus is using phrases from the Old Testament (2 Chronicles 15:6 and Isaiah 19:2) whose original context was of describing God's activity among the nations. And the same images are used in Revelation following the vision of God as sovereign on his throne (Revelation 4—6). Jesus' warning of these events is to allay a sense of disorientation; God is working his purpose out, despite all appearances to the contrary.
- **God is faithful** (vv. 12–19). When faced with opposition from the powers-that-be and betrayal from those closest, God will continue faithful. There will be physical suffering (see Mark 13:9) but God will guard that which matters (verse 18 is again an Old Testament phrase—see, for example, 1 Samuel 14:45; 2 Samuel 14:11).

'Though the earth may shake me, though my friends forsake me—I believe in you' (Bob Dylan).

JP

CHRIST THE KING

YEAR A

Ezekiel 34:11–16, 20–24

Secular writers of ancient times described kings and rulers as shepherds of their people, so it is not surprising that Moses and David both have this title.

More frequently the leaders of Israel are castigated as *bad* shepherds. Ezekiel condemns them for neglecting and exploiting the people, as shepherds who feed *on* the sheep instead of feeding the sheep, who leave the flock to wander and be attacked.

Against this background, God himself, the true King, comes as the Good Shepherd to the rescue of Israel. He will search out and bring home those in exile. He will provide for them in abundance in their own land, ensure they rest in safety from their enemies, heal them and care for the sick and defenceless.

The leaders/shepherds are not the only ones to feel the edge of God's anger. Some of the sheep are greedy and ruthless.

Not all the people of Israel will share this idyllic restoration. Those who have exploited the invasion and the exile to grow rich at the expense of their fellows will find that a just leader is not to their liking. But God will send a descendant of the house of David as a true shepherd to establish the rule of righteousness.

Ephesians 1:15–23

Paul longs that the Ephesians may fully grasp their amazing privileges, all that God has done for them in Christ:

- **They are called and chosen by God** (cf. 1:4). They have hope—not vague optimism but the confident certainty of eternal life.
- **They are 'saints'**, being made holy to enjoy the presence of God, with a rich inheritance of glory to look forward to.
- **They have power**, the limitless power of God working in them and through them.

'In the heavenly places' (v. 20) stands for the invisible, spiritual environment of human life as distinct from the visible, tangible environment we call earth. 'Rule, authority, power and dominion' denote spiritual forces manipulating the different structures of earthly society: religion, politics, law, culture. With the resurrection and exaltation of Christ, their grip over human beings has been broken.

The key to the passage lies in the link between 1:20 and 2:6. Because Christ reigns in glory, we who are 'in Christ' share privileges now which are a foretaste of untold glory to come. In Christ, God's divine nature is seen in all its fullness. This is his gift to the Church, and through the Church to the whole of creation.

Matthew 25:31–46

The sheep and the goats are hardly more than a passing analogy, for the main canvas Matthew paints is an awe-inspiring judgment scene.

Is Jesus to judge everyone, believer and unbeliever alike, on the grounds of how they have treated any of the poor and needy in the world? Or is the rest of the world (the usual meaning of 'all the nations') to be judged on the basis of how they have cared for poor and needy Christian disciples— because this is a measure of how they respond to Christ himself? Probably the latter is the more appropriate understanding of this particular passage, although elsewhere Christian believers are often challenged to show human-itarian concern.

More fundamentally: what sort of king is this, who is encountered in the poor, the weak, the prisoner and the stranger? Yes, he is the Judge, holding supreme authority. Yes, he is the King; he reigns in glory. But, as Martin Luther suggested, this is a hidden glory, veiled to those who live by the world's values. He will be recognized only by those who know their own spiritual poverty and need, whose hearts and minds are open to receive him in faith.

And again, the basic premise remains, uncomfortable but unavoidable: there *will* be division.

GS

YEAR B

Daniel 7:9–10, 13–14

This passage was used extensively by Jesus, and the very early Church, to throw light on the identity of Christ.

Daniel predicts that a human figure will be brought to the Father and will have power and kingship conferred upon him (v. 13). That this figure is human is indicated by his description as 'one like a son of man' (NIV) or, as the NRSV rather lamely has it, 'one like a human being'. However, this human figure also has a divine quality. This detail is suggested by a comparison of Daniel's vision with the pagan Baal myth. In this Canaanite myth, the god Baal is brought to the god El and has authority conferred on him by which he may destroy chaos. In Daniel's polemic reinterpretation of this myth, the divine figure Baal is replaced by the one like a son of man. Thus Daniel 7 presents a picture of a divine/human figure who is commissioned by God to conquer evil and chaos and to reign as king. It is this figure that Jesus appropriated to himself.

Revelation 1:4b–8

When water starts to break through a dam, the process starts with just one drop emerging on the far side. Once the initial breach has been made, the process will continue, if repairs aren't made, until the whole structure collapses and a torrent rushes through.

Revelation celebrates Jesus as the firstborn of the dead (v. 5) (the first one to breach the dam of death), and looks forward to the process by which his heavenly Kingdom, won by his faithful death, floods all other realms. The doxology of this passage (vv. 5b–7) is spoken from the point of view of those who watch as the natural order of things, made unnatural by the dam of sin and death, is broken down and the injustices of the old kingdoms are wiped away.

The descriptions of God as 'him who is and who was and who is to come' (v. 4), and the, 'Alpha and Omega' (v. 8), express the eternal truth that it is in the very nature of God to be over all that is in time and space. Consequently, dominions that attempt to hold out against him must always come to nothing.

John 18:33–37

Jesus has a habit of replying to straightforward questions in ways that seem to be disconnected from the initial thread of the conversation (vv. 33–34). Pilate wants to establish whether or not Jesus has committed the crime of setting himself up in opposition to the rule of Rome. Jesus, on the other hand, is totally uninterested in this issue.

Jesus explains that his Kingdom is not from this world (v. 36). This is one of two valuable snippets of information that we receive about his Kingdom in this passage. The fact that it is not from this world demonstrates that it is not bound by national borders as other kingdoms are. The second snippet is Jesus' remark that 'everyone who belongs to the truth listens to my voice' (v. 37). This suggests that membership of Christ's Kingdom has something to do with listening to Jesus' voice.

Pilate, who has the privilege of hearing Jesus, thus also has the opportunity of *listening* to him, and thus also of belonging to the truth. We, too, hear Jesus regularly in the words of scripture, but we may be as far from grasping the point as Pilate was.

A G

YEAR C

Jeremiah 23:1–6

Scrooge himself could scarcely have made a more gloomy greeting for Advent: 'Woe,' says God, 'things are bad and will get worse.' Yet we cannot appreciate the wonder of the coming of the King until we see the dark background against which the light shines.

Thus from a dark pit in the nation's history, with a feckless king, and exile on the horizon, Jeremiah in a leap of faith tells of the coming of a king who will sit on David's throne. Three things will mark his glorious reign. First, he will create a society marked by wise and just administration (v. 5). Second, he will restore the broken unity of God's people: Judah and Israel will be reunited (v. 6). Third, his people will be 'saved'—a rich word which recalls their great rescue from Egypt and points forward to that greater rescue still when Immanuel will tread the dragon underfoot and save his people from death and hell (v. 6).

Moreover, this is no passing blink of sunshine: God himself pledges the honour of his name. That name is Yahweh, the covenant Lord who is committed to his people by promises which he cannot and will not break. His 'righteousness' will ensure that his Kingship is eternal.

Colossians 1:11–20

The language here, as so often in Paul, is doctrine set on fire; it is doxology as he praises Christ the King whom the prophet had foretold and whose advent has staggering consequences for the whole of creation. The astonishing thing is that this transformation takes place 'through his blood, shed on the cross' (v. 20, NIV). By descending into the stifling and claustrophobic darkness, the King will destroy the enemy, dispel the darkness and open the Kingdom to all who believe. Something of the wonder of this is conveyed in that gripping passage from C.S. Lewis' *Out of the Silent Planet* where the plan of salvation is encapsulated and 'Maleldil' (the incarnate God) destroys 'the Bent One' (the Devil) in 'Thulcandra' (Earth): 'They say he has taken strange counsel and dared terrible things, wrestling with the Bent One in Thulcandra'.

Thus the passage tells us:

- **Who the King is**: God himself come into time and space; the Creator of all things visible and invisible, without whom the universe can be neither understood nor properly appreciated (vv. 15–17).
- **What the King does**: Not only does he take away sin but he makes us a transformed society and gives the power to endure and live in the light (v. 14).
- **What the King will do**: His resurrection and defeat of the cosmic powers ensure the safety and victory of the Church but also the renewal of the universe and a new creation more glorious than the old (v. 20).

Luke 23:33–43

A medieval baron, grown old in wickedness and cruelty, was mortally wounded on the battlefield. As he fell dying from his horse, his whole life flashed before him and, in agony, he called to God for forgiveness in that fleeting second, before his lifeless body struck the turf. The old rhymester describes it thus

> *Between the saddle and the ground,*
> *Salvation sought, salvation found.*

Such an experience is described by Luke in an incident unique to his Passion narrative. As the King dies, one of the criminals realizes, in an astonishing leap of faith, that while there is no hope whatever of escaping earthly punishment and death, there is every hope of escaping eternal death because the King has come.

Let us not scorn this ultimate example of 'deathbed' repentance because Luke is telling us profound things about the advent of the King.

First, he is showing what allegiance to the King, or conversion, means. What this man did was to fly in the face of all the apparent evidence and reverse the verdict of political, military and ecclesiastical establishments. This battered and dying figure on the cross he recognized to be the 'very God of very God', the King whom every tongue would confess and to whom every knee would bow. He was, in effect, anticipating the verdict of the last day (v. 42).

Second, Luke shows us that we must choose one or other kingdom. One criminal was saved, thus none need despair; but only one, thus none dare presume.

Third, in darkness, in the apparent triumph of evil and the choking despair, he points to the certainty of the Kingdom: 'Today you will be with me in Paradise'.

RF

THE NAMING AND CIRCUMCISION OF JESUS
(1 JANUARY)

EUCHARIST

Numbers 6:22–27

The readings for New Year's Day start, appropriately, with a blessing. This short prayer is probably one of the oldest poems in the Bible, linking us with all those who for thousands of years have depended on God in their hopes and fears for the future.

Blessing is a broad concept, but covered very practical and definite expectations in the Old Testament. God blesses his people by giving them children, prosperity, land, health—and his presence. When God 'makes his face shine' upon his people, he delivers them from all their troubles, including enemies, sickness or sin. When he 'lifts up the light of his countenance' upon them he is paying attention to their needs and giving them *shalom*, peace which embraces total well-being and wholeness.

The priests pronounced this blessing at the end of the daily morning service in the temple and later in the synagogues. So they put his 'name'— his presence, his character—on the people: Yahweh, the Lord, in threefold repetition.

The New Testament affirms that Jesus is Lord, bearing the 'name' and bringing the presence of God among his people, making peace in all its fullness.

Galatians 4:4–7

According to Paul, Jesus is born 'under the law'.

Born of a woman, he became fully human. Born into a Jewish family, he became fully a Jew, inheriting too the obligation to fulfil the law of God. But more than this, Paul has already spoken of the 'curse' of the law (3:10, 13). So the Son of God, who himself rejoices in freedom to fulfil the law perfectly, voluntarily accepts the guilt of others who have failed to keep the law, and so sets them free.

Between Christ and the Christian is a constant interchange. Because Christ is acknowledged as righteous, believers are justified; and because Christ is declared Son of God, believers are given the name of sons. As children of God, they too can use the children's name for father that Jesus used: 'Abba'. (In Roman law, the adopted son had the same legal inheritance as those who were sons by birth; cf. v. 7).

Christians often make New Year's resolutions like everyone else. To resolve to live according to the law of love in Christ, however, is no longer to be '*under* the law'. And failure to keep our resolutions meets with forgiveness.

Luke 2:15–21

The angels have gone. Life is back to normal—the cold, the darkness and the sheep.

Christmas is over. Work and routine are about to start again. Will the new year be much like the old?

The shepherds could not leave it at that. They tested out the angels' message and they passed on what they had heard—that this helpless infant was to be the Saviour of the nation, the Messiah, the Lord. They were in a state of great excitement. Mary was left wondering...

In the days and weeks that followed, Jesus was absorbed into the normal life of an ordinary Jewish family. He was circumcised, the sign of being a member of the covenant people of God, subject to the covenant law. Yet he will inaugurate a new covenant and give a new commandment.

He was named 'Jesus', the name given by the angel to Mary, confirmed and explained to Joseph: 'He shall save his people from their sins'. Jesus was a common enough Jewish name. Yet, in this very normal-looking child, it is invested with a new significance.

'Behold, I make all things new.' After the first Christmas, nothing would ever be just 'more of the same'.

GS

THE CONVERSION OF PAUL
(25 JANUARY)

EUCHARIST

Jeremiah 1:4–10
Jeremiah's life was apparently mapped out before him. As the son of a priest (1:1), he would have been expected to follow in his father's footsteps. God interrupts this plan by calling Jeremiah to a life devoted to prophecy. Like Moses (Exodus 4:10–13) and Gideon (Judges 6:15), Jeremiah responds to the call reluctantly. His culture did not expect a young man to teach older people, so he believes that his youth is an obvious disqualification (he may have been about twenty years old). God's response (vv. 7–10) emphasizes that he does not call people on the basis of their natural or acquired qualifications, the power to do the job comes from God, not from man.

Jeremiah's ministry was one of the hardest endured by an Old Testament prophet. He had constantly to battle against the deafness of his audience or the derision and abuse he received from them. Jeremiah, however, was able to continue without wavering because he had experienced God's call. A brief survey of the experience of various great characters within the biblical accounts would show that the tougher the assignment given by God, the more vivid the experience of call that is provided.

Acts 9:1–22
On his mission to Damascus, Saul undoubtedly believed himself to be carrying out the purpose of God in stamping out the followers of the Way

(v. 2). If Saul had a qualification for being chosen to be Christ's apostle to the Gentiles, then his enthusiasm to carry out God's purposes must have been it. His zeal was, of course, dangerously misguided. However, it is interesting to note that Christ was able to take that fervour and turn it to his true purpose. This suggests that if we too have a definite desire to serve God's purposes in the world, then God is capable of directing that enthusiasm in the right direction, even if we may start off on entirely the wrong course ourselves. This is perhaps a warning to those of us who prefer a rather more moderate attitude to discipleship and are critical of our 'over-zealous' neighbours.

The fundamental problem with Saul's enthusiasm was that it was born of a personal motivation. To be used by God, he had to be stopped (vv. 3–4) and emptied (vv. 6–9). He became, in fact, an entirely helpless man for three days (v. 9). From this state of emptiness God was able to fill him and send him, in the Spirit's power rather than his own. In our plans to serve God, we also need to be sure that we are fuelled by God's Spirit and agenda, rather than our own.

Matthew 19:27–30

Jesus' explanation of the cost of discipleship was fully experienced by Paul, a man who renounced his place in Jewish intellectual society, his right to marriage and his right to life itself. Paul's reward, as we read from his letters, was a great deal of heartache but also a great deal of blessing. The churches that he founded and nurtured were to him a crown, a sign that his life had been to a good and joyful purpose.

Writing our own obituary is an excellent way of discovering what are our true priorities for life. Paul's obituary would surely be filled with the people that he touched. His forthright manner should not blind us to the depth of his love for those to whom he ministered. The tearful response of the Ephesian elders to the news of his final departure is just one testimony to the deep relationships that Paul built in the course of his ministry (Acts 20:17–38). Ultimately it is achievements of this kind that last to eternity.

Galatians 1:11–16a

The power of Paul's testimony had much to do with the fact that his faith was his own. For most of us, our faith begins as the faith of other people, such as our parents or our peers. Only if this faith becomes something that is entirely a product of our personal relationship with God can it survive isolation and hardship.

A further important characteristic of Paul's faith was that it was shaped by a wholehearted embracing of the revelation that he received (v. 12). Most of us, when we are introduced to a new idea, tend to try to keep hold of our old thoughts and behaviours at the same time as taking on new things a little at a time. Paul, on the other hand, was capable of fully living out the consequences of his new view of the world, without trying to hold on to the things that he had previously held dear (v. 14).

Paul thus affirms that what he had to offer his hearers did not come from his own inner resources. It came from the resources that God gave him. If we are to have something worthwhile to offer our neighbours, then it must come from God and not from ourselves.

AG

JOSEPH
(19 MARCH)

EUCHARIST

2 Samuel 7:4–16

The collect for St Joseph's day begins with the words: 'God our Father, who from the family of your servant David raised up Joseph the carpenter to be the guardian of your incarnate Son and husband of the Blessed Virgin Mary...' This links this humble and godly man with the line of great David himself and with our Old Testament reading which focuses on the Davidic covenant. This is a rich passage and our reflection will centre on the use of the word 'house'.

The first nuance is the temple, which is to be the work of David's son rather than David himself. The emphasis here is on the fact that a permanent temple is not an absolute necessity, and indeed later generations were to find it a snare (see the 'temple sermon' in Jeremiah 7). The initiative for building must come from the Lord. Notice, further, that though David's plan is rejected, he is not; verse 5 calls him 'my servant', a title given to few and notably to Moses.

The second nuance is house as 'dynasty' (v. 11ff). The future of this 'house' is guaranteed (v. 16). Historically it all went sour: the temple and Torah, apart from a few bright lights, notably Hezekiah and Josiah, were neglected and treated lightly. When the exile brought to an end the Davidic dynasty, it seemed as if the covenant had irreparably failed.

Yet in Jesus Christ came the true temple and tent (see comment on the Gospel reading for Christmas Day, Set III) and in him came that descendant of David who would reign for ever. Thus 'great David's greater son' would fulfil and embody that covenant and build that house which would now be destroyed. By the cross, the 'temple of his body' was killed, but by raising him again, God ratified his covenant.

Romans 4:13–18

In this chapter, Paul has already spoken of David and has especially referred to his psalms which speak of the blessedness of those whom God has made righteous by faith. Most of the chapter, however, including our reading for today, focuses on Abraham and the covenant God made with him in Genesis 15. The essence of all covenants is a relationship, and Joseph, like all others in the family of faith, is called to that life which Abraham characteristically exemplifies.

Our reflection will particularly focus on verse 17. How do we know that God gives righteousness in response to faith, and how do we know that God can raise the dead? Paul tells us that we can know these things because God is the Creator. He alone can and does give life, whether it is physical or spiritual.

The barrenness of Sarah proved no obstacle to bearing the promised child because, in all births, God is the ultimate Creator and humans only co-operate with the life he has given. Here, as in Matthew 1, Abraham and David are part of that line which was to culminate in the child who was to be the Saviour of the world.

It is God's word which itself gives life: 'God... calls into existence the things that do not exist' (v. 17). When God speaks, his words are life-giving and consequences follow. Joseph, caught up in this great drama, exercises similar faith to Abraham's. God's word both creates faith and makes possible that response which is the essence of a loving covenant relationship. Joseph's part in this drama is an honoured one, as we shall see in our Gospel reading.

Matthew 1:18–25

We often reflect on the role of Mary in this great drama of the incarnation. Today we think a little of the part played by Joseph, that good and generous man who opened his home to the Son of God. From a human point of view, the legitimacy of Jesus' claim on David's throne depended on the willing-ness of Joseph, who was the legitimate heir, to accept him as his son.

Joseph is a sensitive man (v. 19) and wants to make things as easy as possible for Mary. He then shows openness and obedience when God appears to him. Like chapter 2 (see comment on the Holy Innocents, 28 December), these verses are full also of deeper undertones.

Once again, scripture is fulfilled, as the mysterious prophecy of Isaiah 7:14 is finally understood. This does not rule out earlier and immediate meanings but catches these up in the great story as the 'last days' dawn and David's son, who is also David's Lord, is born.

Once again the Creator is at work. As the Holy Spirit brooded over the chaos waters and brought life, so now life is conceived in this young Jewish girl. That same Spirit spoke through the prophets and is the source of all life.

Joseph is a model to us all. His compassion and gentleness as well as his strength and his faith, and his exemplary conduct as a loving husband and father as well as his openness to God, are qualities all of us could well emulate.

RF

THE ANNUNCIATION
(25 MARCH)

EUCHARIST

Isaiah 7:10–14

King Ahaz of Judah is faced with some pressing political problems. Two of his neighbours have allied themselves against him and present a serious threat (7:2). Isaiah is told to assure Ahaz that their onslaught will not be successful, and God offers to give the king any sign he chooses to confirm this promise (7:10–11). Ahaz, however, is not prepared to trust the situation to God. He prefers the assurance of an alliance with another power, Assyria (cf. 2 Kings 16:7–10). Isaiah 7:17–20 predicts that this arrangement will ultimately prove disastrous.

The sign chosen by God against Ahaz is that of a child who will be called Immanuel. The sign is said to apply to Ahaz and his immediate situation and it measures the time from the birth of this child until it reaches the age of decision. By the time the child reaches thirteen, Isaiah predicts, the enemies feared by Ahaz will be no more (v. 16).

Matthew (1:23) takes this sign and reapplies it to Jesus. This small and vulnerable child will once again signify God's mighty action in the world, to the surprise of all his enemies.

Hebrews 10:4–10

Hebrews 10:1–18 forms the closing summary of the central doctrinal section of the book (note the 'Therefore' in 10:19, as the next section considers the practical consequences of the doctrine discussed in 5:11—10:18). Hebrews 10:1–18 emphasizes the effect of Christ's total obedience to God in his complete offering of himself (vv. 5–7); this perfect sacrifice brings to an end the ceaseless round of sacrifices and makes it possible for us all to enter the Most Holy Place where God is present (10:19f.).

Christ's total giving of himself is a model for all who follow him. The words of Psalm 40:6–8, quoted in Hebrews 10:5–7, are supremely applicable to Christ, but they may also be said by anyone who seeks to serve God. Mary's response to God is consistent with this psalm. In the sphere to which she was called, Mary did not stop at sacrifices and offerings (vv. 5–6). Instead she was prepared to 'do God's will' (v. 7) in service that demanded the wholehearted commitment of her body, her life and her emotions.

Luke 1:26–38

The annunciation to Mary, while unquestionably unique, reveals certain elements that are a model for our own experience of God.

First, there is the remarkable way in which Almighty God invites a girl without status to become a co-worker in his plan for humanity. In this act, God repeats his pattern of involving frail, often unlikely, human beings in his purposes.

Second, Mary experiences, perhaps more than any other, the pain of sharing in God's purpose. Thus, while it is a sign of favour to be chosen to bear Christ's body into the world, this privilege does not come with a pain-free guarantee. Quite the opposite is true. To share with God in his work, we must also share with him in his pain. Simeon later predicted that a sword would pierce Mary's own soul too (Luke 2:35), as certainly must have happened at the crucifixion.

Third, Mary was a conduit of Christ, but she was more than just an empty channel through which he could pass into the world. Mary had something genuinely and uniquely of herself to offer in the process. When God uses us to do his work, he uses real, unique people.

AG

GEORGE
(23 APRIL)

EUCHARIST

Revelation 12:7–12

In this chapter, the seer on Patmos throws the veil aside and shows us the high command of good and evil. The underlying cause of evil and suffering and the cause of the hostility towards God's people is the rage of Satan. We are left in no doubt of the identity of the great Adversary (v. 9). This text charts the conflict of good and evil from the time that the 'ancient prince of hell' (from Luther's hymn '*Eine Feste Burg*') hurled defiance against God to the end time, when he continues to harry God's people. Of that conflict and its imaginative impact, the story of George and the Dragon is one echo. The dragon, the embodiment of ancient evil, is overthrown by the saint who trusts in God.

Michael, the archangel (see Daniel 10—12; Jude 9), leads the heavenly hosts in the great battle which may be the heavenly counterpart of Christ's victory on the cross. Three consequences flow from this victory.

First, the Christians overcome 'by the blood of the Lamb'. This does not mean repeating the words as a kind of mantra or formula; rather that the ground of their success is that Jesus died and thus they can face the Accuser.

Second, they overcome 'by the word of their testimony'. This is by the continual proclaiming of the truth of the gospel and by making it known in all possible ways.

Third, they are willing to die for their faith—'they did not cling to life even in the face of death'. Satan's ultimate defeat is certain but in the interim he can still inflict enormous damage on believers. Thus there is a need to be strong, to believe and to realize that Christ has conquered.

2 Timothy 2:3–13

Like Revelation, this passage also calls for endurance. This is no call for a grim and 'stiff upper lip' stoicism; the call to endure is, as in Revelation, linked to the death and resurrection of Jesus Christ which will give the necessary strength and incentive.

Three illustrations show the nature of Christian endurance. The soldier's priority is to please his commanding officer: so must the Christian soldier's first loyalty be to Christ. The athlete must compete within the rules: so must the Christian practise personal discipline. The farmer works hard to secure an abundant harvest: so must the Christian labour so that the fruit will be plentiful. All this requires careful and diligent meditation so that the Lord will enlighten the heart (v. 7).

The reason that this endurance is not only possible but transforming is brought out in verse 8: 'Remember Jesus Christ'. Two great facts are highlighted. The first is that he is the living, victorious Christ. History belongs to him and he is both the strength and the goal of Christian serving. The second is that he is 'a descendant of David'. He is the centre of the great biblical story from creation to new creation, which manifests itself in time and space.

All this gives the point and purpose of Paul's own suffering, which is the blessing of eternal glory for all who believe. Then, as so often in the pastoral letters, we have a fragment of a hymn introduced by the 'trustworthy saying' formula. This moves the whole call to endurance on to the plane of worship, as Paul celebrates Christ's faithfulness which is the ground for the faithful endurance of his followers.

John 15:18–21

Stories such as George and the Dragon capture something of the thrill of battle and have a swashbuckling feel to them reminiscent, for earlier generations, of Errol Flynn and, at the time of writing, the adventures of Zorro! Nevertheless the actual reality of the Christian battle is costly and painful. Our passage here, without denying the glory, reminds us that the cross comes before the crown. John here particularly analyses the hatred of the world, the anti-god, self-centred attitude, ultimately devilish, which opposed Christ and continues to oppose his disciples.

The first cause of the world's hatred is that it resents any lack of conformity. The Christian, by definition, is under the Lordship of Christ; the world by definition is not. This is not a narrow-minded exclusivism, rather the conviction that if God has truly revealed himself in Jesus Christ then there is an absolute standard.

The second cause of the world's hatred is that it hated Jesus Christ. If the Master suffers, then the servants must expect the same treatment. This means that as Christians we have no right to expect trouble-free and unopposed lives; that would be setting ourselves above Christ.

The root of all this is in verse 21: 'They do not know him who sent me'. Not recognizing God in Jesus is at the heart of the world's darkness.

All our passages today are a stirring call to courageous faith, such a faith and courage as are exemplified in the stories of St George.

Faith overcomes! In Jesus' love abiding,
We yield ourselves to follow his commands,
Willing to suffer for his name, confiding
Our needs and hopes and fears into his hands.
Christopher Jones, College Hymn of St John's College, Durham

RF

MARK
(25 APRIL)

EUCHARIST

Proverbs 15:28–33

Much of the book of Proverbs consists of short couplets, individual sayings that can stand alone. They are pithy, pointed, even punchy snippets of wisdom that weave practicality and piety into the fabric of sensible everyday godliness. In many sayings, the paths labelled 'righteous' and 'wicked' open like a fork in the road. These are two ways of living, with the prospect that our habitual choice of one or the other will eventually shape our whole character. Most of this short section is about learning.

- **Learning from ourselves** (v. 28). If we always speak before we think, our mouth will be like a rubbish chute. Pausing for thought lets us hear the wisdom of our own experience.
- **Learning from others** (vv. 31–32). When we learn from the advice and warning of neighbours, we become wiser. If we are too proud to learn, we cheapen ourselves.
- **Learning from God** (v. 33). Recognizing that God is great and we are small makes us stable rather than fragile. It gives us a rock and refuge, reason for prayer, and a ready hearing when we pray (v. 29).

Scripture portrays St Mark as a learner first, before he was a teacher (see comment on Acts 15, below). He learned well. The good news he brought has refreshed many lives (v. 30).

Acts 15:35–41

Christians quarrel too. It is not always easy to find a settlement. The 'sharp disagreement' (v. 39) over John Mark broke up a good working partnership between Paul and Barnabas (vv. 35–36).

Barnabas was a pastor, always ready to support people who were overlooked or misunderstood (9:26–27; 11:21–24). Mark was his cousin (Colossians 4:10). Although Mark had dropped out midway through an earlier missionary journey (v. 38; cf. 13:13), Barnabas looked on him as a trainee, who should be given another chance (v. 37).

Paul was a pioneer, keen to spread the gospel quickly and effectively across the Greco-Roman world (Romans 15:18–20). If Mark could not handle the hardships of itinerant work, Paul viewed him with suspicion. It would be unwise to risk him again (v. 38).

The dispute found no easy resolution: both men stuck to their opinions, so firmly that they separated (vv. 39–40). Paul's commitment to the advancement of the work, and Barnabas' desire to deal sensitively with the individual, collided and split.

The project and the person: both matter. Happy the church whose leaders can hold these two concerns in creative tension. But even our quarrels sometimes end in peace: Mark appears later as Paul's trusted associate (Colossians 4:10; 2 Timothy 4:11), and an ancient (and reasonable) tradition identifies this Mark as the writer of Mark's Gospel.

Ephesians 4:7–16

We may think of our service in the Church as our gift to Christ. The capacity to serve is his gift to us—all we can do is give it back, with love. Several New Testament passages list gifts of service, to be used for Christ (Romans 12:6–8; 1 Corinthians 12:8–10, 28–30; 1 Peter 4:10–11). The lists address different situations and needs, so they complement and overlap one another. One such list, here at verse 11, mentions apostles, prophets, evangelists, pastors and teachers.

Jesus Christ, ascended in glory (vv. 7–10), shares his wealth and equips particular people to make his love known. The gifts listed here are seed gifts, intended to bear fruit, to set the Church on a solid footing, to energize and activate its whole life. They include active mission (apostles), openness to the mind of God (prophets), telling the Christian message (evangelists), caring for the Church (pastors), and explaining the faith (teachers). These ministries can give Christ's people the confidence to be effective in their Christian living (v. 12); they impart understanding, to prevent Christians being prey to shallow ideas and fast talkers (vv. 13–14); they foster love, to bind the Church together (vv. 15–16).

Mark was an evangelist. His written Gospel is a gift to the Church from God. So is every faithful preaching of the gospel—yours included.

Mark 13:5–13

Chapter 13 of Mark's Gospel looks ahead from the time of Jesus to the struggles and challenges that would beset his followers. It addresses—in the words of Jesus—the Church of Mark's own day, possibly a generation later. More widely, it sets the whole of Christian life in a framework of hope and warning.

- **Timetables** (vv. 5–8). It is always hard to look beyond the immediate crisis. Earthquakes, battles, famine—sweeping changes of any kind—darken the horizon and hide the view ahead. They remind us that time and history are fragile and finite, that the end of all things lies in the hand of God. But we do ourselves a disservice if we expect that ending too soon. Christian teachers who concentrate too narrowly upon dates and times may be a disturbance and distraction rather than a benefit (vv. 5–6).
- **Testing** (vv. 9–13). Christianity is not always a comfortable faith. The Church has regularly come under pressure from outsiders, so that fellowship and even family loyalty have fractured (v. 12). Yet persecution has often given momentum and credibility to the Church's message, and hastened the spread of the faith (v. 10). Mark urges Christians to keep the faith, to endure patiently, to hope, and not to fear to wait (v. 13).

JP

PHILIP AND JAMES
(1 MAY)

EUCHARIST

Isaiah 30:15–21

When God's purpose seems hard to understand, panic and fright can easily take over our lives and lead us to act out of character.

The leaders of Judah felt threatened. They were sandwiched between two major military powers, Egypt and Assyria. Alliance with Egypt offered some protection (30:1–2). The Jews could buy arms—Egyptian cavalry horses (v. 16; 31:1). But Egypt would prove a fickle ally. She would not help when she was needed (30:7), and Judah, who had shaped her policies by fear, would find that same fear returning to paralyse her. Her courage would fail under challenge (v. 17).

Isaiah's positive word for the occasion was, 'Trust God.' God is just and gracious (vv. 15, 18). He may allow his people to meet hard times, and his purposes may seem clouded, but in time the skies will clear (vv. 19–20). God's steady presence will give guidance to those who need it (v. 21).

Fear often distorts our judgment. Some alliances, some deals, some compromises may owe more to panic than to practicality, more to fright than to faith. God is still to be reckoned with, still involved and concerned for our good.

Ephesians 1:3–10

These verses unfold a broad and splendid vision of God—as creator and lover, redeemer and friend.

- **Creator**: When all was formless and void, God began to shape his purpose (v. 4). The universe is his, and he will draw it together, to find its full goodness and security within the love and leadership of Jesus Christ (v. 10). This purpose stretches beyond the edges of time, yet in its centre is the Christian Church.
- **Lover**: God intends the Church, the company of people gathered by Jesus, to know the intimacy of his Father-love (v. 5), and to reflect that love in their own lives (v. 4), as they serve and speak his praise (v. 6).
- **Redeemer**: God's gracious love found visible focus in the death of Jesus. God's purpose, beginning before time and reaching into eternity, pivots on that moment in history. Love took human flesh, and by his dying he ransomed his people and pardoned their sins (vv. 7–8).
- **Friend**: Finally God draws the Church into his own circle of friendship: they begin to understand his ways (v. 9; cf. John 15:15); he shares with them his own sense of purpose. For God will not waste what he has made, but will joyfully include earth and heaven in the final glory of Christ (v. 10). The Church may see and serve that vision, trust it and travel towards it, express and explore it now, and enjoy it for ever.

John 14:1–14

The Gospel passage, from the upper room, links today's three readings together. Philip and James were fearful, along with all the other apostles. They could not understand what Jesus was doing. Yet he had called them into his circle of friendship and love, and now he tells them enough of his purposes and plans to steady their spirits and calm their fears.

The upper room conversations, tense and perplexing as they are, take us into the calm and clarity of the relationship that binds Jesus to the Father. We are led from human puzzling and fear, into holy mystery and faith.

- **Losing touch.** Jesus is going away (13:33). His friends are afraid of losing him (v. 1). Yet Jesus will not disappear for ever. He will make a place where they can share his company (vv. 2–3; cf. 15:4). There will be another meeting (v. 3).
- **Seeking the way.** Meanwhile Jesus is their map, their route and their destination. To know him is to know the way to God, and to know God (vv. 5–7). Indeed—and this is the answer to Philip's anxious question (v. 8)—the disciples have met God already, in Jesus: his voice has been speaking God's words; his deeds are God's own activity (vv. 9–11).
- **Finding and being found.** So paradoxically the disciples will find the way to Jesus, through Jesus, after he has gone. The friends who recognize God's presence in Jesus, and pray in his name, will discover that he has not left them stranded. The power and goodness of his life will fill theirs (vv. 12–14). They thought he was withdrawing from them. In fact, he was preparing to share himself with them more deeply than ever.

JP

MATTHIAS
(14 MAY)

EUCHARIST

Isaiah 22:15–25

Snakes and ladders in King Hezekiah's civil service. Shebna enjoyed all the prestige of high office (v. 16) but did his job deplorably (v. 18). Ultimately he was dislodged and Eliakim installed in his place (vv. 20–23). The switch is portrayed not simply as the fortune of political life, but as God's doing. God's concern for the quality of human leadership (e.g. 1:23) was especially acute in Israel, who had been called to model his life and goodness in the world.

Eliakim is described as a father (v. 21), exercising his authority in a manner unmistakably motivated and shaped by love. He will be an effective administrator (v. 22): his plans will be well thought-out; friends will not need, and enemies will not manage, to disturb them. Jesus later uses this image of a trustworthy key-holder for Simon Peter (Matthew 16:19), and even for himself (Revelation 3:7).

Eliakim will be an anchor man, a person to depend on (v. 23). So what is meant in verse 25, when he crashes as abruptly as Shebna had done? Are we meant to recall that all human leadership, even the best, must perish? Did power eventually corrupt even Eliakim? Do the references to 'ancestral house' (v. 23, 24) hold the clue: had Eliakim's flesh and blood dragged him down, by expecting favours from their man at court?

Acts 1:15–26

That Matthias had to be appointed at all was a tragedy. The shadowy figure of Judas had been fully involved in the apostolic group, then had made a not wholly explicable, and ultimately heartbreaking, compact with the enemies of Jesus (vv. 16–17). The ugly details of his death would indicate to Luke's sophisticated readership that this was no dignified or creditable suicide (vv. 18–19; cf. Matthew 27:5).

The figure of 'righteous sufferer' in many of the psalms spoke eloquently to early Christians of the tribulations endured by Jesus himself. Verses from two such psalms, calling down the due judgment of God on those who hate and harass the psalmist, are applied to Judas, and to the need for his place in the apostolic circle to be taken by another (v. 20).

Matthias had begun to follow Jesus in the period when John was baptizing (portrayed in John 1:35–51). He had remained in contact with the apostolic group right up to the ascension (vv. 21–22). In his new role, he would be both a witness that the Lord had been raised, and also a guardian of the gospel tradition, able to ground new Christians in the teaching of Jesus and to preserve the memories of his ministry in an expanding fellowship.

(See the Seventh Sunday of Easter, Year B, for further comment.)

1 Corinthians 4:1–7

This passage is about leadership and responsibility in the Church, how we look at those who lead, and how we carry responsibility ourselves. Some in Corinth were inclined to foster rivalry and choose favourites among the preachers who had brought the faith to them (3:1–5). Paul suggests three reasons for a different attitude.

- **Leaders work for Christ**, as 'servants'—this word was used in synagogues for the person who looked after the scripture scrolls (Luke 4:20). They are also 'stewards'. They must deal faithfully and carefully with God's gospel; it is their responsibility but not their property (vv. 1–2).
- **Leaders are judged by Christ.** A steward's management is assessed by the master, by Christ when he comes. His verdict is far more important than any human opinion (v. 3). Jesus Christ sees more deeply than we know ourselves (v. 4): he reads the human heart, he will give praise as

each is due (v. 5). Any human summing up of work done for Christ is bound to be premature.

- **All Christian experience is a free gift**, from God's grace (v. 7). If we recognize that, we shall understand better that Christian responsibility, our own and other people's, is not fit material for pride or rivalry, or for any sense of self-sufficiency (vv. 6–7).

John 15:9–17

The Church started on the initiative of Jesus. He gave it life, by the loving relationship into which he called his followers (vv. 9, 13). He chose the twelve who would become its first leaders (v. 16; Acts 1:2). He called them friends, and shared his thinking with them (v. 15).

So this inner group of apostles were committed to a relationship. They were to abide in his love, to sustain the bond of friendship and trust that joined them to him (vv. 9–10). That meant two commitments: to a particular lifestyle, to keeping the commands he had given (vv. 10, 14); and to one another (vv. 12, 17). Love was not an option; it was the lifeblood of their common life.

And the intended outcomes? Their lives would count, their fruit would last (v. 16). Their confidence in prayer would grow, as their lives reflected his purposes (v. 16). They would know an extraordinary joy (v. 11; cf. 16:22–24).

Christian leadership remains a privilege, never a right. It still requires the double commitment, to the pattern of Christ's commands and the people of Christ's community. It has the same targets: fruit that lasts, helping people to put their own deep roots into Christ; and a deep walk with God in the leader's own life. We do not strive for joy; that comes as a gift.

(See the Sixth Sunday of Easter, Year B, for further comment.)

JP

THE VISIT OF MARY TO ELIZABETH (31 MAY)

EUCHARIST

Zephaniah 3:14–18

Zephaniah's short book of prophecy echoes many of the other prophets in his warning of coming destruction, not only on Judah's neighbours, Philistia,

Cush and Assyria, but also on Judah and Jerusalem. He emphasizes the coming great day of the Lord, a day identified both with the coming of the Messiah and with the end of time. His particular targets are those with wealth and power. It is those who are haughty and proud (v. 11) who will be removed, not the meek and humble (v. 12), echoing the words of the Magnificat. Then with verse 14 the prophet looks beyond the corruption and the idolatry (1:4–5), beyond the great day of judgment, to the day of restoration. This restoration involves forgiveness (v. 15), joyous worship (v. 14), justice (v. 19a), care of the handicapped and refugee (v. 19b) and vindication (v. 19c). It is these kinds of prophecies that inform the sense of joy and shocked surprise in the story of Mary and Elizabeth. Verse 17 is full of the kind of motherly 'lullaby' love that will be called out from both women when their babies are born, and is also the love of a parenting God to us.

Romans 12:9–16

After all the powerful doctrinal and theological arguments of the previous chapters, Paul turns to love in the family of God. In chapters 12—15 he encourages the Roman Christians to let love undergird all their relationships. He has focused until this point on the love of God through Jesus Christ, but now he turns to the love that Christians demonstrate.

Verses 9–13 include exhortations that appear in many of Paul's letters, while in verses 14 and 15 the teaching of Jesus is echoed (Matthew 5:44). Each crisp command requires a lifetime of practice!

But it is also a picture of 'ordinary' love between friends—a picture of shared commitment to working out what love means in daily lives. Elizabeth, her son the forerunner, honours her very much younger cousin, whose son carries even greater promise. The two women demonstrate the kind of love Paul describes, *devoted* to one another, *honouring* one another, *rejoicing* with spiritual fervour and prayer, *practising* hospitality. Also from the Gospel story we know that both Elizabeth and Mary are *patient* in affliction.

If this kind of love is to flourish in the Church, we have to ask what kind of structures and programmes of communal life have to be in place to make it happen.

Luke 1:39–49 [50–56]

It is interesting to look at what these two women have in common. They are both pregnant in miraculous ways, with babies heralded by angels. They are both at a high point of excitement, knowing that God is acting and that they are part of the fulfilment of his purposes in a way they could never have anticipated. Both praise the Lord in similar style, in words that echo Old Testament prophecy.

But there are differences. One is very old and the other probably very young. One is at last about to produce the son for which they had longed, who would carry the family future. The other is pregnant before marriage, threatening the future of her own married life in a small community. They encourage each other for three months, full of expectation and joy. But a rosy future is not now guaranteed; their sons will not fit the patterns of family life, they will not marry, they will fall foul of authority and both will be executed in early manhood. All Christians are called to the highest of joyful expectation in the purposes and promises of God, but often live to see hopes dashed and promises still unfulfilled. Yet Mary glimpsed the fulfilled promises when she saw her risen son (Acts 1:14).

MK

BARNABAS
(11 JUNE)

EUCHARIST

Job 29:11–16

Barnabas was a 'good man' (Acts 11:24). Job was another good man, honoured as an elder in his community for his good deeds. He expected to remain so honoured until his death, ripe in years and in his own bed. But he has been struck down. Despite his goodness and social righteousness, he is now despised and considered a sinner. Why else should he be so afflicted?

Job's goodness is that of the high-minded, socially conscious citizen; he takes his place at the city gate, the place of justice. He cares for the disadvantaged and the vulnerable and he tells us that he has been effective in this (v. 13). He has cared about righteousness and justice—in obedience to God, he has extended God's Kingdom.

But he is brought up sharply when his life does not proceed smoothly into his just reward. Bad things happen to good people. In this world, justice and reward are not guaranteed. There will be vindication one day, but meanwhile, 'He has told you, O mortal, what is good; and what does the Lord require of you but to do justice, and to love kindness, and to walk humbly with your God?' (Micah 6:8), whatever the outcome in this world.

Acts 11:19–30

Acts 4:36 tells us that Barnabas was a Jew, a Levite, and a Cypriot. It was the Cypriot Christian Jews who, in preaching to the Greeks of Antioch, were carrying on the revolution that had begun with Peter and Cornelius (v. 20). 'So then, God has granted even the Gentiles repentance unto life' (v. 18).

Antioch, a large and beautiful city with a cosmopolitan population, called the third city of the empire by Josephus, is the site for the first Christian church with both Jews and Gentiles. Barnabas sees the great number there who have turned to the Lord (v. 23). He is glad and, true to his name (Acts 4:36), encourages them. He then becomes another fruitful and Spirit-led evangelist, and again 'a great number' join the church (v. 24).

Barnabas then plays a crucial part in God's plan—he fetches Saul from Tarsus. Their teaching is an essential element in the growth to maturity of the young Church, a maturity which leads them to respond with generosity to the need of the Judean church (v. 29). The role of this 'good man' is to be an encourager, full of the Holy Spirit and faith, a gifted evangelist, a strategist and a maintainer of good relations between Jewish and Gentile Christians and churches.

John 15:12–17

Six billion people on one small planet and they all need love. This short reading requires that we stop and think what love means. Just to limit such research to the songs the world sings would give us an amazing amount of material. We are surrounded by the images of romantic love and sexual love, and our news is full of what happens when love is distorted, when people have never been loved, when there is hate.

Jesus told this intimate gathering of his closest friends that they must love one another and that the love they give each other should be sacrificial. They are not servants or employees in a relationship of orders given and obeyed, but friends who are loved, friends who share deep and intimate knowledge of each other, who are chosen as an adopted child is chosen to be loved, and chosen for work of privilege and honour. 1 Corinthians 13 defines Christian love. This kind of love, worked out in the Church in practical ways, could draw in many of those who live in a world where love so often fails.

Galatians 2:1–10

Barnabas accompanied Paul on missionary journeys, sharing in the dangers. He had encouraged and supported Paul on his first difficult return to Jerusalem after his conversion (Acts 11:30) and had brought him into the teaching ministry on his own initiative (Acts 11:25). He was an encourager. Paul is called to go to Jerusalem, to resolve the first great challenge to the gospel. Do Gentiles have to become Jews first? Even Barnabas succumbed to the tensions involved in this issue (v. 13).

Paul was an independent preacher of the gospel, but he was not a maverick who wished to carve out his own territory without reference to the Church as a whole. He impressed on the Galatians, who were divided on the issue of Jewish practice, that there was unity among the Church leaders; that he had debated the whole issue in Jerusalem and it had been settled. He demonstrated this unity by going as a team with Barnabas—a Jewish Christian—and the uncircumcised Titus. His team was a living example of the gospel of unity and freedom he was preaching. He demonstrated the truth he was defending. Barnabas took part in an enterprise that must have involved a great inner battle. When he first encouraged Paul, he could have had no idea where the Lord was leading him!

MK

BIRTH OF JOHN THE BAPTIST (24 JUNE)

EUCHARIST

Isaiah 40:1–11

Here is a banner headline of good news, a ringing royal decree for Israel from God (v. 9). Exile is over. For two generations, through most of the sixth century BC, many thousands of Jews lived as prisoners in Babylon, hundreds of miles from home. But after hardship came mercy. The long punishment ended (vv. 1–2). There would be a road home. God would lead his people across the dry wilderness, and the world would know his power (vv. 3–5).

God is both mighty and tender. Beside the frailty of human life and the passing splendour of our days, his promises endure (vv. 6–8). His word will achieve its purpose, his people will come home (cf. 55:10–13). The strong arm of God will deliver on his promise, as his gentle shepherd hands lead his people back to where they belong (vv. 10–11).

The New Testament likens John the Baptist to Isaiah's 'voice in the wilderness' (e.g. Luke 3:4–6). There are two links: his desert preaching prepared the way for Jesus (v. 3); then his message—carried forward by Jesus—was a word of restoration and return. God's might and tenderness, and the hope of a prodigal world coming home to God, are shown in the clearest light in the gospel of Christ.

Acts 13:14b–26

This reading sets John the Baptist at the hinge between Old Testament and New, the last link in a long chain of preparation, and the herald who launched the ministry of Jesus. The passage is an excerpt from a sermon to a Jewish synagogue congregation in Pisidia (central Turkey) (vv. 14–16). It is quite tightly argued, weaving together several themes and episodes from the Old Testament.

The first movement is historical, tracing Israel's journey from slavery to promised land, and the varied patterns of leadership that followed (vv. 17–21). The climax of this section is King David, who was—at least potentially—an ideal ruler, a king 'after God's own heart' (v. 22; cf. 1 Samuel 13:14).

Then there is a pivot from Old Testament to New. Jesus, born within the line of David (v. 23), has come as Israel's Saviour. The ancient ideals for leadership have come to fulfilment in him (vv. 32–33). The heritage and history are not abandoned, but their hopes are realized more profoundly and fully than was ever the case in earlier times (v. 39). That is good news indeed (v. 26).

John the Baptist launched this era of promise. He blazed a trail for Jesus, preaching the righteousness that Jesus would echo (v. 24), while pointing ahead to the 'one who would come after' (v. 25).

Galatians 3:23–29

This passage is about preparation and release. God's ancient law, observed by Israel for centuries before Christ, led the way towards his coming. It was a tutor, expressing God's love at second hand, as it were (v. 24). Yet it also restricted, it divided humanity, and seemed to exclude the Gentiles from the scope of God's grace.

The law was always meant to be temporary (vv. 19, 23). Its job was done with the coming of Christ. He was born within its rule (4:4), his teaching fulfilled its best intentions (5:14), and his new life burst its tight boundaries (v. 26). God's promise to Abraham, given long before the law (v. 17), now came alive through Abraham's 'seed' and heir Jesus Christ (v. 16). All the nations would find blessing (Genesis 12:3), through what God had begun in Abraham and completed in Jesus.

So the Christian gospel, grasped in faith (vv. 25–26) and sealed in baptism (v. 27), would extend God's family. People of all races would be called his children (v. 26) through their belief in Jesus Christ. The fault-lines of race, class and gender would not divide this new family, for its identity and unity are formed in the purpose and promise of God (v. 28–29). This is still the Church's charter, made possible by the cross of Christ (vv. 13–14) and activated among us by the Holy Spirit (4:6).

Luke 1:57–66, 80

Neighbours and relatives are usually glad to celebrate a birth (v. 58). But the arrival of this child gave people even more to talk about than usual (vv. 65–66). The great age of the parents, too old—you would think—to start a family (1:7), would surely arouse comment. The unusual name, not shared by anyone in the extended family, seemed odd to some (v. 61), but the parents insisted (vv. 60, 63). The name John (Hebrew *Johanan*), chosen months before, means 'God has been gracious'. For God had answered the ageing couple's longing for a child (1:13), and Israel's desperate prayer for new hope and promise (vv. 68, 72; cf. 2:25, 38). A prophet child was born (v. 76).

The father had plenty to shout about. He had lost his voice through unbelief (1:20). But the months of silence had quickened his faith. When he wrote down the name the angel had given (v. 63), then praise flowed free. His child would be the roadmaker for God (v. 76).

For another child was stirring in the womb (1:31), the Saviour and leader for whom Israel had waited. John would prepare his way, by his own bold and costly ministry. So before very long John went into the desert (v. 80). A prophet must learn to live alone. God wanted time and seclusion, to prepare this young man for the work ahead.

JP

PETER AND PAUL
(29 JUNE)

EUCHARIST

Zechariah 4:1–6a, 10b–14

The lampstand, with seven lamps and each lamp with seven lips (v. 2), sheds light brightly and widely. It represents the seeing eye of God, reaching across the world (v. 10). All human life is lived within his view, and his sight is like a lamp. To be seen by God gives dignity and solemnity to our days and deeds. There is a kind of glory in the light of God's eye.

Two olive trees stand right and left of the lampstand (vv. 3, 11), not for decoration, but to fuel the lamps. Oil pours out through golden pipes (v. 12). These are two anointed servants of God (v. 14). Zechariah probably meant Joshua and Zerubbabel, Israel's spiritual leaders of his time (3:6–9; 4:6–10), but this image of two witnesses is taken up elsewhere (Revelation 11:3–4). In the context of today's festival, we think of Peter and Paul, Christ's great apostles to the Jews and to the Gentiles. The apostles' message fuels the Church's witness, and the Church serves as God's lampstand in the earth (Revelation 1:20), called to radiate his truth and love. Ultimately the light is Christ's (John 8:12), yet the Church must let it shine (Matthew 5:16). As a lampstand stood in Israel's ancient temple, so the Church now lights the holy place that is God's world.

Acts 12:1–11

The word of God is not bound (2 Timothy 2:9)—but the people who believe and obey it have often had to suffer threats to their liberty, and sometimes to their lives. Here the main player is Herod Agrippa I, who ruled Palestine from AD41 to 44. He wanted to advance his public image (vv. 3, 20–23), and if persecuting the Church would help, so much the better. He targeted the leaders of the Jerusalem church, killing James son of Zebedee (vv. 1–2) and arresting Peter, whom he held in prison for a while—an execution during the sacred Passover season might have caused undue disturbance (v. 3).

Other forces, however, were at work: the church was praying (vv. 5, 12). We have no precise understanding of the chemistry of prayer, but the Christians who prayed that night surely discovered fresh confidence that it works. God had indeed answered. A shaft of joyous amazement punctured the darkness, prompting Rhoda's surprised absentmindedness, and the group's reaction—'He can't have escaped. We've been praying for him' (vv. 12–16).

Peter moved on to a safer place (v. 17), and a wider mission (v. 19). Chains, gates and guards had not held him (vv. 6–11). The memory of that night would help him to meet suffering—which would surely come again— in faith and hope (1 Peter 4:12–19).

2 Timothy 4:6–8, 17–18

This is Paul's view from prison (2:9), looking back at his life's work, forward across the threshold of death, and upwards to God. The whole letter is very practical and positive in outlook and in the advice it gives. So the final verses are not mere sentiment or nostalgia, but an honest appraisal of a life lived in the presence of God.

Paul probably expects execution. He looks on his coming death as a 'libation' (v. 6), the pouring out of his life-blood as an offering to God, to complete the sacrificial service of his days. He has kept going like a long-distance runner, right to the finish line. He has held the faith steadily in his heart and in his preaching to others (v. 7; cf. 1 Corinthians 9:26–27). Now the long race is ended, and the faith he has held still holds him.

So he looks upward to God, and forward to the final triumph of Jesus Christ (v. 8), with hope and confidence and joy. His recent legal defence was a lonely business (v. 16), but he was able to testify to the gospel and to trust God for the outcome (v. 17). When death eventually comes, he will not be afraid. God's strong hands will still be there, to bring him through to glory beyond (v. 18).

Matthew 16:13–19

The Church stands by its faith when it recognizes and trusts God's unique saving presence in Jesus. For that is what it means to say, 'You are the Messiah, the Son of the Living God' (vv. 15–16). To affirm this, amid the myriad opinions of earth (vv. 13–14), is a gift from God (v. 17).

The passage is full of resonances, both in scripture and word-play.

- The name Peter—or a word very like it—means 'rock'. Like Abraham, the first believer of a former era (Isaiah 51:1–2), Peter is the rock that founds the Church.
- God's ancient promise to David spoke of an enduring royal household (2 Samuel 7:13, 16). So Christ's Church will be a house and kingdom built to last.
- Peter—and the leaders who come after him—must be faithful stewards of Christ's message and people (v. 19; cf. Isaiah 22:22).

The Church will be battered, but never broken (v. 18). The powers of evil will not hem it in, and the Church itself will open doors of life to many, through the good news (cf. Acts 15:7). The gospel will open and shut, 'binding and loosing', as it shapes and limits the life of God's people (v. 19). And it started when Peter said, 'You are the Christ.'

JP

PETER *alone*
(29 JUNE)

EUCHARIST

Ezekiel 3:22–27

These two readings especially for Peter alone connect through the theme of silence—arising from hardship and opposition.

This passage recalls Ezekiel's earlier vision (1:1—2:7). Again there is no promise of instant success, only of restriction and difficulty. He would have to act out the tragedy that beset his nation (4:1–8), and bear in his own soul their hard resistance to the word that he brought (2:6).

Jerusalem was under siege, and many Jewish people were confined in exile. Ezekiel too would shut himself in, and bind himself with harsh cords (vv. 24–25; cf. 4:1–8). His own bitter silence would one day echo his people's sorrow (v. 26; cf. 24:15–27).

These verses seem also to outline a call experience, a symbolic cameo of Ezekiel's own ministry. The walls that hemmed him in (v. 24) and the silence that held him fast (v. 26) were signs, a warning that his word would have no free course among the people. In time God would move him to speak, but even then the response would only be patchy (v. 27).

Yet the vision of God's glory, utterly overpowering at first (v. 23), did not paralyse him. It prepared him to know that however intimidating his ministry might be, however exhausting the people's stubbornness, however encompassing the gloom of their unbelief, he was supported by light and power from above and beyond himself.

1 Peter 2:19–25

Christians who form a minority in society may encounter suspicion and even ill-treatment (2:12). They need an outward calm, and deep inner strength. This first-century passage speaks to Christian slaves—who would be especially vulnerable—about the hardships that would come their way (v. 18). Peter is not supporting slavery, but offering positive Christian advice about survival under pressure.

Obedience is important (v. 18), and honesty (3:13). Do not ask for trouble, and avoid wrongdoing (v. 19). But if ill-treatment comes anyway, there is no shame in it; it is an honourable pattern, set for the Christian by the suffering of Jesus Christ (vv. 20–21).

411

For the cross speaks to the Christian in two ways. It is a majestic example of patience and faith under appalling hardship, of silence that speaks more powerfully than any words (vv. 22–23). It is also 'for you' (v. 21), the pardoning of our sins, wholeness for broken lives, homecoming for the lost (vv. 24–25). A church that trusts in Christ's salvation need not be afraid to live by his example. Those who feel the weight of Christ's cross will know too its grace and power.

Persecution is not just a fact of history. Some Christians still endure it. They deserve our care, prayers, and—where we can—active help.

JP

THOMAS
(3 JULY)

EUCHARIST

Habakkuk 2:1–4

The apostle Thomas has become an unofficial patron saint for all doubting Christians. He manages to remain faithful to his Lord, through a difficult period of uncertainty and disappointment. When we cannot trace God's purpose or presence in our own situation, it is hard to hang on to faith. Yet even under strain, faith makes a difference—as this Old Testament passage shows.

Habakkuk had heard of the Chaldean army (1:6–11). They were cruel and strong. No one could stand in their way. His own Jewish people were under threat. Was this really the judgment of God? Habakkuk burst out in complaint and distress (1:13–17). Then he waited for God's answer (2:1).

In time, through vigilance and patient prayer, a new understanding became clear. Habakkuk was to write a vision, clearly enough to be read at a glance (v. 2). The vision, graphically portrayed in chapter 3, outlined God's final victory. God's glory, judgment and triumph will one day be seen. 'The earth will be filled with the knowledge of the glory of the Lord, as the waters cover the sea' (2:14).

Meanwhile the present crisis was a time for faith, for hanging on to God (v. 4). When we see no obvious sign of God's active presence, faith is the stubbornness that will not sink into unbelief or despair. To maintain this faith is to sustain inner life, to sharpen vision, and to foster hope. Dogged obedience often leads to clearer understanding—as Thomas discovered (John 11:16; 20:28).

Ephesians 2:19–22

Several images for the Church are here, portraying different aspects of the life God gives. The fragile faith of Thomas and his fellow apostles brought an expanding, solid and lively fellowship into being.

- **Belonging** (v. 19). The 'strangers and aliens' are surely this letter's Gentile readers, who had not known the special stream of God's grace that flowed in Israel's life (v. 12). But now Christ has included them (v. 13). They belong to God's holy fellowship, as citizens belong to their nation. For Israel, in particular, the nation is thought of as one great family. Christians are part of God's family, members of his household.
- **Building** (vv. 20–22). The language of 'household' develops into the idea of house-building. The Church is like a temple, a dwelling for God, formed by the living stones that are human lives. Jesus Christ is the base-stone, the rock on whom the whole structure rests. (The possible alternative 'corner-stone' may mean the top-stone of an arch—the highest honour belongs to Jesus. But probably 'base-stone' makes better sense.) The leaders of the first generation form the first layer of stones, around and upon that base. Thomas and those with him, so uncertain to start with, have laid a strong foundation for the Church to come.
- **Biology** (v. 21). The building grows. It is alive. No static image is wholly sufficient. The language of organic, animated life is needed, to describe the Christian fellowship where God makes his home.

John 20:24–29

Thomas speaks three times in John's Gospel. At 11:16 he commits himself to follow Jesus, while muttering darkly that this journey to Jerusalem will surely be the death of them all. He seems to have missed what Jesus said about raising Lazarus (11:11–15). At 14:5 he asks about the route Jesus is taking, again missing the thrust of Jesus' words, yet surely wanting to follow and struggling to understand. He does not easily think in a religious way. The language of symbol and prophecy is not his kind of speech. He wants a reality he can see and touch.

Then we come to chapter 20. Thomas cannot grasp what his friends tell him. What do they mean? His Lord is dead. He knew it would happen. He needs something more solid than a story to lift him out of his grief.

Then Jesus does meet Thomas, in a way that he can understand, a resurrection appearance just for him. Suddenly Thomas has no need to touch (vv. 27–28). He has struggled to understand, and now he worships Jesus—directly, simply and profoundly (v. 28). The person who believes quickly and easily may not be the one to whom faith comes most surely and deeply. (See the Second Sunday of Easter 2, Year B, for further comment.)

JP

MARY MAGDALENE
(22 JULY)

EUCHARIST

Song of Solomon 3:1–4

The Bible has so many different modes, genres and literary forms. Doctrine, propositional truth, theological treatise, historical narrative, worship songs, pithy aphorisms, story and parable all weave together to give us the truth of God. But here in the middle of it all there is a book which is a love song, even perhaps a description of sexual intercourse. No mention of God, no mention of marriage or social obligation, just human sexual love. Here is the drive and urge we share with most of the animal kingdom; the urge that leads to the greatest delight and self-sacrifice and to the worst exploitation and abuse.

We should delight in the poetry, in the rich imagery, in the passion of this book, encouraging Christians to be positive and open about this gift from God. But we should also protect and respect its power and its vulnerability. The fall has distorted all God's gifts, all his world, all his creatures, and unless we are aware of that, aware of the need to seek forgiveness and his redeeming love even in our most passionate loves, we too shall be those who look 'for the one my heart loves' but do not find.

2 Corinthians 5:14–17

Christ's love compels us, urges us on. Mary Magdalene's brief and incomplete story, as told in the Gospels, illustrates the compulsion of love. She stands beneath the cross and endures the crucifixion (Matthew 27:55) and then experiences her moment of despair at the empty tomb (John 20:1, 11), compelled to do so by her love and gratitude for the healing love of Jesus. After the resurrection she must have been part of the group that experienced the coming of the Holy Spirit in power, and then may have spent the rest of her life serving, witnessing and loving because she was compelled to do so.

Mary Magdalene was a new creation (v. 17). We do not know what she had been delivered from, whether it was a physical, mental or moral problem, but the implication is that she was seriously in need of healing. Now 'in Christ' (v. 17), the old having gone, having died to the past (v. 14), with a radically changed view of the world (v. 16), Mary was indeed a new creation compelled by love. This is a description of wholehearted and radical discipleship. There is no compromise; every perspective has to change. Are we new creations, compelled by love?

John 20:1–2, 11–18

Mary Magdalene (from Magdala in Galilee?) appears first in Luke 8:2, where she travels with Jesus and his other followers. She had been delivered from seven demons, information repeated in Mark 16:9. Apart from this reference, she appears only at the crucifixion (Matthew 27:55) and the resurrection. There are no grounds for identifying her with any other women in the Gospel accounts.

The devotion and dutiful love of Mary Magdalene and the other women who waited and watched by the cross, and then waited for the end of the Sabbath so that they could pay their last acts of love to their Lord, shine out in the Passion narratives. How appropriate that they are the first to meet the risen Lord!

The power and emotional impact of this encounter between Mary and the Lord begins with the question, 'Why are you crying?' (v. 13). So often Jesus asks questions rather than making statements or giving information. He gives her opportunity to explain and time to express her love, that offers even then to retrieve the dead body and return it to the tomb. In the voicing of her name she recognizes him, and then, after he gently tells her that their relationship has changed, she receives the commission to tell the disciples. A woman is the first witness.

MK

JAMES
(25 JULY)

EUCHARIST

Jeremiah 45:1–5

Baruch had a very hard time. He was Jeremiah's scribe, and it is worth reading chapter 36 to understand the difficult job he had and the risks he took in being a faithful disciple. In this little interlude, Jeremiah responds to Baruch's heartfelt groaning at being caught up in sorrow and pain directly from God. Jeremiah emphasizes that what he has to say comes from the Lord. They are both caught up in the working out of God's punishment and judgment on the people of Israel; they cannot escape that, but God will protect Baruch from untimely death.

The Bible, as well as subsequent Christian history, is full of examples of faithful disciples who have very difficult and unrewarded lives. There is no guarantee of earned comfort and prizes. The pressures may have become unendurable for Baruch, but he shares Jeremiah's vocation of suffering with the people, even as he warns them of their disobedience and idolatry. Paul said of the servants of Christ that 'it is required that those who have been given a trust must prove faithful' (1 Corinthians 4:2) and for Baruch, James and countless others, we can add, faithful whatever the cost.

Acts 11:27—12:2

Against the background of the spreading gospel and growing Church, we have the second wave of persecution, the first having scattered the Christians to all corners so that new churches sprang up (Acts 8:1). Now, the unity of believers and their love for each other sends support back to the Judean church (v. 29). ('From each according to his ability, to each according to his need', a slogan from the writings of Karl Marx, was probably taken from Acts!)

'King' Herod, a title given to him by Caligula, is the nephew of the Herod who tried Jesus. Insecure in his authority both with the Jews and the Romans, he is anxious to preserve the peace to keep in with Rome, and to persecute the Christians to keep in with the Jews. So James, the son of Zebedee, the fisherman from Galilee, is killed (v. 2). Those who remembered Jesus' words, 'You will indeed drink from my cup' (Matthew 20:23) must have realized afresh that their lives were in his hands. Stephen is already dead, but Peter is miraculously rescued. The death of those who seem to have key jobs to do, great gifts to contribute, can raise many questions about the sovereignty and plans of God.

Matthew 20:20–28

A mother's ambition leads to some radical and subversive teaching on social status. The desire to do well and to achieve necessarily requires someone else to have done less well or to have failed. All human relations, from family through church to government and global institutions, have leaders, an ordering which puts someone on top—bosses, generals, kings, bishops. It is difficult to imagine a world where this does not happen. But the Church is called by her Lord to attempt to grapple with the implications of this passage: how to be servants, even when we are called to lead.

The implication of this request is that James and John, or at least their mother, did not want any of their fellow disciples to have the best seats in heaven, although they may not have thought of it like this. Their willingness to 'drink the cup' did not arise out of obedient discipleship, but out of a desire to get to the top.

Their mother kneels before the Lord and asks for seats in heaven for her sons. In a way she is praying in faith, sure that he can give her anything. It is interesting that he does not immediately deny her request. He answers with firmness but gentleness, helping her to understand the way it will be, and he only rebukes the disciples.

2 Corinthians 4:7–15

In verses 1 and 16, Paul uses the phrase, 'We do not lose heart'. We may be weak jars of clay (v. 7), but we do not lose heart, because our weakness makes the Lord's power more apparent. Christians may suffer any number of troubles, but they do not lose heart. The idea behind verse 10 is that those who belong to Jesus bear in their own lives his dying, which is both part of the world of pain and suffering and its cure. But they also carry his risen life, because his life and death are inextricably linked. The treasure is the light of the knowledge of the glory of God in the face of Christ (v. 6).

There is a note of triumph in these verses, but not the triumphalism that ignores injustice and suffering. Paul's pairs of contrasts—hard pressed but not crushed, and so on—arise out of some pretty bad experiences, which he lists in 2 Corinthians 11:23–28. There are two ways by which the Christian can live through such blows. First, 'these light and momentary troubles' (v. 17) are 'achieving an eternal glory that far outweighs them all'. Second, Christians are called not just to endure and wait for eternity, but also to mitigate the effects of evil, to fight for justice and bring relief for suffering.

MK

THE TRANSFIGURATION
(6 AUGUST)

EUCHARIST

Daniel 7:9–10, 13–14

The striking images of Daniel's vision provide part of the Old Testament background to the transfiguration of Jesus.

Two figures appear in this passage. First, the Ancient of Days (vv. 9–10) represents God himself, ruling and judging in majesty. Dazzling white clothing (v. 9) is a characteristic of heavenly figures in scripture, so this feature of the transfigured Jesus would have brought to mind straight away references like Daniel 7, and affirmed Jesus' unique relationship with God.

The second figure (vv. 13–14) is 'one like a son of man', or 'like a human being', who is given authority, glory and everlasting power. The identity of this figure is unclear but the crucial point is that he brings God's justice to earth, decisively and for ever. So the passage would have provided the persecuted Jews for whom Daniel was written with encouragement in their suffering and hope for the future.

These links are part of the huge, complex mosaic of Old Testament prophecy which finds fulfilment in Jesus. Jesus is God's definitive response to the hopes and fears of his people over previous centuries. Keeping that perspective is vital if we are to grasp fully and communicate effectively the way Jesus meets needs today.

2 Peter 1:16–19

2 Peter was written in response to false teaching which doubted the reality of God's promise to bring about a new age of peace and justice, and which also doubted the second coming of Jesus (the *parousia*). The transfiguration is one of the key planks in the letter's defence of the *parousia*.

The accounts of the transfiguration are reliable, not clever inventions (v. 16). The glory given to Jesus on the mountain is therefore a reality, which will be seen definitively by everyone when he returns. The phrasing given here of God's statement from heaven echoes Psalm 2:6–7, and therefore makes clear that Jesus is the one appointed by God to bring in his Kingdom, a task he will finally fulfil at the *parousia*.

Doubts about the *parousia* are still a problem today, almost two thousand years after the ascension of Christ. Seeing the transfiguration of Jesus in the context not only of the past but also of the future sharpens its relevance for the present. The glory of Jesus, momentarily revealed on the mountain, is still a hidden reality until his return. Meanwhile, the transfiguration gives us evidence for hope in the saving power of God, past, present and future.

Luke 9:28–36

The transfiguration of Jesus gives us clear pointers to his identity, each of which are still central today in our relationship with him.

First, he is the royal Son of God. His sonship is explicitly affirmed by God's voice (v. 35), and his dazzling appearance reveals his heavenly origin (see the notes on Daniel 7 above). So he is revealed as the one to whom our loyalty and worship are due.

Second, he is the chosen one of God (v. 35), the one anointed by God to save his people. More specifically, the language recalls the description of the Servant in Isaiah 42:1. The Servant in Isaiah is also chosen by God to bring salvation, but is humiliated before his final vindication. There is a link here to Jesus' coming death, to which he has just referred in 9:22. Jesus is revealed as the one who has given himself for us and saved us.

Third, Jesus is the prophet of God. The presence of Elijah the prophet witnesses to the superiority of Jesus; the voice from the cloud commands the disciples to listen to Jesus. He is revealed as the one who brings the message of God which is to be obeyed.

MG

THE BLESSED VIRGIN MARY
(15 AUGUST)

EUCHARIST

Isaiah 61:10–11

These two verses are a description of the characteristics of God's action from two points of view, that of the one who experiences that action personally (v. 10), and that of those who see that action from the outside (v. 11). In both cases, it consists of a display of divine righteousness, which leads humans to respond with praise. Where God declares an individual right-eous, which could involve forgiving sin or dispensing justice or blessing that person in some other way, that person will be moved to praise God (v. 10).

Where, too, the world sees the righteous hand of God at work, including in the lives of other people, this will elicit praise from all those who see it for what it is (v. 11).

Both of these aspects can be applied to the story of Mary, the mother of Jesus. God's choice of her to bear a unique Son is, first of all, a personal declaration to her that she is righteous in the eyes of God, a declaration that moves her to a response of praise as seen in the Magnificat (Luke 1:46–55). But it is also a declaration to the world of God's righteousness in providing a Saviour, and as such it will cause the whole world to respond with praise.

Revelation 11:19—12:6, 10

This curious, dream-like picture is part of a symbolic representation of the battle between good and evil, in which, although the power of evil is great and terrifying, it is shown as being unable to defeat the designs of the power of good. Just before the picture begins, the ark of the covenant is seen in heaven, accompanied by storm phenomena (11:19). For the people of Israel, the ark and the storm were symbols of God's presence, and so here they are a reassurance of the presence and power of God throughout what follows. The figure of the woman (12:1) represents the nation of Israel, her child (12:5) is the Messiah, and the dragon (12:3–4) represents the powers of evil and chaos which threaten to destroy the Messiah but which are thwarted by God. Christ is snatched up to heaven out of the clutches of the dragon (death) to become king of the universe (12:5). This seals the fate of the power of evil, and although there is still a battle to be fought, it is no surprise to hear the subsequent declaration of victory for God and Christ (12:10). The message: victory is not instantaneous but, by the power of God in Christ, it is assured.

Galatians 4:4–7

Paul's meditations on the nature of salvation in Christ here have a double thrust. The first is the sense of the maturing of God's plans in God's own time (v. 4). The arrival of Christ on the world scene was no mere haphazard accident, but the result of long foreknowledge, careful planning and complete control by the ruler of the universe. The second aspect is how this transformation of human nature occurred: God's son became as humans were, sharing in the relationships of a human family, so that humans could share the relationship he shares with God (vv. 4–5). Indeed, so human was God's son that he took the normal route into life that all humans take: he was born of a woman (v. 4), with all that that implies about helplessness and dependence.

The net result is that the humanity of human beings who believe in him is changed for ever, and they can now count themselves children of God and therefore heirs of everything that God has to give them (v. 7). Proof of their new status is that they are enabled to call God 'Father' in a way that is no mere metaphor, but is the spirit of God-in-Christ within them, calling out to his divine Father (v. 6).

Luke 1:46–55

Mary's song of joy gives classic expression to many of the major themes of the gospel message. The song is dominated by the concept of a God who defies all worldly expectations by honouring the poor and humbling the rich (vv. 48, 51–53). Normally the poor and helpless would be seen as cursed by God, and the rich and powerful as enjoying God's favour. However, there was another way of thinking that regarded the poor as favoured by God, because in the absence of human support they were forced to rely on divine power. Certainly the emphasis in Mary's song is entirely on the work of God's power, which is shown particularly brightly when it exalts the humble who fear God (vv. 48, 50) and shatters the illusion of security surrounding the rich and powerful who trust in themselves (v. 51).

The song ends on the theme of God's faithfulness as displayed in remembrance of the promises to Abraham (vv. 54–55). In this way, the miraculous conception in the womb of a humble woman is affirmed as part of God's ongoing plan of salvation through the nation of Israel. This unique event is not a one-off, but no more than we would expect from a God of such overwhelming grace!

DR

BARTHOLOMEW
(24 AUGUST)

EUCHARIST

Isaiah 43:8–13

Bartholomew was with Jesus, as one of the Twelve (Mark 3:18). Afterwards, by all accounts, he travelled north and east, spreading the faith and eventually suffering martyrdom for his Lord. Some records suggest that he died in Armenia, which later became (in AD301) the first nation publicly to adopt the Christian faith.

This Old Testament reading calls the nations of the world to hear about God, who would rescue Israel from exile and plant her back in her own land (vv. 1–7). That would be a sign for the world, that Israel's God was alive and at work. Let the nations gather and recognize that they had not realized the reach of God's love (v. 9). For the Jewish people—who had seemed blind and deaf (v. 8; cf. 42:18–20)—will be able to witness for God: that no other god compares with him (v. 10), saves like him (v. 11), speaks as he does (v. 12), or protects with his strength and consistency of purpose (v. 13).

This missionary message takes new shape in New Testament times. In the life, death and resurrection of Jesus, God shows with fresh and startling clarity how he can speak, save and restore. This is the gospel Bartholomew took, to open the eyes and ears of the whole world.

Acts 5:12–16

In the early days after the ascension, Jesus' apostles were an influential group in Jerusalem. They had experienced suspicion and opposition from the Jewish leaders (4:1–3), but among the bulk of the population their reputation was growing. They gathered in Solomon's Porch, on the outer edge of the temple complex, a place where Jesus himself had taught (John 10:23). This central site was accessible to pilgrims and to local people, but was also a place where the apostles would attract further unwelcome attention before long (5:17–18). Sometimes there is a cost in making the gospel known, a cost which the Church is better to face than to avoid.

Perhaps the earlier incident involving Ananias and Sapphira (5:1–11) and, more importantly and consistently, the powerful healing ministry, created an aura of awe around the apostolic group. Outsiders took them seriously, and either kept their distance (v. 13) or drew near to listen and believe (v. 14). Similarly today, the Church's practical care for needy and hurting neighbours will regularly make a public impact. A church that is united in itself and committed to loving service (v. 12) is always likely to draw respect (v. 13) and to win new believers for Christ (v. 14).

1 Corinthians 4:9–15

Who would be an apostle of Christ? Paul's words have a sarcastic edge, as he writes to the proud members of the Corinthian church. The circumstances of his ministry are so very different to theirs. People look on him as a hopeless wretch, like a criminal going to an early death (v. 9), mere human rubbish (v. 13). His public image is that of a fool, a man of no power in the world (v. 10). He is destitute, despised, and often desperately poor (v. 11). Preaching is no leisurely life; the time it takes must be squeezed from a routine of subsistence manual labour (v. 12).

Yet Christ's apostles have an inner toughness. They can face ill-treatment with patience and good cheer (vv. 12–13). There is a supernatural life in them, the life of Jesus Christ, and their business is to pass this life on. Their job satisfaction is in their spiritual children, the people who have been won to faith through their work (vv. 14–15). The Corinthians should take this paradoxical sort of Christianity seriously—for they owe their lives to it (vv. 16–18).

To represent Jesus Christ in the world—as every Christian does—may still be a rough ride. But the love of Christ, seeping out from battered lives, remains as contagious as ever.

Luke 22:24–30

There is no great kudos, no high status to be found in following Jesus. Patterns and hierarchies learned from royal courts, where greatness is shown in command and control, and rulers draw the fawning praise of the ruled, have no place in the Christian community. This is an upside-down kingdom. Importance is measured differently here. There is no special merit in seniority: every disciple must be like an apprentice, glad to do the task at hand and to learn through doing it. As to leadership, if our contribution is to count, we should be like a domestic servant, content to serve others humbly and patiently, without attracting attention to ourselves (vv. 25–26). Good Christian leaders don't mind getting dirty fingernails.

For this is the last supper and Jesus is himself a servant (v. 27). He has just washed his friends' feet at the table (John 13), and tomorrow he must be the Servant supreme, suffering to make others whole. The disciples have followed him practically into the shadow of the cross (v. 28). They have shared his troubles—and there will be more suffering ahead—but they will celebrate with him too (v. 29). Their costly service is no dead-end street. This is the measure by which the world will be judged (v. 30; cf. 1 Corinthians 6:2).

JP

HOLY CROSS DAY
(14 SEPTEMBER)

EUCHARIST

Numbers 21:4–9

This strange story is taken up in John 3 as a sort of blueprint, an early sketch of the cross of Jesus Christ. The obvious point of comparison is that both the bronze serpent (v. 9) and the crucified Jesus were raised up on a stake. In both situations there is healing from sin, or from its consequences (v. 7; cf. John 1:29). In each case, salvation comes through a kind of faith, the helpless look of hope and trust (vv. 8–9; John 3:15).

Perhaps there is a deeper likeness to the story of Jesus. The antidote against the snakes' venom is actually a copy of the source of the trouble. The serpent was an unclean creature for the Jews (Leviticus 11:41–42); in the creation story it represents the evil and deceit at large in the world (Genesis 3). So Moses' bronze serpent is a picture of evil, identified with the cause of the very suffering that it heals. This corresponds to the biblical description of Jesus, as sent 'in the likeness of sinful flesh, and to deal with sin' (Romans 8:3). Degraded by the humiliation and misery of the cross, 'made... sin who knew no sin' (2 Corinthians 5:21), he draws the poison of sin and death. 'Lifted up' to die, he lifts his people into eternal life.

Philippians 2:6–11

The supreme example of humble service, and pattern for all our Christian living (v. 5), is the crucified Christ. Spanning heaven and earth, linking glory and suffering, showing royal dignity in the obedience of a slave, and returning like a parabola to the heights, the path taken by Jesus Christ invites our worship and awe.

'Though he was in the form of God' (v. 6), the divine nature in Jesus expressed itself in love. He reached out to creation, took our nature, and died our death—the despised and lingering death of a slave (vv. 7–8). Yet this 'emptying' (v. 7) was not an abandonment of his bond with God, but a profound and visible sign of God's gracious care.

'Therefore' (v. 9) God raised Jesus up. He is drawn back into the glory and honour that belong to God alone (v. 10; cf. Isaiah 45:23). The praise of all creation honours what he has done. God's love has touched earth in the humanity and humility of Jesus. So now the sacrificial self-giving of Jesus is the lifeblood of the Church, the template and inspiration for our worship and work. His distinctive example, of majesty taking flesh, and God nailed to a tree, gives shape and meaning to all our service.

John 3:13–17

This is the climax of Jesus' conversation with the Pharisee Nicodemus. The cryptic exchanges of the early verses are over. Jesus is speaking freely, of the reasons for his coming and the scope of his ministry.

- **He comes as revealer** (v. 13). He brings the life of heaven among us, and comes to teach us about things we cannot see for ourselves (v. 11).
- **He comes as life-giver** (vv. 14–15). This man of heaven is 'lifted up', like the bronze serpent of Numbers 21. Jesus will be raised up on the cross—apparently part-way to heaven, yet representing all that is ugly and wretched on earth—that many may find healing and wholeness through him.
- **He comes as God's love-gift** (vv. 16–17). As the cross exposes human sin, it displays too the greater reality that is God's love. Here is the heart, the fulcrum, of a generous and holy purpose. Human life turned away from God will surely sour and shrivel. Yet the life that Jesus Christ offers is whole and firm, fresh with the clean air of heaven, laden with love, and reaching past death into eternity.

Jesus came to draw people to God (12:32). He died our death that we may live his life.

JP

MATTHEW
(21 SEPTEMBER)

EUCHARIST

Proverbs 3:13–18

God's wisdom does not simply displace 'worldly' wisdom, but contains two important ambiguities.

First, there is an ambiguity of **content**. God's wisdom appears to be very different from the world's (1 Corinthians 1:17–25), not always 'deep' and esoteric, but embracing some basic disciplines (see v. 9). Yet parts of

Proverbs are indistinguishable from the 'secular' wisdom of the day, and the text often appeals to enlightened self-interest—this passage is hardly a call to asceticism! God's apparently foolish wisdom is not completely alien—neither is it the same as incompetence! It does make sense, but it is a sense that requires humility and realism to grasp. The distinction between the wise and the fool is not based on intellectual ability or social status, but on readiness to listen (cf. Psalm 53:1).

Second, there is an ambiguity of **consequence**. Riches are promised (v. 16)—but no, something far better than riches (v. 14). Wisdom gives what we desire—no, something much better than we can even imagine desiring (v. 15). God is neither tyrant nor slave. He longs to fulfil our desires (Psalm 37:4) but will not satisfy our greed for 'prosperity'. God's wisdom must shape our desires at least as much as it satisfies them—what wise parent simply gives what a child wants?

Ultimately the wisdom of God is found both in the liberating power and the humble self-giving of Jesus.

2 Corinthians 4:1–6

In what is perhaps Paul's most personal disclosure of himself and his ministry, he sets out some of the paradoxes of Christian ministry.

There is both **discouragement** and **affirmation** (v. 1). The discouragement comes from failure certainly, but here most pointedly from opposition, and that from his fellow Jews whom he most longs to see come to Christ (Romans 9:3, 10:1). But God's affirmation ('by God's mercy') is fundamental to Paul's work.

There is both **freedom** and **constraint** (v. 2). Whilst Paul revels in the freedom he has in Christ (Galatians 5:1), he will not practise cunning (literally 'do everything')—there are limits imposed by the responsibility he has, the limits of integrity.

There is the reality of **failure** even for Paul (v. 3) in the battle with spiritual forces of darkness. Yet there is also the **joy** of being agents releasing the light of God's creative power (v. 6, 2 Corinthians 5:17) into others' lives.

Finally, there is both **ignominy** and **glory**. The ignominy of being the slave of others for the sake of making Jesus known (v. 5; cf. John 3:30) involved being criticized, taken advantage of and ignored. But there was also glory (v. 6)—the weight, character and dynamic presence of God as revealed in Christ, the very image of God (v. 4).

Matthew 9:9–13

There is no reason to suppose that this was the first time that Matthew (Levi, Mark 2:14, Luke 5:27) had heard of or met Jesus. But now he hears the call to discipleship, and he has seen enough to respond without hesitation.

On tax collectors and sinners (v. 10), see comment on Luke 15, the Gospel reading for Proper 19, Year C. In the days before fast food and public restaurants, eating with someone was a significant social act—it showed friendship or common cause (see 1 Corinthians 5:11). The act of reclining around a low table, rather than sitting on chairs, enacted this intimacy.

The Pharisees cannot bring themselves to quiz Jesus in person about the company he keeps (v. 11); but perhaps the disciples were asking themselves the same question, for it comes to Jesus (v. 12). Jesus quotes Hosea 6:6 in Greek (v. 13); the Hebrew has 'loving faithfulness' (*hesed*). But the two ideas are not so far apart. As we love God, we reflect his mercy to others.

Jesus exercises *hospital*-ity: the place of welcome he offers is the doctor's waiting room as much as it is a seat at the dinner table (v. 12). Jesus loves us and accepts us as we are, but he loves us too much to leave us as we are. Unlike the Pharisees, who fear being made unclean by associating with the unclean, Jesus brings holiness to the unholy—it is his holiness rather than their uncleanness that is the more infectious. If we are to share this ministry of Jesus, we too need to be among the unclean with the infectious holiness of God's mercy.

IP

MICHAEL AND ALL ANGELS
(29 SEPTEMBER)

EUCHARIST

Genesis 28:10–17

This passage highlights the transformations brought about by encounter with God.

There is transformation of **place**. Jacob is on the run, fleeing from his brother's wrath (27:43). The lonely fugitive is in between his threatened home and his place of refuge. But the touch of God makes this place holy (v. 17). The presence of God's messengers show that heaven has to do with earth, and that Jacob's place is not as desolate as he thought.

Second, there is a transformation of **person**. Jacob has got where he is by trickery (of which there is still more than a trace: 'If God...' v. 20). But God has attached himself to Jacob, regardless of his deceit, and Lord in spite of it. The promise of 'God with us' begins a process of change that is not complete until his later encounter in chapter 32.

Third, there is a transformation of **purpose**. The thin assurance of another person (vv. 3–4) is superseded by the substantial promise of God—his gracious commitment to fulfil his purposes in Jacob (v. 15, cf. Philippians 1:6). Such hope is the bedrock of personal security in the face of an uncertain future.

Revelation 12:7–12

The figure of Michael here acts out Christ's victory over Satan won on the cross—verses 7–12 retell in Jewish terms what is alluded to in the 'snatching away' of verse 5, and in turn are explained as the victory of God's people 'by the blood of the Lamb' (v. 11). This retelling teaches us at least three things about Christ's victory:

- **It is the climax of hope.** Michael, whose name means 'Who is like God?' (see Exodus 15:11; Revelation 13:4), was the hero of God's people (Daniel 12:1). His victory is described here as fulfilling the Jewish hope of the triumph of God's justice through the coming of his Kingdom ('no longer any place for them', v. 8, comes from Psalm 37:36 and Daniel 2:35). The Christ of the cross is Israel's true hero, and it is he who will 'satisfy the needs and aspirations of east and west, of sinner and of sage' (William Fullerton).
- **It is costly.** The victory was won by no less a cost than the blood of the Lamb (v. 11), and all who share in the free gift of his life follow in his way. The book of Revelation is at every point a call to faithful witness (*martyria*) after the pattern of Jesus (1:5; 17:14; 19:11).
- **It is clear, but awaits completion.** The Enemy—the Accuser—has no place in the sphere of God's ultimate reality (v. 8). This brings the real joy (v. 12a) of experiencing God's sovereignty in our lives, real anticipation as we wait for its full realization (Revelation 21), and requires real endurance (Revelation 1:9) in the meantime.

John 1:47–51

In contrast with the Synoptic Gospels, here Jesus' disciples need no second opportunity to respond—they discover from the first his true identity.

Nathanael (probably another name for the apostle Bartholomew) is stunned by Jesus' supernatural knowledge of him. He is a true Israelite—

neither a 'Jew', John's term for those who reject Jesus, nor a 'Jacob', one trying to grasp what is promised by his own cunning and resourcefulness—an ever-present tendency of God's people.

His conversation with Philip (vv. 45–46) and the mention of the fig tree (associated with the 'day of the Lord', Micah 4:4; Zechariah 3:10) show him wrestling with the question of the Messiah, and his acclamation expresses Messiahship in strong but nationalistic terms (v. 49).

Jesus then calls him to move on (v. 51), in the first place beyond the merely spectacular (wouldn't it be a nice problem in our churches to have to move beyond the spectacular and miraculous?!) but also in his understanding of who Jesus is.

He is a king, yes, but one who is crowned on the cross (John 19:19). He fulfils the aspirations of Israel from the time of monarchy, but he also takes up Israel's beginnings (in Jacob) and Israel's destiny—in human weakness, trusting in God alone for vindication (Daniel 7:13). He becomes not only God's person, but God's place, the meeting point of heaven and earth. The true stairway to heaven—and not just for one nation—is his death on the cross. He is truly the king for all those who are truly Israel.

Hebrews 1:5–14

This string of Old Testament quotations supports the sequence of affirmations in verses 1–4. Together they lay the foundation for the argument that the covenant in Jesus' blood, while in continuity with the Mosaic covenant, is superior to it (3:3) since its mediator is superior to the angels, mediators of the Mosaic covenant (2:2). Jesus is:

- **'The appointed heir of all things'** (vv. 2b, 5–9; Psalm 2:7; 2 Samuel 7:14; Psalm 45:6–7). Jesus not only fulfils Israel's hopes of deliverance, but also fulfils all God's promises. He is the one who perfectly embraces God's righteousness and makes it available to us.
- **The mediator of creation** (vv. 2c, 10; Psalm 102:25). As the one through whom the world was created (John 1:3) and so was master over it (Mark 4:35–41), only he can make sense of this world and return it to its proper order.
- **Of unchanging and eternal nature** (vv. 3a, 11–12; Psalm 102:26–27). We can trust ourselves to him for our eternal future, since he shares God's unchanging nature (see 13:8). Trust in Jesus is neither temporary nor negotiable; as the 'exact imprint of God's very being' (v. 3), it is he alone who shows us what God is like.
- **At God's right hand** (v. 3b, 13; Psalm 110:1). It is through Jesus that God exercises his kingly rule in our lives.

As in Revelation, the truth about Jesus is discovered in worship; all these texts come from the Greek Psalter, the hymn book of both synagogue and early Church.

JP

LUKE
(18 OCTOBER)

EUCHARIST

Isaiah 35:3–6

This closing section of the long collection of oracles (from 13:1) adumbrates many of the themes of Isaiah 40—66. God will intervene decisively to deal with:

- **Fear** (vv. 3–4). Drooping hands (thrown up in horror?), shaking knees and trembling hearts will all be calmed. God will come as judge, not least to vindicate his people. If on the cross Jesus bore our sins, it means he stands with the sinned against and bears their pain, as much as he stands with sinners and takes their punishment. His perfect love drives out fear (1 John 4:18).
- **Failure of understanding** (v. 5). Though carrying at least some literal force, the images of the blind and deaf have much metaphorical significance. The people who refused to understand (Isaiah 6:9–10) will at last be healed (cf. Jeremiah 31:33–34).
- **Infertility** (vv. 6–7). The 'lame' and the 'desert' were classic Old Testament images of barrenness, of lifelessness (e.g. 2 Samuel 9:1–8). But it is here that the sudden and dramatic intervention of God will be seen most clearly. The image of the desert blooming (v. 1) has both political and personal potency. God delights to bring life where there is no life.

These three are resolved with God's 'coming' (v. 4)—in the return from exile, in the ministry of Jesus (Luke 7:22; John 7:37–38), in God's people calling others to share with them redemption and holiness (vv. 8–10) and finally and fully in the return of Christ, which will complete all of these. And in Luke's account of God's coming in the birth of Jesus, fear, failure and infertility are distinctively present (Luke 1—2).

Acts 16:6–12a

This is the moment when Luke joins Paul's missionary team ('they', vv. 6–7; 'we', v. 10). Their work is marked by:

- **Listening**. The Spirit's intervention is the most striking feature of this passage, in the first instance telling the team what *not* to do (vv. 6–7). We too need to listen to what Jesus is saying to us through his Spirit ('Spirit of Jesus', v. 7; cf., for example, Revelation 2:1, 7)—often to hear what we must stop doing before we can hear what we must start doing.
- **Unity**. As soon as Paul had seen the vision of the man of Macedonia, the call became the whole team's. Paul had earlier changed his team because of disunity (15:39–40); he was clear that there must be shared vision and trust if they were to work effectively together.
- **Obedience**. Once the direction was clear (v. 10), they immediately sought to follow God's lead.
- **Strategy**. Paul might earlier have wanted to head straight for Ephesus, to establish a strategic base for the evangelizing of the Aegean coast of Asia Minor. The Spirit took them on a detour through Greece before they finally reached Ephesus. But Paul has not abandoned strategic thinking—he heads for what appears to be a significant city, Philippi.

Through the combination of listening, united obedience and strategic thinking, Paul and his team in the end accomplish far more than they had perhaps intended.

2 Timothy 4:5–17

Facing death, Paul is able to look back and see his life as a whole, and he shows us the marks of a life given to Christian ministry.

There is **loneliness** as Paul is left high and dry by the human weakness of others (v. 16). There is **sacrifice**: Paul sees all his hardship and self-giving as a drink-offering poured out (v. 6)—presumably on the sacrifice of Christ, not adding to it but sharing in it (Philippians 3:10). And there is **struggle** and **hard work** as Paul has strained with every fibre of his being to make Christ known and to build up the church (v. 7).

But there is also a **graciousness** to those who have let him down (v. 16b), born of a **testimony** of God's life-long faithfulness (v. 17) and power to save (v. 18; cf. Daniel 3:17–18) and a conviction that the whole enterprise is not Paul's but God's ('kingdom', v. 18). And there is great **confidence** as Paul not only looks back but looks forward to meeting face to face the one he has served (v. 8). The chapter is over, but the story has only just begun.

His ministry might be different in degree to ours, but it is a ministry which all who are Christ's share (1 Corinthians 12:4–7). Is there any more satisfying way to be able to look back on one's life? What should I be doing now that will enable me to look back and look forward with the confidence Paul has?

Luke 10:1–9

Coming at the beginning of Luke's special section of Jesus' teaching and ministry on the way to Jerusalem (see Luke 9:51), Jesus' deployment of the seventy teaches us seven straightforward lessons in mission:

- Jesus sends us to the places he himself intends to go (v. 1). Since we are his body, we are his agents for reaching others. This should not lead us to arrogance, but to urgency.
- People are hungry for spiritual reality (v. 2). Whenever the possibility of encounter with God, the touch of his love, and the life-giving call to discipleship is made clear, people will be drawn to it. The Church's frequent failing has been to get in the way.
- Mission is spelt R-I-S-K (v. 3). It is much easier to stay in our buildings, our homes and our familiar places and not expose ourselves to the vulnerability of sharing Jesus. But 'in-drag' is not the same as 'outreach'.
- It must be clear that we are not interested in personal gain (v. 4). Evangelism is not a recruitment drive to fill the pews (and so the collection plate), nor is our witness to be a demonstration of our personal piety.
- Bless first, ask questions afterwards (v. 5). To take part in Jesus' mission, we need to be like him—generous of spirit, open of heart.
- Don't go around searching for the best deal, but stay in the place to which God has led you (v. 7). Faithfulness is more effective than constant searching for success.
- Don't criticize or appear superior (v. 8); pray for others and let them see God's power; and be honest about the demands and delights of knowing God (v. 9).

IP

SIMON AND JUDE
(28 OCTOBER)

EUCHARIST

Isaiah 28:14–16

The 'covenant with death' referred to in verse 15 is the alliance which Judah had concluded with Egypt against Assyria. This alliance was to prove a dangerous mistake (36:1–10).

In contrast, God is laying a 'tested stone' in Zion (v. 16). That God's way is 'tested' combines two meanings. First, it brings assurance, because God is 'tested' in the sense that he is faithful and dependable. He is reminding the people that their hope lies not in dubious foreign alliances, but in him. In fact, God does later rescue Jerusalem from the Assyrians when King Hezekiah turns back to him (ch. 37). Second, it is a challenge, the standard against which the people and their leaders will be judged (see Isaiah 8:14).

This combination of assurance and challenge is similar to that which Jesus poses to the disciples, including Simon and Jude, in our Gospel reading: he challenges them to follow him and testify to him, but assures them of his presence through the Holy Spirit. The call to base our lives on God's 'tested stone' rather than on anything else also brings to mind today's reading from Ephesians, with its image of God's people as a living building, founded on Christ.

Ephesians 2:19–22

Why commemorate apostles like Simon and Jude? This passage gives us three reasons.

First, the apostles, those who were specially commissioned by the risen Jesus to testify to him, are part of the foundation of our faith (v. 20). In other words, it is through the reliable testimony of the apostles that we have the good news of Jesus. Today, that reliable testimony is included in the New Testament documents. We can—and must—go right back, in the company of eye-witnesses, to Jesus himself and the message he proclaimed and entrusted to the apostles.

Second, God used the preaching of the apostles to spread the gospel among the Gentiles, and consequently to bring into being a united people, undivided by race or nationality (v. 19). So the ministry of the apostles reminds us again of our calling to minister and witness to all, regardless of their background.

Third, the wonderful image of the growing building, founded on Christ, in which all believers belong, emphasizes the unity we share with our fellow Christians across the world and down the ages (vv. 21–22). In a fast-changing and individualistic culture, reminders of our common heritage stretching back to the apostles (and beyond) are vital compass bearings.

(See Proper 11, Year B, for further comment.)

John 15:17–27

Jesus reminds the disciples of his unique and controversial claims. He is the one sent from God (v. 21), so that accepting or rejecting Jesus means accepting or rejecting God himself (vv. 22–24). Jesus also calls on the disciples to testify about him and his claims (v. 27). As his followers today, we have that same responsibility. Some will accept our message, some will reject it (v. 20).

If this prospect is daunting, remember three things. First, the response we experience reflects the response Jesus himself experienced (v. 20): he knows what acceptance and rejection feel like! Second, he is with us in power through the Holy Spirit (v. 26). Third, Jesus will equip us for his service, whoever we are. We know virtually nothing about Simon and Jude. This Simon is 'Simon the Zealot', who only ever appears in the lists of the twelve apostles. Jude is another one of the Twelve about whom we know little; he might have been the same Jude who was the brother of Jesus and who wrote the letter of Jude, but we do not know. Yet Jesus chose them and used them, just as he chooses us and uses us today, whoever we are and whatever our gifts.

MG

ANDREW
(30 NOVEMBER)

EUCHARIST

Isaiah 52:7–10

Israel's sin had led to exile in Babylon and the ruin of Jerusalem. Out of this misery, Isaiah looks forward to the time when, as the people turn back to God in faith, he will redeem them in power. The relationship between God and Israel is joyfully restored. The picture Isaiah uses is of a runner approaching Jerusalem bringing news of a great victory won by God to rescue his people. Encountering God brings deep joy to those who have been alienated from him (vv. 8–9). How often is the Church today faintly embarrassed about its message? The gospel is the best news our neighbours could hear, not an irrelevant imposition!

The messenger with the good news for Jerusalem is not on his own: God himself is returning also (v. 8). As God's people, we are all bearers of his good news (v. 7) as Andrew was, living and working for him. It is greatly encouraging that God does not ask us to do this by ourselves; he is with us by his Spirit.

Hold on to the big picture (v. 10)! The Kingdom of God keeps on growing throughout the world, and the ultimate establishment of his peace and justice is certain.

Romans 10:12–18

Like Andrew, we are called to spread the gospel. But many do not listen or accept it. What do we make of this? Is it failure on our part?

God's salvation in Christ is offered freely to everyone, regardless of background (vv. 12–13). But many of those to whom the gospel has been preached have rejected it. Has God given up on them? No, says Paul. God has done everything he could to bring the gospel to them. He has sent preachers (v. 15), so they have been able to hear the message (v. 14). The problem is that many in Israel have not believed the message, and therefore have not called on God to save them through Jesus (v. 14).

When those around us appear not to respond to the gospel, there are two things here to remember. First, God goes on loving us and those to whom we minister, whatever their present response to him (v. 21). Second, do not count it as personal failure: our task is to go on showing the love of Christ to others and to be ready to give an account to others of the hope that we have (1 Peter 3:15). The rest is between God and them.

Matthew 4:18–22

The apparently simple story of Jesus' calling of Andrew and the others contains profound truths about what following Jesus really means.

Following Jesus means acknowledging his supreme authority. This is the first time the disciples meet Jesus. Yet his authority is so compelling that they follow him immediately. In a culture which understandably values individual choice, do we take seriously enough the Lordship of Jesus in our private and public lives?

Following Jesus brings the privilege and responsibility of sharing in his mission. This has implications for who we *are*, as we walk in his way to become more like him in commitment to God and others, and implications for what we *do*, as 'fishers of men' proclaiming his message to bring others to salvation (v. 19).

Following Jesus is costly. Leaving their nets implied that loyalty to Jesus now took radical precedence. No other tie, whether to livelihood, family or anything else, was to interfere with following him (vv. 20, 22). There would be other costs—hardship (8:19–20), perhaps even death (16:24). Tradition has it that Andrew was crucified for his faith on a diagonal cross, shown today in the flag of Scotland, of which country he is the patron saint.

MG

STEPHEN
(26 DECEMBER)

EUCHARIST

2 Chronicles 24:20–22

Joash had been a good king up until the death of the priest Jehoiada (24:17). Under the subsequent influence of the officials of Judah, however, he lost his way and the country reverted to Canaanite cults (24:18).

The people's reaction to the prophecy of Zechariah (Jehoiada's son) (v. 20) against this situation is characteristic of the reaction of those who object to having their wrongdoing pointed out. The demand to hear God's call and to return to him is met by an even greater act of lawlessness (v. 21). As Zechariah dies, he predicts that God will act in judgment against his attackers (v. 22). This is fulfilled in the demise and death of Joash (24:23–25) and it is also a theme that Jesus takes up when he mentions the death of Zechariah in Matthew 23:35.

It is worth remembering that the purpose of Zechariah's prophecy was to bring about a restoration. In this sense it is something of a compliment, although an unpalatable one. That is to say that no one seeks to restore a relationship if they have no interest in being close to the person concerned. God speaks hard words to us sometimes because he seeks our restoration, not because he enjoys the prospect of our condemnation.

Acts 7:51–60

Stephen's speech and martyrdom are given a great deal of prominence by Luke. As the first martyr, Stephen demonstrates a model of Christian discipleship. As a deacon, he is an approved servant of the community (6:5). His ministry, full of grace and power, provoked a reaction in those around (6:8–9). He was full of the Spirit and wisdom so that he could successfully debate with those who confronted him (6:9–10). His lifestyle and teaching, however, provoked a murderous plan among his enemies (6:11–12), who brought false witnesses against him (6:13–14). In all these details, Stephen is a small replica of Christ. In his speech before the Sanhedrin, Stephen spelt out the whole plan of God's salvation and was executed for his supposed blasphemy by those who claimed to be righteous. He mirrors Christ even in his final words as he asks God to receive his spirit and to forgive his attackers (vv. 59–60).

Stephen's pattern of faithful death must have made a powerful impression on the watching Saul. In a world full of cynicism, individuals and churches who live what they preach, regardless of the consequences, will always make an impact beyond what they can imagine.

Matthew 23:34–39

The two murder victims mentioned by Jesus, Abel and Zechariah (v. 35), are the first and the last to be cited in the Hebrew canon (where 2 Chronicles is the final book). In both of these cases, their deaths are accompanied by a call for vengeance (Genesis 4:10 and 2 Chronicles 24:22).

The pattern of response that was experienced by the prophets of the Old Testament was also experienced by Jesus, and Jesus predicts that it will be the experience of Christian prophets, wise men and teachers (v. 34). (Stephen was the first to fulfil these words.) There is an irony here in that the prophets are sent to the city precisely because it is beloved, but its continual rejection of them results in the ever-increasing inevitability of judgment. This situation provokes a response of heartfelt sadness from Jesus (v. 37).

Galatians 2:16b–20

This passage occurs within Paul's description of his dispute with Peter over whether or not Jews could share common meals (the eucharist) with Gentiles (vv. 11–21). The difficulty that Peter, Barnabas and the other Jews faced was that, according the customs they had inherited, a Jew's righteousness would be impaired if he or she shared a meal with people on a lower level of adherence to the law. Paul has a gift for perceiving the natural consequences of a new situation and points out that the righteousness of all concerned is dependent on their faith in Christ, and not on adherence to the law (v. 16). In these circumstances there is no basis for separating Gentiles from Jews.

Grasping the full consequences of a new situation can be extremely difficult. Paul describes it as a dying to the old system (v. 19), and death is always painful. The benefit, however, is the possibility of new life in Christ (v. 20). That commitment to dying to our old life and taking on a new life is one that we reaffirm every time we receive Holy Communion. By taking the bread and wine, we express our allegiance to Christ in both his death and his resurrection.

AG

JOHN
(27 DECEMBER)

EUCHARIST

Exodus 33:7–11a

Meeting God is at the heart of our readings for today, and our Old Testament passage is one of those which tell us about both the preparation for such a meeting and the effects it has. Three matters call for comment.

The first is that effort had to be made. While God is everywhere, it was necessary for people to undertake the journey to the 'tent of meeting' to show that they were serious about him. Today that remains a important principle. To say that God is everywhere is often an excuse to avoid him anywhere.

The second is that this was no mere subjective exercise. Verse 9 speaks of the pillar of cloud, the symbol of God descending on the tent. God always responds to those who are serious in searching for him. The grace of God is always available to those with the faith to believe and the diligence to seek.

Third, this experience is more than sensation and feeling. 'The Lord used to speak to Moses face to face as one speaks to a friend.' This reminds us of the significant place of Moses in salvation history. He is the archetypal prophet who hears and passes on the words of God. He foreshadows Christ who is himself the Word of God, a title of Christ which is at the very heart of John's writings. All meeting with God is saturated with these elements: the grace which reaches out to us; the faith which responds to that grace; and the relevation which embodies and focuses these experiences.

1 John 1

1 John, in a deliberate echo of the Prologue of John's Gospel, proclaims positive and uncompromising affirmations about Jesus, the Word of life. John's technique here is to begin with the historical and tangible reality of Jesus (vv. 1–4) and then to begin to spell out the implications for living which flow from this (vv. 5–10).

Two things stand out in verses 1–4. The first is the personal encounter with the living Word. This is no imagined experience, such as the Gnostics might have advocated. Not only have there been a voice and a seeing but there has been physical contact. The word 'revealed' strongly points to the pre-existence of Christ, the eternal Word embodied in the flesh of Jesus of Nazareth.

The second thing is that this is more than a truth to believe; it is a gospel to proclaim—'declare to you the eternal life that was with the Father' (v. 2). This is a reality which must be shared, and that sharing brings disciples into a fellowship marked by deep and lasting joy.

The second section begins to spell out the practical implications of that experienced and proclaimed gospel. 'God is light' (v. 5) is a text on which a meditation is based. It is impossible to have a relationship with God unless we 'are walking' (continuous) in the light, which implies complete integrity and sincerity. This has two consequences. One is true fellowship and the other is the continual experience of forgiveness through the blood of Christ.

This is closely bound up with confessing our sins (v. 9). The plural suggests not merely a general acknowledgment of sin but a specific spelling out of particular sins which we know hinder our fellowship with God. Both treating sin lightly and despair at how sinful we are find their remedy in this passage.

John 21:19b–25

At the end of this great Gospel, the themes of the beginning are echoed. 'Follow me' is an echo of the initial call to discipleship of chapter 1 and a reminder that the initial following must be renewed day by day.

This delightful little dialogue reinforces the motif of discipleship by reminding us that the Master cares for each disciple with individual attention. There is no belittling of either Peter or the beloved disciple; each is given a demanding, painful but ultimately rewarding task and each is assured that this lies in the will and goodness of Christ.

Yet the final emphasis is not on discipleship but on Jesus himself. The work of both disciples, even of all disciples, is only a minute part of the importance of Jesus. This Gospel, with all its profundity, is only a fraction of all that Jesus has done. The significance of Jesus can never be exhausted.

Just as, at the beginning, John the Baptist had pointed away from himself to Christ, so the beloved disciple bows out, leaving Christ centre stage. No one must ever think that the story is complete. Since Jesus is the Word who utters the inner reality of God, nothing less than eternity could suffice to declare him.

RF

Holy Innocents
(28 December)

Eucharist

Jeremiah 31:15–17

Jeremiah, in one of his most beautiful and poignant lyrics, summons a voice from the ancient past. Across the centuries, Rachel weeps for the lost children of Israel, including the current generation who are to go into bitter exile. This personification of agony is one of the most effective of Jeremiah's powerful messages (v. 15). We are to hear this note again in our Gospel reading.

God's words (vv. 16–17) both address the immediate situation and point to that greater end of sorrow and drying of tears (see also Isaiah 25:8; Revelation 7:17; 21:4) which will be a mark of the world to come. More immediately, this refers to the bitterness of exile, a trauma which probably is matched only by the Holocaust in its searing effects on Jewish life and consciousness.

Two aspects of this are striking. First is God's providence, which is not legalistic or mechanical but especially reveals itself in companion and mercy. No book is fiercer in its denunciation of evil than Jeremiah, yet none is more tender and welcoming to the returning sinner.

The second is the human response. The people will return—an action initiated by God but calling out a response (see also comment on readings for the Second Sunday of Christmas). There is a blend of the importance of the past—'There is a reward for your work'—and hope for the future, and the rest of this chapter is dominated by such phrases as 'The days are surely coming'. New life, so savagely butchered, will spring up again. Rachel's children 'are no more', yet they will return.

1 Corinthians 1:26–29

The slaughter of the innocents reminds us of the brutal power of the state and the helplessness of the chosen victims. Here Paul shows how the cross was the supreme example of that, and yet at the same time a demonstration of God's power which, working through weakness, establishes another kind of power that is life-changing and eternal. Three important truths emerge.

First, the weak and uninfluential can be transformed by God's grace: 'You were called' (v. 26, NIV). It is not that weakness and insignificance are being praised *per se*; rather that God by his converting love transforms such people into agents of his Kingdom. The thrice-repeated verb 'chose' (vv. 27–28) emphasizes God's sovereign love as he works out his purposes.

Second, the purpose of this calling is to 'shame the strong' and reduce to nothing the things that are' (vv. 27–28). Without God, nothing has any real substance or enduring value. This is a powerful message to a church all too ready to trust in showy gifts and 'charismatic personalities'.

Third, the message of the cross creates a fundamentally humble attitude —'so that no one might boast in the presence of God' (v. 29). Boasting and self-seeking were all too common in Corinth and too often the true source of gifts and talents was ignored.

This passage helps us to see Holy Innocents day in proper context. God revealed in Jesus is a perpetual opponent of worldly power, whether it appears in military swaggering or in over-confidence in gifts and personalities.

Matthew 2:13–18

These few verses with a few vivid and colourful phrases raise vast and profound issues. Three of these will form the basis for today's meditation.

The first is the nature of revelation. For the second time in this chapter, God speaks through a dream. This dream is specifically linked with the quotation from Hosea 11:1, 'Out of Egypt I called my son'. It is also linked with Joseph's immediate response: 'He got up, took the child and his mother by night, and went to Egypt'. Here we have scripture, supernatural messages and practical action combined. Scripture is the normative revelation, but guidance, sometimes supernatural, is needed for specific situations and obedient action must follow.

The second issue is the mystery of Providence: why did God allow this ghastly slaughter, which has all too many extensive and chilling parallels throughout history? Mystery remains, and yet this child who is to suffer the fury of a later Herod and of Pilate is both to be cruelly killed and yet, by dying and rising, to create another kingdom.

The third is the fulfilment of the Old Testament. It is not that Matthew rewrites the story of Jesus or even invents it to demonstrate alleged parallels between his story and the earlier scriptures. Rather, Matthew is showing how Jesus, the true Son of God, recapitulates the story of Israel who is also the son of God. In him the failures of Israel are transformed and the true meaning of the Bible's plot-line unfolds. All Herod's machinations prove ultimately futile because he responded not with worship but with fury.

RF

INDEX OF BIBLE PASSAGES

THE PEOPLE'S BIBLE COMMENTARY

A daily commentary for Bible readers

General Editors: Richard A. Burridge, Henry Wansbrough, David Winter

The *People's Bible Commentary* (PBC) is designed for all those who want to study the scriptures in a way that will warm the heart as well as instruct the mind. To help you, the series distils the best of scholarly insights into the straightforward language and devotional emphasis of Bible reading notes. Explanation of background material, and discussion of the original Greek and Hebrew, will always aim to be brief.

- If you are involved in regular preaching and teaching, you can find invaluable 'snapshots' of a Bible passage through the PBC approach.
- If you are feeling 'burned out' on the Bible, this series could help you recover the wonder of scripture.

The series is designed for use alongside any version of the Bible. You may have your own favourite translation, but you might like to consider trying a different one in order to gain fresh perspectives on familiar passages. The Notes section at the back of each PBC volume provides space for you to write personal reflections, points to follow up, questions and comments.

Each *People's Bible Commentary* can be used on a daily basis, as an alternative or complement to Bible reading notes. Alternatively, it can be read straight through, or used as a resource book for insight into particular verses of the biblical book.

To help build your *People's Bible Commentary library*, there is a special voucher scheme. Each PBC volume includes a voucher on the back page which you can cut out and attach to a form, also printed in the book. Every four vouchers that you collect entitle you to a free PBC commentary, which you can obtain from your local Christian bookseller or from BRF direct.

All PBC volumes are priced at £7.99.

1 & 2 SAMUEL
Harry Mowvley
ISBN 1 84101 303 8

The intertwined stories of Samuel the prophet and David, arguably greatest of the kings of Israel, have fascinated people ever since they were first written down, more than two thousand years ago. From God's gift of a son for Hannah to the last days of King David, the books known as 1 and 2 Samuel tell of larger-than-life heroes, desert warfare, political intrigues, adultery, murder, wise women, undying friendship, and the powerful bonds between parent and child.

Throughout all that happens, the storyteller's aim is to show God at work—bestowing and removing his blessing, bringing both success and disaster, guiding human events to fulfil his promises to the people of Israel.

1 & 2 KINGS
Stephen B. Dawes
ISBN 1 84101 118 5

The stories that appear in the books of 1 and 2 Kings are part of a longer tragedy. Together with the books of Joshua, Judges and Samuel, they tell how the people of Israel moved from a bright beginning across the Jordan River into, and then out of, the Promised Land, and away to exile in Babylon.

Throughout the books of Kings, the repeated message is the importance of faith in God and faithfulness to God, demonstrated in the lives of those who reigned over both Israel and Judah. There is a lesson to be learned. Righteousness brings its rewards—usually—and so does failure to walk in God's ways. Along the way, we encounter such memorable characters as Elijah and Elisha, Queen Jezebel, and Solomon in all his dangerous glory.

CHRONICLES TO NEHEMIAH
Michael Tunnicliffe
ISBN 1 84101 070 7

'If my people who are called by my name humble themselves, pray, seek my face, and turn from their wicked ways, then I will hear from heaven, and will forgive their sin and heal their land.'

Written after the nation's exile to Babylon, the books of Chronicles, Ezra and Nehemiah show the faithfulness of God at work in the history of Israel through years of gradual decline and final, terrible fall. 1 and 2 Chronicles retell with special emphasis the story of King David's royal line, first set down in 2 Samuel and 1 and 2 Kings. In Ezra and Nehemiah, the story encompasses the hope of restoration, as the exiles start to return and rebuild the broken city of Jerusalem. Running throughout these books is the message that what God seeks from his people is true worship and obedience, and that as they turn their hearts back to him, so he will bring them home.

PSALMS 1—72
Donald Coggan
ISBN 1 84101 031 6

PSALMS 73—150
Donald Coggan
ISBN 1 84101 065 0

To understand the Psalms, we need to remember that we are treading on holy ground. The writers of these extraordinary songs were in touch with God, the Holy One. Sometimes they raged at him, sometimes they adored him. Often they consciously did neither, but just got on with living a godly life, keeping an eye Godwards all the while.

In these two volumes, we explore the Psalms, pondering their meanings, savouring their poetry, and joining with the communities of faith who over the years have used them in worship.

PROVERBS
Enid B. Mellor
ISBN 1 84101 071 5

'As a door turns on its hinges, so does a lazy person in bed.'

'Do not boast about tomorrow, for you do not know what a day may bring.'

'Pleasant words are like a honeycomb, sweetness to the soul and health to the body.'

One of the world's most famous books of wisdom, Proverbs is a collection of poems, wise sayings and short parables, showing how to apply godly principles to daily life. The 31 chapters cover everything from business ethics to family life, and while some parts speak directly to young people, others advise the leaders of the land. From first to last, however, we are reminded that the source of true wisdom and understanding is knowing God himself.

NAHUM TO MALACHI
Grace Emmerson
ISBN 1 84101 028 6

These six prophets delivered their messages from God approximately 2,500 years ago, but their words still resonate in today's world. Now, as then, God cares passionately about injustice and oppression. He still declares judgment upon individuals, rulers and nations that defy his love and his authority, and treat harshly those they should protect.

The justice of God is always tempered with mercy, however, and these prophets called their hearers—and still call us—to repent. Across the many centuries, they speak of the unimaginable blessings and the miraculous restoration that God promises to all who leave their sinful ways and return to him.

MATTHEW
John Proctor
ISBN 1 84101 191 6

Matthew was a Jewish Christian, writing close to the time and the places where Jesus lived. He told his version of the story of Jesus' birth and life, cross and resurrection, with the aim of encouraging, challenging and stirring up the Christians he knew.

The message of Matthew's Gospel is thoroughly practical, with Jesus' teaching about lifestyle and relationships having a very prominent place. Commitment in all areas of life was clearly important to this writer. At the same time, he wrote a deeply spiritual Gospel, emphasizing how the events surrounding Jesus clearly fulfilled old Testament prophecy about the coming Messiah, and telling of the Son of God who is 'with you always, to the end of time.'

MARK
Dick France
ISBN 1 84101 046 4

Mark's Gospel is the shortest of the four books telling the story of Jesus of Nazareth, yet it is the most vividly told. Mark writes of eager crowds and impressive miracles, of dramatic confrontation with opponents both human and demonic. He shows the disconcerting influence of Jesus on his often bewildered disciples, and how their world was turned upside down by the revolutionary values of the kingdom of God.

Studying the Gospel reveals what a well-written story it is, and how skilfully the writer builds towards the final showdown in Jerusalem, where the cosmic drama of death and resurrection is played out.

LUKE
Henry Wansbrough
ISBN 1 84101 027 8

Luke's Gospel contrasts with the other Gospels—the energy of Mark, the mystical poetry of John, the specifically Jewish focus of Matthew. He writes with the dignity and calm of contemporary historians.

Luke moves in a richer, more sophisticated world than do the other evangelists. This may be why he puts such stress on the dangers of wealth and on God's blessing for the poor. Acceptance of the gospel means a complete reversal of worldly standards of success. And throughout his Gospel, Luke shows by constant little touches his awareness that the Good News of Jesus will spread beyond the people of Israel—as he will narrate in his second volume, the Acts of the Apostles.

JOHN
Richard A. Burridge
ISBN 1 84101 029 4

John's Gospel is often given to people as a readable account of Jesus of Nazareth, yet it is also a sublime masterpiece that has occupied theologians and mystics for centuries. It has been described as 'a book in which a child may paddle but an elephant can swim deep'. At the same time, however, it is still a story—the story of Jesus' deeds and words, his signs and teaching, and how these led to his arrest, death and resurrection.

By following the flow of John's narrative, and showing how it is patterned and devised, this commentary unpacks the text to help the reader grow in understanding and faith.

ROMANS
James D.G. Dunn
ISBN 1 84101 082 0

'All have sinned and fall short of the glory of God; they are now justified by his grace as a gift, through the redemption that is in Christ Jesus...'.

The apostle Paul had not visited the church in Rome when he wrote his letter to them. In doing so, he not only introduces himself but sets out the gospel message, from the fallen state of humankind to the limitless gift of salvation made available through the death, resurrection and Spirit of Jesus Christ. And the consequences of salvation are then explored—the combination of freedom from sin and death and of submission to God that should characterize the new believers, and what it all means both for Israel and for their common life together.

1 CORINTHIANS
Jerome Murphy-O'Connor
ISBN 1 84101 122 3

Here is a description of the problems and challenges facing a young church. What does 'freedom in Christ' mean? How should believers practise the gifts of the Spirit? And what is the role of women in the worshipping community?

Paul wrote to help the Corinthian Christians live out their faith in one of the largest and most notorious cities in the ancient world. His words of confrontation, correction, reconciliation and blessing still resonate in our lives today.

2 CORINTHIANS
Aída Besançon Spencer
ISBN 1 84101 073 1

'But we have this treasure in clay jars, so that it may be made clear that this extraordinary power belongs to God and does not come from us.'

Paul's second letter to the young church at Corinth is forged in the heat of difficult circumstances. False teachers were challenging the apostle's authority and he also had to present a defence of the practice of church discipline for those who had in some way strayed. Throughout this passionate letter, despite the believers' failings, their lack of commitment and their criticism of his ministry, Paul's love and concern for them shine through.

GALATIANS AND 1 & 2 THESSALONIANS
John Fenton
ISBN 1 84101 012 X

Written with Paul's characteristic energy and passion, the letters to the churches in Galatia and Thessalonica addressed different and specific problems arising in the new congregations of believers. While the Galatians wrestled with the relationship between Jewish law and Christian teaching, the Thessalonians were confused about the imminence (or otherwise) of Christ's return. In answering these issues, Paul teaches how Christians should seek to live: celebrating their freedom while mindful of the call to holiness.

TIMOTHY, TITUS AND HEBREWS
Dick France
ISBN 1 84101 119 3

Unlike most of the letters of Paul, 1 and 2 Timothy and Titus are written not to church communities but to individuals caught up in the midst of challenging situations. Hebrews, on the other hand, is a quite distinctive letter, with its compelling presentation of how, in the coming of Jesus, God has given us something 'better' than all that had gone before in the Old Testament period. All four letters are written, however, to help churches to develop the distinctive lifestyle of Jesus' followers in an often hostile world. Theological questions are interwoven with pastoral concerns as the writers seek to guide the growing congregations towards maturity.

JAMES TO JUDE
Francis J. Moloney
ISBN 1 84101 092 8

These seven letters towards the end of the New Testament are a diverse collection, addressed by their writers to widely scattered groups and individuals. They cover topics that range from the meaning of authentic Christian living (as distinct from following Jewish cultural norms), to encouraging perseverance among believers suffering persecution from the authorities. Above all, the writers seek to clarify what is true and what is false teaching—and to instruct the young church as to how to tell the difference.

REVELATION
Marcus Maxwell
ISBN 0 7459 3297 5

The most mysterious book in the Bible, Revelation holds out a shining vision of the final triumph of God's kingdom and the eternal life which God offers to his creation. Handel's 'Hallelujah' chorus from his *Messiah* takes its words from Revelation: 'Hallelujah: for the Lord God omnipotent reigneth.' Against this background of hope stand dire warnings of judgment for a world which ignores its Redeemer and Creator: polluted seas, dying trees, droughts and famines. The risen Christ sends a powerful message to the Church in this age: shake off the temptations to complacency and compromise; be God's army of faithful witnesses, spreading the word of hope to an unjust world.

REFRESHING WORSHIP
Brian & Kevin Draper

Many people involved in church life are on the lookout for ways of keeping weekly worship fresh and vital. Over the last few years, several groups have pioneered inventive new services and ways of doing and being church, with the aim of creating truly authentic worshipping communites. Brian and Kevin Draper, who helped dream one such service into life, ask what we can learn from our experience of church worship, whether it is in new or traditional settings. They consider the theoretical and practical implications of revitalising worship for people of all ages and, throughout the book, they provide many examples of how, in very simple ways, we can all start to make a difference. With fresh vision and resources, we can inspire not only those with whom we worship regularly, but even those outside the church altogether.

ISBN 1 84101 146 0   £5.99

MASS CULTURE
Eucharist and mission in a post-modern world
Edited by Pete Ward

Eucharist... Holy Communion... the Lord's Supper... Mass... Breaking of Bread... different labels, each with different resonance, for the act of worship that lies at the heart of Christian faith. While church teaching varies as to its exact significance, and while it is celebrated with a variety of words and gestures, almost all Christians agree that it is—in one way or another—an encounter with the living God. At the same time, however, it takes place within a very human creation of music, liturgy and ritual. In the context of our late modern—or post-modern—society, *Mass Culture* examines how these familiar cultural forms might evolve and develop.

This book brings together seven contributors, each speaking from within their own church tradition and experiences, to examine the impact that this ancient act of worship can have on believers—and outsiders—today. It is a book that will challenge, provoke and inspire.

ISBN 1 84101 069 3   £6.99

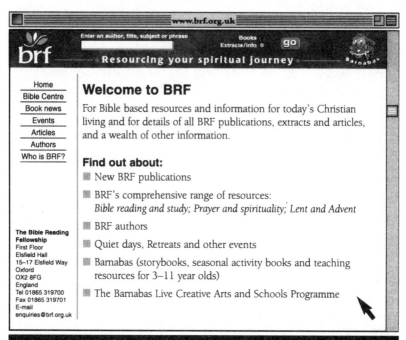

www.brf.org.uk

brf

Enter an author, title, subject or phrase

Books
Extracts/Info

go

Resourcing your spiritual journey

barnabas

Home
Bible Centre
Book news
Events
Articles
Authors
Who is BRF?

The Bible Reading Fellowship
First Floor
Elsfield Hall
15–17 Elsfield Way
Oxford
OX2 8FG
England
Tel 01865 319700
Fax 01865 319701
E-mail
enquiries@brf.org.uk

Welcome to BRF

For Bible based resources and information for today's Christian living and for details of all BRF publications, extracts and articles, and a wealth of other information.

Find out about:

▪ New BRF publications

▪ BRF's comprehensive range of resources:
  Bible reading and study; Prayer and spirituality; Lent and Advent

▪ BRF authors

▪ Quiet days, Retreats and other events

▪ Barnabas (storybooks, seasonal activity books and teaching resources for 3–11 year olds)

▪ The Barnabas Live Creative Arts and Schools Programme

Visit the BRF website at www.brf.org.uk

BRF is a Registered Charity

ORDER FORM

REF	TITLE	PRICE	QTY	TOTAL
303 8	PBC 1 & 2 Samuel	£7.99		
118 5	PBC 1 & 2 Kings	£7.99		
070 7	PBC Chronicles to Nehemiah	£7.99		
031 6	PBC Psalms 1 – 72	£7.99		
065 0	PBC Psalms 73 – 150	£7.99		
071 5	PBC Proverbs	£7.99		
028 6	PBC Nahum to Malachi	£7.99		
191 6	PBC Matthew	£7.99		
046 4	PBC Mark	£7.99		
027 8	PBC Luke	£7.99		
029 4	PBC John	£7.99		
082 0	PBC Romans	£7.99		
122 3	PBC 1 Corinthians	£7.99		
073 1	PBC 2 Corinthians	£7.99		
012 X	PBC Galatians and 1 & 2 Thessalonians	£7.99		
119 3	PBC Timothy, Titus and Hebrews	£7.99		
092 8	PBC James to Jude	£7.99		
3297 5	PBC Revelation	£7.99		
146 0	Refreshing Worship	£5.99		
069 3	Mass Culture	£6.99		

POSTAGE & PACKING CHARGES			
Order value	**UK**	Postage and packing:	
£7.00 & under	£1.25	Donation:	
£7.01–£30.00	£2.50		
Over £30.00	free	**Total enclosed:**	

Name _____ Account Number _____

Address_____

_____ Postcode _____

Telephone Number _____ Email _____

Payment by: Cheque ❏ Mastercard ❏ Visa ❏ Postal Order ❏ Switch ❏

Credit card no. ❏❏❏❏ ❏❏❏❏ ❏❏❏❏ ❏❏❏❏ Expires ❏❏ ❏❏

Switch card no. ❏❏❏❏❏❏❏❏❏❏❏❏❏❏❏❏❏❏

Issue no. of Switch card ❏❏❏❏ Expires ❏❏ ❏❏

Signature _____ Date _____

All orders must be accompanied by the appropriate payment.

Please send your completed order form to:
BRF, First Floor, Elsfield Hall, 15–17 Elsfield Way, Oxford OX2 8FG
Tel. 01865 319700 / Fax. 01865 319701 E-mail: enquiries@brf.org.uk

Available from your local Christian bookshop.   BRF is a Registered Charity